MINNESOTA TRAVEL COMPANION

MINNESOTA TRAVEL COMPANION

A Guide To The History Along Minnesota's Highways

By Richard Olsenius
Book Design by Author

Cartography by
Sona Karentz Andrews, Ph.D.
Department of Geography, University of Minnesota

Bluestem Productions—Wayzata, Minnesota

Printed in the United States of America at
North Central Publishing Company, St. Paul.
Published by Bluestem Productions
Box 334, Wayzata, Minnesota 55391

Library of Congress Card Catalog Number: 82-72658

ISBN: 0-9609064-0-1

Second Printing, 1983

ACKNOWLEDGMENTS

Trying to thank all those who helped in the process of compiling this book, is something like photographing waves on the ocean. It doesn't seem to do justice to the reality. First off, I would like to show my appreciation for the patience shown by the library staff at the Minnesota Historical Society, who answered my endless questions and requests. I would like to also thank Bonnie Wilson and her staff at the Audio-Visual Library of the Historical Society. They made the process of looking at thousands of photographs as painless as possible. Few also realize the easy access that can be had to thousands of photographs in their collection. This project was worth the effort just for the chance to look through all the early photographs.

I want to thank Sona Andrews, for her guidance and cartographic skills in the preparation of the maps. Before this book, I had little understanding of what went into the making of maps. To me, they were always something that just sat in the glove compartment. They are beautiful, Sona!

I also want to thank Judy Zerby for the energy and time she put into helping with the final editing and picture selection of this book. Without her efforts and consultation, it is doubtful the book would have ever been finished on time. Judy and I also plan to combine our energies on a Wisconsin book next.

And to my wife, Christine, who helped write the information on some of the towns, special acknowledgment is due. She assisted in almost every aspect of this book, while still maintaining her job as Coordinator of the Freshwater Society. I want to thank her for her support, guidance, patience and love.

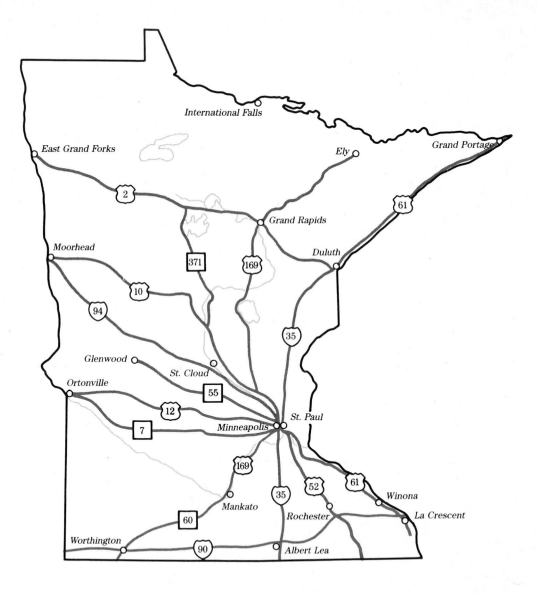

TABLE OF CONTENTS

INTRODUCTION

It was a couple of years ago, when I was working for the MINNEAPOLIS TRIBUNE as a photographer, that I developed the idea for this book. For 12 years I had assignments that took me to every corner of the state and then some. A curiosity developed about how this state came to be, and how the towns were settled and named. It was obvious how little I knew about my state; I didn't even know the year it received statehood. Part of the problem I guess, is the young age at which I received my state history. For one reason or another, it didn't sink in. Well, it is quite surprising to see how this curiosity has led me into one of the more interesting projects of my life.

I never intended to do a book, but when I started looking around for a resource book to help me out, I became frustrated. Certainly there are history books that cover this state in expanded volumes, but what I wanted was a book that I could carry with me in the car or have at home to answer my questions in a simple direct way.

I sensed there was a need for this type of book, so for the past year, I have spent much of my time at the Minnesota Historical Society, going through the old county history books, gathering information about the towns and villages of this state.

The concept of this book was not to tell people where to go or what to see, but to select frequently traveled routes and explain how the history of the state unfolded along those roads. There are enough books that explain where to see the Paul Bunyan statue in Bemidji, but few that tell about the early days in that wilderness area. This book is designed to be a companion on your trips through Minnesota, explaining the passing towns and rivers with anecdotes and brief histories. I guess I would call it snap-shot history; trying to give enough information, without burdening you with a multitude of facts.

I also wanted to assist the reader in seeing the relationship between the towns and rivers, so I commissioned maps to be drawn that would detail every 30-mile section along the route. As it turned out,there are some 80 maps covering 2,500 miles of Minnesota highways. I also wanted to add warmth to the book, so 160 photographs of Minnesota scenes were selected by culling through the seemingly endless files of the Minnesota Historical Society. I tried for the most part to select photographs and information on as many towns as possible, but the size of the book became a determining factor as to how much could be included. I hope you come to discover this beautiful and interesting state as I have. See you on the highways.

FINAL NOTE: Throughout this book, all references to the Sioux and Chippewa Indians are made using their indigenous names–Dakota and Ojibwe. Also, all maps are scaled 1" to 4 miles and north is always at the top of the page. The routes start at the Interstates of 494 & 694, fanning out from the Twin Cities. All Minnesota Historical Society Photographs are credited MHS.

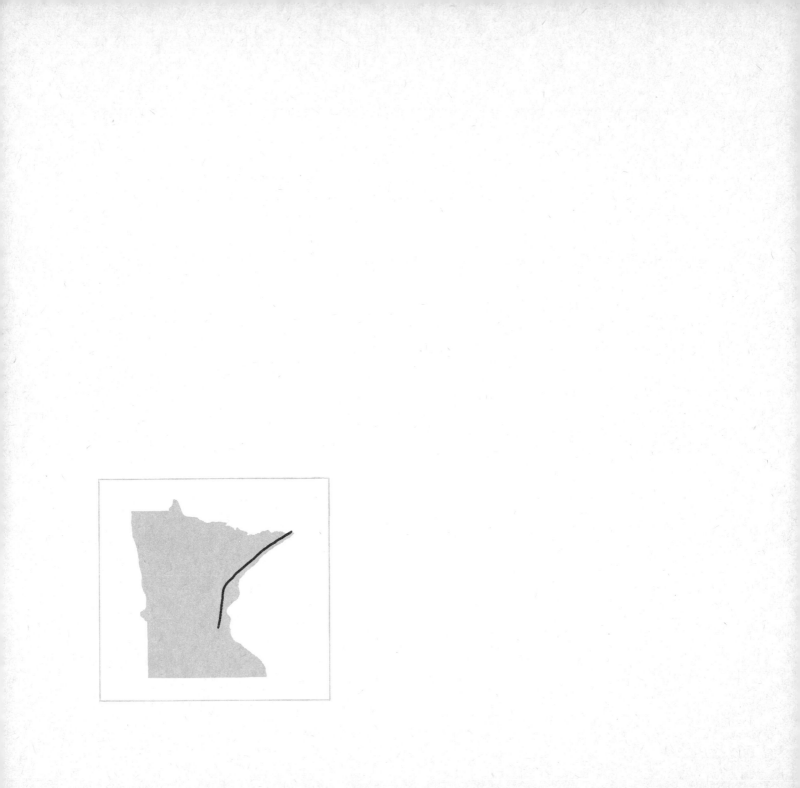

4

ROUTE I-35, 61 NORTH TO CANADA

Massive log jam below Taylors Falls, on the St. Croix River. Photo/John Runk, 1880.

MHS

This route runs north where towering white pine once covered the land for as far as the eye could see. Though Father Hennepin and Sieur Du Luth were exploring the territory in the mid-1600's, the white man didn't make his permanent entry into the region until the 1850's. At that time, the first lumberjacks journeyed up the St. Croix and started to harvest the large stands of pine that stretched between the Mississippi and the St. Croix rivers. Scandinavians immigrated to the Taylors Falls area, a region that reminded them of their native country. Many worked the boom sites and sawmills and some began to clear land for farming.

In the 1860's, a military road was cut north along the St. Croix River, connecting St. Paul to the village of Superior on Lake Superior. A few years later a railroad was built to Duluth, a town whose future would be governed by iron ore and lumber.

The freeway ends at Duluth and U.S. 61 travels north along beautiful Lake Superior, the largest freshwater lake in the world. It was across Superior that the Ojibwe came from the east, into the land of the Dakota. Here the struggle for these rich hunting lands of the north lasted some 200 years, before the Dakota were driven permanently to the prairie. The lake also carried the explorers Radisson, Groseilliers and Du Luth, who were searching for furs and a way west to the Pacific Ocean. Not long after, the French voyageurs developed a trading network that stretched from Montreal almost to the Pacific. It was at Grand Portage, on the tip of the Arrowhead, that furs were exchanged for knives, blankets and other goods.

Iron ore was shipped to Lake Superior from the Vermilion and Mesabi ranges during the late 1800's. This ore fed the blast furnaces in a society that was changing from wood to steel. Lumber was also an important part of the North Shore, helping Duluth grow from a small trading post at Fond du Lac to a major inland port.

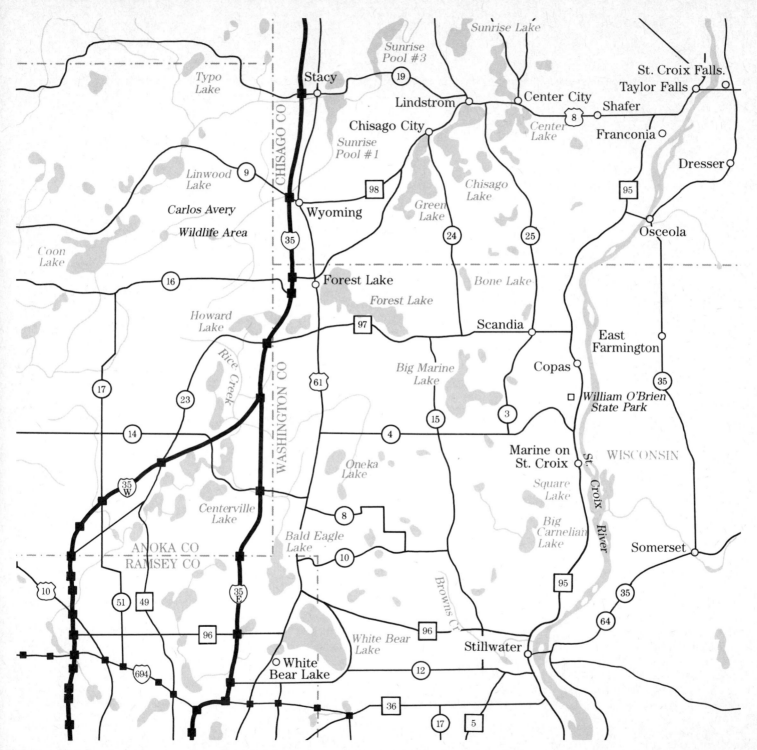

WHITE BEAR LAKE, Pop. 22,538

Since the early days of Minnesota, especially after St. Paul began to grow during the 1850's, the village of White Bear Lake was popular as a resort town. Located along a 2,400 acre lake, the town didn't become incorporated until 1881. The Dakota, who hunted along its shores, called the lake "Mah-to-me-di," or White Bear. The name developed from a legend about the wife of a warrior who had been attacked by an incredibly huge white bear. Rushing to her defense, the brave slayed the bear whose spirit is said to have inhabited the lake ever since. The Indians named the large island in the lake, "Spirit Island," which today is called by its original Ojibwe name, Manitou Island. The lake is a popular fishing lake for walleyes, bass and bluegills.

BALD EAGLE LAKE

When government surveys were taken in this area during the 1800's, a small island in the center of the lake had bald eagles nesting there. Because of this, the surveyors named the lake Bald Eagle.

FOREST LAKE, Pop. 4,596

Before the Ojibwe had pushed their way across Lake Superior and into Minnesota, the Dakota occupied most of the state. Seven Dakota tribes occupied land from Minnesota west to the Tetons. It was the Mdewakanton band that controlled Minnesota, with their main village or cultural center named Kathio, at the mouth of the Rum River on Mille Lacs Lake. Kathio is the oldest Indian village name known in Minnesota. From here, the Dakota hunted, fished and maintained many villages throughout the region.

The Ojibwe began to exert their strength in Minnesota during the 1700's, as they pushed westward across Lake Superior. The Ojibwe had faced pressure in the East from the Iroquois Nation and white settlement. In 1745, a decisive three-day battle between the Dakota and the Ojibwe at Kathio forced the Dakota to flee down the Rum River, beginning the Dakotas' nomadic existence on the prairie of southern Minnesota until their expulsion from the state following the Sioux Uprising of 1862.

The Dakota and Ojibwe continued to launch attacks against one another. In 1837 the Ojibwe gave away their rights to the lands of eastern Minnesota. But the area between White Bear Lake and Forest Lake continued to be a land of confrontation. In 1856, the Ojibwe built a fort at the outlet of Forest Lake in anticipation of an attack by the Dakota. The battle never occurred, however, and the fort's wood was later used by Michael Marsh who built the first hotel in the little village of Forest Lake. In 1868 Marsh was assured that the railroad being built to Duluth would pass in front of his new hotel. However, the tracks were laid hundreds of yards to the west, making his patrons walk a fair distance.

Forest Lake took its name from the ash, elm, basswood and cottonwood that line the lake's shoreline. For the early settlers, the area had abundant wild rice, hay meadows for their cattle, and many sloughs alive with waterfowl.

MHS

Gaff-rigged sailboats glide along White Bear Lake on a moonlit night. Photo/Ingersoll, 1908.

STILLWATER, Pop. 12,290

Stillwater has been referred to as the birthplace of Minnesota and the "cradle" of the white pine lumbering industry. The name Stillwater, referring to the still waters of Lake St. Croix, was proposed by John McKusick in 1843. It reminded early settlers of their previous homes in Stillwater, Maine. Joseph Brown, Stillwater pioneer, came to Minnesota at the age of 14 with a detachment of troops who were building a fort at the confluence of the Mississippi and St. Peter (Minnesota) rivers. The year was 1819 and the fort would later be called Fort Snelling. In 1839, Brown laid out the first townsite at the head of Lake St. Croix and named it Dahkotah. This site was about a half-mile above the original site of Stillwater.

The Territory of Minnesota was born here at a public meeting called the "Stillwater Convention of 1848". The convention was held to organize the new Territory. In order that their request for territorial status be taken seriously, John Catlin, former secretary of the Wisconsin Territory, assumed the role of acting governor of the St. Croix Delta. After establishing his residence at Stillwater (as if it were the capital), he called for a delegate to be elected to represent their interests before Congress. Fur trader, Henry Sibley, was chosen. One year later in 1849, Sibley's campaign to establish the Territory of Minnesota was successful.

Stillwater's first sawmill was built in 1844. A decade later the town had become the major lumbering center of the territory. Stillwater became one of the Territory's three largest towns, along with St. Paul and St. Anthony (later called Minneapolis). The town continued to be the lumbering capital of the state until the mid-1800's when the mills of Minneapolis surpassed the output of those at Stillwater. Yet lumbering remained important until the 1890's, due in part to the St. Croix Boom Corporation. (Booms were places where logs were caught and measured).

In 1856, Isaac Staples and his business partners began the construction of a boom on the St. Croix, a short distance north of Stillwater. At this place, millions of logs were sorted according to ownership marks; then measured and rafted to down-river sawmills. One spring it was estimated that the logs covered a nine mile stretch of river. The first frame house in St. Paul was built with lumber from the Stillwater mill. Some of this lumber was also used in the construction of the dam at the Falls of St. Anthony in 1847.

The territorial Legislature chose Stillwater as the site of the region's first prison. It was built in Battle Hollow, a place where an Ojibwe chieftain was buried after a bloody, one-to-one battle with a Dakota chief. New buildings were erected at nearby Bayport after the turn of the century. Of the original buildings, only the 14-room, warden's house still stands.

Steamboat call at Stillwater. Photo/John Runk, 1911.

MHS

ST. CROIX VALLEY

The upper St. Croix Valley was once a forest of centuries-old white pine. Today this sandy region is in its second growth, along the valley where the river winds and twists over numerous rapids. The river maintains a split personality dating back to post-glacial times when melting ice shaped two immense lakes. Glacial Lake Grantsburg extended from Grantsburg, Wisconsin, to east-central Minnesota. Torrential runoff from this extensive body of water flowed southward from St. Croix Falls to the Mississippi, carving the wider, and more fertile lower valley. Later in geologic time, the upper St. Croix was formed when a vast reservoir of water from Glacial Lake Duluth (forerunner of Lake Superior) gouged a path south through the Brule River and upper St. Croix. The fast-moving water cut through the basalt rock by Taylor's Falls, which had been formed by lava flows in the region some 750 million years ago. This turbulent melting water from Glacial Lake Duluth eroded the lava formations, leaving strange rock features for which the St. Croix Dalles is famous.

In Indian times, the St. Croix Valley was a neutral, no-man's land between the warring Ojibwe and Dakota. No permanent villages were established here by either nation, since at any time the area could turn into a battle ground. Zion's Hill, near the center of Stillwater, was the scene of an Indian battle between an Ojibwe and Dakota chieftain. The endless warfare between these nations had begun to alarm the two enemies. It was decided therefore, that warfare should be ended by hand-to-hand combat between the two chiefs. After a long, brutal battle, the Ojibwe chief died, deciding the battle in favor of the Dakota. But before dying it was reported by Indian Trader, Thomas Connor, that the chief had made a prophecy: "the white man is coming and will soon be here...He will build buildings; one to settle his quarrels in...where the children will learn to be good and not fight as I have done today."

The Washington County Courthouse now stands on Zion's Hill. Built in 1867, it is the oldest Minnesota courthouse still in use. The original courthouse was built on the corner of Fourth and Chestnut in 1849 and was the first courthouse in Minnesota Territory. The treaties between the U. S. government and the Indians, which covered the St. Croix Valley, were not completed until 1837. But white settlers soon began to push into the area in anticipation of development.

NAMING THE ST. CROIX

The Dakota had referred to the river and lake as "Hoganwahnkay-kin," meaning "the place where the fish lies." It marked the place where a Dakota hunter was supposedly transformed into a large fish after drinking water from the river. The white explorers preferred a different name. Father Hennepin referred to it as the "river of the tomb" because a band of Indians had left the body of one of their dead warriors there. In the 1700's, French explorer Le Sueur was the first to call the river, St. Croix, because a Frenchman of that name was shipwrecked at the mouth of the river. Others state that it was called St. Croix because a cross had been planted over the remains of a voyageur. The St. Croix is nearly 170 miles in length.

MARINE ON ST. CROIX, Pop. 543

The great lumbering industry of western Wisconsin and Minnesota had its beginning in the small village of Marine, the oldest civilian town in Minnesota. Built in 1838, this was the sight of the first sawmill in Minnesota to cut and market lumber commercially. The previous year the Marine Lumber Company had been formed by Lewis Judd and David Hone, of Marine, Illinois. They selected this area for a mill site while on a steamer trip up the St. Croix.

Fort Snelling was the nearest post office until one was established here in 1845. Prior to this time, the mail had been carried monthly between the fort and Marine by a man named Philip Aldrich. The town of Marine was officially organized on October 20, 1858. The second death recorded in Marine was Mrs. B. T. Otis in the winter of 1847. One day when Mr. Otis went into the woods, leaving his wife with the James Brown family, Mrs. Otis became sick with ague. Mr. Brown was sent to buy some calomel. During his return, he put two packages of similar size and shape in his pocket; one containing calomel and one containing strychnine. Tragically, his memory failed him and Mrs. Otis was given the strychnine.

MHS

The last logs collected at the St. Croix boom in 1886. Photo/John Runk.

VASA

Vasa was a town named in honor of the Swedish king, in hopes of attracting Scandinavian settlers. The town encompassed some 300 acres of land a short distance above present-day William O'Brien State Park. It was leased to land agent, Francis Register, from Benjamin Otis of Marine. Advertisements in the Stillwater and St. Paul newspapers spoke of a town with a good steamboat landing, a sawmill and several stores. The St. Croix Union predicted Vasa would have growing prosperity. But the sawmill failed after a partner pocketed what little money there was. The town name was changed to Otis because another town by the name of Vasa had been organized in Goodhue County.

In 1860 the post office was discontinued and Marine voted a re-annexation of the area. Today the name "Copas" has replaced the names Vasa and Otis. This name was taken from an early storekeeper, John Copas. The Crabtree Kitchen restaurant and the 1875 schoolhouse along Highway 95, lie in the heart of old Vasa. Vasa was typical of settlements planned and platted by land speculators. These towns lasted only a few years; often becoming the victims of hard economic times.

COPAS

Copas adjoins the former site of Vasa. Indian burial mounds were once numerous throughout the lower St. Croix Valley, especially near Copas and Osceola, Wisconsin. But over the years, farming has leveled these archaeological treasures. A short distance from Copas is William O'Brien State Park, a beautiful wooded area of 1,273 acres adjoining the St. Croix River.

SCANDIA

The rural community of Scandia, five miles north of Marine on St. Croix, was the home of the first Swedish settlers in Minnesota. Scandia takes its name from the Roman term for southern Sweden. Carl Fernstrom, Oscar Roos and August Sandahl were the first immigrants to stake out claims just west of Hay Lake in 1850. (Today a granite obelisk stands on the site as a monument to those early settlers.) In 1851 they sold their farm to Daniel Nilson. Nilson has been called the "founder" of Scandia since his home became the nucleus of the community. The early Swedish pioneers were a devout group and they held worship services at the Nilson cabin.

In 1856 the community's first church was built, but with the continued arrival of new settlers, it was quickly outgrown. Four more churches preceded the present-day Elim Lutheran Church, located in the heart of Scandia. Some of the earlier buildings were destroyed by fire and one was struck by a tornado. Each time, despite economic hardships, the Swedish community quickly rebuilt their church. It was not until the late 1920's and early 1930's that services at Elim were conducted in English. This major change from the exclusive use of Swedish occurred during the pastorate of Joel Olsenius, the grandfather of this author.

FRANCONIA

Three miles south of Taylors Falls lies the deserted village of Franconia. The first settler here was Ansel Smith, who came in 1852 and named the town for his former home in the White Mountains of New Hampshire. The first white pines logged on the St. Croix were cut here, made into rafts, then towed down river.

The town had numerous stores, hotels, factories, saloons and a four-story, stone flour mill, built in 1864 by Paul Munch, an immigrant from Luxembourg. A sawmill and ship-building yard was located by the river's edge. During the 1860's, a number of lumber and wheat barges and several paddle-wheel steamboats were constructed at Franconia. In 1865, the Taylors Falls Register noted that Franconia was sure to become a place of note. The town depended on lumber and the river transportation of wheat and was quite successful as commerce remained brisk. But by the mid-1880's, the St. Croix Boom Company had gained an economic strangle hold on the valley and made no attempt to keep the steamboat channel open. Slowly, the saw and flour-milling towns above Stillwater were left to a quiet demise. In 1881, the Northern Pacific railroad missed Franconia, and Taylors Falls became the leading trading spot in the region.

MHS

Two friends pose for the camera of John Runk.

By the turn of the century, Franconia had sold its jail and other property, and quietly gone out of business. In recent years, the community has become the location of a few summer and year-round homes, taking on the flavor of Marine on St. Croix.

TAYLORS FALLS, Pop. 623

Taylors Falls was named for Jesse Taylor, who arrived in 1838 to establish timber claims. The town was first called Taylor's Place and later Taylors Falls. The apostrophe was officially removed by a legislative act.

The town's first settlers didn't arrive until the early 1850's. Many packet river steamers tied up at the lower dalles of the river or a few hundred yards below the present inter-

Timber ready for skidding down the St. Croix. Photo/John Runk.

MHS

state bridge. The old iron rungs of the steamboat companies can still be seen in the rocks. These boats carried many immigrant pioneers who eventually made their way overland to Center City.

In 1851, the first frame building was constructed by independent logger and valley historian, William H. C. Folsom. Three years later, Folsom built another home with a beautiful view of the valley. It can be reached by taking Government Street, at the junction of Highways 8 and 95, to the top of Angel's Hill. The home is open to the public, afternoons from June through September.

As the lumber industry's demand for logs grew, so did Taylors Falls. In 1881, the town experienced a boom-type growth when the Northern Pacific Railroad opened a branch line from Wyoming to Taylors Falls. Today, the town is heavily dependent on tourism, brought about largely by the spec-

tacular beauty of the St. Croix Dalles. (Dalles is a French name meaning "slab of rock"). The Dalles is now a part of the St. Croix Interstate Park.

SUNRISE RIVER

This major tributary to the St. Croix River once carried away the meltwater of glaciers. The river, which begins in the Carlos Avery Wildlife Area, a 23,000 acre parcel of land, has been dammed in a couple of locations, flooding an extensive area to provide waterfowl habitat. This managed area is full of song birds, ducks, geese, grouse and deer. It is used by both hunters and non-hunters alike. Carlos Avery was named after the state's Game and Fish Commissioner during the early 1920's. The Sunrise River flows through the refuge northward, to the early St. Croix town of Sunrise. The Ojibwe called this river "Me-mo-ka-ge," or "Sun-Keep-Rising."

CENTER CITY

This town was platted in 1857 and is the seat of Chisago County. Because of its central position between Chisago City and Taylors Falls, it was given the name Center City. Eric Norberg was one of the first white men to travel to this region in 1850, lured by the Indian descriptions of the numerous lakes and abundant fish. By 1851 he had returned with a group of Swedish settlers. By 1854 these pioneers established the Chisago Lakes Lutheran Church, the first church in the entire region. The church is listed in the National Historical Registry of buildings. Today a monument near the church commemorates its founding and the development of the Minnesota Conference of the Augustana Lutheran Church.

LINDSTROM, Pop. 1,972

In 1853, Daniel Lindstrom traveled from Sweden to a Swedish settlement in Moline, Illinois. With the help of a young churchman, Dr. Eric Norelius, Lindstrom came to the lake region of Chisago County in 1854. He purchased 134 acres of land at $1.25 per acre. His log cabin and windmill were located where the Dinnerbell Restaurant now stands. He later built a home on the present site of the Lindstrom Bakery.

There was a heavy concentration of Swedish settlers in this region, partly because the land, lakes and climate are so similar to southern Sweden. The chain of lakes here was often called "Swede Lake", but it was decided that the area should keep the Indian name for the largest of its lakes, "Ki-chi-saga," Ojibwe for "large and lovely." Through pronunciation and clerical errors, the name became Chisago.

The Lindstrom homestead covered what is now the business section of town. A. C. Tumbler was the first businessman to settle on this site. He operated a general store and sold supplies to nearby farmers. Tumbler and Lindstrom convinced the St. Paul and Duluth Railroad Company to build a station in Lindstrom, and the town began to grow. Lindstrom began to plat and sell portions of his homestead for businesses and homes. The railroad brought many people to the lake region, making it a popular resort area.

From the turn of the century to the mid-1920's, the Chisago Lakes area did its biggest business in potatoes. Every town in the county had potato warehouses along the railroad tracks. In winter, the farmers made a living selling cord wood, shipped by the train loads cross-country. Dairy farming became a principle occupation when wood and potato production had run its course. The railroad made its last run between Wyoming and Taylors Falls in 1948. The Lindstrom tracks and station were removed, marking the end of an important era for the region.

Lindstrom, Center City and Chisago City were considered to be the nucleus of Swedish culture and religion. A statue of Karl Oskar Nilsson, still stands in Lindstrom as a symbol of all immigrants who came to the United States. Nilsson is the legendary character in Wilhelm Moberg's trilogy—"The Emigrant Saga", the story of Swedish settlement in America. Seven miles northeast of Lindstrom, the Yesterfarm of Memories Museum has an extensive collection of pioneer memorabilia.

CHISAGO, Pop. 1,634

When the county was formed in 1851, names of the lakes and rivers were collected from the Indians. Many liked the name "Ki-chi-saga Sagiagan," meaning large, fair and lovely lake. So Chisago became the choice for a county name. In 1851 there were no roads for the settlers traveling to Still-water for supplies, except for canoeing or rafting down the St. Croix. The Point Douglas road was constructed through Chisago County on its way to Superior in 1853, greatly aiding travel through this region.

The first Swedes came to this area in 1851 and settled between Chisago and Green Lakes. Speculators bought land from the government for $1.25 an acre—and sold it for much more. A hotel was soon built, followed by a saw and grist mill. Prosperity grew around Chisago City so fast that the county seat was moved there from Taylors Falls in 1865. Later it was moved to Center City. When a branch of the St. Paul and Duluth Railroad was built from Wyoming to Taylors Falls in 1878, it passed a mile north of Chisago to avoid the lake and swamps. Consequently, the town also moved a mile north and re-formed around the new depot.

WYOMING, Pop. 1,559

A farming colony emigrating in 1855 from a region in Pennsylvania known as Wyoming Valley, gave this township and village its name. The St. Paul and Duluth Railroad made its way from Forest Lake in 1868 and a village formed around the station shortly after. Ten years later, tracks were laid as far east as Taylors Falls. Wyoming is an Indian word for "expansive plains."

STACY, Pop. 996

Stacy formed around the station of the St. Paul and Duluth Railroad in 1875 and was named after Dr. Stacy Collins, who moved here from the East to improve his health. The town grew as an agricultural marketing center during the 1900's, but the number of farms has decreased and many supporting businesses have folded.

(left) Twin City & Lake Superior Railroad Workers clear right-of-way to Duluth.
(bottom) A picnic along the St. Croix Valley.

NORTH BRANCH, Pop 1,597

It wasn't until after the Civil War ended in 1865, that the North Branch area began to draw settlers. By 1870, with the coming of the Lake Superior and Mississippi Railroad from St. Paul, its location was secured on the north branch of the Sunrise River. One of the major reasons that people began to settle here, and in other areas of Minnesota, was the passage of the Homestead Law in 1862. This law gave 160 acres to anybody who would settle and farm land for at least five years. The railroads had also received incentives to build and were given sections of land that adjoined the tracks. In turn, the railroads sold much of their land cheaply, encouraging further settlement and use of their line.

Many agents and land speculators traveled to Europe and Scandinavia, promoting these new Minnesota lands and encouraging immigration. Between 1840 and 1930, over 1 million Swedish immigrants came to the U.S., with many coming to the Chisago region. The reasons for such a large Swedish exodus were many. But religious persecution and a life of subsistence living were among the main factors.

A young station agent named Richard Sears worked at the North Branch railroad station for a couple of years. While here, he bought an unclaimed load of watches and sold them by mail to other agents, all for a good profit. Sears had sparked an idea about selling through the mail and went on to found the Sears and Roebuck Company of Chicago in 1893.

At Wyoming in 1896, two people were killed in a restaurant holdup. The armed robbers ran up the railroad tracks to North Branch, and were captured after a brief shootout. The leader of the group, named Kelly, was hung, making his the first lynching in the county.

About thirteen miles east of North Branch, at the confluence of the St. Croix and Sunrise rivers, is the 6,000 acre St. Croix Wild River State Park, with 30 miles of trails and 73 campsites.

SUNRISE CITY

One of the stops on the government road from Point Douglas (near Hastings) to Superior, Wisconsin, was Sunrise City. This town is located a short distance from the confluence of the St. Croix and Sunrise rivers. The name "Sunrise" was derived from the Ojibwe name for the lake and river, "Memo-ka-ge," meaning "sun-keep-rising". The township was organized in 1858, and by 1869 it had reached its peak, with over 300 inhabitants, a sawmill, two gristmills, four hotels, two stores, a schoolhouse and one saloon. The regional land office for the public sale of acreage in the St. Croix Valley was located at Sunrise and was largely responsible for its growth.

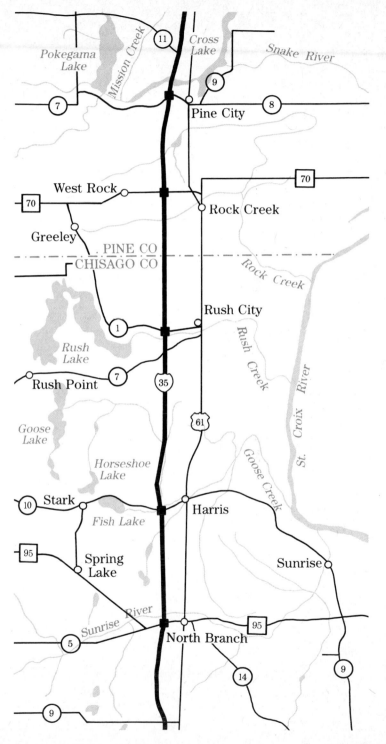

Neighboring newspapers, from towns in competition with one another, had another view of Sunrise. In 1867 the Osceola POLK COUNTY PRESS advised the settlement to rename itself "Sunset", for it was "not of rapid growth, nor fortunate in its settlers." An editor of the STILLWATER MESSENGER advised that the town's name be changed to "Sundown", since "The sun doesn't rise there until three or four weeks after it makes its appearance at other places."

In the 1860's, the railroad was built through North Branch, ten miles west of Sunrise. After that the town began a steady decline. The land office was moved down river to Taylors Falls. When trains began running from St. Paul to Duluth, the heavy traffic on the government road came to an end, and so did the growth of Sunrise. The newspapers' prophecies came true. Today there is little left of Sunrise City, except its claim to being the birthplace of movie actor Richard Widmark.

MHS

A Dakota mother and child. Circa. 1899.

HARRIS, Pop. 678

In 1870, the village of Harris formed along Goose Creek by the Lake Superior and Mississippi Railroad depot. The town was named after Philip S. Harris, an officer of the railroad. Residents of the town traded hay, wheat, potatoes, wood and rail ties. At one time, Harris had two hotels, three grain elevators, four general stores and two blacksmith shops.

RUSH CITY, Pop. 1,198

Settlement by whites first began here in 1855 when the military road was built across a shallow spot in Rush Creek. A man named George Folsom built a wayside house to feed travelers who rode the stages that ran between St. Paul and Duluth. The stopping point became know as Rushseba. Seba is an Ojibwe word for river. A sawmill was built along Rush Creek in 1868 by Samuel Martin. This mill also provided lumber for the town of Rush City that was growing around new railroad tracks that had been laid just west of Rushseba. Rushseba faded quickly as Rush City continued to grow.

The railroad from St. Paul to Rush City became known by depot agents as the "Skally" line. The story goes that Swedes arriving in St. Paul were asked where they were going; they replied, "ve skal go to Rush City."

The first settlers of Rush City were Patrick and Thomas Flynn, brothers who came here to operate a trading post on Rush Creek. For a time, they traded with the Ojibwe, who brought beaver pelts to exchange for guns, salt pork, tea and flour. The flour was ground at a mill located at the small settlement of Sunrise, until a one hundred barrel-a-day mill was built at nearby Rushseba. The Flynns built much of early Rush City, including the huge Merchant Hotel with its balconies and ballroom, making it the town's pride.

Potatoes became a major cash crop for area farmers, with the Twin Cities markets providing the major incentive. Potato acreage continued to increase through the late 1800's, with Rush City being the northeast limit of the potato belt. At one time this town had eleven potato warehouses.

In 1883 tracks were laid across the St. Croix River from Rush City to Grantsburg. This route became known as the "Blueberry Special," since it was quite popular to take the train into Wisconsin and pick berries. Wood was cut by area farmers who cleared the land for fields and stacked wood piles near the tracks, hoping to sell as much as they could for the wood-burning locomotives.

PINE CITY, Pop. 2,489

As you drive north towards Pine City, the soil changes from a sandy loam to a sandy clay, and the oak, elm and maple trees become more interspersed with pine, spruce and tamarack. Years before the whites settled in this area, the Ojibwe maintained a village here which they called "Chengwatana," or Pine City. When trading started with the Indians, several posts were maintained here and at Pokegama Lake, by the Snake River. Even though the British had lost the Revolutionary War, The Northwest Fur Company, a British company, traded here with the Ojibwe in 1804. Today a replica of the post is maintained by the Minnesota Historical Society.

When the military road was built through this region in 1854, a station for changing horses was constructed, giving added importance to this town. Chengwatana became the county seat in 1856, two years before Minnesota was admitted as a state. But when the Lake Superior and Mississippi Railroad passed on the west side of Cross Lake, a new town formed with an English translation of Chengwatana (Pine City) as its name. It was only a short time before the county seat was moved from Chengwatana to Pine City. By now the Ojibwe had been transferred to the White Earth Reservation and Chengwatana faded away.

By 1880 the lumber companies were cutting the huge white pine forests that stretched across the Snake River basin. For years, the Snake carried the logs down the St. Croix and fed the mills of Stillwater, Winona and beyond. Pine City became an outfitting center for the hundreds of men working in the forests. In the fall, the city filled up with a rough crowd of lumberjacks waiting for the ground to freeze so they could begin their work. The lumber industry believed these expansive forests were inexhaustible. By the late 1890's however, the logging industry was moving north, looking for the trees they thought would never disappear. The problem now was what to do with the cut-over, decimated land they left behind.

The railroads, with their own interests in mind, began promoting this area as a farming region. This promotion attracted a number of Bohemian immigrants who came here to farm. Tourism started to affect Pine City and the nearby lakes. By 1900 it became a fashionable weekend retreat for people from the Twin Cities and St. Cloud. They came here to dance and dine at places like the "Tuxedo Inn." Steamboats even carried resorters around Lake Pokegama. Pokegama is an Ojibwe word meaning, "water which juts out from another water." This is in reference to the closeness of Pokegama lake to the Snake River.

Lumber crews in 1885 were fed from riverboats, called wannagans.

MHS

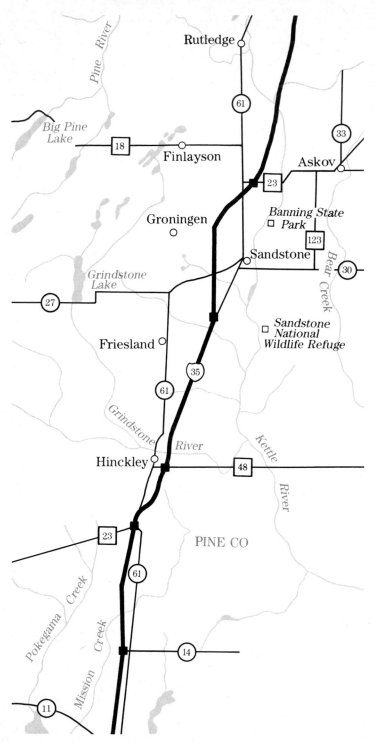

HINCKLEY, Pop. 963

By 1857 the government road from St. Paul to Superior, Wisconsin was completed and stages began regular service between the two towns. One of the principle relay stations on this route was about three miles east of present-day Hinckley, at the Grindstone River. Here passengers were fed and lodged at the station house, while stage drivers changed horses. Hinckley lies in a richly-forested area with a number of streams draining into the St. Croix River. The Dakota Indian first hunted under these towering pines, but by the mid-1700's they were pushed out by the Ojibwe, who themselves were feeling pressure in the eastern states and had begun moving into the rich hunting areas of Minnesota by way of Lake Superior.

The Indians sold their furs at trading posts located at Lakes Pokegama and Mille Lacs. One Ojibwe band led by Chief Cowatossa, wintered at Mission Creek, not far from where State 23 joins the Interstate. A mission was started there in 1838, but an attack by a Dakota war party destroyed it three years later. Located between the Snake and Grindstone rivers was a large Ojibwe burial ground of over 100 graves.

In the summer of 1870, the Lake Superior and Mississippi Railroad was built through Hinckley, bringing carloads of lumberjacks to this region. (In 1877, the Lake Superior and Mississippi Railroad became the St. Paul and Duluth line; by 1900 it was run by the Northern Pacific.) Many of the lumbermen stayed at the huge Depot Hotel. It had 20 beds and two dining rooms with a seating capacity of 500. During the winter months, hundreds of men worked in the woods, skidding out the logs that floated down the Kettle River during the spring's high water. Hinckley grew as a railroad division point and also became a supplier to the logging and milling industries of the region. Until the great fire of 1894, some 400 men were employed at the McKane Bros. sawmill. The town also had several other large hotels, three churches and a hospital.

GREAT HINCKLEY FIRE

In the summer of 1894, a persistent drought dried up many of the rivers and turned the forests tinder-dry. Debris and slash left by the loggers lay scattered through the entire region, with little effort made to clean it up. The Hinckley residents were nervous, and when a small fire started September 1st, at the hamlet of Mission Creek (located a few miles south of Hinckley), their fears were realized. Fanned by a strong wind, the fire rapidly spread through the trees and brush towards Brook Park and Hinckley. Before long it was evident that Hinckley and its 1,200 residents were in danger. A train, engineered by Jim Root, rushed to Hinckley from Sandstone and loaded some 300 passengers. Unable to turn, Root backed the train through a wall of flames, running it out of town, across the burning Grindstone bridge. Five minutes after it was crossed, the bridge collapsed. It was a race then to see which would make it to the Kettle River first–the train or the fire. But Root brought the train out safely, though his hands were badly burned from holding the hot metal throttle. In the aftermath, both Hinckley and Sandstone had been destroyed, and over 400 people perished before the fire burned out. Hinckley's economy never recovered to those early boom-days.

SANDSTONE, Pop. 1,594

The sandstone ledges lining the Kettle River, were known to be of some value to the early settlers. However, it wasn't until William Grant came here and started a quarry in 1885, that the town of Sandstone began to form. Although there were many lumber camps in the area, it was the payroll from the quarries that gave the town its will to exist. A railroad spur was built from the main line at Sandstone to the quarries and was called Sandstone Junction.

Sandstone, with its five saloons and location near the lumber camps, provided lumberjacks with a place they called home. The great fire of 1894, which destroyed Hinckley, also swept over Sandstone. Many died, but most of the residents found safety in the Kettle River. The area was totally burned, taking on an almost moon-like appearance. The future seemed bleak for the burned-out and homeless residents. But help soon came, and some 50 homes were built with state relief-aid and the Red Cross. A number of Swedes started clearing the blackened stumps for farming, while still working ten hours a day on the railroad to pay for their land. The quarries started up again and before long, 100 railway cars were being loaded daily. By 1910 Sandstone had a population of 1,800, with 600 men working in the quarries and creosote plant. The stone quarries closed down when structural steel started replacing stone in buildings.

ASKOV, Pop. 350

This part of Pine County was basically a forested wilderness until the Great Northern Railroad was built here in 1888, en route from Hinckley to Duluth. Lumbering started shortly after, with logs being sent down the Kettle and Sand rivers. Around 1900, a number of German settlers began to clear land for farming. Unable to make a profit, the farms were sold and the Germans moved away. A few years later, a Danish organization purchased land here to build a town. Over the next ten years, news about this town spread throughout Europe and some 1,000 people immigrated here. At first the town was named Partridge; later it was changed to Askov. Askov formed several co-ops, one being their own fire insurance company, due to the extremely high rates for this fire-prone region. Their most important effort, though, was forming a creamery co-operative in 1911. At one time, this region carried the dubious distinction of being the rutabaga capital of the nation.

FINLAYSON, Pop. 202

Finlayson was named after Scotchman, Dave Finlayson, who came here about 1880 to run a sawmill. Activity at that time was centered around harvesting the white pine. During the Depression of 1893, a number of Finns settled here from the northern coal mines of Wyoming and the Mesabi Range. In 1907, a co-operative creamery was started, and at one time Finlayson had a 25-piece, brass band.

KETTLE STAGE STATION, RUTLEDGE & WILLOW RIVER

During the 1850's, a stage stop was established where the Interstate crosses the Kettle River. This stop ran along the military road that linked Duluth and St. Paul. A small settlement of whites and Indians formed here. But when the Lake Superior and Mississippi Railroad came through in 1870, it rapidly faded away. A couple of miles up stream, the town of Rutledge formed along the railroad. Rutledge had some boom years during the height of lumbering, but after the lumberjacks moved on, the town became just another small settlement along the Kettle River. A short ways up the Kettle River, the small town of Willow River formed, at a point where the Willow River enters the Kettle.

KETTLE RIVER

The Ojibwe called it "Akiko-zibi" or Kettle River, because of its 82 mile journey over a scoured river-bed. The river was often bordered in many places by ledges and cliffs made of sandstone. In 1973 the Minnesota Legislature passed the Wild and Scenic Rivers Act; two years later the Kettle River became the first stream designated under this law.

The Kettle flows through what was once, one of the richest pineries in the Northwest; a place where lumbermen saw only money when they cut the trees, not the desolation they were leaving behind. Today, a second growth of birch, aspen, poplar, and wide range of brushy undergrowth, has made this land a rich wildlife habitat. The towering pines (the sign of a mature forest) had blocked the sun, giving little chance for the undergrowth needed by the deer, grouse and other animal species.

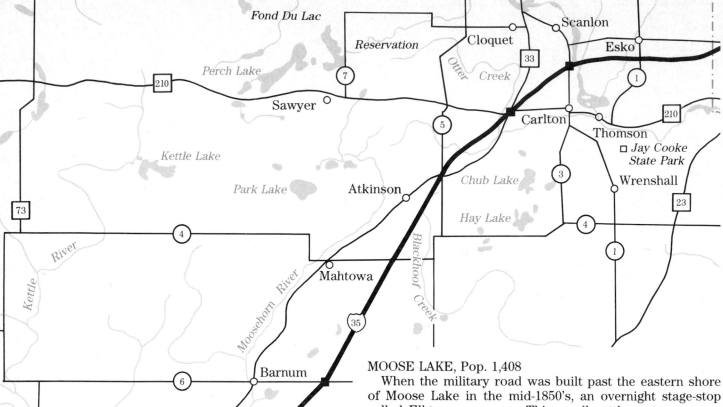

MOOSE LAKE, Pop. 1,408

When the military road was built past the eastern shore of Moose Lake in the mid-1850's, an overnight stage-stop called Elkton sprung up. This small settlement was comprised of little more than a meager hotel, a stable, a few log cabins and a band of Ojibwe Indians living nearby. In 1870 the Lake Superior and Mississippi Railroad was constructed just three miles west of Elkton. The residents picked up stakes and formed the new town of Moose Lake. Like most towns of this region, logging provided the only income during those first years. But when logging decreased in the 1800's, an influx of Scandinavian farmers began to work the cleared land. The village continued to grow, and by 1910, another railroad, the Soo Line, passed through town.

A replay of the tragic fire that destroyed Hinckley and Sandstone in 1874, took place October 12, 1918, after a long dry autumn. A number of forest fires broke out across St. Louis and Carlton Counties, causing the greatest damage the state has ever known. Fanned by 60 mile-an-hour winds, the fires consumed anything and everything that would burn. Cloquet, Carlton, Moose Lake and other smaller villages were leveled, and 453 people lost their lives in the holocaust. Because of these tragic fires, legislation was enacted to deal with the slash from logging, requiring permits to burn and mandatory spark protection from train locomotives. The cemetery in Moose Lake has a 28-foot granite spire, to commemorate those who died in the tragic fires.

BARNUM, Pop. 464

Barnum, a small railway village, found its early economy centered around its lumber mill and the woodsmen that resupplied at the stores. The village was platted in 1887 and named in honor of George G. Barnum, a paymaster of the railroad. Today this railroad right-of-way is vacant.

When lumbering died out, dairying and poultry began to develop. One frustrated and unemployed lumberman brought 2,000 chickens to raise at Barnum. A hard winter killed 1,500 of them. Still he persisted, and within a few years, Barnum was one of the largest egg-producing centers in the state. In 1904, H. C. Hanson developed a purebred Guernsey cow called the "May Rose Guernsey." The milk production from this breed helped make the Barnum Creamery one of the nation's largest. Hanson later helped develop a purebred strain of the White Leghorn chickens.

Barnum, located on the Moose River, offers excellent walleye and northern pike fishing. Just north of Barnum lies the divide between the Mississippi and Lake Superior Basin, where rain showers falling on the south side of the divide, flow to the Mississippi and the Gulf of Mexico. On the north side of the divide, the water drains through the Great Lakes into the North Atlantic.

CARLTON, Pop. 862

When the first traders passed up the St. Louis River on their way from Lake Superior to the Upper Mississippi, the Carlton area was occupied by Ojibwe Indians. Few whites traveled here, until the military road passed through Scotts Corner, Wrenshall and the small village of Superior. A number of "paper towns" were platted along this route as speculators tried to entice people to purchase land in their towns. One of these towns was called Komoko. The Lake Superior and Mississippi Railroad was built through Komoko in 1870. That winter, a group of men stood around a bonfire at the small hamlet, and threw in the first dirt to commemorate the spot from which the Northern Pacific Railroad would eventually reach the Pacific Coast. It was Jay Cooke, a Philadelphia promoter and financier, who carried the bonds for the building of the Northern Pacific.

At the junction of the Northern Pacific and the Lake Superior and Mississippi tracks, a new town formed, a mile east of Komoko, called Northern Pacific Junction. Across the river, the town of Thomson developed and later became the county seat. These two villages fought over the county seat until the

Northern Pacific Junction residents crossed the St. Louis River and stole the county records and safe. The Junction was renamed Carlton after Reuben Carlton, a settler in the early trading village of Fond du Lac (later a part of Duluth). Lumbering and railroads were Carlton's backbone as the Northern Pacific trains ferried workmen and lumber to areas such as Brainerd, Aitkin and McGregor.

ST. LOUIS RIVER

The St. Louis River was a much smaller river during its early history, with most of it draining into the Mississippi rather than Lake Superior, as it does today. But thousands of years of erosion from tributaries such as the Cloquet and Whiteface rivers carved a new channel to Lake Superior. Today the St. Louis extends some 160 miles into the quiet wilderness of northern Minnesota, where jack pine, aspen and birch have now grown back following years of lumbering. The St. Louis has developed a poor reputation over the years as a polluted river. But that problem can only be seen after it passes the towns and industry of its lower portion. A large sum of money is being spent to clean up pollution from the Cloquet paper mill.

This river was an early portage for the Indians and traders who came from Lake Superior to the Mississippi basin. Daniel Greysolon Sieur Du Luth traveled the St. Louis as early as 1679. Later, important expeditions of Cass and Schoolcraft passed here in 1820 and 1832, respectively. The river was most likely named by Sieur de la Verendrye, a French ex-

Dairy farmers bringing milk to the Barnum creamery. Circa. 1900.

MHS

(right) Ojibwe village at Fond du Lac.
(bottom) Forest fire devastates Northern Minnesota town in 1890.

MHS

MHS

plorer who traveled this region in 1731. For Verendrye and others, the portage along the St. Louis River, up the hill from Lake Superior, was the most difficult. The river drops nearly 500 feet along a rock-strewn channel as it tumbles down the hills bordering the lake.

Canoes and goods were carried along the banks of the St. Louis until more placid and rock-free waters could be reached. At the junction of the St. Louis and East Savanna rivers, near Floodwood, the explorers headed west along the Savanna into the Big Sandy, where trading posts had been established. From Big Sandy it was only a short portage to the Mississippi. This 70-mile route was used for some fifty years by both British and American fur traders.

The upper sections of the St. Louis and its tributaries, were channels for the large number of pine being harvested during the late 1800's. The lumbermen would have floated their logs all the way to Duluth, but the last stretch of the St. Louis made it impossible. Consequently, Cloquet prospered as a sawmilling town, at least until the railroads carried ore from the range, and began hauling lumber to Duluth. But the "inexhaustible" supply of pine peaked in 1902. Considerable decline was seen during the next couple of decades. During this time, the iron mines of the Mesabi Range were in full production while the numerous lumber camps began to fade away.

FOND DU LAC INDIAN RESERVATION

On an autumn day in 1854, several hundred Ojibwe Indians gathered on Madeline Island of Lake Superior, to sign an important treaty. The small settlement where they signed is called La Pointe. At one time, it was the most important village of the Ojibwe Nation. It was here that ten tribes ceded most of northeastern Minnesota to the whites, thereby opening the area for settlement. The Ojibwe were given the Fond Du Lac Reservation and a million dollars for the ceded land; later it would be worth billions for its mineral deposits and timber.

CLOQUET, Pop. 11,142

During the 1700's, traders passed up the St. Louis River on their way to western posts. But Cloquet wasn't an attraction, until the lumbermen realized that the water potential of the river made this an ideal place for milling. In 1870, a sawmill was hauled here and logs started descending the Whiteface, Floodwood and Cloquet rivers, eventually coming to rest in this growing village. The town of Cloquet was first platted as Knife Falls, but in 1883, it was changed to Cloquet. During this period, the lumber companies owned every house in town.

Cloquet was destroyed in October, 1918, by the same fire that swept across the entire region, killing some 400 people. The town was later rebuilt, but at a time when the white pine was just about depleted. Struggling to stay alive, the lumber companies started to work with wood that was once considered waste. A large paper mill now operates in Cloquet, utilizing the pulpwood of the north.

SCANLON, Pop. 1,050

Scanlon developed as a lumber manufacturing village in the late 1870's and is situated between Cloquet and Carlton on the St. Louis River. It was named for M. Joseph Scanlon, whose company held substantial lumber investments in the village.

ESKO

This village formed as a Finnish dairy community, which grew around a strong co-operative creamery. The early Finns that settled here, kept to themselves, and practiced what many thought was a pagan form of religion. It seemed that many Finns were often spotted in white robes, walking to little houses or shrines behind their barns. As it was later discovered, the Finns were not practicing some strange religion; merely taking their daily "sauna."

JAY COOKE STATE PARK

A good portion of this 9,500 acre park was donated in 1915 from the estate of Jay Cooke. Cooke was considered one of the richest men in the United States before the great "Panic

of 1873." His financial company floated the bonds that built the Northern Pacific Railroad, which had its start in 1870 just outside of Carlton. When the panic struck in '73, the tracks were almost laid across Minnesota when construction came to a halt. The railroad was eventually re-organized and the golden spike, connecting Duluth with Puget Sound, was struck at the half-way point of Helena, Montana, in the fall of 1883.

The park is an area of woodlands and jagged rocks. Here the St. Louis River drops 395 feet from the uplands, in just a few miles. Near the end of the last ice age, when the two-mile thick, glacial ice began to melt, much of the water began to flow south through the St. Croix Valley. But as the ice melted and its incredible weight diminished, the land around the St. Louis River began to rise, causing the St. Louis River and the glacial lakes of the Arrowhead to drain into Lake Superior. These rushing rivers carved out deep rugged gorges. However, this beautiful area was not a favorite place of the early explorers and traders as they passed up from Lake Superior. They followed a trail along the rocky rapids, struggling with their canoes and goods until they reached the quieter waters above the gorge. They cynically called this, the "Grand Portage."

MHS

A river crew works to dislodge logs, 1865.

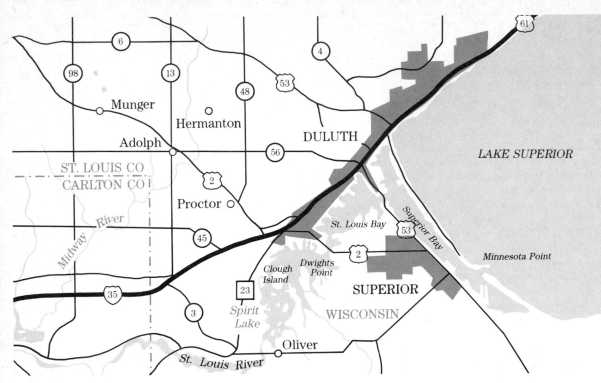

LAKE SUPERIOR

The dark rocky hills, against which Duluth is built, were formed by lava flows and are some of the oldest surface formations on this continent. These hillsides also formed the shoreline of ancient Glacial Lake Duluth, a body of water much larger than today's Lake Superior, the largest freshwater lake in the world.

Glacial Lake Duluth was at least twice as high as the present lake. Much of the initial drainage of this huge body of water was south through Wisconsin, where it carved out the St. Croix Valley. At Hastings, this massive drainage of Lake Duluth, joined the Glacial River Warren, which drained Lake Agassiz in northwest Minnesota. From there the combined rivers continued down the Mississippi, carving out its broad river valley. The actual basin of present day Lake Superior was formed by a succession of glaciers, each one carving a deeper and wider basin.

The Ojibwe called the lake, "Kitchigumi", meaning "Great Water." The early French called it Lac Superieur, since it laid at the head of all the Great Lakes. However it was called, this grand lake was the first route used by the explorers as they pushed westward, looking for a passage to the Pacific. Superior soon became a conduit for an intricate fur-trading network that strung from the Pacific Northwest, eastward to

Montreal. During the early 1900's, the whale-back ore boats started crossing Superior for the steel mills of Michigan, feeding the blast furnaces of a nation whose needs were changing from wood to steel. Today, Lake Superior continues to provide the Midwest with a deep-water port for the ships of the world. There is also a growing challenge for those concerned with preserving the pristine beauty of the lake. Though Superior is the largest freshwater body in the world, its ability to replenish itself from pollution is very poor, requiring over 190 years for a complete exchange of its waters.

PROCTOR, Pop. 3,180

The town formed in 1894 around the Duluth, Missabe and Northern Railroad that had begun hauling ore down from Mountain Iron, one of the first areas to be mined on the Mesabi Range. At first, Proctor was considered part of Oneota, a shoreline village on the St. Louis Bay that was later annexed by Duluth. Proctor contains a number of train repair shops and 57 miles of tracks. These tracks lie in classification yards, where ore cars are prepared for the six-mile downhill trip to the ore docks of Duluth. The railroad is still Proctor's major industry.

At one time the town was called Proctor Knott, after a U.S. Congressman from Kentucky who ridiculed the town of Duluth on the floor of Congress in 1871. Knott was opposed to a land-grant bill that kept the towns of Duluth and Superior at each other's throats. Knott sarcastically referred to Duluth as the "center of the universe." His speech continued until the Congressmen were rocking with laughter, giving Duluth immediate, if not humiliating, recognition. Years later, the town dropped "Knott" from its name.

DULUTH, Pop. 92,811

Lying in a narrow band from the mouth of the St. Louis River for some 25 miles along Lake Superior's shore, is the city of Duluth. Flanked by lava bluffs that rise 800 feet above the lake, Duluth is affected by the lake's own weather system. While the rest of the state cooks under a summer sun, a cool breeze is usually drifting off the lake, re-affirming Duluth's nickname as the "air-conditioned city."

When the first explorers paddled to the head of Superior in the mid-1600's, they found the Ojibwe pushing their way into Minnesota, the long standing territory of the Dakota Nation. This conflict between the Ojibwe and Dakota never really ended until the 1850's. Radisson and Groseilliers are credited with being the first whites to visit this part of the lake, during the years from 1654-1660. One of the early settlements was a small Ojibwe village located on the north side of the St. Louis River, which was called Fond du Lac, meaning "head of the lake."

Daniel Greysolon Sieur Du Luth visited the Indians here in 1679 to try to establish peace between the warring Dakota and Ojibwe. It was to the fur-traders' benefit to prevent any disruption of their trade. Fond du Lac soon became the gateway to the fur-bearing lakes and streams, as traders made their way up the St. Louis to the important portage at Big Sandy Lake, where they crossed to the Mississippi. Many colorful people traveled through Fond du Lac on their passages into the "interior," but few made it their permanent home.

It wasn't until 1854, when rumors circulated that copper and ore were being found on the North Shore, that a number of people came to the Duluth area. The rumors were short-lived and Duluth, along with a couple of other small villages, continued to grow slowly. That same year the Ojibwe ceded the entire Arrowhead region to whites at their old capital on

Shanty-town of Duluth in late 1850's.

MHS

Madeline Island in Lake Superior. In 1857, the village of Duluth had only 14 buildings. And that year, the national monetary panic closed them—for the next ten years. The small number of residents that persisted, traveled by boat for supplies to the small town of Superior. As if life weren't bad enough, a scarlet fever epidemic swept through the small community the following year.

By February 1865, only a few houses were occupied in Duluth, and Beaver Bay had become the only permanent town between Duluth and Grand Portage. It seemed inevitable that Duluth would become a ghost town. But Duluth had seen the bottom. 1869 became a banner year when the Lake Superior and Mississippi Railroad was approaching completion from St. Paul to Duluth. The town's population swelled from fourteen families nestled on Minnesota Point, to 3,500 by that summer. By 1870 you could reach Duluth from St. Paul in only 16 hours, and immigration to this new town took off. 1870 was also the year Jay Cooke, an eastern financier, decided to support the building of the Northern Pacific Railroad from Duluth to the Pacific. At the same time the railroad was pushing west from Duluth, the city fathers became concerned about the harbor access and decided to cut a channel through Minnesota Point, saving boats from making the seven-mile trip to the natural opening at Superior Cut. But the town of Superior obtained an injunction from the Army to halt Duluth's digging. Word came to Duluth on a Friday that the injunction would be served that following

Monday. Through the weekend Duluthians shoveled and spaded, so that by Monday, as the injunction was being served, the small tug, Fero, steamed through the little channel to the lake.

However, in 1873, Duluth's bubble broke when the the financial empire of Jay Cooke collapsed. The Northern Pacific had almost reached the Dakota border, but work stopped immediately. Within 60 days, half the people doing business in Duluth were out of work. The town's population shrunk from 5,000 to 2,000. The city was so far in debt that it burned its bonds, dissolved the council, and returned the city to a village status.

RECOVERY OF DULUTH

Five years later, Duluth was on its way again. The farms of the Red River Valley began shipping large quantities of No. 1 hard wheat back to Duluth on the Northern Pacific. Grain elevators were being built and capacities continually increased. By 1885 there were nine large elevators doing business in Duluth. Sawmills also began to cut the lumber that was now being shipped by train or brought down the lake into town. In 1893, another era started to unfold when the Duluth, Missabe and Northern Railroad began to creak along the Superior Uplands with iron ore from the newly discovered Mesabi Iron Range. Docks were built and whaleback ships began to haul wheat and ore. By 1920, some 2,000 ships passed out of the harbor, with ore shipments totaling

Late 1800 harbor activity in Duluth.

MHS

Incline railroad, 3,000 ft. long, running along Duluth's 7th Avenue.

thirty million tons. It has been said that the Mesabi Range with its high-grade ore, won the two World Wars for the United States.

Everything seemed to be working for Duluth during the early 1900's. United States Steel came to town and purchased 1,000 acres for a steel plant. They built Morgan Park as a company town and upwards of 3,500 men worked the blast furnaces and coke ovens just down the block from their homes. Portland Cement came to town in 1916 and set up shop next to the steel mill. A large number of Finns and Scandinavians, first attracted to the Duluth region because of the lumber industry, turned to shipping and mining when the white pines were depleted. Iron ore continued to be pulled from the "range" for a nation that had developed an appetite for steel. When the first predictions came that the iron would be depleted, the ground shook under Duluth and the entire range. During the 1950's, unemployment spread along the Arrowhead, until the process of removing low grade ore and forming it into taconite pellets, was developed by Henry Davis, a professor at the University of Minnesota. Today, all ore shipped from Duluth is taconite.

NAMING OF DULUTH

A missionary by the name of Reverend Joseph Wilson was offered two lots in the newly platted village along Lake Superior, provided he could come up with a name to everyone's satisfaction. Wilson scoured through some Jesuit narratives and finally came upon the accounts of Greysolon Sieur Du Luth's travels around Lake Superior. The name had a nice ring, so it became the village of Duluth, and Wilson got his two lots.

NAMING OF THE ARROWHEAD

In 1924, the Northeastern Minnesota Civic and Commerce Association decided it needed a more catchy name for this region, which would soon have a paved highway from Duluth to Grand Marais. A national contest was unleashed and over 3,000 entries were taken in. The contest was won by a Philadelphian who compared the physical boundaries of this region to the shape of an arrow's point.

LESTER RIVER

This river was called "Busabika zibi" by the Ojibwe. This is interpreted as "a river that comes through a worn hollow in the rock." The Lester, named after an early pioneer, extends some 15 miles back into the upland bogs. The river was a favorite stream for netting smelt, a small fish which was first stocked in Lake Michigan in the early 1900's, and quickly spread to Superior. Beginning sometime in April, the fish migrate at night up the North Shore streams, in an attempt to lay their eggs. It is quite a sight watching the thousands of people who spend the night standing in the frigid, shallow streams of Lake Superior, netting these minute fish by the bucketful.

Just north of the Lester, the highway divides into an expressway to Two Harbors, and a scenic two-lane route along the lake. Along the lakeshore road, there is a a paved shoulder designated as a bicycle route.

Searching Lake Superior shoreline for agates. Photo/B.F. Childs.

FRENCH RIVER

In 1848, French River was the site of a copper ore discovery. News spread quickly to St. Paul and signaled a rush of prospectors to the area, with some coming from as far away as Michigan. Test pits were sunk and many started to mine the small veins of copper. There was little commercial value to the ore, however, and French River settled back into oblivion for the next twenty years. French River became a railway station when the Duluth and Iron Range Railroad was built from Two Harbors down to Duluth in 1887. The river is only 12 miles long and flows out to a flat pebble beach. There are numerous picnic spots along this scenic route, making it an ideal place to stop for lunch.

Located next to the French River, off the highway, is a fish hatchery for the Department of Natural Resources. Here the DNR raises trout, walleyes, suckers and other game fish. Most of the lake trout are spawned in southern Minnesota at Lanesboro and trucked here to grow. There are no guided tours, but visitors are welcome to wander around the site and visit the buildings where hundreds of aerated containers house the hatching eggs.

KNIFE RIVER

Located by a river of sharp-edged stones that the Ojibwe called "Mokomani zibi," Knife River was first settled by pro-

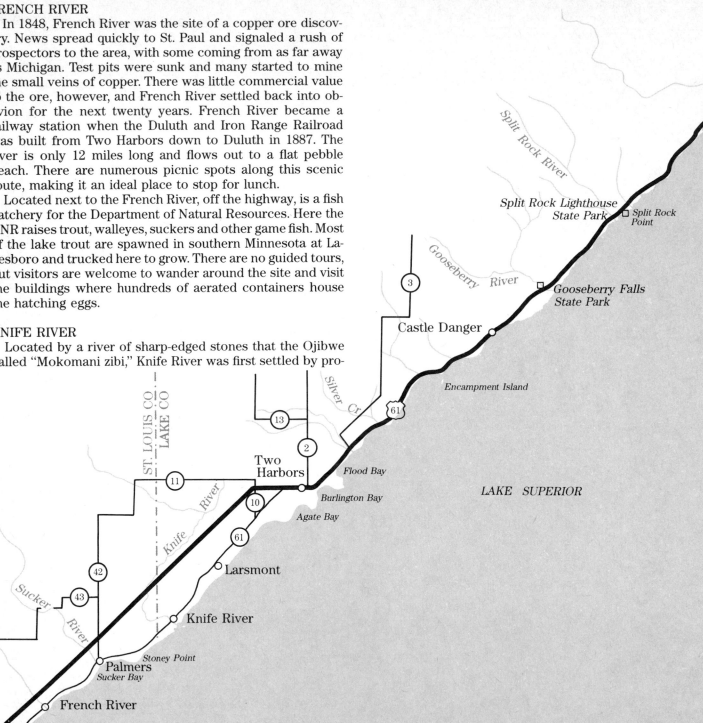

spectors looking for copper. Most began arriving around 1854, about the time the Ojibwe were signing away the North Shore in a treaty session at La Pointe, on Madeline Island. Copper was never found in paying amounts, so the prospectors moved away. But in 1898, the Knife River became the logging headquarters for a Michigan lumber company named Alger, Smith and Company. From Knife River, a railroad was built along the North Shore to the Cascade River, over which some 300 cars traveled, pulled by 20 locomotives. The railroads began to haul lumber from deep in Cook County. Occasionally, large rafts of logs were floated down the shore to be milled in Duluth, but great care had to be taken to avoid storms that could easily break up the rafts, spreading thousands of logs across the lake. A dock was built at Knife River in 1909, so lumber could be directly shipped on pulpwood steamers to the demanding eastern markets. In the 1970's, the harbor was enlarged and a breakwater was built by the Corps of Engineers to provide a harbor of refuge.

Knife River is an unusual stream in that it flows parallel to the lake for a number of miles before it cuts sharply back and empties into the lake. A record-breaking, 17 pound rainbow trout was taken from this river in 1974. There is little remaining at Knife River today except the marina, a number of homes, a store and a couple of places to buy fresh Superior fish. There is also a nice crescent-shaped beach from which to watch the sailboats enter and leave the scenic harbor.

TWO HARBORS, Pop. 4,039

The prevailing winds and waves of Lake Superior have carved two bays from the lava coastline of the North Shore. Two Harbors was the name given to this hamlet when it was platted in 1888. But years before that, the Ojibwe called it "Wass-we-wining," or "a place to spear by moonlight." The first white settler was Thomas Saxton, who in 1856 lived along what is now called Agate Bay. In the adjoining Burlington Bay, another village sprung up in 1857, near a sawmill. Financial panic later that year wiped out the settlements of Agate Bay and Burlington. For the next twenty years, the only real activity here was a little commercial fishing and some logging.

With the discovery of iron ore at Lake Vermilion in Ely, Agate Bay soon recovered. A Philadelphia investor named Charlemagne Tower heard of this discovery and quickly bought land in northern Minnesota. Knowing that the country would need increasing amounts of iron ore, he formed the Minnesota Iron Co. The Duluth and Iron Range Railroad was also built to carry the mined-ore to Two Harbors. In 1884, a ten-car train came down the hill to Agate Bay, loaded with 220 tons of Vermilion ore. The first ore dock on Lake Superior

was built here, and with a length of 1,388 feet, it became the largest in the world.

The town of Two Harbors is east of the highway, down by the docks. Here the old depot, built in 1907, houses the Lake County Historical Society Museum. Nearby you'll find some old locomotives on display that were used on the early ore trains. This is also a good spot for watching the loading of ore boats.

DISCOVERY OF IRON RANGE ORE

The discoverer of iron ore at Vermilion Lake in 1865, was credited to state geologist, Henry Eames. The ore he wrote about was found at the mouth of Two Rivers, on Lake Vermilion, and consisted of veins some 60 feet thick. Since that time it has been known as the Vermilion Range. The story goes that when Eames came upon an iron deposit, at what would later become Babbitt, he told one of his associates, "to hell with iron...its gold we're after."

In 1865, another man, named George Stuntz, was prospecting for gold in the Lake Vermilion area. He discovered what would later become the first bed of iron to be mined in Minnesota. The mine was called Breitung and its first shipment of ore went out by rail in 1884. The deposits were in narrow veins running vertically into the ground, thus making it necessary to mine in the traditional underground method. As it turned out later, ore deposits were discovered to the south of the Vermilion ore, and lay so close to the surface that they could be scooped out in open-pit mines. Because of this difference and the ease of ore extraction, this southern range, called the Mesabi, easily out-produced the Vermilion once it was in operation.

Early 1900 steamer taking on pulpwood at Knife River. Photo/Roleff.

MHS

Split Rock Lighthouse, guardian of the North Shore through 1969. Photo/National Archives.

MHS

CASTLE DANGER

This hamlet was supposedly named after the ship, Castle, which sank here on an off-lying reef. No evidence of the ship has ever been found to prove this, however.

GOOSEBERRY FALLS STATE PARK

This is one of Minnesota's more popular parks and was established in the late 1920's. Today, this park has six miles of trails bordering a spectacular series of falls that drop over 100 feet. There is picnicking, 125 campsites, a naturalist, interpretive center and trout fishing. The velocity of Gooseberry River has for centuries cut through the coarse basalt rock. The Ojibwe called this place "Shabonimikani-zibi," or "Place of Gooseberries." The interpretive center is located on the west side of the highway, with the camp grounds on the east side, along the lake.

SPLIT ROCK LIGHT HOUSE

A short distance northeast from Gooseberry Falls, the road climbs up to the headlands of Split Rock State Park. Perched on a cliff 168 feet above Lake Superior, this 370,000 candle-power light has helped captains navigate their boats safely through an area of magnetic interference which rendered their compasses useless. The increased ore boat traffic during the 1900's, coupled with a bad storm that drove two boats on the rocks and threatened many others, provided an increasing need for a lighthouse. Plans were approved for a facility and the project was completed in 1910. The supplies and construction materials for the lighthouse were hoisted from the lake with a huge derrick. For 60 years, this heavily-visited landmark, flashed at 10-second intervals.

In 1901, a mining company started to work the cliff below Split Rock for an abrasive material called corundum. Some buildings were located at the base of the cliff, and the operation continued until it merged with the Minnesota Mining and Manufacturing Company (3M). After that it was shut down and operations were moved to St. Paul.

The Coast Guard abandoned Split Rock Lighthouse in 1969 because today's navigational equipment allows ships to pinpoint their position more precisely. For the small boater though, the lighthouse structure still remains a valuable landmark from which to navigate along the North Shore. The view from the lighthouse is one of the best along the lake, and the climb up the spiral staircase to the tower's top is worth the effort. On a clear day at Split Rock, the faint lines of the Apostle Islands can be seen across the lake.

Lake Superior Schooner in 1870. Photo/Childs.

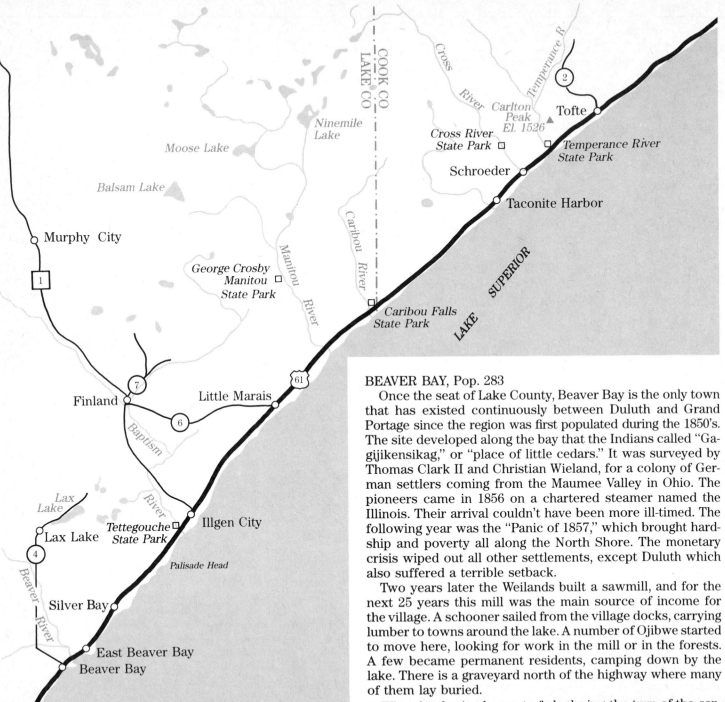

Ninemile Lake

Moose Lake

Balsam Lake

COOK CO
LAKE CO

Cross River

Temperance R.

Carlton Peak
El. 1526

Tofte

Cross River
State Park

Temperance River
State Park

Schroeder

Taconite Harbor

Murphy City

Caribou River

George Crosby
Manitou
State Park

Manitou River

Caribou Falls
State Park

LAKE SUPERIOR

1

7

Finland

6

Little Marais

61

Baptism

Lax Lake

River

Lax Lake

Tettegouche
State Park

Illgen City

4

Palisade Head

Beaver River

Silver Bay

East Beaver Bay
Beaver Bay

BEAVER BAY, Pop. 283

Once the seat of Lake County, Beaver Bay is the only town that has existed continuously between Duluth and Grand Portage since the region was first populated during the 1850's. The site developed along the bay that the Indians called "Ga-gijikensikag," or "place of little cedars." It was surveyed by Thomas Clark II and Christian Wieland, for a colony of German settlers coming from the Maumee Valley in Ohio. The pioneers came in 1856 on a chartered steamer named the Illinois. Their arrival couldn't have been more ill-timed. The following year was the "Panic of 1857," which brought hardship and poverty all along the North Shore. The monetary crisis wiped out all other settlements, except Duluth which also suffered a terrible setback.

Two years later the Weilands built a sawmill, and for the next 25 years this mill was the main source of income for the village. A schooner sailed from the village docks, carrying lumber to towns around the lake. A number of Ojibwe started to move here, looking for work in the mill or in the forests. A few became permanent residents, camping down by the lake. There is a graveyard north of the highway where many of them lay buried.

When lumbering began to fade during the turn of the century, the small village reverted to farming and some fishing.

(right) Northern Minnesota Indian family.
(bottom) North Shore vista. Photo/Childs.

MHS

MHS

More recently, a taconite concentrating plant has been constructed here, along with some shipping docks.

SILVER BAY, Pop. 2,917

This town was built in 1954 by the Reserve Mining Company. Reserve built it for the workers in their taconite processing plant, located on the shore of Lake Superior. Silver Bay was the focus of one of the longest-running court cases: the State of Minnesota vs the Reserve Mining Company. For many years, Reserve dumped an average of 67,000 tons of taconite tailings daily, directly into Lake Superior. Concern had been mounting about the effects of the asbestos fibers from these tailings being found in Duluth's drinking water, as well as the general degradation of the lake. Finally in 1974, Reserve was ordered to stop dumping and make plans for on-land disposal. From the day the suit was filed, dumping continued six more years, as the legal process ground on. In 1977, Mile Post 7 was selected, an area just seven miles up the railroad line from Silver Bay, and in 1980, the tailings finally stopped flowing into the lake.

The town of Silver Bay, basically a one industry town, has been plagued by the roller coaster economics of the steel industry for the last decade. The slightest ripple in the economy is felt by its residents.

PALISADE HEAD

Rising some 348 feet above Lake Superior, is an 80 acre precipice of reddish lava, forming one of the most striking features along the North Shore. The column-like rock formation of Palisade Head, is caused by the repeated heating and cooling of the rocks by the sun. A small sign here marks the narrow and winding road to a little wayside park on the top. It is worth your time to drive up, to what might be one of the more spectacular views of the lake. You can also have your picnic there, but keep a close eye on young children.

BAPTISM RIVER & TETTEGOUCHE STATE PARK

Located between Palisade Head and Little Palisades, is one of the most beautiful spots along the North Shore. This river, first called "Au Bapteme" by French traders, drops some 700 feet from the surrounding headlands and has the sheerest drop (70 feet) of any falls in Minnesota. The park was recently renamed Tettegouche, after one of the mountain-like lakes in the nearby uplands. The park has four miles of trails, but no camping is allowed. Brown Trout is most likely to be found in the river, if your plans include fishing.

CRYSTAL BAY

In 1902, five men from Two Harbors built a six-story crushing plant here to mine and crush what they thought was the mineral corundum, an abrasive used in grinding and sanding. They mined for several years and built docks for boats to carry away the ground-up rocks, before discovering that it wasn't really corundum they were mining, but something closely resembling it. Consequently, they closed the plant and turned their interests into making sandpaper down in St. Paul. The company's name was the Minnesota Mining & Manufacturing Company (3M). It became one of the largest corporations in the state.

ILLGEN CITY

The highway north from Illgen City is known as the Finland-Ely Trail and runs 61 miles north to Ely, through some of this state's most beautiful wilderness area. From U.S. 61, travel 2.4 miles up State 1 until you get to Illgen Falls, a beautiful 50-foot falls located on the Baptism River. A few miles up the road, the town of Finland was founded. A number of Finns came to work in the lumber industry and settled here along a logging railroad.

LITTLE MARAIS

This small resort village, whose French name means "little marsh," was named by traders passing by the small marsh along the Superior shore. Little Marais was once used as a place to collect logs in rafts, which were towed along the North Shore to Duluth.

MANITOU RIVER

This river, one of the longer North Shore rivers, extends into the hills some 17 miles. The last few miles, it rushes down to Lake Superior through a gorge with eight waterfalls. Located up river a few miles is the George Crosby-Manitou State Park, a park which can be reached only by backpacking along the river, or by the access off of State 1 and County 7. There are 23 primitive campsites and nine miles of trails. The Manitou River is considered one of the better trout streams along the North Shore. Manitou is the Ojibwe word for "spirit" and probably got this name from the mist that forms along the falls and rapids, when conditions are right.

CARIBOU FALLS

This twelve-mile long river, named for the Caribou that once roamed this state, has for centuries flowed down the lava bedrock, creating several beautiful waterfalls. A wayside stop at Caribou Falls is maintained by the state with picnic tables, trout fishing, and three miles of trails. From here, the highway generally follows along one of the beach terraces formed by Glacial Lake Duluth during the end of the Wisconsin Ice Age, 11,000 years ago. During 1910 and 1926, major fires burned along the North Shore, destroying most of the remaining pine and allowing the birch and poplar to grow in its place.

TACONITE HARBOR

The docks and shipping facilities of the Erie Mining Company are located at Taconite Harbor and are connected by

Crews warming up in North woods lumber camp. Photo/Roleff.

MHS

rail to their processing plants on the Mesabi Iron Range. An observation road just south of the railroad bridge, brings you down to the harbor. Under the shadows of the giant ore dock, you might also catch a close-up view of a "laker," (ore boat).

SCHROEDER & CROSS RIVER

The small village of Schroeder was named after John Schroeder, a lumberman from Wisconsin, whose company sent thousands of logs down the Temperance and Cross rivers to be floated to mills. To bring logs down these rivers, dams were built across the streams at their headwaters. During the spring melt these dams were opened, sending the logs crashing down to Superior where they were later collected in large rafts and towed across the lake to Ashland, Wisconsin. Railroad tracks were extended into Cook County to haul out timber, but these were abandoned during the turn of the century when the pine became scarce and too far from streams and tracks.

The Cross River State Wayside is located near Schroeder. The river was named "Tchibaiatigo-zibi" by the Ojibwe, meaning "wood of the soul river." This was inspired by a Catholic priest named Frederic Baraga, known as the "Apostle of the Ojibwe." In 1846, Baraga set off across the lake from Madeline Island for the North Shore, to minister to the Ojibwe.

On the crossing he encountered a difficult storm which threatened to sink his small boat. (The water temperature of Lake Superior hovers in the 40's even during the summer and death comes quickly to those caught in the water.) Baraga survived the storm and upon landing, he nailed a small wooden cross to a tree by the river, giving thanks for his safe passage. The wooden cross has been replaced by one of granite and is located at the mouth of Cross River. In 1850 Father Baraga published the first grammar book of the Ojibwe language.

CARLTON PEAK

Northeast of Schroeder, the land is relatively flat. When approaching Tofte, though, a prominent landmark named Carlton Peak can be seen. It is named after Reuben Carlton, an early settler at the Fond du Lac village, who was once located at the mouth of the St. Louis River. Seen from the lake, Carlton Peak marks the southern limit of a ridge of hills whose serrated profile has given rise to the name, "Sawtooth Mountains." The ridges resulted from the erosion of alternating, hard and soft layers of rock.

TEMPERANCE RIVER

The Temperance is one of the longest streams on the North Shore watershed, running some 25 miles into the Sawtooth Mountains. Most rivers of the North Shore have bars of gravel and sand formed across their entrances into Lake Superior. But the Temperance rarely has a sandbar. Subsequently, in the late 1800's the name Temperance, or "No Bar" River, was applied. In the last few miles of its downhill journey, the Temperance cuts a deep and narrow gorge. In some places it is only a few feet across, yet deep enough that only the sound of rushing water can be heard. Located here is a state park, with 51 campsites and six miles of walking and cross-country ski trails.

At the resort town of Tofte, the Sawbill Trail passes a national park campground and ends at Sawbill Lake in the Boundary Waters Canoe Area. At one time, this trail was called the Temperance Trail and was used extensively by loggers.

Quiet moment along the North Shore. Photo/Childs.

MHS

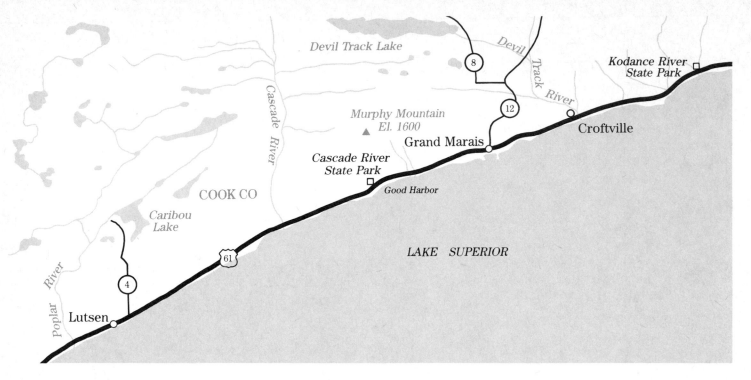

SUPERIOR NATIONAL FOREST

Lumbering continued unchecked during the late 1800's, and by 1900 much of the white pine had been cut in the Arrowhead region. A growing concern arose that some tracts of natural forest should be set aside, but the lumber companies threatened to pull out, leaving many newly arrived settlers without work. A Civil War general, named Christopher Andrews, stressed the need to protect the wilderness and helped establish the state and national forest system. He also promoted the need for preserving historical sites.

In 1909, his ideas became reality with the establishment of the 36,000 acre Superior National Forest. Today, that forest system encompasses over three million acres, and together with Canada's Quetico Provincial Park, provides a matchless recreation, canoeing and wildlife area.

LUTSEN

During the late 1890's, Lutsen was an important stop for tugs taking rafts of logs to Duluth. The town was named by Swedish settlers, after a German town where the King of Sweden, Gustavus Adolphus, was killed in a battle with Austrians during the mid-1600's.

CASCADE RIVER

Situated by a series of beautiful rapids is the Cascade River State Park, with 38 campsites and 15 miles of trails. In its final few miles, the Cascade drops some 900 feet. A number of Scandinavian fishermen used to maintain shacks along the lake here, where they ran small commercial operations.

GOOD HARBOR BAY

During the last period of volcanic activity in Minnesota millions of years ago, lava flowed extensively from cracks in the earth's crust and was pushed up from the floor of Lake Superior. At one point the entire region sank again and was submerged in water. During this period, sandstone was formed under water by sediment washing down from the hills. When the lava flows resumed, the sandstone was buried by new molten rock. Examples of these successive volcanic and sedimentary formations appear in many places from Duluth to Grand Portage. At the wayside overlooking Good Harbor Bay, red sandstone can be seen between the dark gray lava flows along the cut near the road.

The beach at Good Harbor Bay is also a good source of thomsonite, a semi-precious stone formed in lava.

CONTROL OF THE SEA LAMPREY

Many years ago, an unusual looking primitive fish (eel-like in appearance), made its way into the Great Lakes. It came from the Atlantic Ocean through the 27 mile-long Welland Canal which connected Lake Ontario with Lake Erie. Finally making its way into Lake Superior, the lamprey feeds by attaching itself to lake trout and steelhead, which once provided a good living to the North Shore fishermen. The sea lamprey multiplied at an alarming rate, so by the early 1950's, the game fish were nearly wiped out. The lamprey spawned in the North Shore streams and it was here that the battle against the parasites was waged. At first electric shocking devices and other traps were used, but eventually, chemicals proved the most successful. Today the fish of Lake Superior are making a successful recovery as the lamprey are kept in check.

mainly to carry on fishing and lumbering. By 1879, a road was finally cut between Grand Marais and Duluth, but many found travel by boat more convenient. Logging continued to play an important role in the economy of the town through the early part of the 1900's. In 1910 much of the North Shore, including Grand Marais, was threatened by forest fires that spread easily along the debris left by the loggers. A number of people were rescued by Coast Guard boats patrolling the coast during this dry season.

GRAND MARAIS GEOLOGY

The harbor at Grand Marais was formed by the unequal

Early Highway 61, along the North Shore.

GRAND MARAIS, Pop. 1,289

A marsh once ran along the bay here, so the early French traders named this protected harbor, Grand Marais, meaning "great marsh." Although only a short distance from the historic Grand Portage, not much fur trading was done at Grand Marais. The American Fur Company operated a fishing station here for several years starting in 1834. Little was heard about Grand Marais until after the area was ceded by the Ojibwe in 1854, in the treaty signed at La Pointe. John Godfrey, considered the first permanent resident, opened a post here in 1856. One of the peaks along the Gunflint Trail was named Mount Josephine, after his daughter. After only a few years, Godfrey became discouraged with his remote post and went back to Detroit.

It wasn't until 1871 that settlers started to arrive by boat,

erosion of two different rocks. One, hard and resistant to Superior's wave action, has become the outer barrier to the harbor. The softer lava, worn away by waves, forms the harbor basin. From the harbor's breakwater, the serrated edge of the Sawtooth Range can be seen behind Grand Marais. This range was also formed by erosion, when the rain and winds wore away the softer rocks, leaving the more resistant ones to form the ridge.

At Saganaga Lake near the end of the Gunflint Trail, one of the oldest granites in North America, called Saganaga Granite, marks the remains of the ancient Laurentian Mountains. These mountains were some of the first on this continent to be uplifted from the vast seas that covered the continent. At one time they reached from southwest Minnesota to the St. Lawrence River.

BOUNDARY WATERS CANOE AREA

The BWCA, a one million acre wilderness area of lakes and rivers, offers one of the more unique outdoor experiences of this country. The Boundary Waters runs for 150 miles along the border of the Canadian Quetico Provincial Park, another wilderness area set aside by Canada. The use of motors is banned in most of the park, and even airplanes are required to maintain a minimum altitude. Over 180,000 people use this park each year. Permits are required between May and September and group size is limited to ten. No cans and bottles are allowed and all trash must be carried out.

GUNFLINT TRAIL

A geological survey of the Gunflint Lake area in 1850, reported the discovery of iron ore. But it wasn't until 1893 that a mine was opened. A road was cut from Grand Marais to the mine which was situated on Gunflint Lake. The present road follows this supply route. Several national forest campsites can be reached from the road and a number of trails lead back into the Sawtooth Range. One trail leads to Eagle Mountain, the highest point in Minnesota (2301 ft). This trail crosses the Laurentian Divide, the skeleton of one of the great mountain ranges of our continent. Millions of years of wind, rain, and glacial activity, have worn this ancient range down to its granite and volcanic core.

To many, the Gunflint Trail is the personification of what the north woods is all about. Wolves, bear, beaver, birds, waterfowl, moose and fish, live in this pristine wilderness. But there is concern now that the rock bottom lakes here, are becoming highly susceptible to acid rain. Sulphur in the air, caused by the burning of coal and other fossil fuels, is combining with moisture in the atmosphere to form sulphur dioxide. These northern lakes have little buffering capabilities and so the Ph of the water becomes more acidic and ultimately destroys the reproductive ability of the fish. This creates a major break in the food chain for this wilderness area.

CHIPPEWA CITY

Just east of Grand Marais is the old St. Francis Xavier Church, a historic landmark. It was built in the French style of architecture in 1895. Xavier had no regular priest, but missionaries from Canada and St. John's, in Collegeville, took charge. Most often they came from Duluth by boat, once a month, to conduct services for the band of Ojibwe that lived just outside of Grand Marais.

KIMBALL & KADUNCE CREEKS

Both of these short streams provide excellent trout fishing and spectacular views. These rivers have flowed for thousands of centuries, cutting their narrow gorges through the forest. Kimball Creek was named in honor of Charles Kimball, a member of a survey party that drowned in a lake accident in 1864, not far from the mouth of the creek.

Kadunce Creek is French for diarrhea and received its name from those that drank the mineral water. Located along Kadunce Creek is Kodonce River State Wayside, a picnic spot which offers stream fishing and trails.

MHS

Ojibwe Indian and child navigate northern Minnesota lake.

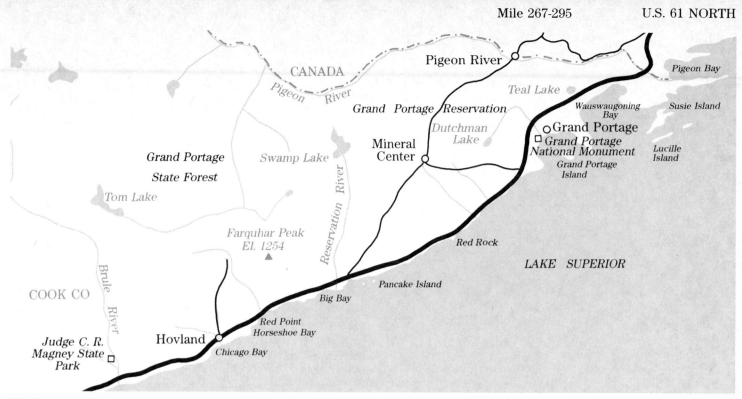

BRULE RIVER

This river has also been called the Arrowhead River, to avoid confusion with the Bois Brule River on Wisconsin's South Shore. Located near the mouth of the Brule is the 4,000 acre Judge Magney State Park. Magney was a Duluth mayor and state supreme court judge who promoted the development of the parks along Lake Superior's North Shore. The Brule is considered by many to be one of the best rainbow trout streams along the shore. The trout enter the stream during the spring and fall, though the spring migration is the only time when they spawn. The rainbow, or steelhead as they are commonly called, are a highly adaptive member of the salmon family and have been able to make their home in the salt water of the Pacific Ocean, as well as the fresh-water of the Great Lakes.

The 38 campsites in the park are situated amongst the ruins of an old Civilian Conservation Corps (CCC) camp. A number of building foundations (almost all overgrown by trees and brush) can still be seen. Some 800 men lived here during the depression years, working for the government, planting trees, and working to reclaim the forests that had been decimated by loggers at the turn of the century.

OLD DOG TRAIL

In 1856, post offices were established at Grand Portage and Grand Marais. Mail was then carried between Fort William (Thunder Bay), Canada and Duluth. During the summer boats were used, but during the winter, dog sleds were the only way to traverse the North Shore. A German named Sam Zimmerman and two Ojibwe brothers, named Beargrease, ran the sleds. By 1895, the road was cleared for logging and horses were used on the mail-route. In 1920, the trail was improved and named Trunk Highway 1. U.S. 61 follows most of the "Old Dog Trail."

GRAND PORTAGE

Grand Portage is the beginning of a nine-mile portage to the Pigeon River on the Canadian border. It bypasses a 20 mile series of impassable falls and rapids. For hundreds of years before the white man set foot here, this trail was used by Indians as they traveled from Lake Superior to the interior waterways. Though Radisson or Du Luth could have visited here as early as 1660 and 1679, it is certain that Pierre La Verendrye, with his sons and some fifty French soldiers, paddled into Grand Portage Bay during one August day in 1731.

During the late 1700's, Grand Portage became the scene of one of North America's more important fur-trading centers. The Northwest Company was British run and traded goods with the Indians on a supply-line that reached all the way to the West Coast. Supplies were brought from Montreal

37

on large 40-foot canoes. Each July the voyageurs, loaded with furs, would arrive here from their distant posts that stretched across the Northwest. They met with officials of the Company to exchange goods and money and establish new rules for the coming winter. With business done, Indians and voyageurs drank and danced in the huge great hall, before they headed back into the loneliness of the north woods.

The voyageurs were mostly Frenchmen, who came from the Montreal area of Canada. They were short, but exceedingly strong. Their loyalty to the trade and honest verbal contracts, made the vast fur-trade network possible. They were colorful men, whose songs, cocked red wool caps, bright sashes, deerskin pants, and pipes, made the Grand Portage legacy one of the most colorful in this nation's history.

During the Revolutionary War, Grand Portage was the only spot in Minnesota to see British soldiers. They were stationed at Grand Portage to protect the interests of the Northwest Company. The Company was moved to Fort William, Ontario in 1803, because of the uncertainty as to whether the post was on American soil or not. The vacated buildings soon rotted away. During the 1930's, the old fort of Grand Portage was re-constructed and in 1960 it became a National Monument. There is a park interpreter here during the summer to answer questions and lead you through the exhibits. A one-half mile trail behind the post takes you 300 feet to Mount Rose, which provides an excellent view of the fort and Grand Portage Bay, the largest bay on the Minnesota shore of Lake Superior. On the northern edge of Grand Portage stands the state's first Catholic mission school, established in 1838 by Father Pierz.

WITCH TREE

Located east of Grand Portage, is one of Minnesota's oldest landmarks. It is a 300-year-old gnarled and twisted cedar, growing out of the rocks and located a few feet above Lake Superior. The tree was growing here before La Verendrye passed by in 1731. Indians believed that the tree was possessed by evil spirits, forcing many to lose their canoes on the treacherous rocks of the point. To appease the spirit, tobacco and other gifts were left at the base of the tree.

Witch Tree can be reached by taking Cook County 17, two and one-half miles east from the stockade. Just before the blacktop ends, a small brown shed marks a footpath that winds a hundred yards northward, through a thick spruce forest to the tree. The tree is on private property, and a dropbox asking for a donation (at this printing, 50 cents) is located at the shed.

SUSIE ISLAND

Located just off of Pigeon Point is a grouping of rugged islands, whose exposure to the rough elements of Lake Superior has given rise to plants normally found hundreds of miles north, on the Canadian tundra. It is uncertain how these plants became isolated here, so far from the tundra. The Nature Conservancy maintains a preserve on the south half of Susie Island and access can only be made by boat. If you go, keep an eye on the weather. During the early 1900's, copper and silver were mined on this island, until a storm flooded the shaft and destroyed the buildings.

Minnesota fur traders.

MHS

PARKERSVILLE

In the late 1700's, a trading post for Indians and traders was located a few miles west of Grand Portage, near the mouth of the Pigeon River. It later became known as Parkersville when a family by the name of Parker operated a store here and collected mail. They also raised potatoes, vegetables and fruit. Several buildings were erected, but the area was abandoned in 1876. All that remains now are cellar holes.

PIGEON RIVER

The Ojibwe called this rugged river "Omimi-zibi" or Pigeon River, because of the passenger pigeons that came to this region in the spring to breed. By 1900 this bird, with its incredible homing instinct, had disappeared forever. The Pigeon River is the largest of the North Shore streams, with the exception of the St. Louis River. Its lower portion is rugged and broken by rapids and spectacular falls. Pigeon Falls, some 70 feet high, is located two miles from its mouth. Other views of this beautiful river area are accessible by trails off the main Grand Portage Trail.

It was 1842 when the Webster-Ashburton Treaty set the Pigeon River as the border between Canada and the United States.

FORT CHARLOTTE

Fort Charlotte was located at the end of the nine-mile portage to the Pigeon River. It was an 18th century, disembarking post where canoes were unloaded and left, while the voyageurs carried their ninety-pound packs of furs to Grand Portage.

MHS

Ice pushed by wind along Lake Superior shoreline.

MHS

1870 Voyageurs across from Ft. William, 35 miles north of Grand Portage.

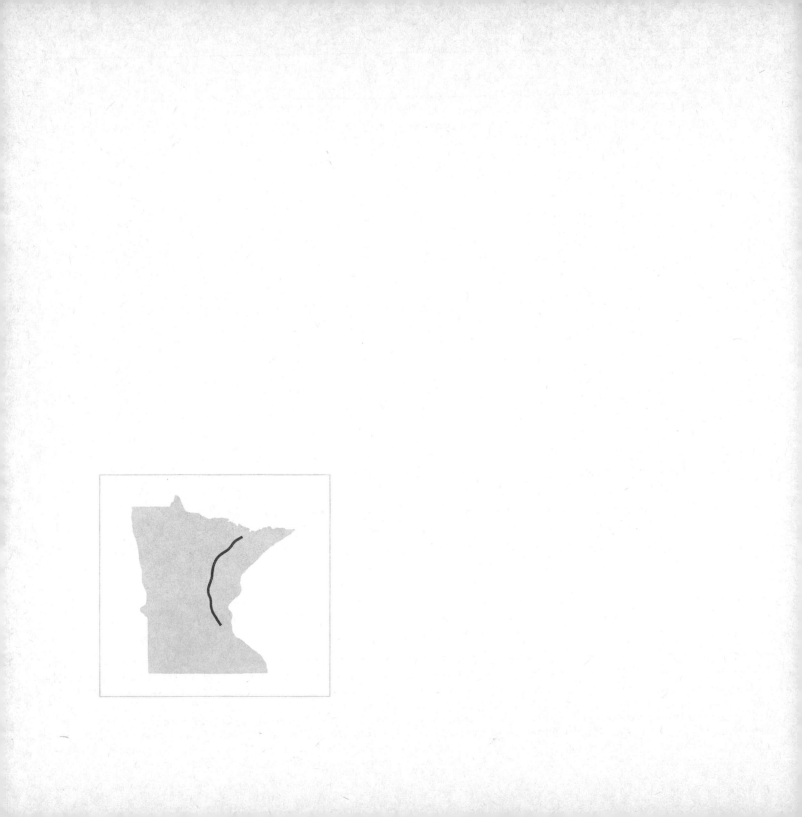

ROUTE 169, NORTH TO ELY

Underground miners at Eveleth, 1915. Photo/Roleff

Route 169 stretches north 220 miles from Elk River to Ely. In its southern portion, the road passes through a land laid flat by glaciers and covered with a sandy soil. After the ice age, white pine flourished as far as the eye could see. Through these forests the Indian traveled on the Rum River, between the Mississippi River and their regional camp at Mille Lacs Lake. The Rum later became an important route for the early white traders and lumbermen.

North of Mille Lacs Lake, the road leaves the tamarack swamps and passes deeper into the forests of northern Minnesota. As the lumbermen cut their way through this virgin pine, few anticipated that the red earth under their feet would yield some of the largest deposits of iron ore ever to be found. The ground northeast of Grand Rapids was swallowed by huge open-pit mines. These mines helped win two world wars and supplied this nation's appetite for steel.

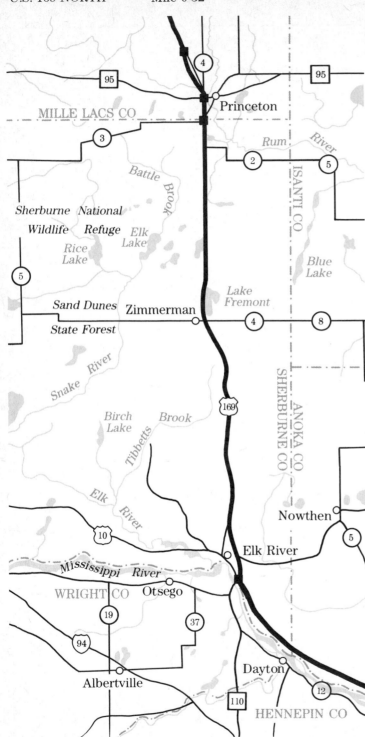

SHERBURNE COUNTY, Pop. 29,908

Sherburne County was named after Moses Sherburne, a lawyer and Supreme Court justice of Minnesota Territory from 1853 to 1857. Eventually Sherburne moved to Orono, a small village which later became part of Elk River.

ELK RIVER, Pop. 6,785

Elk River was named by Zebulon Pike after the herds of Elk once found here. Pike passed along the Mississippi during the fall of 1805 on a government expedition. Forty-three years later, Pierre Bottineau, a French trader, built a small trading post on a bluff overlooking the Elk River near Lake Orono. A couple of years later, Bottineau built a hotel to service settlers and oxcart drivers that were beginning to push northwest along the river.

A hamlet named Orono, developed along the north side of Elk River, which old timers still call "lower town." Orono became the practical site for a grist mill, and it wasn't long before a dam was built across Elk River. A ferry operated between Orono and Otsego at one time, but when the railroad put a station at Elk River, people began moving out of Orono, nearer the station. In 1880 both Elk River and Orono became one.

ANOKA SAND PLAIN

North of Elk River is an area known as the Anoka Sand Plains, a triangular region of some 858 square miles. In some places, winds have eroded away the thin topsoil and formed sand dunes reaching up to 20 feet in height.

Just east of Zimmerman is the Sherburne National Wildlife Refuge. This refuge covers 31,500 acres, a third of which is scheduled for flooding to provide a waterfowl habitat. Currently, the refuge is developing a Canada goose population that, hopefully, will return yearly to nest. There are several trails in the park that wind through the reserve, past prehistoric Indian sites. Numerous spots here are ideal for nature photography.

ZIMMERMAN, Pop. 1,074

Zimmerman was built on a small rise of land, as a railroad village, during the late 1800's. It was first called Lake Fremont, after a nearby lake. But when the Manitoba Branch of the Great Northern Railroad was completed, they renamed the village after Moses Zimmerman, a local farmer.

LUMBERING IN MILLE LACS COUNTY

For many years, lumbering dominated Mille Lacs County. The first logging started east of here at Cambridge in the fall of 1847. For the next three years, crews worked on removing

Cutting seed potatoes near Princeton. Circa, 1920.

MHS

driftwood obstructions along the Rum River, to make it navigable from Elk River to Lake Mille Lacs. The West Branch of the Rum, which joins the main stream at Princeton, was also cleared that same year (1850). Lumbering operations soon began on a large scale and the banks of the Rum River were dotted with lumber camps. Logs continued to flow down the Rum for the next 60 years.

PRINCETON, Pop. 3,144

The town of Princeton formed at the junction of two branches of the Rum River. The first house, of sorts, was built in 1849, by a man called "Banjo Bill." The house was used as a resting place between his treks into the woods as a lumberjack. The village wasn't settled until 1854, and was named after John S. Prince, a St. Paul fur-agent who helped develop the town. The early settlers were mostly from the eastern states and Canada. While some chose to clear land and farm, most depended entirely on the lumber industry.

In 1856, a steam sawmill was built at Princeton. Then, in 1890, a much larger mill was built. At one time, Princeton boasted of two flour mills and a brewery. This small settlement was only a few years old when financial panic swept across the nation in 1857. Besides having little money to buy food, the settlers' gardens were laid bare by grasshoppers. Flour and sugar were used only on special occasions; corn meal and venison provided the main sustenance. Although the local pine forests provided millwork for residents, farming eventually became more realistic. The Great Northern Railroad finally reached Princeton in 1880, connecting the town directly to the Twin City markets.

BRICKTON

A mile north of Princeton, a plaque marks the spot where the village of Brickton once stood. Years ago, Brickton was a thriving village of some 400 people with stores, a sawmill, school, post office, boarding house and a railroad depot. But the main business in town was a brickyard. From the years 1889 to 1929, this factory turned out 20 million bricks annually. Shortly after 1929, the operation closed down and the town was plowed under for farming.

LONG SIDING

The small village of Long Siding sprung up when the railroad was built through here on its way to Milaca, in 1880. The town was named after Edgar Long, an early lumberman in the area.

FARMING IN MILLE LACS

Early farming in Mille Lacs County was done mainly to supply food for the individual settlers. Women and children worked the plots of prepared ground while the men spent time working in the woods, or taking logs down the Rum. If enough food was raised, it was easily sold to the lumber camps. But farming progressed slowly, and as late as 1890, there were only 180 farms in the county. Today, there are mostly dairy farms around Mille Lacs County.

Logs must be moved before the spring thaw.

MHS

43

PEASE

This was once a station on the Great Northern Railroad line between Elk River and Milaca. It was named Pease by railroad officers. The railroad does not extend beyond Princeton, but you can see the old right-of-way, to the west of the highway.

MILACA, Pop. 2,104

At first, Milaca was known as Oak City, but town fathers wanted something more innovative, so they rearranged the letters from Mille Lacs Lake and came up with Milaca. Milaca, resting on the banks of the Rum, began as a lumber center for a company owned by James J. Hill. As the region became deforested, farming and dairying took over.

In Milaca, the county courthouse is an attractive, rustic structure, with a bas-relief of local history set over the front door and murals of past logging days painted on interior walls. These art works were sponsored by the Federal Arts Project during the Depression.

RUM RIVER

The Rum begins in Lake Mille Lacs and winds its way 70 miles south to Anoka. Mille Lacs was first called Spirit Lake by the Dakota, who lived along its shores. When the first whites began using the river, they mis-translated Spirit to mean, rum. This was an obvious mistake since Rum liquor was being traded heavily to the Dakota at that time.

The Rum was a familiar route to traders who traveled between the Mississippi River and the populous Indian villages on the shores of Lake Mille Lacs. More thorough knowledge regarding the Rum River country was obtained during the fall of 1847, when Daniel Stanchfield, and some helpers, were sent to the area to assess the lumber potential. Stanchfield climbed a tree in the area of Princeton and as far as he could see, there were pine. He was quoted as saying, "It

MHS

1854 Dakota Indian Camp. (Daguerreotype).

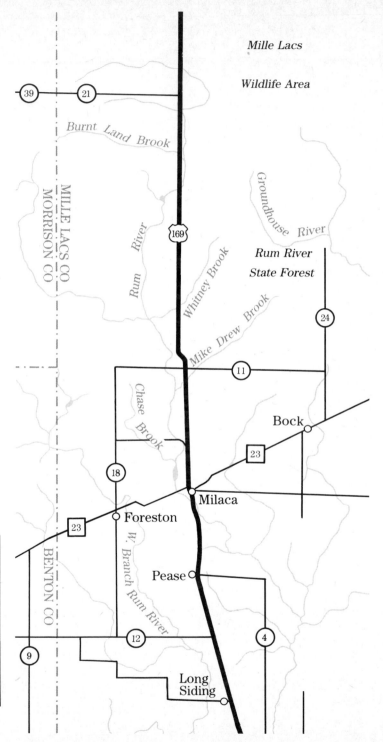

would take seventy mills, seventy years, to exhaust the white pine along the Rum." The first logging on the Rum occurred in 1822 when a number of soldiers, building Fort Snelling, came here to cut logs and float them down to the fort located at the mouth of the Minnesota River.

The Rum later developed as an important highway for lumbermen who came to harvest the pine between the Mississippi and St. Croix rivers. For twenty years, starting in 1850, logs flowed down the Rum on their way to the sawmills of St. Anthony. Today, the Rum is a recreational river, bordered not by white pine, but by oak, elm, ash, maple and poplar. The Rum is also an excellent river for canoeing and smallmouth bass fishing.

MARKING THE LOGS

As the pines were cut and sent down the Rum, it was necessary to mark them with a brand of some design which would show ownership of the log. At St. Anthony, and other places along the Mississippi, boom sites were made to collect the floating logs and prepare them for sawing. At these boom sites, men walked the logs calling out measurements and brands to another person, who recorded the information and tallied the results. This was an important process since the lumberjacks, working miles upstream, wanted to be sure that they were getting credit for their efforts. One of the lumberjack's skills was knowing what side to put the brand on, so when logs floated down the stream the brand would be facing up.

RAILROADS

The region became more populated and prosperous as the railroad developed. The first railroad to enter the county was the Minneapolis and St. Cloud, which in 1882 passed through Milaca, connecting St. Cloud and Hinckley. Four years later, a branch of the St. Paul, Minneapolis and Manitoba line reached Milaca from Elk River. Finally, in 1908, the Soo Line passed through the Onamia area, on its run between Brooten and Superior.

Northern Minnesota logging crew taking a lunch break.

MHS

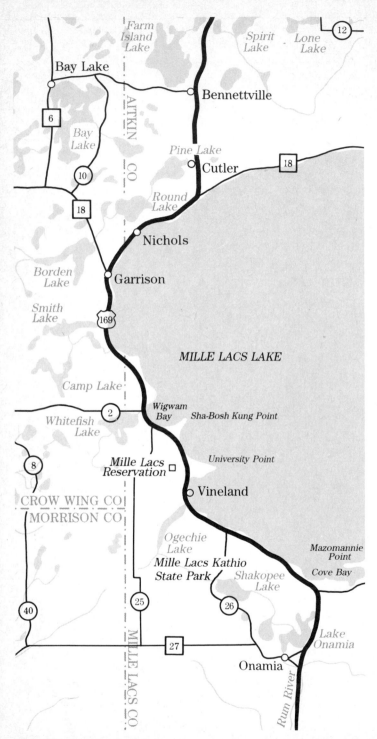

ONAMIA, Pop. 691

Onamia, a railway village along the Soo Line route from Brooten to Superior, takes its name from the lake on the northwest side of town. The Rum River flows through the west side of town, on its journey to the Mississippi. Onamia is the site of Crosier College, a Catholic Seminary founded in 1913 by Belgium priests.

MILLE LACS KATHIO STATE PARK

Located along Lake Ogechie, just opposite Mille Lacs Lake, is the beautiful Kathio State Park. Situated among wooded hills and meadows, it includes the area where the Dakota and Ojibwe battled for control of northern Minnesota. There are 71 campsites along Ogechie Lake, interspersed with Indian mounds. The park has an incredible array of trails for hiking, skiing, horseback riding and snowmobiling. There is also an interpretive center describing the Indian history of the area.

KATHIO VILLAGE (VINELAND)

Before the Ojibwe had pushed their way across Lake Superior into Minnesota, the Dakota occupied the country surrounding Mille Lacs Lake. Kathio, the main village or cultural center for the Dakota Indians, was located at the mouth of the Rum River, near what is now Vineland. It is the oldest Indian village name known in Minnesota. The first white visitor was Daniel Greysolon Sieur Du Luth, a French nobleman, who had come from Montreal in 1678 on his search for a route to the Pacific Ocean. Here Du Luth spent the winter and claimed the entire area for France.

The following summer, when Father Hennepin traveled up the Mississippi, he was captured by Dakota warriors at Lake Pepin. Some wanted to kill him, but instead he was brought on a long, grueling trip to Mille Lacs. At times, Hennepin claimed he was carried on the backs of his captors. It was during this period, that Father Hennepin discovered and named the Falls of St. Anthony.

The Ojibwe began to exert their strength in Minnesota during the 1700's, and in 1750, a three-day battle between the Dakota and Ojibwe at Kathio Village, forced the Dakota to flee down the Rum River. This battle marked the beginning of the Dakotas' nomadic existence on the prairie of southern Minnesota. Later, they were expelled from the state, following the Sioux Uprising of 1862.

For many years, the Dakota and Ojibwe continued to launch attacks against each other, with heavy casualties taken on both sides. In 1837 the Ojibwe gave away their rights to the land around Mille Lacs. When they were told to move to the White Earth Indian Reservation, many refused to budge. This

(left) Ojibwe Indians setting up a 20-ft. birchbark canoe. Photo/T.W. Ingersoll. (bottom) Chief Good Thunder, a Dakota Indian with family and Rev. Knowlton, 1900.

MHS

group of Ojibwe became know as the "Non-Removal Mille Lacs Indian Band." In 1926, after a long controversy, the group was deeded a small reservation along the lake.

MILLE LACS LAKE

For some 20 miles, U.S. 169 follows the shore of Mille Lacs Lake, one of the largest and most beautiful lakes in Minnesota. The lake is famous for walleyes and northern pike, but bass, perch and crappies are also fished. A prehistoric people lived along the lake many years before the Dakota and Ojibwe made their claims. Some 1000 mounds have been discovered in the region.

This lake has many legends. One is that the Dakota felt Mille Lacs was inhabited by spirits. At night, their low, sighing moans could be heard across the waters. Vague, distorted forms were also seen in the shadows of the forest. The Ojibwe called the lake, "Minsi-sagaigon" or "everywhere lakes," because of the number of lakes that dotted this region. The French translated this into Mille Lacs, meaning "thousand lakes."

MILLE LACS LAKE GEOLOGY

This part of Minnesota was covered by glacial ice, several thousand feet thick, on at least four occasions during the last million years. As the glaciers moved in from Canada, they brought with them enormous quantities of sand and deposited them along their leading edges. It was this deposit of sand and gravel which blocked the normal southward drainage of water, creating the second largest lake in the state. Mille Lacs is 18 miles long, 14 miles wide, and only 30 to 40 feet deep. The lake drains to the Mississippi through the Rum River.

MHS

VINELAND

Located at the mouth of the Rum River, Vineland was named after an early Norwegian settlement on the northeast coast of Canada. Today, Vineland is a trading post for a small band of Ojibwe Indians living on the reservation here. Adjoining the post, is an Ojibwe museum, with many exhibits depicting Indian culture.

GARRISON

This small resort village was named after Oscar Garrison, who also platted the town of Wayzata. Garrison worked along the Upper Mississippi as a surveyor for the U.S. Government. The town really comes to life during the summer as a resort village, providing lodging and boat rentals to vacationers. Ice fishing during the winter also supplies the town with resort income. On the south side of Garrison, there is a wayside park on the lake–an excellent spot to stop for lunch.

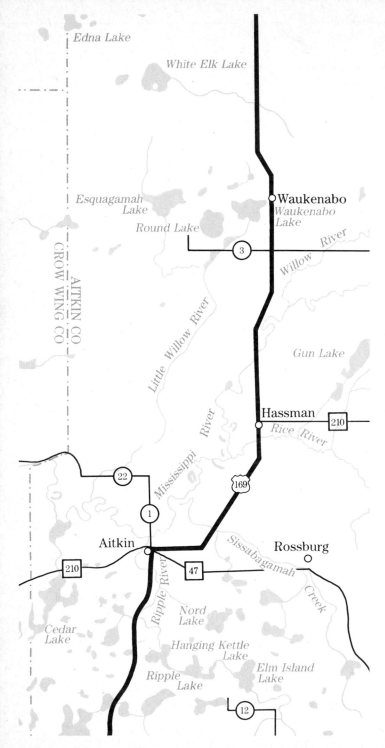

AITKIN COUNTY, Pop. 13,404

Many years before white explorers set foot in what is now Aitkin County, the Indians were using a well-known route from Lake Superior. They came up the St. Louis River to Big Sandy Lake via the East Savanna River. From the Big Sandy, it was only a short distance to the Mississippi. It was along this route that the explorers, traders, and missionaries entered Minnesota and reached the Mississippi. Sieur du Luth most likely came down the Mississippi from Sandy Lake when he visited the Indians of Mille Lacs in 1679. The Northwest Company, a British post established on Big Sandy Lake in 1794, was one of the first trading centers in the region west of Lake Superior.

The county was named after William A. Aitkin, a fur trader who came here in 1802, as a teenager from Scotland. For years, Aitkin traded with the Ojibwe at the trading posts of the American Fur Company, on the west side of Big Sandy Lake. Aitkin also helped establish a school for the Indians here in 1832. The teachers were missionaries, Frederick Ayer and Edmund Ely.

AITKIN, Pop.1,770

The Dakota hunted this region until they were driven from Lake Mille Lacs in the mid-1700's, by the well-armed Ojibwe. Early explorers, such as Radisson and Groseilliers, passed what would later become Aitkin as early as 1655. Du Luth also camped in the area on his way to Mille Lacs in 1679.

The first white settlement of this region was comparatively late. In the fall of 1870, Nathaniel Tibbetts, a member of the Great Northern survey crew, filed a claim on the present site of Aitkin. The tracks were laid to this point a few months later, providing the incentive for a new town to begin. A passenger station was constructed, as was a store and trading post. Tibbetts helped the cause by building a hotel called the "Ojibwe." For the next few years, lumbering was the predominant activity, with millions of feet of lumber carried out on flats of the Great Northern Railroad.

Up to 1875, the town was mainly filled with men working in the lumber camps. The population was 165; all but 20 of them, men. The region developed slowly, and as late as 1880, there were only 366 people living in the entire county.

For a number of years, steamboat traffic increased between Aitkin and Grand Rapids along the Mississippi. The trip could be made in a day, if the conditions were favorable. But when the water-level was down, passengers often had to climb off and help push. With the unbearable mosquitoes, and a trip strung out to five or so days, the passengers were happy to finally reach their destination. When the forests were stripped around Aitkin, the settlers had little choice but to start farming. Many Swedish and German settlers were attracted to the rich soil here, during the late 1800's. Besides dairying, the Aitkin area farmers raised turkeys for the eastern markets.

An ancient glacial lake covered much of Aitkin County and the town of Aitkin. A sandy beach of this huge lake existed about one mile south of town and formed a three to five-foot high ridge of sand. The lake was only about 20 feet deep and was eventually drained by the Mississippi. When approaching Aitkin from the south, you can see the rolling well-drained land change to a flat, poorly-drained glacial lake bottom.

CUYUNA IRON RANGE

U.S. 169 crosses the northeastern limits of the Cuyuna Range, a narrow range of iron ore that was discovered in 1904. One day, a crusty old prospector named Cuyler Adams, noticed that his magnetic compass was acting funny. Adams, along with his dog Una, had been prospecting in the Deerwood area when he made the discovery. This iron range was then named after Cuyler and his dog Una.

The late discovery of the Cuyuna ore (some 30 years after the Vermilion and Mesabi ranges), was due to the thick glacial deposits covering the iron-bearing rocks. The Cuyuna deposits differ from the Mesabi Range to the north, in that they do not form one continuous strata that can be easily mined. A unique aspect of the Cuyuna ore is that it contains manganese, a metal scarce in the United States. During World War II, 90 percent of the country's supply of manganese came from the Cuyuna Range.

MISSISSIPPI RIVER

North of Aitkin, U.S. 169 traverses the old lake bottom of Glacial Lake Aitkin and runs parallel to the Mississippi for several miles. The Mississippi is an Ojibwe word meaning "great river" or "gathering of all waters." Along this stretch, the river winds through a region of hardwoods and pine, where it has formed many ox-bow lakes. (Ox-bow lakes are bends in the river which have broken off from the main stream.) Along the shores, ruffed grouse, muskrat, beaver and deer are abundant, while the waters are home for northern pike, and large and smallmouth bass.

WAUKENABO

The lake and small village are named after an Ojibwe word meaning "broth of moss growing on rocks or trees." During long winter months when game was hard to kill, many Indians ate the moss on the trees and rocks to stay alive.

Steamer "Irene" near Aitkin on Mississippi River. (Aitkin Co. Hist. Soc.)

Harvesting barley on once-forested land, near Aitkin.

MHS

MHS

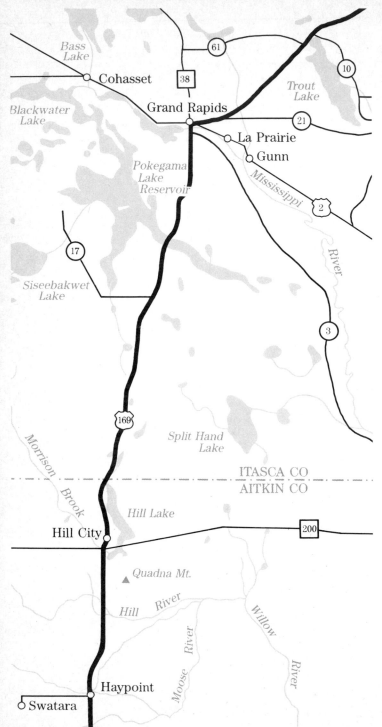

HILL CITY, Pop. 533

Hill City takes its name from a hilly region to the southeast, originally formed by mounds of glacial debris. The Ojibwe referred to this hilly region as "Piquadinaw," meaning, "it is hilly." When lumbermen started working here, they called the larger hill of this group "Poqoudenaw Mountain," which has since been shortened to Quadna Mountain. During its early years, Hill City manufactured wooden pails and other wood products. Today, a large lumbermill rests on the west side of town.

ITASCA COUNTY, Pop. 43,006

The county, established in 1849, was named after Lake Itasca, the source of the Mississippi River. The Ojibwe called the lake "Omushkos," their word for elk. But Henry Schoolcraft, the first white explorer and writer who discovered the true source of the Mississippi in 1832, wanted a better name for such an important lake. One day, while canoeing with a friend, they came up with two Latin words; "veritas," meaning truth, and "caput," meaning head. Schoolcraft combined the two words, dropped three letters from the front and back of the combination, and arrived at the name of Itasca.

GRAND RAPIDS, Pop. 7,934

It wasn't long after 1865 that lumbermen started taking advantage of the giant pines growing along the Mississippi. The real activity started in 1870 though, when Leonard Day came to the region wearing his plug hat and riding a fancy carriage. Day and his sons developed a logging industry that soon had the woods filled with over 600 men, cutting and removing timber.

The lumberjack was a skilled ax-man whose importance went beyond just muscle. He had to know how to drop a tree in the right direction, while at the same time, wasting as little of the important trunk as he could. He made as much as $40 a month, until the invention of the crosscut saw brought in a less-skilled woodsman who was paid $25 a month. The crosscut saw was faster and could cut closer to the ground, leaving more of the important trunk-wood for milling.

The railroad reached Grand Rapids in 1890. Many settlers came in its wake and the town was incorporated the following year. In 1894, the Pokegama Hotel boasted of having the first electric lights in the city. A large paper mill was built here in 1902 and was eventually taken over by the Blandin Paper Company. Located a couple of miles west of Grand Rapids, is the new Forest History Center, run by the Minnesota Historical Society. It is situated in a new building with displays and information on the early days of the lumbermen. Here you can also tour a reconstructed turn-of-the-century logging camp.

MESABI IRON RANGE

There is some evidence that a few French missionaries and explorers, venturing through the Mesabi region in the 1700's, suspected there was iron here. Before the ore was discovered, however, the region was drawn on Joseph Nicollet's 1841 map of the state and labeled, "Missabay Heights." This is an Ojibwe name that means "giant," or "big man hills." The name refers to a ridge of land that divides the drainage between Hudson Bay and Lake Superior. But whether or not there was any knowledge of the ore, it was gold and copper that were on the minds of the early prospectors.

The first iron deposits were discovered at Lake Vermilion in 1865 and became known as the Vermilion Range. These deposits were positioned vertically, and shafts had to be sunk to extract them. But when the Mesabi Range was discovered in 1890, it turned out to be the largest concentration of iron-ore deposits in the world. Unlike the deep veins of ore in the Vermilion Range, the Mesabi deposits were stratified horizontally near the surface, enabling it to be mined from open pits. These remarkable mines that dotted the range gave up ore that was close to 50 percent iron. During the 1940's, the mines shipped over one-third of the world's ore. These rich deposits have been depleted now, but taconite (a low-grade iron of 20 to 30 percent), is now being processed successfully.

How the ore was formed was a complicated process that spanned hundreds of millions of years. The elements that helped precipitate the iron into these unusual concentrations were the ancient seas which left layers of deposited sand, the heat from lava streams that formed the North Shore, and finally years of erosion which brought these deposits close to the surface.

MINING TOWNS

The towns and villages along the range had a common beginning in an industry that made them more alike than different. Yet for all their similarities, the particular setting and style of this area and its people, cannot be found anywhere else in the Midwest.

The gaping holes of the formerly-active mines can still be seen near most of the range towns. Trees now grow along the steep spoil banks (waste rock remaining after ore removal). Rusting pieces of machinery lie neglected under water which has drained into the pits. It takes little imagination to hear the noise of the steam shovels digging down into the earth, or the chugging of the locomotives, winding their way out of the pits and onto the docks of Lake Superior. The highway from Grand Rapids bends through a scarred landscape; where distant hills are more likely to be man-made

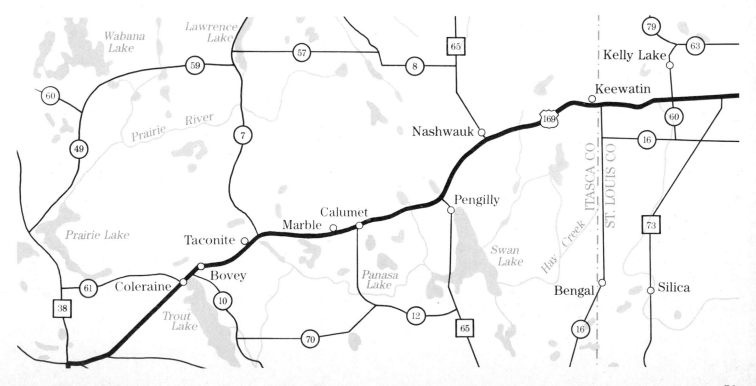

MHS

Minnesota mine workers, 1910. Photo/J.C. Amundson.

spoil banks, than formations of ancient glaciers. New growth is everywhere; poplar, aspen—all the signs of a land that has been disturbed.

COLERAINE, Pop. 1,116

In 1905, John Greenway, a superintendent for the Oliver Mining Company, stopped at the shores of Trout Lake and planned a new mining town. It was named after Thomas F. Cole, president of the new company. The Duluth, Missabe and Northern Railroad reached here the following year, and Coleraine developed as a mining and railway village.

Coleraine marks the western limits of Mesabi ore deposits which run northeastward to Virginia. Because the ore was mixed with sand, the region around Coleraine was ignored until the Oliver Iron Mining Company developed a process to remove the sand.

EARLY SETTLEMENT

Those early years on the range saw many conflicts between the lumbermen and miners. The range had fast become a melting pot of foreign immigrants, creating tensions and abrupt social change. From the eastern seaboard, labor agencies dumped Slavs, Germans, Greeks, Italians, Finns, and Swedes into this intensive labor market. Many could not read or write, and the number of different languages forced the common use of English. As the rich concentrations of iron ore were being removed, it seemed ironic that only a short eighty years before, in 1826, the Ojibwe had exchanged all mineral rights for a few gifts and a $2,000 annuity.

BOVEY, Pop. 813

Bovey was the first town to be developed in the Canisteo District, an area comprised of sandy ore. Grand Rapids was the closest town, so teams of exploration parties came up the road to Bovey and made it their headquarters. When the town was incorporated in 1904, there were barely enough residents to meet the legal village requirements. But the new settlement started to attract businesses, and when the Oliver Iron Mining Company successfully started to wash the sand from the ore, the Canisteo Mine opened, just outside of town. In three years, the work force in the mines pushed the town's population to 1,200. During the early 1900's, three major mines were working in the area. They were the Canisteo, Danube, and Harrison mines.

TACONITE, Pop. 331

The small village of Taconite was the site of the old Home-Cliffs Mine, which has been inactive for a number of years. This area had one of the first mining operations on the Mesabi and also had the first experimental ore-washing plant.

MHS

Early railroad bed through deep north woods.

MARBLE, Pop. 757

This was another railway village built by the Oliver Mining Company when ore was found underneath the thick growth of forest. The town was literally cut out of the forest. The first open-pit mine called the Hill Mine, began operations here in 1908.

CALUMET, Pop. 469

Calumet was the last of the towns constructed in the Canisteo District, an area of ore deposits laced with sand. After the Oliver Mining Company's successful removal of sand from the ore, the company started to expand into the Calumet area. A company called the Powers Improvement Company, platted the town and erected a hotel. In 1909 the town was incorporated. The community's early income came from the Hill-Annex Mine, which operated on a state lease. The state had passed a law that Sections 16 and 36 of every township, was to be set aside for recreation. As it turned out, the Hill-Annex mine rested on section 16.

The Hill-Annex Mine was one of the first to use electricity in its mining operations. Today, state-run tours are conducted into the now-inactive mine, which produced over 75 million tons of ore during its 67-year history. The old employee clubhouse is now an interpretive center.

The town takes its name from a French word which describes the ceremonial pipe smoked by the Ojibwe during important occasions. One such occasion might have been in 1854, when the Ojibwe ceded the entire Arrowhead region to the whites.

NASHWAUK, Pop. 1,419

In 1890, Nashwauk was the site of a large logging camp in the midst of a thick pine forest. The camp had a problem, however. There were no rivers or streams to float away the logs. The Wright-Davis Lumber Company solved this problem by building a railroad to the town of Jacobson, where the Swan River enters the Mississippi. Here they could ship the logs and then float them downstream to the mills. James J. Hill later bought out their interests and incorporated the line into his railroad empire.

It wasn't until 1900 that the Itasca Mining Company discovered ore at Nashwauk, which then became known as the Hawkins Mine. The extension of the Great Northern Railroad from Nashwauk to Grand Rapids was completed in 1909. With the opening of the nearby La Rue and Headley Mines, Nashwauk became one of the larger towns in Itasca County. At the head of its main street, there is an observation stand where you can look down into the water-filled Hawkins Mine. Outside of Nashwauk, the Hanna Mining Company still runs a large taconite pellet operation.

KEEWATIN, Pop. 1,443

In 1904, large amounts of ore were discovered in the Keewatin area. But several years lapsed before mining was to begin on any scale. Keewatin is an Ojibwe word meaning "north," or "north wind." The Mississippi and Bennet Mines were operating here by 1912, and during the 1930's, the Hanna Ore Company was operating the Mesabi Chief and Mississippi 2 mines. During 1939, the Mesabi Chief produced 6.6 million tons of ore.

ST. LOUIS COUNTY, Pop. 222,229

Settled during the 1850's, St. Louis County is named after the largest river that enters Lake Superior. St. Louis is also the largest county in Minnesota, with slightly more than four million acres. It wasn't long before lumbering and farming were over-shadowed by the iron mining industry. The present mining of taconite accounts for over 90 percent of all minerals mined in this state. It has been said that the iron mines of Minnesota, won the two World Wars for this nation. Those days have long passed though. The "can do" spirit was shaken when word came during the 1940's that the ore would soon be gone. In the late 1970's, mining stopped altogether on the Vermilion and Cuyuna ranges. Only taconite (a lower grade of ore) was being mined on the Mesabi. With state tax incentives being given, the taconite industry revitalized some of the old mining towns; building taconite processing plants at Iron Mountain, Nashwauk, Keewatin, Hibbing, Eveleth, Silver Bay, and Hoyt Lakes.

Many of the towns that grew alongside the mines declined after World War II, and the centers of trade moved to cities like Hibbing, Virginia and Grand Rapids, leaving behind bedroom communities with decaying business districts. The highway then became the link between the communities and the jobs.

KELLY & LEETONIA

These are two railroad villages that formed along the Great Northern Railroad, when it was built from Hibbing to Grand Rapids in 1909.

Chandler Mine on Vermilion Range, Ely, 1895.

MHS

HIBBING, Pop. 21,193

1892 was an incredible year on the Range. It was the year the first ore was shipped from the Iron Mountain Mine. The Oliver Mining Company was formed (Oliver later became part of United States Steel). Virginia, McKinley, and Biwabik developed as villages, and Frank Hibbing discovered ore at a spot where he decided to build a town.

That town quickly became a mix of miners and lumbermen from almost every corner of Europe. A portable sawmill had been hauled through the woods and began milling the countless number of white pine. Stores and shacks collected around this makeshift operation.

It wasn't long before there were more saloons than stores in Hibbing. Crew captains of the lumber companies picked their workers from the drunks "sleeping it off" on the bar floors. The roads to Hibbing were poor, easily turning to slush and mud, and making the needed trips for supplies tedious. Feed for the horses working the woods became more of a priority than the nutrition of the men. There were also problems in finding safe drinking water; cases of typhoid were common.

The Swan River Lumber Company built a large mill one mile east of town and employed 1,500 men. Logs were brought to this mill and the finished products were shipped by rail to the Swan River, then floated down the Mississippi.

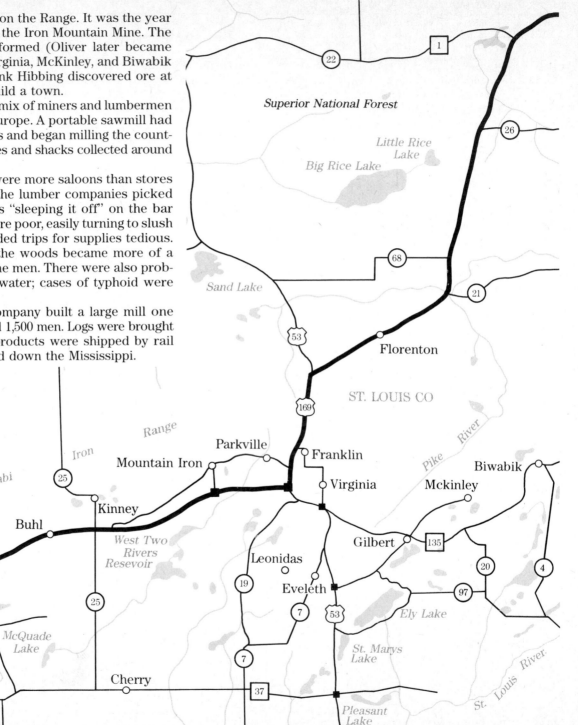

The nation-wide panic of 1893 almost destroyed the future of Hibbing, but with the railroad completed to the Mahoning mine, just outside of town, prosperity started to return to this destitute village. It took twenty years of hard work before the now famous, Hull-Rust-Mahoning mine became one of the biggest, richest, iron-ore mines in the world. During WW II, young boys and women were working this gigantic mine, since many of the men were away fighting. The mines worked day and night as they extracted the red earth from the ground.

Today, an observation area is maintained on the edge of the now-inactive mine, once the largest open-pit iron mine in the world. It is certainly worth the stop, for no one can quite imagine a man-made hole this expansive, until you stand on its edge and see it for yourself.

HIBBING IS MOVED

It was apparent by 1910, that the original Hibbing would have to move off the rich deposits that lay underneath a good portion of the town. A location one mile south, called Alice, was selected, and in 1919 buildings started to be dismantled and moved.

A car salesman named Carl Eric Wickman, needing a better way to earn a living, started a bus service between the old and new towns of Hibbing. Wickman called it the Mesabi Transportation Company but later changed its name to the Northland Greyhound Line. His successful company eventually evolved into the national carrier, Greyhound Lines.

During the early 1900's, some 70 mines worked the Mesabi Range, creating a wealth that many felt would continue forever. But it was soon evident that rich ore deposits were limited. A process was developed that extracted the more abundant, lower grade ore embedded in rock, crushed it, then suspended it in liquid and removed the iron magnetically. It was then dried and shaped into pellets, containing about 60-65 percent iron.

LAURENTIAN DIVIDE

Just north of Hibbing, there's a small rise of land topped by a simple plaque. This spot marks an unusual geologic occurrence, where three major drainage basins come together. When a rain shower falls on this spot, one-third of the water flows north to Hudson Bay, another third drains east into Lake Superior and the Atlantic, and the final portion flows south to the Mississippi and into the Gulf of Mexico.

Millions of years ago, the surface of northern Minnesota was being pushed and vaulted into a rugged, mountainous terrain. This range once reached from southwest Minnesota to the St. Lawrence River. For hundreds of centuries, wind and rain slowly eroded these mountains down to a resistant ridge of very old granite. This 400-foot ridge, called the Giants Range or Laurentian Divide, runs east near Virginia and up along the North Shore.

IRON RANGE INTERPRETATIVE CENTER

Located on Highway 169 between Chisholm and Hibbing, is the Iron Range Interpretative Center, a living museum situated on the edge of the abandoned John S. Pillsbury open-pit mine. The displays here are sensitively done and utilize modern audio-visual techniques which bring the unique iron-range history to life. It is definitely worth the stop.

CHISHOLM, Pop. 5,930

Archibald Chisholm came to the United States from Canada and worked as an accountant and paymaster on the Vermilion Range. When ore was found south on the Mesabi Range, Chisholm headed for Hibbing and became the discoverer of a number of Mesabi mines. One was in the Chisholm area, and a town was organized by the Chisholm Improvement Company in 1901. The town quickly grew, and in six short years the population had swelled to 6,000. Many of the workers were from Yugoslavia, Finland, and Italy, making the process of educating their children extremely difficult. The push for education almost became an obsession with the mining town. At one time, 46 percent of the population had gone through the Chisholm educational system.

In the dry fall of 1908, a brush fire swept into town backed by a strong wind. The buildings were made of wood and the town was mostly destroyed. By the following year, seventy new fireproof brick buildings lined the main street.

First street in Hibbing. Spring of 1893.

MHS

At one time, 45 mines were shipping ore from this district, with the deepest open-pit mine reaching 400 feet into the ground. Today, Chisholm is ringed by the gaping holes of these now-inactive mines.

BUHL, Pop. 1,284

Mining operations had started on the western Mesabi by 1900, but in the vicinity of Buhl, loggers were still harvesting the tall stands of norway and white pine. In 1900, prospectors for the Sharon Mining Company of Pennsylvania, decided that a new town was in order. They platted a 40-acre site in honor of Frank Buhl, former president of the company. Eight mines once operated near Buhl. When production started to decline, many of the miners turned to dairy farming.

KINNEY, Pop. 447

Located near the southern border of the Superior National Forest, Kinney grew up on the edge of the open-pit mine (now inactive) that bears its name. It was shortly after the Buhl mines had begun production, that O.D Kinney discovered ore here. The property was leased to the Republic Iron and Steel Company, and the population of Kinney grew to 1,200. The mine became inactive, though, and the town is now a bedroom community for Hibbing and Virginia.

MOUNTAIN IRON, Pop. 4,134

The city of Mountain Iron marks the birthplace of the Mesabi Range. For years after iron was found on the Vermilion Range near Ely, prospectors crisscrossed the Arrowhead region, looking for new discoveries. Few ever conceived though, that for a hundred miles along the highland region the early explorer Nicollet called, "Missabay Heights", lay the largest concentration of ore in the world just under the forest floor.

A family of brothers named Merritt, was committed to the search for iron. For some twenty years they were led by Leonidas Merritt, as they combined lumbering with their search for ore. But the early theories on mining taught them that minerals were embedded in hard rock, and that mine shafts had to be sunk to extract it. No one suspected that the red powdery substance just beneath the surface could be ore, because it fell outside the old concepts.

In 1890, the Merritts had spent most of their money in test pits and returned, defeated, to Duluth. One of their crew leaders was also leaving the Mountain Iron region, when his wagon wheel cut into some red powdery soil. Scooping up fifty pounds of the stuff, he brought it back to Duluth, where an analysis showed an iron content of 64 percent. More discoveries followed, and in one short year the Merritts had

organized the Duluth, Missabe, and Northern Railroad. By October 1892, the first ore shipment left Mountain Iron for the port of Superior.

As operations started in the Mountain Iron Mine, an 80-acre townsite was platted and named Grant, after the contractor who was building the railroad. When Grant was incorporated a short time later, it took the name Mountain Iron. Only a couple of years later, the Merritts had considerable financial trouble raising capital and paying off their debts. They lost control of the mining operation to oil magnate John D. Rockefeller, who brought out the Merritts' stock. In the late 1890's when mining was in high gear, Rockefeller bought numerous ore companies, lands and leases on the Range.

IRON RANGE MERGERS

During the early 1900's, there was a favorable mood in the United States for the merger and consolidation of large business interests. The Mesabi Range was no exception. There was Carnegie and his holdings in the Oliver Mining Company, James J. Hill and his Great Northern Railroad, and the Lake Superior Consolidated Iron Mining Company, under John D. Rockefeller.

It was during this period that J. Pierpont Morgan came onto the scene and began buying ore leases from most of these companies, with the exception of James J. Hill's railroad. Morgan spent close to $1.4 billion setting up his empire of steel plants, mines, blast furnaces, railroads, coal lands and ore vessels. All of this later became known as the United States Steel Corporation.

VIRGINIA, Pop. 11,056

As ore-fever swept across the Range in the late 1800's, the area was inundated with prospectors and lumbermen. In 1892, Captain Cohoe, a prospector for the Merritt brothers, found ore at what soon became the Missabe Mountain Mine. With this discovery, a company was formed to develop a town in one of the richest ore and lumber regions of the Arrowhead. The company called itself the Virginia Improvement Company, after the home state of Alfred E. Humphrey, its founder.

While some members of the company were busy hacking an 80-acre plot out of the dense pine forest, others were busy selling lots in Duluth for $300 to $400. Lumbering was the primary force in early Virginia, as lumberjacks, timber cruisers, investors, and milling companies flocked to the new town. When the Duluth, Missabe and Northern Railroad reached here in 1893, both ore and timber were shipped out of the area. Soon, Virginia became one of the major lumbering towns of northern Minnesota.

Main Street, Eveleth Minnesota, 1895.

In just a few short years, this boom-town sprouted a population of 5,000. But misfortune came to Virginia one hot summer day in 1893. A forest fire raging through the area destroyed the entire village. Following the fire, a financial panic swept the nation, forcing many to lose their holdings in the mines. Work came to a standstill and many people left, unable to pay their bills. But in spite of the hard times, Virginia was rebuilt. Then seven years later, the tragedy was repeated as residents of Virginia watched another fire, that started in the Finlayson Mill, roar through town.

By now residents had learned their lesson. Main street was reconstructed with stone, brick and concrete. What is ironic about Virginia is that it grew from the wealth of both lumbering and mining. But when the forests were depleted, the growing national hunger for steel provided an even stronger economic base. As many as 20 mines worked the region of Virginia during the early 1900's. Shipping over 7,000 tons of ore a day, the Missabe Mountain Mine soon grew into one of the largest open-pit iron mines in the country. But a one-industry region is vulnerable to swings in the economy. One of the worst periods for Virginia and the Range was the depression of 1932, when 70 percent of the work force was jobless.

EVELETH, Pop. 5,042

Calling itself the "Hill Top City," Eveleth was named after lumberman, Erwin Eveleth. Eveleth came here from Michigan in 1883 to purchase forested lands for lumbering. That same year, ore was discovered and a town was platted.

But the town of Eveleth was forming when the national economy was at a standstill. Only four buildings lined main street. At times, food was so scarce that most survived only on the food that men brought back from hunting. Yet Eveleth continued to grow and by 1910, 7,000 people had made it their home.

As mining continued in 1895, Eveleth found itself sitting on valuable ore deposits. A few years later, the entire town was moved about a mile northeast. One of the main concerns was where to relocate the cemetery, since no one wanted to disturb the graves a second time. A number of sites were tested before they found a site devoid of ore, where they could bury their dead.

SUPERIOR NATIONAL FOREST

Lumbering continued unchecked during the late 1800's and by 1900 much of the white pine had been cut in the Arrowhead. There was a growing concern that some tracts of natural forest should be preserved, but the lumber companies threatened to pull out, leaving many without work. A Civil War general, named Christopher Andrews, stressed the need to protect our wilderness, and helped establish the state and national forest system. He also promoted the need for preserving parks and historical sites.

In 1909, his ideas became reality when 36,000 acres were established as the Superior National Forest. Today, this forest system encompasses over three million acres, and together with Canada's Quetico Provincial Park, they provide a matchless recreation, canoeing and wildlife area.

LAKE VERMILION

Situated in the center of the Vermilion Iron Range is Lake Vermilion, a pristine, rock-bound lake, whose 186 miles of shoreline, granite ledges, and islands make it one of the more beautiful lakes in the state. It is part of the eroded core of the Laurentian Mountains that once stood out like the Rocky Mountains. But millions of years of wind, rain, and glacial activity has left little more than a rise of rock, dividing the flow of water between the Hudson Bay and Lake Superior.

As the fur trade expanded across northern Minnesota, posts were established on Vermilion to trade with the Ojibwe. During the 1740's, the Ojibwe fought bitterly with the Dakota for control of northern Minnesota and the valued hunting grounds of Vermilion. The lake had the long Indian name of, "Sah-Ga-Ee-Gum-Wah-Ma-Mah-Nee", meaning, "Lake of the Sunset Glow."

At the Ojibwe capital on Madeline Island, the Indians signed a treaty in 1854 which many called the "Miners' Treaty." In this treaty, the Ojibwe gave the mineral and pine-hungry settlers most of the North Shore region that came to be known as the Arrowhead. For this, the Ojibwe were given a reservation west of Cloquet, called Fond Du Lac.

Vermilion is the fifth largest lake in the state, not counting Superior.

LAKE VERMILION GOLD RUSH

Governor Alexander Ramsey took special interest in assessing the region's wealth in 1850, but interests were directed toward gold and copper, not the red ore that lay under the forest floor.

In 1865, a rumor surfaced that gold was found on the northeastern side of Lake Vermilion. That winter a number of "gold companies" rapidly formed, and by May of 1866, some 300 men were working the rocky region around the lake. What is unusual about this minor event, is that no trace of gold was ever found. Yet during this futile search for gold, considerable deposits of iron ore were discovered.

FIRST DISCOVERY OF IRON RANGE ORE

The honor of being the first discoverer of the Vermilion Range ore went to Henry Eames, a state geologist. In 1865, Eames wrote about iron ore he found at the mouth of Two Rivers on Lake Vermilion. It consisted of two, 60-foot-wide veins. From then on the deposits became known as the Vermilion Range. It was reported that when Eames came upon an iron deposit at what would later become Babbitt, he told an associate, "To hell with iron...its gold we're after."

That same year, a man named George Stuntz, prospecting for gold in the same area, discovered what would later be-

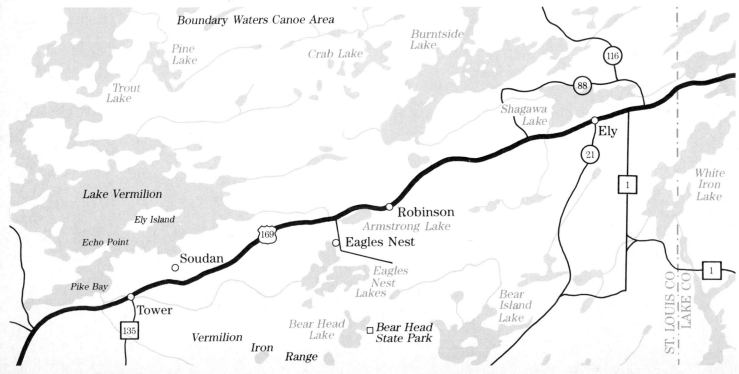

come the first iron to be mined in Minnesota. The mine was named Breitung. The first shipment of ore went out by rail in 1884. The ore deposits were in narrow veins, running vertically into the ground. These had to be mined in the traditional underground method.

TOWER, Pop. 640

It was prospector George Stuntz, who brought iron-ore samples to Duluth in 1875. He enticed financiers, George Stone and Philadelphian, Charlemagne Tower, to invest money in a Vermilion iron mine. Finally getting financial support in 1882, Stuntz went back up the rugged Vermilion Trail (a narrow path through the woods connecting Vermilion with Duluth), and platted a town named after Tower. The Minnesota Iron Company was formed by Tower, Stone and Stuntz. They also bought the rights to the fledgling Duluth and Iron Range Railroad. Tower then proceeded to buy thousands of acres of land in the Arrowhead, where he thought ore might be found.

In the meantime, the small shanty town of Tower was built to provide services for those that would work at the Soudan Mine, a short distance away. The activity around Tower attracted many from the copper mines of Michigan and a number of Swedish immigrants.

Those first years were difficult for the workers, since the trip from Duluth took two nights and three days. Supplies and mail delivery were unpredictable at best. Even the miners' payroll had to be sent from Duluth, nailed shut in a wooden box. Besides the inconvenient distance from supply points, the winters added another hardship. During one long cold-snap, a storekeeper requested a six-foot thermometer that wouldn't freeze at minus 40 degrees.

The railroad was essential to the development of the new Soudan mine. Consequently, great effort was spent laying tracks from Two Harbors. In August 1884, the first ore from the iron range was shipped from the Soudan mine to Two Harbors in a small, 10 car train. As the train pulled away, every miner stood alongside it and threw in a chunk of ore for good luck.

SOUDAN

The Soudan mine is the oldest and deepest mine in the state. When it stopped production in 1963 because of high production costs and reduced profits, it had reached 2,400 feet into the earth. This mine produced some of the richest ore on the Range, with the veins running at 65 percent metallic iron. The method of underground mining was similar for all the mines. Some 1800 men worked this mine during

its peak in 1892, hauling out 568,000 tons of ore. Over 1.5 million tons of ore is still left in the mine.

During its heyday, Soudan had a population of 800 people who lived and worked next to the mine. Soudan never had any stores or merchants because the village of Tower had worked out an agreement that none could be established in Soudan, not even a gas station. In trying to think up a name for the town, the mine's manager played on his sense of humor. He picked the name of a region whose weather greatly contrasted with their bitter winters. He came up with Soudan (Sudan), Africa.

Today, the Tower-Soudan Mine is a 1,000 acre state park, donated by U.S. Steel. The main feature of the park is the mine tour, where mining cars are ridden three-quarters of a mile into the mine. A guide explains the mining process and there is an interpretive center on the surface. All-in-all, the Tower-Soudan State Park is an interesting and unique experience. Tours continue from early May through Labor Day.

ELY, Pop. 4,820

This village rests along the shores of Shagawa Lake, once known as the "Capital of the Vermilion Range". Ely is now the gateway to one of the most beautiful wilderness areas in this country. The town lies within the 3.7 million-acre Superior National Forest, just a short distance from the Boundary Waters Canoe Area. Before Ely became an important jumping-off spot for those seeking solitude in the surrounding maze of lakes and woods, this area was the center of iron mining, dotted with the black lift-towers that marked the mines.

Ore was discovered at Ely in 1886 at what became the Chandler Mine. A town was platted the following year and named after Arthur Ely, an Ohio businessman who helped finance the mines and railroad. At first the only access to Ely was from Tower, where supplies were brought across the frozen lakes and bogs during the winter, hoping to avoid travel during the wet summer months. A trail was eventually cut to Ely and in 1888 the railroad connected Ely to Tower. At one time, there were five underground mines in operation, employing over 1,500 men. A couple of blocks north of Ely's main street, you can see the huge sunken depression of the old Chandler and Pioneer Mines. The land over the mines was once flat, but during the last 60 years the honeycombed tunnels underneath have collapsed, causing this huge depression.

Ely has lost its mines, but the tourist industry has provided the region with a new economic base. The town is now filled with outfitters and suppliers for the nearby Boundary Waters Canoe Area, a one million acre wilderness.

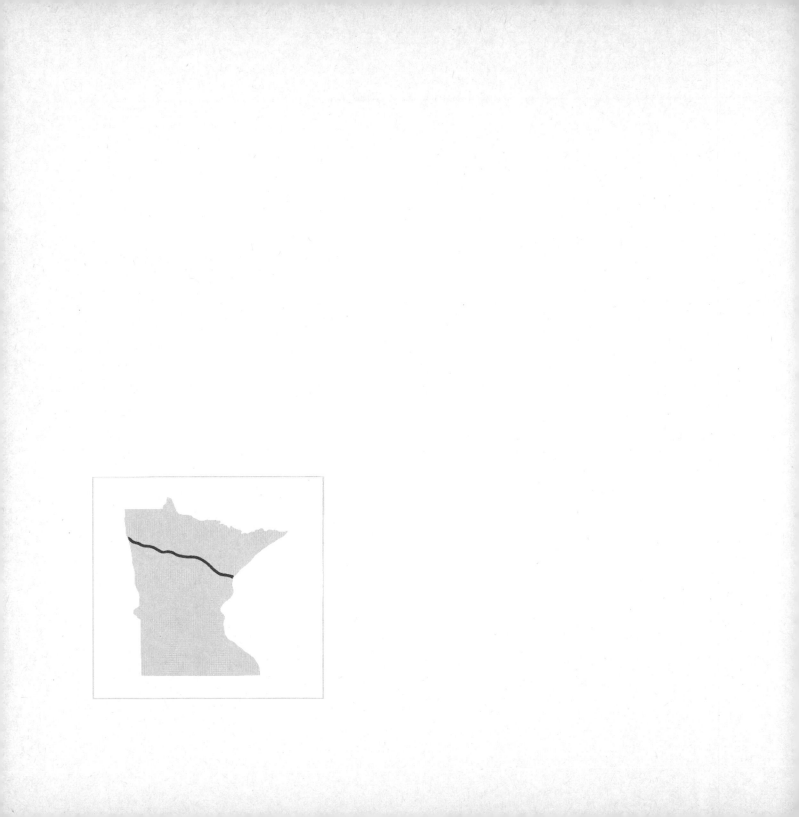

ROUTE 2, DULUTH TO EAST GRAND FORKS

Wheat threshing in 1905.

This northern route leaves the Lake Superior basin, over hills that once formed the ancient shoreline of Glacial Lake Duluth. The route soon passes the St. Louis River, a historic waterway that the early explorers used as they made their way to the Misssissippi. U.S. 2 continues on through the Arrowhead region, a land where white pine forests once extended westward to the plains of the Red River Valley. Today, the 650,000 acre Chippewa National Forest, a remnant of the early wilderness, encompasses the large and beautiful Leech, Winnibigoshish and Cass Lakes. From there the route passes through the Bemidji resort area and on to the Red River Valley, a region situated in the basin of an ancient glacial lake, which today supports some of the most productive farmland in Minnesota.

LAKE SUPERIOR

The dark rocky hills against which Duluth was built, were formed by lava flows and are of some of the oldest surface formations on this continent. These hillsides also formed the shoreline of ancient Glacial Lake Duluth, a body of water much larger than today's Lake Superior, the largest freshwater lake in the world.

When Lake Duluth was formed during the ice ages, it was at least twice as high as the present lake. Much of its initial drainage was south, through Wisconsin, where it carved out the St. Croix Valley. At Hastings, this massive drainage joined the Glacial River Warren, which was draining Lake Agassiz in northwest Minnesota. Together they continued down the Mississippi River, carving out its broad river valley. The actual basin of present day Lake Superior was formed by a succession of glaciers, each one carving a deeper and wider basin.

The Ojibwe called the lake "Kitchigumi," meaning "Great Water." The early French called it Lac Superieur, since it lay at the head of all the Great Lakes. However it was called, this grand lake was the first route used by the explorers as they pushed westward looking for a passage to the Pacific. Superior soon became a conduit for an intricate fur-trading network, that strung from the Pacific Northwest, eastward to Montreal. During the early 1900's, the whale-back ore boats set out across Superior for the steel mills of Michigan. Today, Lake Superior continues to provide the Midwest with a deep-water port for the ships of the world.

A growing challenge exists for those concerned with preserving the pristine beauty of this lake. Though Superior is the largest freshwater lake in the world, it's ability to replenish itself from pollution is very poor, requiring over 190 years for a complete exchange of its waters.

DULUTH, Pop. 92,811

Lying in a narrow band from the mouth of the St. Louis River, some 25 miles along Lake Superior's shore, is the city of Duluth. Flanked by lava bluffs that rise 800 feet above the lake, Duluth is affected by the lake's own weather system. While the rest of the state cooks under a summer sun, a cool breeze is usually drifting off the lake, reaffirming Duluth's nickname as, the "air-conditioned city."

When the first explorers paddled to the head of Superior in the mid-1600's, they found the Ojibwe also pushing their way into the state. Minnesota had long been the Dakota Nation's territory. The conflict between the Ojibwe and Dakota continued until the 1850's. Radisson and Groseillier are credited with being the first whites to visit this part of the

lake, during the years 1654 to 1660. One of the earliest settlements was a small Ojibwe village, located on the north side of the St. Louis River which was called Fond du Lac, meaning "head of the lake."

Daniel Greysolon Sieur Du Luth visited the Indians here in 1679 to try to establish peace between the warring Dakota and Ojibwe. It was to the fur-traders benefit that they prevent any disruption of their trade. Fond du Lac soon became the gateway to the fur-bearing lakes and streams, as traders made their way up the St. Louis to the important portage at Big Sandy Lake. Here the traders crossed to the Mississippi. Many people traveled through Fond du Lac on their way into the "interior," but few made it their permanent home.

It wasn't until 1854, when rumors circulated that copper-bearing ore was being found on the North Shore, that a number of people came to the Duluth area. The copper rumors were short-lived, and Duluth, along with a couple of other small villages, continued to grow slowly. That same year, the Ojibwe ceded the entire Arrowhead region in a treaty signed at their old capital, on Madeline Island (a part of the Apostle Island chain of Lake Superior).

In 1857, the village of Duluth had only 14 buildings, and the national monetary panic of that year closed them for the next decade. A small number of residents persisted here,

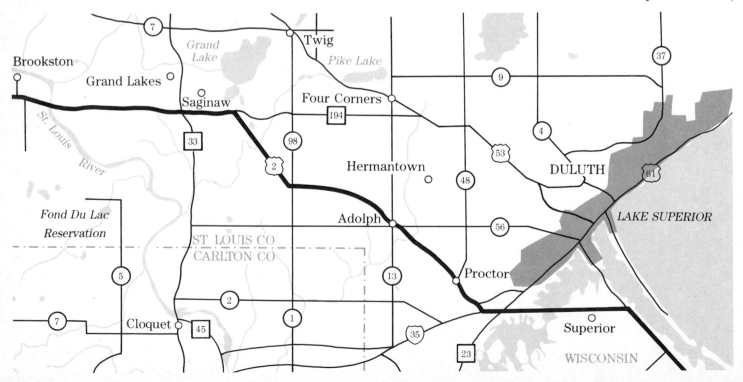

traveling for supplies by boat to the small town of Superior. As if life wasn't bad enough, a scarlet fever epidemic swept through the small community the following year. By February 1865 there were only a few houses being occupied in Duluth. Beaver Bay became the only permanent town between here and Grand Portage. It seemed inevitable that Duluth would soon become a ghost town.

But Duluth had seen the bottom. 1869 was a banner year, for it was during that year that the Lake Superior and Mississippi Railroad was approaching completion from St. Paul to Duluth. The town's population swelled from fourteen families nestled on Minnesota Point, to 3,500 by that summer. By 1870 you could reach Duluth from St. Paul by rail in only 16 hours. Immigration to this new town took off. 1870 was also the year Jay Cooke, an eastern financier, decided to support the building of the Northern Pacific Railroad from Duluth to the Pacific. At the same time that the railroad was pushing west from Duluth, the city fathers became concerned about the harbor access, and decided to cut a channel through Minnesota Point, saving boats the seven mile trip to the natural opening at Superior Cut. But the town of Superior obtained an injunction from the Army to halt Duluth's digging. Word came to Duluth on a Friday that the injunction would be served that following Monday. Through the weekend Duluthians shoveled and spaded. As the injunction was being served on Monday, the small tug Fero, steamed through the little channel out to the lake.

But in 1873, Duluth's bubble broke when the financial empire of Jay Cooke collapsed. The Northern Pacific had almost reached the Dakota border, but work stopped immediately. Within 60 days, half the people doing business in Duluth were out of work. The town's population shrunk from 5,000 to 2,000. The city was so far in debt that it burned its bonds, dissolved the council, and returned the city to a village status.

RECOVERY OF DULUTH

Duluth was on its way again by 1878. The farms of the Red River Valley began shipping large quantities of No. 1 hard wheat back to Duluth on the Northern Pacific. Grain elevators were being built and capacities continually increased. By 1885, there were nine large elevators doing business in Duluth. Sawmills also began to cut the lumber that was now being shipped by train or rafted down the lake into town. In 1893 another era started to unfold, when the Duluth, Missabe and Northern Railroad began to creak down from the Superior Uplands with iron ore from the newly-discoverd Mesabe Iron Range. Docks were built and whaleback ships began to haul wheat and ore. By 1920, some 2,000 ships passed out of the harbor, carrying 30 million tons of ore. It has been said that the Mesabi Range, with its high-grade ore, won the two World Wars for the United States.

Everything seemed to be working for Duluth during the early 1900's. United States Steel came to town and purchased one thousand acres for a steel mill. They built Morgan Park as a company town and 3,500 men worked the blast furnaces and coke ovens, just down the block from their homes. Portland Cement came to town in 1916 and set up shop next to the steel mill. A large number of Finns and Scandinavians, first attracted to the Duluth region because of the lumber industry, turned to shipping and later mining, when the white

Whaleback ships in Duluth harbor.

pines were depleted. Iron ore continued to be pulled from the "range" for a nation that had now developed an appetite for steel. When the first predictions came that the iron would be depleted, the ground shook under Duluth and the entire Range. During the 1950's, unemployment spread along the Arrowhead, until the process of removing low-grade ore and forming it into taconite pellets was developed by Henry Davis, a professor at the University of Minnesota. Today, all of the ore shipped from Duluth is taconite.

NAMING OF DULUTH

A missionary, by the name of Reverend Joseph Wilson was offered two lots in the newly platted village along Lake Superior, provided he could come up with a name to everyone's satisfaction. Wilson scoured through some Jesuit narratives where he came upon the accounts of Greysolon Sieur Du Luth's travels around Lake Superior. That name had a nice ring, so it became the village of Duluth, and Wilson got his two lots.

NAMING OF THE ARROWHEAD

In 1924, the Northeastern Minnesota Civic and Commerce Association wanted a more catchy name for the region which would soon have a paved highway from Duluth to Grand Marais. A national contest was held and over 3,000 entries accepted. The contest was won by a Philadelphian who compared the physical boundaries of this area to the shape of an arrow's point.

PROCTOR, Pop. 3,180

Proctor developed in 1894, along the tracks of the Duluth, Missabe and Northern Railroad, the first railroad that began hauling ore down from the Mesabi Range. At first Proctor was considered part of Oneota, a shoreline village on St. Louis Bay. Oneota was later annexed by Duluth, and the little town on the hill became known as Proctor Knott. Proctor Knott was a U.S. congressman from Kentucky, who ridiculed the town of Duluth on the floor of Congress in 1871. Knott was opposed to a land-grant bill that had kept the towns of Duluth and Superior at odds. Knott sarcastically referred to Duluth as the "center of the universe." His speech kept the congressmen rocking with laughter, giving Duluth immediate, if not humiliating, recognition. Years later, Proctor dropped "Knott" from its name. Proctor now contains a few shops and some 57 miles of tracks, where ore cars are prepared for the six-mile, downhill trip to the docks.

HERMANTOWN, Pop. 6,759

This town was named by its German settlers after Herman, a hero who fought against the Roman invasion of Germany, during the time of Christ. (A statue of Herman exists in the town of New Ulm.)

MHS

Wagon bridge on St. Louis River near Thompson, 1885.

CLOQUET, Pop. 11,142

During the 1700's, traders passed up the St. Louis River on their way to western posts. But this area had little attraction for settlement, until the lumbermen realized that water power from the St.Louis River made this an ideal place for milling. In 1870, a sawmill was hauled here and logs started descending the Whiteface, Floodwood and Cloquet rivers, into this growing village. Actually, the town was first platted as Knife Falls, but it was changed to Cloquet in 1883, a period when every house in town was owned by the lumber companies.

In 1918, Cloquet was destroyed in the same county fire that killed some 400 people. The town was later rebuilt, but at a time when the white pine was just about depleted. Struggling to stay alive, the lumber companies started to work with wood that was once considered waste. A large paper mill now operates in Cloquet, utilizing the pulpwood of the north.

MUNGER

Munger is a railway village that formed at the junction of the Burlington Northern and the Duluth, Winnipeg and Pacific Railroads. The village was named after Russell Munger, who came to Duluth from St. Paul in 1869, doing business in lumber, grain and steel. As president of the Imperial Milling Company, Munger helped make Duluth one of the major grain capitals of the country.

SAGINAW & GRAND LAKES

These are two railway villages located on the Duluth, Missabe and Iron Range Railroad line, connecting Duluth with the Mesabi Range.

ST. LOUIS RIVER

The St. Louis River was a much smaller river during its early history. Most of it drained into the Mississippi, rather than Lake Superior as it does today. But thousands of years of erosion from tributaries such as the Clouquet and Whiteface rivers carved a new channel to Lake Superior. Today the St. Louis extends some 160 miles back into the quiet wilderness of northern Minnesota. Here the jack pine, aspen and birch have grown back from a time when lumbermen stripped the area. The St. Louis has developed a poor reputation as a polluted river. But its problem only develops after it passes the towns and industry on its lower portion. A great amount of money is being spent to clean up the pollution caused by the Cloquet paper mill.

The St. Louis River was an early portage for the Indians and traders who came up from Lake Superior on their passage to the Mississippi basin. Du Luth traveled the St. Louis as early as 1679. Later, important expeditions of Cass and Schoolcraft passed here in 1820 and 1832, respectively. The river was most likley named by Sieur de la Verendrye, a French explorer who traveled through here in 1731. For Verendrye and others, the portage along the St. Louis River, up the hill from Lake Superior, was the most difficult. The river drops nearly 500 feet along a rock-strewn channel, as it tumbles down the hills bordering the lake. Canoes and goods were carried along its banks until the more placid and rock-free waters could be reached.

At the point where the St. Louis and East Savanna rivers connect, near Floodwood, the explorers headed west, into Big Sandy, where trading posts had been established. From Big Sandy, it was only a short portage to the Mississippi. This 70-mile route was used for some fifty years by both British and American fur traders.

The upper sections of the St. Louis and its tributaries, were channels for the large number of pine being harvested during the late 1800's. The lumbermen would have floated their logs all the way to Duluth, but the last stretch of the St. Louis made it impossible. Consequently, Cloquet prospered as a sawmilling town, at least until the railroads, carrying ore from the range, began hauling lumber to Duluth. But the "inexhaustible" supply of white pine peaked in 1902, and harvests steadily declined for the next couple of decades until the pine was totally gone. By then, the iron mines of the Mesabi Range were in full production and hundreds of lumber camps passed quietly away.

FOND DU LAC INDIAN RESERVATION

On an autumn day in 1854, several hundred Ojibwe Indians gathered on Madeline Island in Lake Superior, to sign an important treaty. The small settlement where they signed is called La Pointe. At one time, this was the most important village of the Ojibwe Nation. It was here that some ten tribes ceded most of northeastern Minnesota for white settlement. In return, the Ojibwe were given the Fond Du Lac Reservation and a million dollars. Few anticipated that later this land would be worth billions, for its iron deposits and timber.

Memorial day parade in Cloquet. Circa. 1905.

MHS

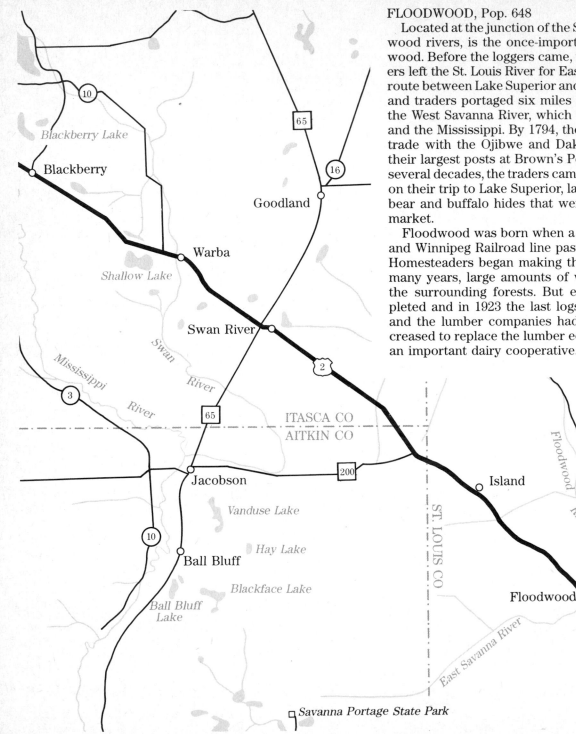

FLOODWOOD, Pop. 648

Located at the junction of the St. Louis, Savanna and Flood-wood rivers, is the once-important, logging town of Flood-wood. Before the loggers came, the early explorers and traders left the St. Louis River for East Savanna, on a well-traveled route between Lake Superior and the Mississippi. The Indians and traders portaged six miles across the marshy divide to the West Savanna River, which led them to Big Sandy Lake and the Mississippi. By 1794, the British had increased their trade with the Ojibwe and Dakota and established one of their largest posts at Brown's Point, on Big Sandy Lake. For several decades, the traders came to the region of Floodwood on their trip to Lake Superior, ladened with muskrat, beaver, bear and buffalo hides that were headed for the European market.

Floodwood was born when a survey crew laid the Duluth and Winnipeg Railroad line past the Savanna River in 1890. Homesteaders began making their claims shortly after. For many years, large amounts of white pine were taken from the surrounding forests. But eventually, the pine was depleted and in 1923 the last logs had gone down the rivers, and the lumber companies had moved out. As farming increased to replace the lumber economy, the town developed an important dairy cooperative.

*(right) Cut-over tim-
berland in northern
Minnesota in 1880.*

MHS

Floodwood was named for the large piles of dead trees
that clogged the junction of the St. Louis and Floodwood
Rivers. Above Floodwood, the St. Louis River passes through
the bogs of glacial Lake Upham, a body of water that covered
one thousand square miles in the St. Louis River basin.

ISLAND
When railroad tracks were laid in the 1890's much of the
area around the railway village of Island was covered with
spruce swamps. One exception was an area of higher land
more suitable for farming. Subsequently, the village became
known as Island.

ITASCA COUNTY, Pop. 43,006
This county was established in 1849 and took its name
from Lake Itasca, the source of the Mississippi. The Ojibwe
called the lake "Omushkos," which means, "Elk." But Henry
Schoolcraft, who discovered Elk Lake in 1832, wanted a better name for such an important lake. One day while canoeing
with a friend, they came up with two Latin words; "veritas,"
meaning truth, and "caput," meaning head. Schoolcraft combined these two words and dropped the first and last three
letters to arrive at the name of Itasca.

An early Minnesota road cut through northern Pine forests, 1901.

MHS

SWAN RIVER, WARBA, & BLACKBERRY
These three villages formed along the Great Northern Railroad line when it passed through in the late 1800's. "Warba"
is Ojibwe for "soon."

LA PRAIRIE, Pop. 536

Located near the mouth of the Prairie River, the small town of La Prairie became one of the first settlements in Itasca County. Lumbermen worked this area extensively and developers promoted the town as the head of navigation on the Mississippi. But steamboats traveling the Mississippi, north from Aitkin, passed by the eager town of La Prairie and stopped at the true head of navigation, the falls of Grand Rapids. La Prairie eventually faded and the buildings were removed, leaving only faint outlines of what was to have been a great town. Today, La Prairie is a bedroom community for Grand Rapids.

GRAND RAPIDS, Pop. 7,934

It wasn't long after 1864 that lumbermen in the Grand Rapids area started taking advantage of the the giant pines growing along the Mississippi. The real activity started in 1870 though, when Leonard Day came to town wearing a plug hat and riding in a fancy carriage. He and his sons soon developed an expansive logging industry that filled the woods with some 600 men, cutting and removing timber.

The lumerjack was a skilled ax-man, whose importance went beyond sheer muscle. He had to know how to drop a tree in the right direction, while wasting as little of the important trunk as possible. He made as much as $40 a month,

until the invention of the crosscut saw brought in a less-skilled woodsman, who was paid only $25 a month. The crosscut saw was faster and could cut closer to the ground, leaving more of the important trunk-wood for milling.

Iron ore was found here in 1890, but had little effect on the lumber industry. The railroad also reached Grand Rapids in 1890. So many settlers came in its wake, that the town was incorporated the following year. A large paper mill was built here in 1902 and was eventually taken over by the Blandin Paper Company.

Grand Rapids is the gateway to the Arrowhead fishing region and the Mesabi Iron Range. Located a couple of miles west of Grand Rapids, is the new Forest History Center run by the Minnesota Historical Society. It is situated in a new interpretive center, with displays and information on the early days of the lumbermen. A reconstructed, turn-of-the-century logging camp can also be toured. The nearby Pokegama Lake is named from an Ojibwe word meaning, "lake that has many bays."

MESABI IRON RANGE

There is some evidence that a few French missionaries and explorers, venturing through the Mesabi region in the 1700's, suspected there was iron here. Before the ore was discovered however, the region was drawn on Joseph Ni-

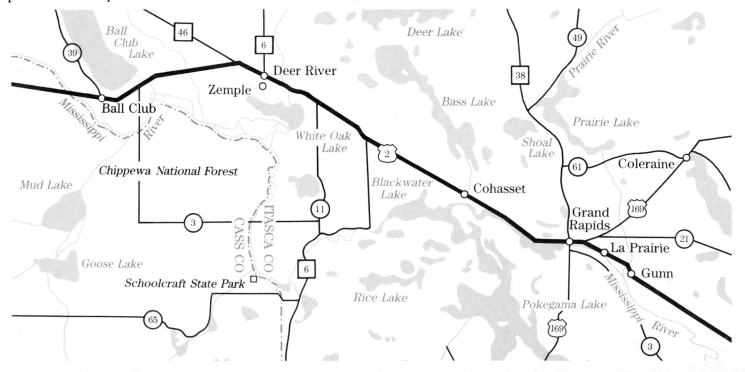

collet's 1841 map of the state and labeled "Missabay Heights." This Ojibwe name means "giant," or "big man hills." It refers to a ridge of land that divides the drainage between the Hudson Bay and Lake Superior. But whether or not there was any knowledge about the ore, gold and copper were on the minds of the early prospectors, instead of this "useless" iron ore.

The first iron deposits were discovered at Lake Vermilion in 1865 and the area became known as the Vermilion Range. These ore deposits were positioned vertically, and shafts had to be sunk to extract it. When the Mesabi Range was discovered in 1890, it turned out to be the largest concentration of iron ore deposits in the world. Unlike the deep veins of ore in the Vermilion Range, the Mesabi deposits were stratified horizontally near the surface, enabling it to be mined from open pits. These remarkable mines that dotted the range, gave up ore that was close to 50 percent iron. During the 1940's, the mines shipped over one-third of the world's ore. The rich deposits have been depleted now, but taconite (a low-grade iron of 20 to 30 percent) is now being processed successfully.

How the ore was formed was a complicated process that spanned hundreds of millions of years. The elements that helped form the iron into these unusual concentrations were the ancient seas which left layers of deposited sand, the heat from lava streams that formed the North Shore, and finally years of erosion which brought these deposits close to the surface.

COHASSET

This is a small hamlet whose Indian name means "place of pines" or "young pine trees." The Minnesota Power and Light Company has a coal-burning power plant here.

DEER RIVER, Pop. 907

When the Ojibwe hunted along this river, they called it "Wawashkeshiwi," meaning "Deer River." The history of this settlement is rooted, like so many others of this region, in the lumbering industry. The white pines began to be cut around 1870, north of here by Deer Lake. They floated down the Deer River. As cutting moved farther from the lake, the Itasca Lumber Company built a railroad spur into the woods to haul out the logs. A number of shacks around this spur became known as Itasca City. Later, the city changed its name to Deer River and in 1907, a highway was constructed between here and Grand Rapids. Deer River was also one of the first areas to popularize wild rice, a grain that grows abundantly in some of the area lakes. At one time Deer River maintained a dormitory for 100 school children, sparing them the hardships of winter travel from their cabins and farms.

BALL CLUB

This village took its name from the nearby lake. The Ojibwe liked to play ball with sticks that the French called La Crosse.

Just west of Ball Club the highway crosses the Mississippi. At this point the river has wound its way 125 miles from Lake Itasca through important breeding areas for wood ducks, mallards, blue-winged teal, goldeneyes and many other waterfowl. The swamps and oxbows, many of which are filled with stands of wild rice and cattails, provide excellent breeding grounds for muskies and northern pike. Bald eagles also make their homes in this area.

CHIPPEWA NATIONAL FOREST

Millions of feet of lumber were removed from this region during the late 1800's, exhausting the forests and laying bare much of the land. A number of Minnesota citizens were becoming alarmed at the depletion of the major forest lands of northern Minnesota. As early as 1898, groups such as the State Medical Society, and the Minnesota Federation of Women's Clubs, pushed to put some of these forest lands aside. The idea eventually grew after a trainload of prominent Twin Citians came here to view the area under consideration.

A portion of the present forest was acquired in 1902 and contained about 312,000 acres. But National Forest status

The "Kate R." on Lake Pokegama, 1889.

MHS

was not acquired until 1928. Through acquistions, the forest boundaries grew to 650,000 acres by 1936. The flourishing towns that had popped up along the railroads and logging trails disappeared once logging declined, and today much of the forest is in its second growth. There are over 450 lakes here, carved out by glaciers, some 12,000 years ago.

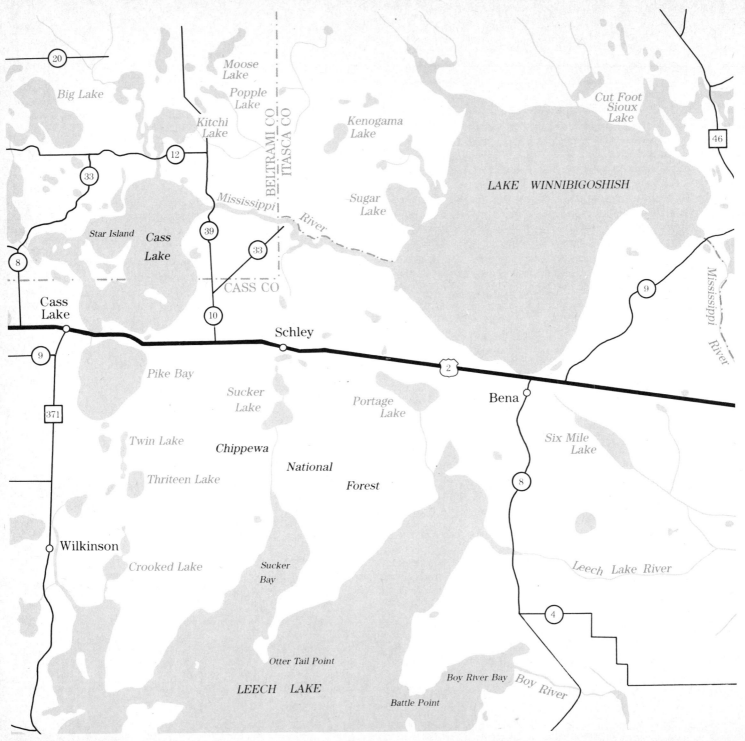

BENA, Pop. 153

Located on the south shore of Lake Winnibigoshish, is a small hamlet named from the Ojibwe word for partridge, or ruffed grouse. The town formed in 1910 and was popular with the Ojibwe for hunting and fishing. Logging was carried out in the vicinity, and a Civilian Conservation Corps camp was located here during the 1930's.

LAKE WINNIBIGOSHISH

This lake was formed some 12,000 years ago, when a large section of glacial ice broke off, forming a basin that filled with water. The lake's level, along with that of Leech Lake, was raised when dams were built across their outlets in 1882, regulating the flow of the Mississippi. The dams were built during the winter and moving supplies to the work sites was a major effort. When the ice was sufficiently thick, sleighs were brought from Brainerd across Leech Lake.

Lake Winnibigoshish is a shallow lake, with an average depth of 20 to 25 feet. During gale-force winds, waves stir up its muddy bottom, making the water extremely cloudy. The lake's name is Ojibwe, meaning "filthy water, bad and miserable."

CUT FOOT SIOUX LAKE

This region was once a favored Dakota hunting ground, before the Ojibwe tried to gain control of the area. A battle between the two nations was fought here in 1748. The Dakota successfully routed the Ojibwe. To celebrate their victory, they built along the shores of Cut Foot Sioux Lake, an earthen mound, 30 feet long, which resembled a turtle. Here the Dakota positioned the turtle's head north, in the direction of the fleeing Ojibwe.

The Ojibwe, determined to take these lands, returned that same summer, killing most of the defending Dakota. After the battle, the Ojibwe built an earthen snake around the turtle, with the snake's head pointing south. This indicated the Ojibwe's continuing push into the Dakota territory. Shortly after the battle, Ojibwe squaws found a dying Dakota brave with a nearly severed foot, lying along the shore of this lake. From then on the lake was called,"Lake of the Cut Foot Sioux."

LEECH LAKE

According to legend, a band of Ojibwe saw a giant leech swimming across the water. From this incident, the lake received its name. Leech Lake, with 154 miles of shoreline, is 40 miles wide and Minnesota's third largest lake. Glaciers covered this area thousands of years ago. During the melting, it is believed that as many as six different lakes occupied the present basin of Leech Lake, with the Mississippi draining through it. In the 1800's, the remains of an oak forest were discovered on the bottom of the lake when lumbermen noticed that the ice had loosened stumps from the bottom, forcing them to shore. A dam was built on the northeast side of the lake in 1884, raising the lake's level by seven feet and submerging many of the old Indian villages built along its shores. Leech Lake is known for its walleye and northern pike, muskellunge, bass and bluegill fishing.

LEECH LAKE INDIANS

It appears that the Dakota were living in the region of Leech Lake as early as 1000 A.D. But the Indians probably didn't gain complete control of this region until the early 1600's. For over a hundred years, they ranged this land of "milk and honey"; fishing, hunting and expanding their influence. But life changed for the Dakota, as an Algonkian tribe called the Ojibwe, were forced westward by Iroquois tribes of the Appalachian area. The Ojibwe passed through the Great Lakes, making their capital at La Pointe, on Madeline Island, in the Apostle Island chain of Lake Superior.

During the 1600's, the Ojibwe (called Chippewa by the traders) became the go-between for the Frenchmen, who were interested in the furs of the Dakota. But the Ojibwe soon decided to take full possession of the Dakota rice fields and hunting grounds. During the 1700's, many fierce battles were fought for the lands around Leech Lake. Because the Ojibwe were armed with rifles, they were successful in their campaign. Finally, during a series of battles that centered at the Dakota capital of Kathio, on Lake Mille Lacs, the Dakota were pushed from the region entirely. Although raids were

MHS

Ojibwe women portrait.

conducted into each other's territory for a number of years, the Mdewakanton band of Dakota became a prairie people of southern Minnesota.

Soon after the Dakota were driven to the south, the Ojibwe faced a new enemy. Smallpox, brought in by the white man, devastated the Ojibwe villages beginning in 1750. There were several other epidemics lasting until 1824. Some of the once powerful villages were reduced to a few wigwams. Vaccination started during the 1830's, and the Ojibwe Nation was able to rebuild.

COMING OF THE WHITE MAN

Fur Traders were active in the Leech Lake region as early as 1775, when the Northwest Fur Company established a post on Otter Tail Point. In 1805, Lieutenant Zebulon Pike was exploring the newly acquired territory of the Upper Mississippi (bought from the French in the Louisiana Purchase of 1803), when he came to the British post on Otter Tail Point. The British, who had been trading in this region for many years, treated Pike and his exhausted soldiers to a generous stay. Before Pike left though, he ordered his soldiers to shoot down the "Union Jack," reminding the British that they were now on American soil.

Pressure from whites trying to gain control of the Ojibwe's land, continued through the early 1800's, and focused mainly on the rich timberlands of the north. At that time, no one knew of the rich iron deposits lying just under the surface. The lumbermen didn't have to wait long, for in 1854 and 1855 the Ojibwe negotiated treaties for all of the North Shore and most of the Upper Mississippi Valley. For those lands, the Ojibwe were given large tracts of land which became the Leech Lake and White Earth Indian Reservations. Some of the important Indian chiefs that made their homes on Leech Lake were, Flat Mouth, Rabbit, Great Cloud, Red Blanket and Hole-in-the-Day of Leech Lake.

LAST INDIAN WAR IN MINNESOTA

In 1898, federal agents from Duluth were seeking witnesses to convict bootleggers who sold whiskey to the Indians. One Indian named Hole-in-the-Day (more affectionately called "Old Bug"), was asked to testify. He refused the invitation because when he previously testified in Duluth one winter, he had to walk home some 100 miles in the bitter cold.

Because he refused to testify Old Bug was arrested, but with the aid of sympathetic friends, he escaped into the woods. The situation was taken seriously by the military, which dispatched two hundred soldiers from Fort Snelling to Walker, to bring Old Bug in. They departed Walker on barges for his cabin on Sugar Point at Leech Lake (today called Battle Point).

Reaching the point, the troops scoured the woods for Old Bug. Finding nothing, they stacked their rifles and had some lunch. When one gun fell over and discharged, a rapid volley of return fire came from the hiding Indians, who thought a battle had begun. When the fight ended, seven of the soldiers had been killed and ten were wounded. Word of the battle spread, and the towns of Cass Lake and Brainerd feared a general uprising by the Indians. Soldiers poured into the area

Cass Lake stockade built during last Indian war. Circa. 1900.

and in a short time most of the Indians, including "Old Bug", had been captured. A pardon for the Indians was issued the following year, which ended the last armed conflict between the Indian and white man in Minnesota.

SCHLEY

This town was formed in 1898 and named after Winfield Scott Schley, a rear admiral in the U.S. Navy, during the Spanish-American War. Schley commanded the "Flying Squadron" and directed the naval battle at Santiago, Cuba.

Waiting to place land claims in Cass Lake, 1885.

CASS LAKE, Pop. 1,001

Located on the western shore of Cass Lake, is the town of Cass Lake, the largest community in the county. The Indians named the nearby lake "Ga-mi-squawakokag sagaii-gun," meaning, "Place of Red Cedars." Explorers passed here in their quest for the true source of the Mississippi, and in 1798 the Northwest Company maintained a trading post on the lake. In 1805, Lt. Zebulon Pike headed a government expedition to this region, to assert American sovereignty over the Minnesota lands acquired in the Louisiana Purchase of 1803.

In 1820, Territorial Governor Lewis Cass, accompanied by Henry R. Schoolcraft, traveled to all the Indian camps in the region to discuss land treaties and also to see what value the area might hold for the government. But Schoolcraft's underlying motive was to discover the source of the Mississippi. On this trip, Cass felt that this lake was the Mississippi's source, but Schoolcraft disagreed. Twelve years later, Schoolcraft returned, and discovered what he named Lake Itasca. It was on this trip that he named Cass Lake in honor of Lewis Cass.

During the 1850's, the region was covered with thick forests of white pine. After Cass County was organized in 1851,

lumbermen dotted the area with camps and sawmills. For years, lumbering was Cass Lake's mainstay. But as the region became cut over, farming and dairying began to develop, along with tourism and resorts. Cass Lake slowly lost its dependence on lumbering. The Cass Lake settlement continued to grow with the arrival of the Great Northern and Soo Line Railroads, in 1899 and 1900.

Today, Cass Lake Village is the headquarters of the Consolidated Ojibwe Indian Agency, which has jurisdiction over seven reservations; Leech Lake, White Earth, Nett Lake, Fond du Lac, Vermilion, Red Earth and Grand Portage. What rights the Indians actually have on these reservations has long been questioned. It wasn't until 1974 that the state Legislature ended a prolonged legal battle over the Indians' claim to exclusive ricing, hunting and fishing rights. Jurisdiction was turned over to the Tribal Conservation Committee to issue licenses, regulate fishing quotas and enforce hunting laws.

CASS LAKE

Cass Lake is six miles long and three to five miles wide. Like other large lakes in the area, the Cass was formed by retreating glaciers that left behind huge sections of ice-blocks, buried in glacial debris. When these blocks melted, they formed depressions that filled with water, creating the lakes. Located just north of U.S. 2 is Star Island, the largest of Cass Lake's islands (1,200 acres). This island contains a lake named Windigo, which was the home of Chief Yellow Head (Ozawindib), the leader of a small band of Ojibwe. Yellowhead was Schoolcraft's guide when he discovered Lake Itasca in 1832.

Bemidji street scene, 1910.

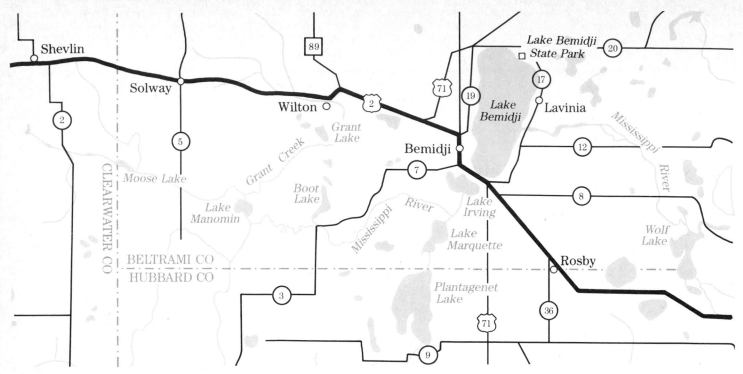

BELTRAMI COUNTY, Pop. 30,982

Although the Ojibwe and Dakota fought for this land through much of the 1700's, white traders did not establish themselves in this area until 1785, when a post was established on the eastern shore of Lake Bemidji. For the next few years, explorers passed through the county looking for the source of the Mississippi. One such explorer was an Italian named Giacomo Constantino Beltrami, who came with an interpreter and two Ojibwe Indians. A short distance above Bemidji, Beltrami crossed a lake he named Julia, claiming that it was the source of the Mississippi. Nine years later, Henry Schoolcraft passed through the county with Indian chief Yellow Head, who led Schoolcraft to Elk Lake (later renamed Itasca), the true source of the Mississippi.

BEMIDJI, Pop. 10,949

A band of Ojibwe, headed by Chief Bemidji, made their homes along the south shore of the lake, which came to be known by the chief's name. Bemidji means "easy crossing" or "place the river flows into and out again." This name was used because the Mississippi flows into and out of the lake near Bemidji. By the time the Mississippi enters Lake Bemidji, the narrow rocky river has already flowed some 60 miles on its 2,500 mile journey to the Gulf of Mexico.

This region was one of the last to be settled along the Mississippi. At first, only traders passed through the county on the old "Red Lake Trail". The path had branches to the Warroad and Pembina settlements. An Indian trail also skirted the lake, passing Chief Bemidji's home and crossing the Mississippi at the present U.S. 2 bridge. The first whites started to settle at Bemidji in 1866, but it took 30 years and an unlikely discovery, before the town started to grow. This small group of residents subsisted on hunting and fishing, since resupplying meant a four day trip to Park Rapids.

On a summer day in 1894, a man tripped over a stone on the shore of Lake Bemidji, uncovering a rock that shimmered in the sun. Thinking he had uncovered a diamond field, he rushed to St. Paul to have the stone analyzed. The specimen was finally sent to New York for analysis while large blocks of land were being bought up around the ramshackle town. As it turned out, the rock was nothing more exotic than quartzite.

The town's location near large stands of white pine, soon brought lumber barons and hundreds of workers, making it one of the rowdiest towns in the Northwest. In a few years, there were 14 sawmills cutting a million feet of lumber daily. In 1897, the Great Northern was cutting its right-of-way into town, guaranteeing its growth. But as lumbering declined, Bemidji became an agricultural and tourist center.

CONTINENTAL DIVIDE

Running just east of Shevlin is the watershed divide between the Mississippi and the Hudson Bay drainage basins.

CLEARWATER COUNTY, Pop. 8,761

This county is named from the Clearwater River which begins near the headwaters of the Mississippi. The Ojibwe called the river, "Ga-wakomitigweia," meaning "clear water." Since many northern Minnesota streams were colored with tannic acid from the decaying plants and trees of the forests and marshes, this clear stream was an obvious exception, and named because of it. The Clearwater became an important logging stream during the late 1800's, as pine flowed to the Red Lake River and on to the sawmills at Crookston.

BAGLEY, Pop. 1,321

A lumberman by the name of Sumner Bagley worked this region during the late 1800's. This railway village and trading center was named after him.

WHITE EARTH RESERVATION

The White Earth Indian Reservation lies just south of Bagley. The reservation was named after the white clay found in many places along the shores of White Earth Lake. The reservation was laid out in accordance with the terms of the White Earth Treaty, signed in 1867. The first group of Ojibwe moved here the following year. Many tribes settled here; the Mississippi band of Ojibwe from Crow Wing and Gull Lake, the Pembina band from the Red River Valley and the Otter Tail Pillagers from Otter Tail Lake. All three bands were of Algonkian stock, from the eastern United States. Pressure from the Iroquois pushed them westward, across Lake Superior into Minnesota. These Indians were known as Ojibwe, but that name became anglicized to Chippewa.

The formation of this reservation is another chapter in the sad history of this country's dealings with the Native Americans. The economic pressures from the whites for lumber, furs and farmland, left little room for the Indians in this society—except on reservations. James Bassett, the Indian agent who led the first group of Ojibwe settlers, wrote "To attempt to civilize a people and at the same time prevent them from adopting any of the arts or advantages of civilization, is to my mind absolutely absurd and ridiculous."

POLK COUNTY, Pop. 34,844

This county is one of the richest farm-producing areas in the state. The reason is that much of the county was part of Glacial Lake Agassiz, that covered northwestern Minnesota 12,000 years ago. The eastern part of the county was not

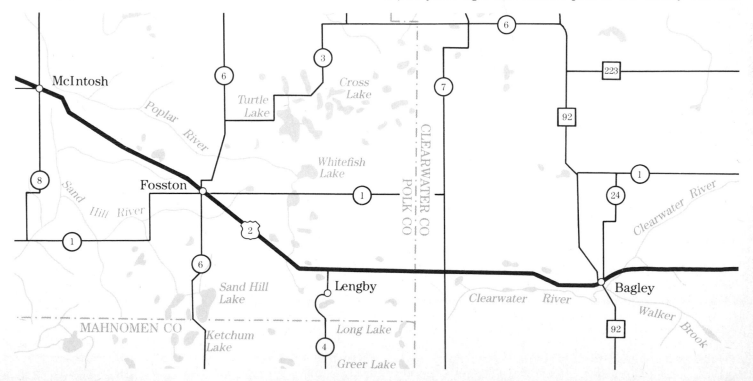

MHS

St. Paul, Minneapolis and Manitoba Railroad stretching west to the Pacific.

submerged by Agassiz, so it became heavily forested and dotted with lakes after the glaciers melted. But the western part of the county was formed differently. As the lake drained, this region was covered with silt, both from the lake and periodic flooding of the Red River after the lake was drained. At first, the early settlers couldn't believe that this black, fine soil would support crops.

It is possible that Vikings passed through this region as they explored southward to the Alexandria area, where the famous Kensington Runestone was found. If the stone is authentic, this handful of Nordic adventurers traveled up the Red River in 1362, some 375 years before the next recorded visit of French explorer La Verendrye.

The Dakota and Ojibwe fought for this land throughout the first half of the 1700's. But the Dakota were finally pushed to the southern plains of Minnesota and the Dakota Territory.

FIRST WHITE SETTLER

The first person to spend any time in this region was a man named Duncan Graham. He operated a trading post in 1817 on the Red River at a place called La Grande Fourche (Grand Forks). To the north, a Scot named Thomas Douglas, Earl of Selkirk, led a small group of farmers eager to start an agricultural community. Graham took them to a place which later became Winnipeg. But the isolation and scourge

of grasshoppers in this northern community, drove many up the Red River into Minnesota. Selkirk was one of the first whites to realize that the route from the Red River to the Minnesota River would be important for trade. These rutted trails later became known as the Red River Trails, and were an economic and political lifeline between the northern settlements and the towns of Mendota and St. Paul.

For years trade continued along these trails, but few stopped to make their homes in Polk County. During the 1870 census, the county reportedly had, "no population." In 1871, some Norwegian farmers began to settle along the Red River, but it wasn't until the late 1870's, when the railroad started to stretch across the fertile plains, that towns formed and the county was homesteaded.

EARLY ROADS

The first roads in this region followed the trails and routes laid out by U.S. soldiers to connect the Indian agencies. One led up from Leech Lake to Cass Lake, then on to Red Lake. Another joined the White Earth and Red Lake Reservations. The railroad was built from Cass Lake to Fosston by the Eastern Railway Company in 1900, and was purchased by the Great Northern Company in 1907.

FOSSTON, Pop. 1,599

This town, founded in 1884, was named after Louis Foss. Foss had been told that the town would bear his name if he would open a store here. Foss opened a general store, but was soon wounded in a holdup attempt. Disgusted, he left town and became a politician in Washington state. Fosston and the neighboring region was one of the last areas to be settled in Minnesota. Because of the financial panic of 1873, the building of railroads came to a halt, giving people little incentive to farm, since there was no way to ship crops to markets.

It wasn't until 1885 that tracks were laid eastward from Crookston to Fosston, where only a couple of shed buildings existed. But Fosston began to grow, and it was soon supplying the lumber camps a short distance to the east. The railroad again provided the farmers with a means to ship their goods, and they started to drain many of the natural wetlands to increase the available acreage. To protect some of the valuable waterfowl areas, the state started purchasing marshlands to create wildlife refuges.

MCINTOSH, Pop. 681

This town was named for a man of Scottish and Ojibwe blood. McIntosh ran a hotel here before he was moved, or forced to move, onto the White Earth Indian Reservation.

ERSKINE, Pop. 585

When this town was founded in 1889, it was named after the president of the First National Bank of Crookston .

LAKE AGASSIZ GEOLOGY

Eleven thousand years ago, when the last glacier began melting and receding back across Minnesota, a large body of water started forming along its melting edge. Eventually, the ice receded across the continental divide, a ridge of land separating the Mississippi and Hudson Bay drainage. The divide is located near Browns Valley in the west central part of the state. Because the ice had retreated to the Hudson Bay side of the divide, the meltwater was blocked. Thus, Glacial Lake Agassiz was created. The maximum depth of Agassiz was 700 feet, and its area was larger than the combined area of today's Great Lakes. Large prehistoric animals roamed the shores of the cool water, feeding on new vegetation. About this same time, these mammals were being hunted by a prehistoric people, who most likely crossed from Asia over the Bering Straits land bridge.

The river that started draining Lake Agassiz was located at Browns Valley and was called the Glacial River Warren. It carved out the broad valley of what is now the Minnesota River. As the northern ice-dam of Lake Agassiz melted, the lake started draining into Hudson Bay. Left behind was a rich sedimentary deposit that now makes up the soils of the Red River Valley region. After years of wave action along the receding shores of Agassiz, a number of gravel and sand ridges were formed. Many settlers used to travel along these old beach ridges. Over fifty have been identified, with most of them located in Canada.

In Minnesota, two main beaches can still be discerned. One, called Herman Beach, was the outermost beach of the lake for 500 years. The other, Campbell Beach, has been there over 2,000 years, creating the most extensive and visible beach in Minnesota. Lake Agassiz finally disappeared about 6,000 years before the birth of Christ.

MENTOR, Pop. 219

Herman Beach of Lake Agassiz ran along the northwest side of Maple Lake, near Mentor. A large stand of sugar maples once grew at Maple Lake and Indians came each spring to collect syrup. When white settlement began, the trees were cut for fuel. Mentor was named after President Garfield's home town in Ohio.

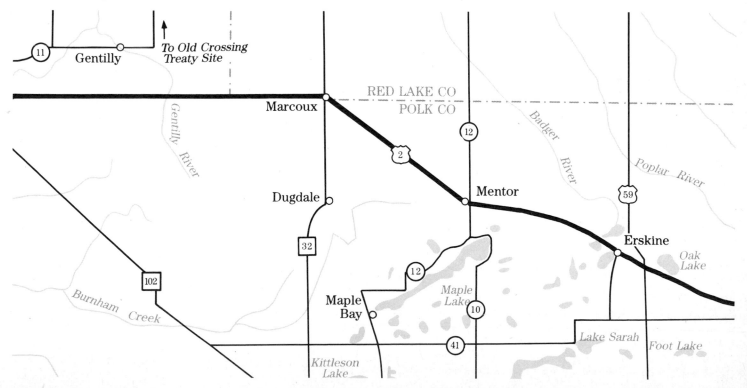

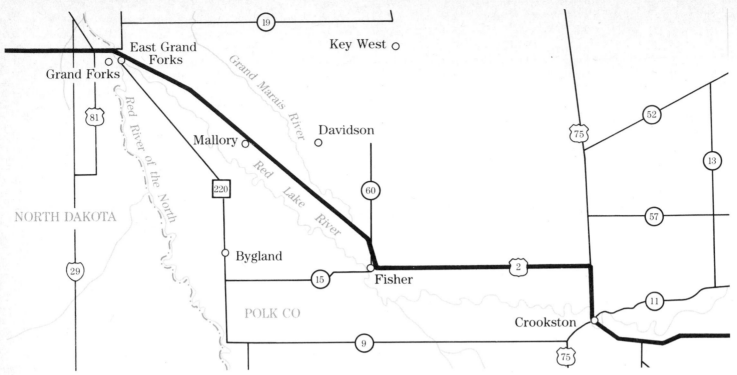

THE VANISHING BUFFALO

By the time local settlement leveled off during the late 1800's, the buffalo had long disappeared. Western Minnesota was once a part of the buffalos' summer feeding range. Though skeletons have been found as far east as Little Falls, the main herds ranged in the west and southwest parts of the state.

It's hard to pinpoint just when the last buffalo disappeared in Minnesota. But it is possible that in the fall of 1868, the last buffalo crossed the Red River to North Dakota with a bullet in its side. A hunter wrote, "The last buffalo I saw was just north of Moorhead and within rifle shot. I got one shot off and followed the trail, but I could only find the drying blood on the grass. That was the last one (buffalo) I saw."

But the memorial to the wanton slaughter of these once mighty herds, was the bleached skeletons that covered the prairie. Many wrote about the way the setting sun reflected off the scattered bones. Shortly after the western counties became settled though, the prairie was picked clean as the buffalo bones were gathered and ground into fertilizer for use in farming.

CROOKSTON, Pop. 8,628

When it became evident that the St. Paul and Pacific Railroad was going to build an extension from the Glyndon-Moorhead area, to a wagon crossing on the Red Lake River, railroad engineers rushed here to buy up the prime property. Houses were built along the tracks and times looked bright for this new town.

But Crookston's future suddenly changed when the financial panic of 1873 ravaged the nation. Construction of the railroad stopped just north of Crookston. Few trains ventured along the newly laid tracks. Once again the Red River became the main link to Grand Forks and the outside world. In 1875, there were about 20 tar shanties in Crookston. Mail came infrequently. Taking matters into their own hands, some enterprising citizens took leftover train wheels and added a platform and sail. It must have been an odd sight to see this strange contraption, gliding silently across the flat, Red River Valley, as supply runs were made some 60 miles south to the railway village of Glyndon.

Crookston recovered slowly, and starting in 1877 a number of boom years followed. The land office was moved here from Detroit Lakes. Even the railroads began selling their land at $2.50 an acre. They were successful in attracting immigrants during this period, and by 1880 the county had grown from zero population to 11,400 people, many of whom were French-Canadians or Scandinavians.

Crookston was known as Hawley in 1872, but a post office

by that name already existed. The postmaster ordered a change. Names such as Aetna, Ames, Davis, and Crookston were suggested. A flip of the coin settled the matter and the town was named after William Crooks, chief engineer who brought the railroad into town.

RED LAKE RIVER

Giacomo Beltrami, who explored this area in 1823, mistakenly thought the Indians referred to the lake and river as "Red" because of conflicts between them and the Dakota. Beltrami called the river, "Bloody River." The Ojibwe reference to red was due to the red reflections on the waters at sunset. The Red Lake River is one of the few good canoeing rivers of this region. This reddish-colored river flows 190 miles, from the Upper and Lower Red Lakes to the Red River at East Grand Forks. The water is colored by the decaying plants of the bogs and marshes. The river was used for many years by explorers and traders, as they traveled through the northwest.

FISHER, Pop. 453

In 1843 a Canadian-born fur trader, named Norman Kittson, began trading with Ojibwe and mixed-bloods called "Metis", hoping they would supply the buffalo hides and furs that were in high demand in the East and Europe. That first year, he bought $2,000 worth of pelts and carted them to Mendota, following the Red River and then the Minnesota River to nearby Fort Snelling. The trip was long, profits small, and the drivers afraid of the Dakota who hunted the plains along the Minnesota River.

Kittson started a new route inland in 1844, crossing the Red Lake River just west of Fisher. This became known as the "Old Crossing of Red Lake River." The best time to bring down the winter collection of pelts was in early spring, before the ground had thawed. Eventually, the trail crossed the river further east, at a ford in the river near the present town of Hoyt. No one used this trail after 1860.

During its early years, this village was called Fisher's Landing, after William Fisher, a railroad official. It was the furthest point that steamboats could navigate up the Red Lake River. After the panic of 1873, The Minnesota & Pacific Railroad laid tracks to Fisher in order to transfer goods to boats trading along the Red River. For a short time, Fisher was more populous than Crookston, until river navigation ceased and the railroad re-laid its tracks to Winnipeg, through Crookston.

OLD CROSSING TREATY

In 1862 the Ojibwe were asked to gather where Kittson crossed the Red Lake River, to discuss abandoning 11 million acres of their land. In return, the whites asked for Ojibwe resettlement at the Red Lake Indian Reservation. But as the negotiators headed for the "Old Crossing," the Sioux Uprising began. Fearing for their lives, the whites turned back for St. Paul. The Ojibwe patiently waited at the crossing until their supplies began to give out. Unfortunately, Norman Kittson happened upon the hungry and frustrated Ojibwe with a train of oxcarts loaded with goods. The Ojibwe rationalized that Kittson had been crossing their lands for years without permission, so they levied a tax and helped themselves to his goods to the tune of $25,000.

The following year, another treaty meeting was called, at a crossing further up the river. It was there that Governor Alexander Ramsey worked out an arrangement, giving the Red Lake Ojibwe $10,000 annually, for all of northwest Minnesota. This treaty ended a 25-year period during which both the Dakota and Ojibwe nations had given up all their land to the white man.

EAST GRAND FORKS, Pop. 8,537

A trading post had been established here as early as 1800. Then in 1863, a man named W. C. Nash was told by his St. Paul doctor that he ought to spend several weeks "roughing it." Subsequently, Nash joined a military expedition leaving Fort Snelling on a search for Little Six and Medicine Bottle (Dakota Indians) in the Red River Valley. (Little Six and Medicine Bottle were both wanted for their participation in the Sioux Uprising.) Camping in the vicinity of East Grand Forks, Nash noticed the richness of the soil and came back to settle here a few years later. The first post office took the name of Nashville. But in 1883 it was changed to East Grand Forks, because of its economic ties to Grand Forks, North Dakota.

MHS

Buffalo disappeared from Minnesota by the 1860's.

ROUTE 371, LITTLE FALLS TO CASS LAKE

Red River carts and drivers, 1860.

MHS

FORT RIPLEY, Pop. 83

This small railway village is located just opposite the river of the original Fort Ripley, which was occupied by a small garrison of soldiers from 1849 to 1878. The fort was previously called Fort Marcey and then Fort Gaines before it was named after a Southern general by the name of Eleazar W. Ripley.

CAMP RIPLEY

Camp Ripley, the Minnesota National Guard camp, was named for old Fort Ripley. The fort originally started as a military post in 1849 on the west bank of the Mississippi River, just below the mouth of the Crow Wing. It was established as an outpost to serve as a buffer between the Ojibwe and Dakota Indians. Another purpose was to keep the Winnebago Indians on their reservation in the Long Prairie area. The fort was usually manned by 30 soldiers.

A sawmill was put into operation during that first winter,

and work continued until several small buildings were finished. These buildings were arranged on three sides of a square, with one side open to the Mississippi River.

During the Sioux Uprising of 1862, a number of settlers, fearing that the Ojibwe might join with the Dakota in their war, sought refuge at Fort Ripley until things cooled down. As it turned out, the Ojibwe did not align themselves with the Dakota. But up to 400 whites were killed during the conflict. Because of the Uprising, the Dakota were banished from the state. All payments they were to have received for lands turned over in treaty settlements were forfeited.

In 1878 the fort was abandoned. After World War II, the state looked for a site to replace Camp Lakeview, at Lake City. They selected 20,000 acres, eight miles north of Little Falls, where National Guard units from all over the Midwest would come in the summer to train.

The older fort was in section 7 of Clough township. But today only the stone ruins of the powder magazine remain.

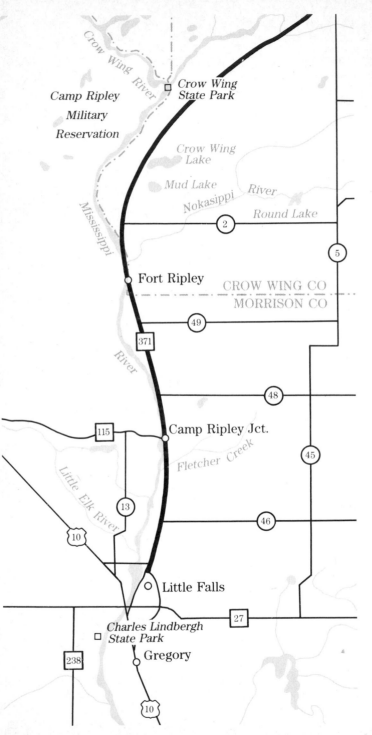

CROW WING

The convergence of the Crow Wing and Mississippi rivers has, for hundreds of years, been a spot rich with history. The Dakota simply called the river the "Pine". To them it was an important hunting ground, providing routes through the tall pine forests. From the early 1700's the Dakota and Ojibwe fought for this land, with the Ojibwe eventually taking control. Battles continued between these two nations for the next 100 years. At the mouth of the Crow Wing, in 1768, the Ojibwe surprised a Dakota war party, beating them badly.

Traders camped occasionally at the mouth of the Crow Wing, collecting furs that the Ojibwe brought in exchange for knives, guns and whiskey. It wasn't until 1835, that a permanent post was inhabited by Clem Beaulieu. Chief Hole-in-the-Day, a strong Ojibwe leader, later made his camp here on the large island at the mouth of the river they called "Kagi-weg-won." Its meaning was "raven's wing," but the English version was incorrectly translated as Crow Wing, probably because the Easterners were more familiar with the crow than the raven.

Traders and Indians started coming to this small settlement regularly and in 1838, several more trading posts were established, including two started by Allan Morrison and William Aitkin. The village grew for the next couple of decades, until there were some 600 people. Crow Wing Village became widely known as an important crossroads for the "Woods Trail", a path winding up the east side of the Mississippi from St. Paul. The Woods Trail crossed at the Crow Wing River and headed west-by-northwest to Pembina, North Dakota. This trail allowed the regular exchange of goods between these remote settlements and the villages of Mendota and St. Paul. A daily stage brought mail from St. Paul. Logging began in 1848, when Henry Rice and Dan Stanchfield paid Hole-in-the-Day fifty cents for every tree that was cut and floated down the Mississippi to the mills at St. Anthony.

The 1860's were the best years for Crow Wing, which boasted of stores, hotels, saloons, churches and a ferry. It was a paradise for trappers, lumbermen, speculators and anyone who felt a need to unload his money. Many a barrel of rotgut whiskey was dispensed, and saloon fights often grew to major brawls in the street.

But difficult days were ahead for Crow Wing. The Ojibwe were getting restless and disturbed by the influx of the white man. Chief Hole-in-the-Day was particularly upset that some of his braves were being enlisted to fight in the Civil War; plus the fact that the lumbermen pushed through a treaty giving them the great pine district between Little Falls and Brainerd.

For many nights the war drums were heard across Gull Lake, causing much fear among the whites at Crow Wing. An Indian agent named Lucius Walker, was keenly disliked by Chief Hole-in-the-Day and Walker knew it. Fearing for his life, Walker took $20,000 of annuity money and fled for St. Paul. A few days later Walker was found dead, just south of St. Cloud. There was no trace of the money. His death is still a mystery. Some speculated that he had been robbed and feeling depressed, killed himself.

But lumbering and settlement by the white man convinced many of the Indians to head for better trapping grounds at the Leech and Red Lake Reservations. The final blow to the Crow Wing Village came in 1872, when the railroad reaching west from Duluth passed to the north, through the new town of Brainerd. The Northern Pacific, which was coming north from Sauk Rapids in 1879, also missed the now dying town. Crow Wing was deserted by the early 1900's and a prairie fire swept through the rotting structures in 1915, leaving only cellar holes and a few tombstones in the grass. In 1962 this area became a Minnesota state park. It is an excellent spot for picnicking or camping. You can still see the depressions from the buildings that once made up the village, as well as the cart tracks imbedded in the prairie by the Red River oxcarts.

POINT DOUGLAS-FORT RIPLEY ROAD.

The military road which ran from Point Douglas at the mouth of the St. Croix to the Crow Wing village, follows State 371 from Little Falls, north. The road was completed in 1858. From old Crow Wing Village to Mendota, the military road followed the well-worn path of the Red River oxcarts. This military road contributed heavily to the settlement of this area. Cart tracks can still be seen along the sandy terraces of the Mississippi and Crow Wing rivers.

Stage traffic along early Minnesota route.

An early view of Crow Wing along the Mississippi, 1863.

83

BRAINERD, Pop. 11,489

The existence of many towns in the new West rested in the hands of the railroad surveyor. Many expected the Northern Pacific to run their tracks further south from Duluth through Crow Wing Village. But the people of Crow Wing watched helplessly, as the road bed was cut through thick pines to a place further north on the Mississippi called the Crossings. This surveyed location was soon named Brainerd, honoring the family name of the railroad president's wife.

The town was first settled by a railroad agent named "Pussy" White, during the summer of 1870. At that time there was only a small shack, a tent and a few lean-tos, supported by some trees. In spite of its humble start, hundreds flocked to this promising site in the following two years. Most were seeking their fortune in lumbering, railroading, or living off the money made by others. Most of the men were unmarried, living in boarding houses and eating at the saloon. In those early years the town became full of railroad men and lumberjacks spending their money as fast as they made it. Gambling flourished; the most popular games were "chuck-a-luck," "high dice," and "mustang."

Brainerd was built on a sandy plain, situated far enough above the Mississippi to avoid serious flooding. Thick pine forests covered the area. An early train traveler wrote about his journey into Brainerd one night…"We first saw Brainerd at night and the view was pleasant and novel. The winds sang through the tops of the pines and the lights from the homes twinkled amongst the many trees…the whole place seemed like a fairy tale."

The town prospered around the railroad, which soon established its general headquarters and repair shops here. But during the "Panic of 1873," Jay Cooke's financial empire which included money for the Northern Pacific, collapsed, leaving many out of work. The town lost half of its population. During the next few years it was very bleak in the once-booming town of Brainerd. But strong, productive years reappeared in the late 1800's, with the population swelling to 14,000.

By 1920, ninety percent of the town was dependent on the railroad. A vicious and prolonged strike took place in 1922. Gangs of striking workers roamed the streets, seeking revenge against hundreds of scabs brought in by the Northern Pacific. It took several years for the scars of that conflict to heal. After the depletion of the forests, iron ore was found in an area later called the Cuyuna Range.

The Burlington Northern once maintained its major repair shops in Brainerd. Lumbering and paper mills are also important. But the tourist industry started having a major impact on this area in the early 1900's, when the automobile brought vacationers to the 500 lakes which circle Brainerd.

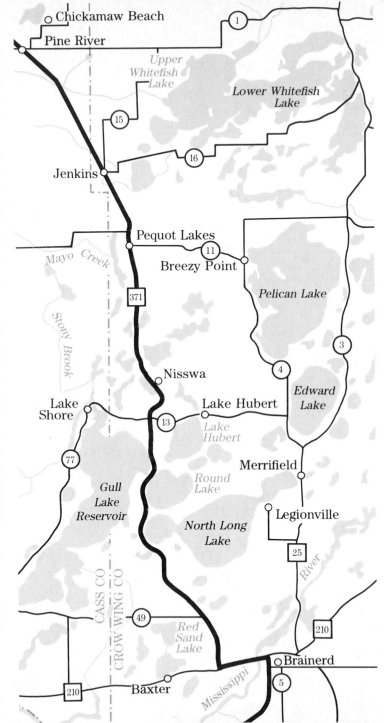

(right) Brainerd, shortly after 1870.
(bottom) End of tracks near Brainerd.

MHS

MHS

GULL LAKE REGION

The region around Brainerd and Gull Lake has been inhabited for the last 4,000 years. The only traces of the first Indian-like people are from a few mounds found along some of the area lakes. When the first whites explored this area, the Dakota were in control of the territory. The Dakota, or Sioux, as they are often referred to, consisted of many tribes whose alliance stretched all the way to the Tetons.

The Dakota that occupied Minnesota were of the Mdewakanton tribe, whose name meant "people of the holy or spirit lake." That is what they called today's Lake Mille Lacs. For some time Mille Lacs was considered the spiritual capital of the entire Dakota Nation. But during the mid-1700's, the Ojibwe started to make their push from the camps around Lake Superior and northern Wisconsin. (Madeline Island, of the Apostle Islands, was the Ojibwe capital in the early 1700's).

For years, the Dakota tried to defend these beautiful and abundant hunting grounds from the better-armed Ojibwe. Gull Lake became a no-man's land during this period. But in the 1740's, decisive battles were won by the Ojibwe at Mille Lacs. The Dakota fought in traditional ways, with clubs and arrows. The Ojibwe, with some aid from the French, used rifles that could cut down their foe without physically engaging him. This was no match for the Dakota, who retreated to the plains of southern Minnesota. From then on it would be a short and sad history for this once proud nation of Dakota.

CHIPPEWA CONTROL

After the decisive battle of Mille Lacs, the Ojibwe retained control of northern Minnesota. As many as five Ojibwe villages centered around Gull Lake. From the Ojibwe, the early lumbermen learned the art of making maple syrup, harvesting wild rice, constructing birch bark canoes and making pemmican, a combination of buffalo meat and lard.

The name Chippewa was developed through the mispronunciation of the Indians' original name, Ojibwe. The Ojibwe first lived in the Lake Huron and Appalachian region and belonged to the Algonkian Indian tribe. Shortly after the Ojibwe took control of the Upper Mississippi, a chief named Hole-in-the-Day, became an important leader. For years, he protected the southern boundary of his people and led attacks against the Dakota as far south as Lake Calhoun. His son, of the same name, took charge after his father died in an unfortunate drinking accident. Because of the growing animosity towards the white man and their practices, Hole-in-the-Day planned an insurrection at Crow Wing. The chief had some difficulty aligning various tribes for his cause. But before the effort faded, the St. Columba Mission, on the south shore of Gull Lake, was burned. Many whites feared that the Ojibwe would join the Dakota, who were fighting the whites along the Minnesota River that same summer. As it turned out, the Ojibwe refused to join forces with their historical enemy.

A Small pleasure boat on a Sunday afternoon cruise.

MHS

GULL LAKE RESORTS

Gull Lake didn't really begin to be developed as a resort area until 1915, when the land around the St. Columba Mission was developed for cabins and resorts. Lake-front property was selling for a dollar a foot. Today, some 10,000 people have summer homes along the 38 miles of shoreline. Minnesota Governors such as Floyd Olson, Luther Youngdahl and C. Elmer Anderson, had cabins on Gull Lake.

During the 1920's and 30's, this region saw the beginning of a number of famous resorts such as Madden's, Grand View, Bar Harbor, Robert's and Ruttger's, the first resort in the state.

PILLSBURY STATE FOREST

In 1899, 1,000 acres of cut-over pine were donated by the John S. Pillsbury estate, making it Minnesota's first established state forest. Extensive seeding had to be undertaken to bring it back to its present condition. Pillsbury was one of the most distinguished and successful men in state history.

NISSWA, Pop. 1,407

This town was once the headquarters for the Mississippi Ojibwe. For a short period, Chief Hole-in-the-Day maintained a five-room house here and kept a white woman as his bride. Although he had several other wives, his most recent wife forced them to live in another nearby house.

Nisswa was first called Smiley, but it was later changed to "Nisswa", an Ojibwe word meaning "in the middle." The train reached here in 1899 and shortly after, the resorts began to develop. When the resorts opened on Gull Lake, people used to ride the train to Nisswa, arriving at 2:30 in the afternoon. From here, they would take a steam-powered launch through a chain of lakes, down to Gull.

HUBERT LAKE

During the early 1900's, this hamlet was a favorite stopping place for tourists. Every afternoon the small station would come to life as people arrived and departed on their vacations. There was just a small store here, but it was the only one around for miles. The railroad was called the Minnesota and International and connected Brainerd to International Falls. This line was later bought out by the Northern Pacific and is now managed by Burlington Northern.

PEQUOT LAKES, Pop. 681

This village was a railway station on the M & I line, starting in 1904. The town was heralded as "a rising star in the new dairy and agricultural county of the Northwest." In 1910, Pequot Lakes had four general stores, a hardware store, drug store, two hotels, one restaurant, two blacksmiths, three lumberyards, two planing mills, a sawmill, lath mill, creamery, feed mill, flour mill, grist mill, two real estate offices, two photo galleries, an undertaker, two doctors, a lawyer, taxidermist, cement-block factory, opera house, school and four churches.

Pequot Lakes was named after a tribe of Algonkian Indians, in New England.

EARLY RESORT HISTORY

Minnesota's clear lakes provided the setting, the trains brought the vacationers, and the local farmers and homesteaders built the resorts. The railroads brought the first resorters, since the few rough and unpredictable roads were used only as lumber roads. The resorts most convenient to the station were the first to be developed. Gull Lake was the farthest from Nisswa, so it was one of the last to be developed.

Ruttger's is considered to be the first resort in the state. Before the train reached Brainerd, fisherman were getting off at Deerwood and walking over to Ruttger's farm on Bay Lake. For awhile Ruttger and his wife fed and put up the anglers for the night, but the financial drain was too great, so they began charging five dollars for the day.

The resort economy took off during the 1920's, after the logging roads were improved and families began exploring the state in their cars.

BREEZY POINT

The flamboyant and famous publisher named Captain Billy Fawcett, who made his money from a magazine called "Captain Billy's Whiz Bang", bought this property in 1922. Fawcett built an elaborate resort, with logs he had brought in by train from the Pacific Coast. The mid-1900's were great years for Breezy Point, with Fawcett bringing in big-name entertainment, such as Gene Autry and current sporting greats. Summer visitors came from all over the country for the fishing and night-life. In 1956 the old resort burned, killing two of its patrons. Today, the rebuilt Breezy Point is a year-round, recreational city, just five miles east of Pequot Lakes.

Indian woman at Cass Lake.

MHS

JENKINS, Pop. 219

This town was named after the lumberman, George W. Jenkins, who laid out this town along the Minnesota and International Railroad. Just east of town, a group of Indian mounds was found. The mounds were three to four feet high, with one mound measuring 700 feet long.

PINE RIVER, Pop. 881

This village was platted along the railroad in 1901, and developed as an important lumber town. During the lumbering era of the 1880's, logs were floated down the Pine River through Whitefish and Cross lakes, and then on to the Mississippi.

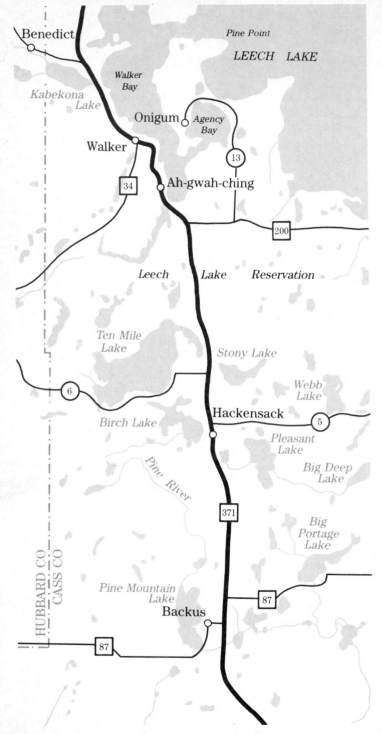

BACKUS, Pop. 255

Backus is another lumber town that grew up along the Minnesota & International Railroad during the late 1800's. It was named for Edward Backus, president of the International Falls Lumber Company.

HACKENSACK, Pop. 285

A small settlement named by its first postmaster, James Curo, most likely after his home town in New Jersey. East of Hackensack, off County 5, is the 6,107 acre, Deep Portage Conservation Reserve which offers public programs on outdoor education and recreation.

TEN MILE LAKE

Distances from the Indian agency at Leech Lake to Brainerd were noted by using some of the lakes as mileage markers. For example, Ten Mile Lake was 10 miles south of the agency. The village of Lothrop, developed on this lake in 1895, once claimed upwards of 2,000 residents. When the M & I Railroad passed some distance away, the town folded, leaving nothing to mark its spot.

AN-GWA-CHING

This name comes from an Ojibwe word meaning "out-of-doors". It was the site of the Minnesota State Tuberculosis Sanatorium which, at one time, had 35 buildings on 886 acres.

WALKER, Pop. 970

This village is located just inside the southwest corner of the Ojibwe National Forest and Leech Lake Indian Reservation. The town was named after Thomas Barlow Walker, a Minneapolis lumberman, who had purchased large tracts of pine in the area. He eventually sold the same land to the Leech Lake Land Company for the purpose of a village. Walker kept the rights to the trees, though, and when he sent a team of lumbermen to the new town the settlers tried to force them away. It was a sore point that took many years to heal. The Park Rapids and Leech Lake Railroad was built in 1897, connecting Park Rapids, Walker and Cass Lake.

LEECH LAKE

According to legend, a band of Ojibwe Indians saw a giant leech swimming across the lake. It was from this legend that the lake received its name. Leech is Minnesota's third largest lake, with 154 miles of shoreline and a width of 40 miles. Glaciers covered this area thousands of years ago and during the melting, it is believed that as many as six different lakes occupied the present basin of Leech Lake. The remains of an oak forest were discovered on the bottom of the lake in the 1800's when lumbermen noticed that ice had loosened stumps from the bottom, forcing them to the shore. A dam was built on the northeast side of the lake in 1884, raising the lake's level by seven feet and submerging many of the old Indian villages along its shores. Leech lake is known for its walleye and northern pike, muskellunge and bass fishing.

LEECH LAKE INDIANS

It appears that the Dakota were living in the region of Leech Lake as early as 1000 A.D. They lived in this land of "milk and honey" fishing, hunting and expanding their influence. But life changed for the Dakota, when an Algonkian group of Indians, called the Ojibwe, were forced westward by Iroquois tribes of the Appalachian area. The Ojibwe passed through the Great Lakes, eventually making their capital at La Pointe on Madeline Island, in Lake Superior.

During the 1600's the Ojibwe became the go-between for the French, who were interested in the furs of the Dakota. But the Ojibwe soon wanted full possession of the Dakota rice fields and hunting grounds. During the 1700's, many fierce battles were fought over the land around Leech Lake. Because the Ojibwe were armed with rifles, they were successful in routing the traditionally-armed Dakota. Finally, during a series of battles that centered at the Dakota capital of Kathio, on Lake Mille Lacs, the Dakota were pushed from the region. Though raids were conducted in each other's territory for many years to come, the Mdewakanton band of Dakota eventually became a prairie people.

Soon after the Dakota were driven south, the Ojibwe faced a new enemy. Smallpox, brought by the white man, devastated the Ojibwe camps, beginning in 1750. Several other epidemics lasted until 1824. Some of the once-powerful villages were reduced to a few wigwams. Vaccination started during the 1830's and the Ojibwe Nation was able to rebuild.

MHS

A gathering of White Earth reservation Indians, 1886.

COMING OF THE WHITE MAN

Fur traders were active in the Leech Lake region as early as 1775, when the Northwest Company established a post on Otter Tail Point. In 1805, Lieutenant Zebulon Pike, exploring the newly-acquired territory of the Upper Mississippi (bought from France in the Louisiana Purchase of 1803), came to the British post on Otter Tail Point. The British, who had been trading in this region for many years, treated Pike and his exhausted soldiers to a generous stay. Before Pike left, though, he ordered his soldiers to shoot down the "Union Jack," reminding the British that they were now on American soil.

Pressure from the whites to gain control of the Ojibwes' land, continued through the early 1800's. The main focus was on the rich timberlands of the north. At that time, no one knew of the rich iron deposits lying just below the surface. The lumbermen didn't have to wait long, for in 1854 and 1855 the Ojibwe negotiated treaties for all of the North Shore and most of the Upper Mississippi Valley. For those lands, the Ojibwe were given a large area that became the Leech Lake and White Earth Indian Reservations. Some important Indian chiefs made their homes on Leech Lake; Flat Mouth, Rabbit, Great Cloud, Red Blanket and Hole-in-the-Day of Leech Lake.

LAST INDIAN WAR IN MINNESOTA

In 1898, Federal agents from Duluth were seeking witnesses to convict bootleggers that sold whiskey to the Indians. An Indian named Hole-in-the-Day, of Leech Lake (more affectionately called "Old Bug"), was asked to testify. His previous experience in traveling to Duluth as a witness had been totally unsatisfactory, so he refused the marshal's invitation. (After his previous appearance, he had been forced to walk the 100 miles home in the middle of winter.)

In an effort to force him to testify, "Old Bug" was put under arrest. With the aid of sympathetic friends, he escaped into the woods. The whole situation was taken very seriously by the military, which dispatched two hundred soldiers from Fort Snelling to go to Walker and bring "Old Bug" in. They departed Walker on barges for Hole-in-the-Day's summer home on Sugar Point (today called Battle Point). Reaching his cabin, the soldiers scoured the woods but couldn't find him anywhere. They decided to stop for lunch, but as they stacked their rifles, one fell over and discharged. A rapid volley of fire came from the hiding Indians, who thought a battle had begun. When the gun-fire had stopped, seven soldiers had been killed and ten wounded. The towns of Cass Lake and Brainerd now feared a general uprising, but their worries proved unfounded. A pardon for the Indians was issued the following year.

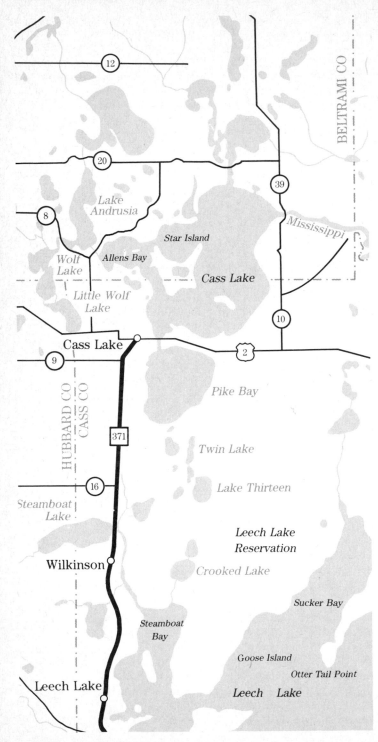

WILKINSON

This village is named after Major Melville Wilkinson, killed during a skirmish on Leech Lake with a band of Pillager Ojibwe.

CASS LAKE, Pop. 1,001

Located on the western shore of Cass Lake, this is the largest community of the county. The Indians named the lake "Ga-mi-squawakokag" meaning, "the place of red cedars." Several early explorers reached Cass Lake in their quest for the true source of the Mississippi. As noted earlier in the Leech Lake description, Lieutenant Zebulon Pike headed a government expedition to this region in 1805 to assert American sovereignty over the lands acquired in the Louisiana Purchase of 1803.

In 1820, Territorial Governor Lewis Cass, accompanied by Henry R. Schoolcraft, visited all of the Indian tribes in the region to discuss land cessions and also to see what value the area might hold for the government. But Schoolcraft's underlying motive was to discover the source of the Mississippi River. Cass felt that this lake was the Mississippi's source, but Schoolcraft disagreed. Twelve years later, Schoolcraft returned and discovered what he named, Lake Itasca. It was on this trip that he renamed the "lake of red cedars", Cass Lake, in honor of his friend.

During the 1850's, the region was covered with thick forests of pine. After the organization of Cass County in 1851, lumbermen dotted the area with camps, mills and planing shops. For years, lumbering was Cass Lake's mainstay. Yet farming and dairying began to develop on the cut-over lands, and along with tourism and resorts, the town became less dependent on lumbering. The Cass Lake settlement grew with the arrival of the Great Northern Railroad in 1899 and the Soo Line in 1900.

Cass Lake Village is the headquarters of the Consolidated Ojibwe Indian Agency, which has jurisdiction over seven reservations: Leech Lake, White Earth, Nett Lake, Fond du Lac, Vermilion, Red Earth and Grand Portage. What rights the Indians actually have on these reservations has long been questioned. It wasn't until 1974 that the state Legislature ended a prolonged legal battle over the Indians' claim to exclusive ricing, hunting and fishing rights. Jurisdiction was turned over to the Tribal Conservation Committee, to issue licenses, regulate fishing quotas and enforce hunting laws.

STAR ISLAND

This is the largest island in Cass Lake (1,200 acres) and it has its own lake named Windigo. It was the home of Chief Yellow Head (Ozawindib) who was Schoolcraft's guide when he discovered Itasca, the source of the Mississippi.

A successful outing for a Leech Lake fishing party.

ROUTE 10, TO MOORHEAD

MHS

A rural Morrison County family, 1900.

ANOKA COUNTY, Pop. 195,998

The topography of Anoka county is flat to gently rolling. Much of this county is underlaid by peat deposits some two to ten feet under the surface. Peat is partially decomposed plant matter that has undergone chemical changes but still retains much of the original carbon matter. Peat also has potential as an alternative source of energy since it can be used as fuel for direct burning or converted to natural gas.

At one time, some 17 percent of this county was covered with wiregrass marshes. Most of the region is covered by a sandy soil deposited by melting glaciers, creating what is called, outwash plains. The soil can sustain plants and crops because, during the dry months, it draws water up from the soil in a capillary action.

Oak and poplar mostly cover the county, and peat bogs support tamarack. Parts of north central Anoka also had large amounts of marketable pine. This area is part of the Mississippi drainage basin, with its most important stream being the Rum River.

White settlement in this county began around the towns of Anoka and Fridley, in 1844 and 1848, respectively.

FIRST WHITE EXPLORER

When Father Hennepin was captured by Indians in 1680, he was brought to Mille Lacs by way of Phalen Creek, through Anoka County and the Knife River Valley. This probably made him the first white person to enter the area. Later, Hennepin joined the Indians on a hunting party down the Rum and Mississippi rivers, where he discovered the Falls of St. Anthony, the future home of Minneapolis. It was during this period that the Mdewakanton Dakota controlled the region, with their capital located on the western shores of Mille Lacs Lake. Starting in the 1730's, the Ojibwe, or Chippewa Indians, began entering the region from Lake Superior. The Ojibwe, with their more sophisticated weapons, began pushing the Dakota from these northern areas into southern and western Minnesota. For many years, bloody battles were fought between these two nations, and Anoka county became a kind

93

of no-man's land, where neither tribe dared linger.

In 1853, another nation of Indians, called the Winnebago, camped a few miles north of Anoka. This tribe was yet another story of a displaced people. The Winnebago were moved from Wisconsin to Iowa and then to the Long Prairie region of Minnesota before being transferred to southern Minnesota, south of Mankato. Finally they were relocated on a reservation along the Missouri River in Dakota Territory. All this because of the white mans' continuing need for land.

ANOKA, Pop. 15,634

A French-Canadian named Joseph Belanger started a one-room trading post at the mouth of the Rum River, in what is now Anoka. Belanger and his comrades carried packs weighing up to 240 pounds as far as Mille Lacs Lake to trade with the Indians. Two men always traveled together for safety while one stayed behind at the post. There were few neighbors in those days as most settlement was focused along the Mississippi between St. Paul and Winona.

Many people were disgusted by the light, sandy soil around Anoka and moved further west. Still the town continued to grow, and by 1855 there were 300 inhabitants. A bridge and dam were built over the Rum River in 1853 with tamarack logs cut near Round Lake, and then floated to the mouth of the Rum. The early settlers figured that Anoka, and not Min-

neapolis, would become the metropolitan center of the state, since its position on the Rum and Mississippi rivers made it an ideal location for milling. It was the development of the Twin Cities as a milling & rail center that dimmed Anoka's prospects.

"A-no-ka," was a Dakota word meaning "on both sides," and was adopted because of the town's growth on both sides of the Rum River.

LAND SPECULATION

Development in the region was slowed by intense land speculation during the 1850's. Everyone that came through the county posted signs on trees, making claims to land on which they never intended to settle. Those that wanted to settle moved to other areas to avoid entanglement in lawsuits over claims.

ANTI-ALCOHOL SENTIMENT IN ANOKA

Anti-alcohol sentiment ran high in Anoka during its early days. In 1859, a saloon keeper named Dudley was asked by locals to close his place down. Ignoring their threats, he was bound and gagged one night while vigilantes destroyed his saloon. Dudley had several men arrested and a trial followed. Halfway through the proceedings, one of the accused lost his patience, stood up, and asked the spectators if they wanted

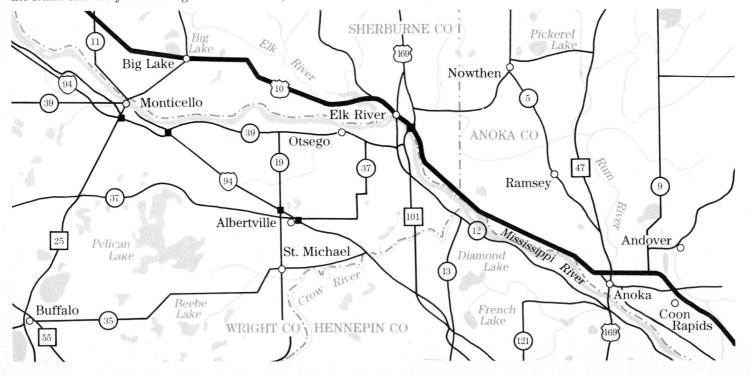

to adjourn this whole mess. The voice vote carried and the courtroom emptied, accused and all.

RUM RIVER

The Rum starts at Mille Lacs Lake and winds its way 140 miles to Anoka. Mille Lacs, which is French for "thousand lakes," was first called "Spirit Lake" by the Dakota. The whites translated spirit to mean rum, which was understandable since rum was the most common liquor traders sold to the Indians. The river was once lined with pine, but after years of lumbering, the Rum is now bordered by oak, elm, ash, maple and poplar.

The Rum River was an important highway for the lumbermen who harvested the great pines on this delta between the Mississippi and St. Croix rivers For twenty years, starting in 1848, logs floated down the Rum on their way to the sawmills of St. Anthony. The logs that were used to build part of Fort Snelling were cut along the Rum in 1822 and floated down to the fort's position at the mouth of the Minnesota River.

Today, the Rum is a recreational river for beginning to intermediate canoeists. It is also a good river for smallmouth bass fishing.

BATTLE OF THE RUM RIVER

In the spring of 1839, a band of 800 Ojibwe were on their way home after being turned away at Ft. Snelling. They had come thinking they would be paid some money that was due them. Passing Lake Harriet, a fight broke out and a Dakota brave was killed by two Ojibwe. Enraged, a number of Dakota followed this band of Ojibwe to Round Lake, east of the Rum River and just north of Anoka. In the early morning mist of July 4th, the Ojibwe, along with their women and children, were attacked as they slept. Seventy were killed. It wasn't until eight years later that the noted lumberman, Daniel Stanchfield, came across the battlefield. Most of the bones had been blackened by prairie fires, but by the time he was through, Stanchfield had stacked close to fifty skulls in a small pile.

RED RIVER TRAIL

A trail from Pembina, North Dakota and other Red River settlements roughly paralled the present freeway to St. Cloud. This trail forded the Mississippi River at Sauk Rapids and followed the river along its east bank. Crude but sturdy carts were drawn by slow-moving oxen, transporting furs and other products of the wilderness. In St. Paul, supplies were loaded for the return trip. It was this movement of goods between Winnipeg, Pembina and other towns, that helped establish St. Paul as a trading center.

As the years passed, these muddy and deeply-rutted paths became the major roads and train routes of today. Townsites began to spring up along the route from St. Cloud to St. Paul. In 1852 a military road was improved from Point Douglas, in Washington County, to Fort Ripley. For the most part, Highway 10 follows this early road.

The Red River carts were always of interest to the people along the route. But one person wrote, "the sound produced by wooden wheels turning on wooden axles without any grease was like a group of swine whose lunch was overdue." The clincher was that at least pigs took time out to breathe.

ITASCA (OLD TOWN)

In 1850, a number of speculators and politicians platted a town in sections 19 and 30 of Ramsey Township. It was hoped that they could turn this into a thriving river port. Governor Ramsey, himself, turned out to be one of the developers. A couple of years later a large hotel and post office were established. A determined effort was made to move the state capital here, and at one time it seemed probable that the bill would pass. But county history states that someone stole the bill until the Legislature had adjourned. Hoping to promote the area, Oliver H. Kelly, founder of the National Grange, established his farm here in 1850. But the town slowly faded away, with the little lake of Itasca now a forgotten remnant of past history.

ELK RIVER, Pop. 6,785

Elk River was named after herds of Elk found here by Zebulon Pike, when he traveled up the Mississippi in the fall of 1805. Forty-three years later, a French trader named Pierre Bottineau built a post on a bluff overlooking the Elk River. Later he built a hotel to service settlers and oxcart drivers.

The town of Orono started to grow on the north side of Elk River. Locals called it "lower town". Of the two settlements, Orono showed the most promise for a grist mill site. It wasn't long before a dam was built across the Elk River. A ferry ran between Orono and Otsego at one time, but when the railroad put a station in Elk River, people began moving closer to it. In 1880, Elk River and Orono merged.

ANOKA SAND PLAIN

North of Elk River is an area known as the Anoka Sand Plain, a triangular region of some 858 square miles. In some parts, winds have eroded away the thin topsoil creating sand dunes that reach up to 20 feet in height.

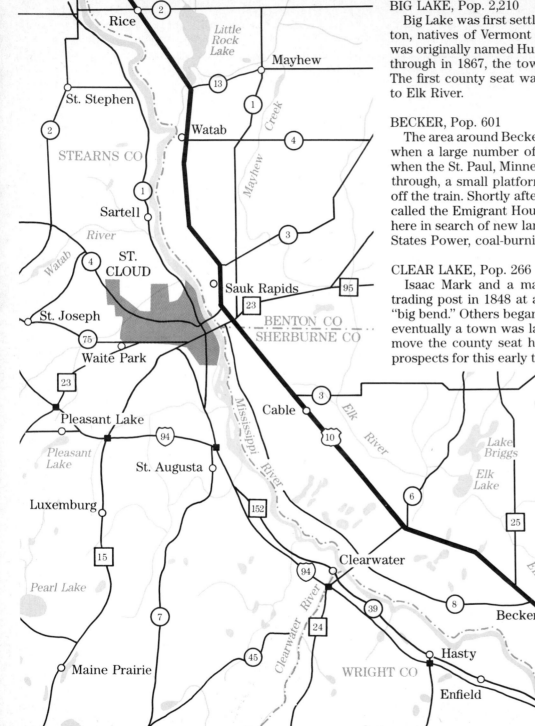

BIG LAKE, Pop. 2,210

Big Lake was first settled by James, Eli and Newell Houghton, natives of Vermont who came here in 1848. The town was originally named Humboldt. But when the railroad came through in 1867, the town was renamed for a nearby lake. The first county seat was at Big Lake but was later moved to Elk River.

BECKER, Pop. 601

The area around Becker was sparsely populated until 1866, when a large number of Scandinavians came here. In 1867 when the St. Paul, Minneapolis and Manitoba Railroad came through, a small platform was built for those getting on or off the train. Shortly after, the railroad built a hotel, of sorts, called the Emigrant House. It was used by settlers stopping here in search of new lands. Becker is the site of a Northern States Power, coal-burning, electric plant.

CLEAR LAKE, Pop. 266

Isaac Mark and a man named White, set up an Indian trading post in 1848 at a spot on the Mississippi called the "big bend." Others began to settle near this post in 1850 and eventually a town was laid out. An effort was later made to move the county seat here, but the attempt failed and the prospects for this early town died. Ten years later, the tracks

A view of St. Cloud in 1885. Photo/E.S. Hill.

MHS

were laid through the county and the railroad established Clear Lake Station, two miles inland from where the original village used to be.

ST. CLOUD STATE REFORMATORY

In the late 1800's the prison conditions in the state were very poor, Many of the county jails and poorhouses were considered unfit for human habitation. A growing need existed for a prison for younger men. Consequently, this site, which was the location of the first quarry in St. Cloud, became a state prison. Inmates did the quarrying, cutting, and placing of the massive granite blocks. The work was completed in 1889.

BENTON COUNTY, Pop. 25,187.

This county was named in honor of Thomas Hart Benton, who served 30 years as a United States Senator from Missouri. Because of his strong support of the Homestead Law, many new counties in the West were named after him.

SAUK RAPIDS, Pop. 5,793

This town was named after a band of Sauk Indians who sought refuge here after being driven by the French from Green Bay, Wisconsin, in 1730. John Baptiste Perrault was said to have stayed here for part of 1789, but the first trading post was established by Robert Dickson in 1805, just below the mouth of the Sauk River. Another post was later built by Henry Rice in 1848. The following year, Jeremiah Russell, the "Father of Sauk Rapids," took over Rice's post and turned it into a hotel.

Highway 10 travels over an old trail that was used long before this area was ever settled. The banks at Sauk Rapids marked the junction point of two Red River oxcart trails. Over these trails, carts loaded with furs and other products of the wilderness, traveled to Mendota at the mouth of the Minnesota River. One such trail, called the "East Plains Trail," crossed the river and roughly followed the present route of I-94 to the northwest. The other route, called the "Woods Trail," continued past Sauk Rapids along the Mississippi to the Crow Wing River, before it headed northwest.

It was at this important ford in the river that trading posts developed, laying out the beginnings of the town and region. Trade picked up when steamboats began to make regular trips between here and St. Anthony Falls in 1850. For 16 years the steamers went unchallenged, until the iron horse chugged its way up the east bank of the Mississippi in 1866. The steamers tried competing with the railroad for a number of years, but the trains lowered their rates, squeezing the boats out of business. The last regular steamboat trip was made in 1874.

ST. CLOUD, Pop. 42,566

Early in 1853, a Norwegian named Ole Bergeson took a claim out on what is now the business district of St. Cloud.

That summer he sold his claim to John Wilson for $250. Wilson, a great admirer of Napoleon, laid out plans for a town, insisting that the place be called St. Cloud, after the city Napoleon built for the Empress Josephine.

During this early period Red River carts were crossing Stearns County to St. Cloud. Fording the river at Sauk Rapids, they rested their oxen at the posts that had developed there. By 1855, the carts began coming into St. Cloud instead of crossing at Sauk Rapids. It was this stream of furs from the northwest that helped St. Cloud grow. Steamboats soon met the carts here and shortened the long trip down the "East Plains Trail" by shipping goods to St. Paul.

Early St. Cloud was divided into three towns; Upper, Middle and Lower. Upper town was organized by General Sylvanus Lowry, a Southerner. Middle Town was settled by Easterners, and Southern Town was occupied by Germans. General Sylvanus and a number of his southern neighbors in Upper Town had slaves, as did their friends who came to visit. Jane Grey Swisshelm, a feminist and editor of the local paper,

MHS

A Morrison County logging camp during winter.

wrote many scathing editorials about this slavery situation. The question of slavery was destined to plunge the nation into civil war. Shortly after one of her editorials, a night raid on the newspaper was led by friends of the general, destroying Swisshelm's press and scattering the expensive type. But with the approach of the Civil War, the Southerners and their slaves soon left the area.

A stage route, which today is followed by I-94, carried the mail from 1851 to 1859 to towns as far away as Breckenridge. This mail was the only form of communication with the outside world. The stage drivers were usually big-hearted, fun-loving men, who were sought out when they rode into

town. They became the eyes and ears of these new settlements.

St. Cloud, also called the "Granite City," is an important quarrying center whose fine-grained granites have been used in notable buildings across the nation, as well as the State Capital and the St. Paul Cathedral. The granites were first quarried in 1868 and in a few years, thousands of tons were being taken annually. Some of Minnesota's granites are among the oldest rocks on the earth's surface, formed under mountain chains that were eroded away millions of years ago.

WATAB

Like its river, Watab was a word taken from the Ojibwe. Watab refers to the long slender roots of the tamarack and jack pine found along this river, which were dug, split and used as threads by the Indians to sew their birchbark canoes. South of Watab in 1825, a treaty was drawn up between the Dakota and Ojibwe at a rock they called "peace rock." This did little to stop the fighting between the two nations however, which continued for another 35 years.

The first claim in Watab was made in 1848 by David Gilman and Asa White. Gilman built a hotel and started the first farm in the county. Trade was brisk with the Ojibwe and Winnebago Indians who lived in this area. In 1848, the Winnebago were relocated from a reservation in Iowa to an area around Long Prairie. The camps around Watab were their favorite. Some of the Winnebago villages contained up to 100 lodges, eight feet high and 10 to 30 feet long. But in 1855, these troubled people were moved again, to a small reservation south of Mankato. They were left alone only until the whites found they needed the land, and after the Sioux Uprising, they were moved one last time to South Dakota.

Stage traffic between St. Paul and Watab began during the early 1850's, bringing new settlers almost every day. Stores were built and a bakery was opened. By 1853, Watab was the most important trading center north of St. Paul. The first bridge across the Mississippi above St. Anthony Falls, was built at Watab in 1856, but a strong wind blew the whole structure off its supports and into the river. It was never replaced. When the town lost the county seat to Sauk Rapids in 1859, it began to die. Today, this once-bustling village, filled with robust oxcart drivers, Indians, and settlers looking for a new beginning, is just a small collection of homes.

RICE, Pop. 499

Rice was named for George T. Rice, a man who maintained a rest stop for the stages that traveled between St. Paul and Little Falls. His name was also given to the extensive prairie that covered this region.

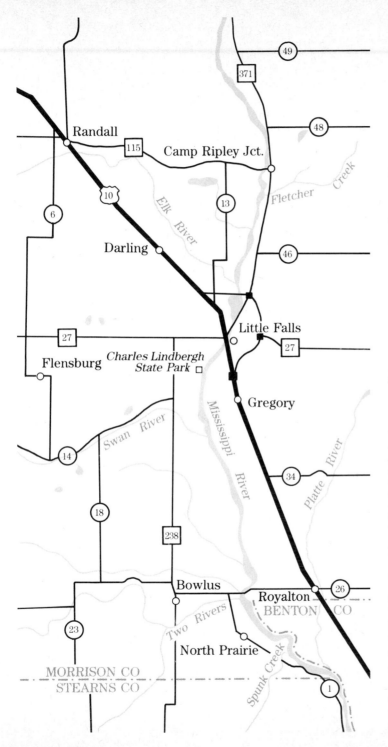

LANGOLA

In 1853, about two miles up from the mouth of the Platte, a townsite had been chosen near a ford across the river. A gristmill was to be built here and a twice-a-week stage stopped, giving rest to those traveling between St. Paul and the now-deserted village of Crow Wing. By 1855, George and Lewis Stone finished the mill and settlers were soon coming to Langola to have their wheat ground or their logs sawn.

The Sauk Rapids newspaper claimed that Langola was in an ideal location and destined to be one of Minnesota's most flourishing towns. But the town's future was short-lived. In 1867, a bad flood carried the whole mill away. The town slowly died, with the last straw coming in 1879 when a log jam of pines coming down the Platte, flooded out the few settlers who had stayed. A few cellar holes are said to be visible at the old townsite.

MORRISON COUNTY, Pop. 29,311

The county was named in honor of two brothers, William and Allan Morrison. William was a trader who roamed the northern regions of Minnesota. His brother, Alan, was in charge of a trading post at the mouth of the Crow Wing River on the Mississippi.

Morrison County is part of the region known as the Upper Mississippi River Basin. The surface of the county is generally level, due to glaciers that slid across its surface some 11,000 years ago, leaving behind 400 feet of sand and gravel.

In many places near the vicinity of Little Falls, flakes of white quartz have been found in the glacial flood plain. It was believed that these were once cutting tools, left by a prehistoric people before the end of the last glacial period. In a more recent time, some 150 mounds have been discovered in the county. These rounded hills point to the occupation of this land by an Indian-like people who were most likely ancestors of the Dakota Indians.

EARLY EXPLORERS

Lieutenant Zebulon Pike was exploring the region of the Upper Mississippi when he was caught in a bad snow storm, a few miles south of where Little Falls now stands. On the west bank of the Mississippi he built a 40-square-foot block-house and waited for better weather. The purpose of his trip was to find the source of the Mississippi and to make peace with the Indians. Citizens of the area built a monument at this site with the chimney stones from the old house.

As early as 1771, traders had established posts up and down the Mississippi where major tributaries entered the river. Missionaries were also active in the early 1800's, trying to bring religion to the Indians.

SETTLEMENT

Around 1847, fur trading began to merge with the settlement of the area and the establishment of lumbering interests. Morrison County was heavily-wooded and many large tracts of white pine were found among the hardwoods. Crews came to the Swan River in 1847 to cut timber for the construction of the St. Anthony Fall's dam. The logs were floated down the Mississippi but unfortunately, most were lost somewhere along the stretch. Logging reached its peak during the 1870's.

Some isolated farming began near the river banks, but it really wasn't until the middle 1850's that people began to come in any numbers. Still, the census of 1860 showed only 618 people living in the county. A number of Germans began to settle here then. Polish settlers came to the area of North Prairie in 1868. During the 1880's, a number of Swedes settled at Upsala, some 20 miles southwest of Little Falls.

ROYALTON, Pop. 660

This town came to life when the Northern Pacific Railroad entered the county in 1877. Royalton actually formed around an old box car donated by the railroad to handle the mail and freight. The name Royalton was taken from the same name given to an old post and mission, located here some 20 years before. The Platte River, a French name meaning, "flat, dull, or shallow," has its beginnings 45 miles north at Platte Lake in southern Crow Wing County. The river flows past Royalton and into the Mississippi just inside Benton County.

SWAN RIVER OR AITKINSVILLE

The old pioneer village of Swan River was located about a mile and a half below Little Falls and one and a half miles west of the Burlington Northern Railroad's Gregory station. In 1848, this spot was once a lively gathering post for Red River carts. Indians interested in trade also came here. The post was first run by William Aitkin, a Scot, who first named this place after himself. When he died in 1851, it was renamed Swan River. The usual frontier stores sprang up, as did a hotel, saloon and mill. This mill was the first in the county to start cutting into the large amounts of white pine being sent down the Swan and Mississippi Rivers.

But Swan River was never destined to survive. Trade was lost when the Winnebago Indians were moved to southern Minnesota, and the movement of goods via the Red River carts was taken over by the railroads. During the Sioux Uprising in 1862, the few townspeople remaining sought safety elsewhere, never to return.

LITTLE FALLS, Pop. 7,250

French traders first called this area of rapids, "Painted Rocks," because of an oddly-colored rock found here. But the Indians called it "Kakabikansing," which literally translates to "little falls with the square cut-off rock." Pike explored this area in 1805, followed by Schoolcraft in 1832 during his successful search for the source of the Mississippi. Stopping at Little Falls, Schoolcraft wrote, "As far as the eye can reach there is one continuous field of grass and flowers waving in the passing breeze. The soil is apparently easy of cultivation, a black earth with a mixture of sand."

In 1849, James Green came here and built the first dam and sawmill across the Mississippi. This triggered rapid growth and in a few years, there was considerable development along the river front. In 1856 a company called the Little Falls Manufacturing Company incorporated and produced flour, lumber and other items. A power company, paper mill and one more lumber company were formed in subsequent years. At one point, the Pine Tree Lumber Company occupied over 50 acres near the Falls.

The old Woods Trail passed through Little Falls and the Red River carts used to camp here. The carts also camped at a place four miles above Little Falls, named Belle Prairie. The noted Ojibwe chief, Hole-in-the-Day, had his village near this spot and was a frequent visitor to the town. Hole-in-the-Day was ambushed along the road from Crow Wing in August 1868, and assassinated by members of the Pillager band of Ojibwe. He was buried at the top of a bluff, north of town. Hole-in-the-Day's name was given to him because of an eclipse that occurred on the day he was born. The darkened sun created a hole-in-the-day.

(FOR THOSE CONTINUING ON STATE 371 NORTH, TURN TO PAGE 81.)

LITTLE FALLS WAR

During the early years of Little Falls, the town grew rapidly with hotels, stores and saloons. Many small shacks sprang up along the river and were lived in by a number of rowdy men. They stayed at Little Falls mainly to take advantage of the large amounts of money being spent during those boom years. Their numbers grew, and by the late 1850's these men seemed to have control of the town. It appeared there was little the average citizen could do. Some of the townspeople tried to organize against them, but they were easily intimidated and ineffective. Things came to a head one night when the town constable, R. L. Barnum, was badly beaten in his

Charles Lindbergh with his famous "Spirit of St. Louis," 1927.

own home by the leader of this gang and a number of his thugs. The law-abiding citizens responded by forming a vigilante committee, arming themselves and forcing the toughs from town. That spring, new elections put the law- and-order group back in office.

CHARLES LINDBERGH STATE PARK

A 294-acre state park has developed around the boyhood home of Charles Lindbergh Jr., the first person to fly solo across the Atlantic Ocean in 1927. "Lucky Lindy" and "Lone Eagle" were nicknames given to the world-famous Lindbergh who helped develop the aviation industry into an international transportation network. Lindbergh lived in Little Falls with his parents, until he graduated from high school and entered the University of Wisconsin. His father practiced law in Little Falls, starting in 1883, and was elected to the U.S. House of Representatives as a progressive Republican. His resistance to entering World War I made him extremely unpopular and Lindbergh Sr. was defeated for his bid to the Senate in 1917. A year later he also lost a bid for the governorship. One more attempt was made, but Lindbergh died before the primary.

The state park has 38 campsites situated in a wooded setting along the banks of Pikes Creek. A 90-foot, 260-year-old white pine stands near the park's picnic area. There is also a new interpretive center on the park grounds, centering on Lindbergh history and regional pioneer life.

RANDALL, Pop. 527

Charles Lindbergh Sr. was the special attorney for this town when it filed for incorporation in 1900. The town was financially squeezed those first years with hardly any revenue to pay its bills. The town fathers decided to grant Nick Rossier a liquor license for $500, to generate some money. But according to the village women, drunkenness increased and they soon organized a successful campaign to dry up the town. A co-operative creamery was established here in 1919 and electric power reached Randall in 1922.

In 1913, iron ore on the western edge of the Cuyuna Iron Range was discovered in the area just north of Randall. But it wasn't until 1950 that the Fontelle Brothers of Ironton, removed up to 55,000 tons of ore and piled it along the highway. For the next couple of years, strip mining was carried out in sections 31 and 32 in Clough township and shipped for processing to Ohio and Georgia. Shipping costs finally proved prohibitive to the venture. The Cuyuna range was discovered by a lonely prospector named Cuyler Adams who was accompanied by his dog Una. Their names were joined together to form Cuyuna.

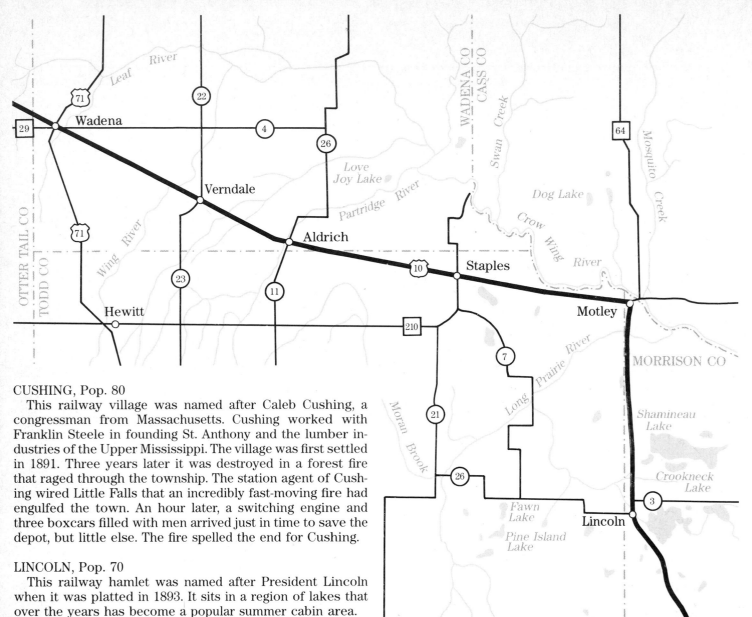

CUSHING, Pop. 80

This railway village was named after Caleb Cushing, a congressman from Massachusetts. Cushing worked with Franklin Steele in founding St. Anthony and the lumber industries of the Upper Mississippi. The village was first settled in 1891. Three years later it was destroyed in a forest fire that raged through the township. The station agent of Cushing wired Little Falls that an incredibly fast-moving fire had engulfed the town. An hour later, a switching engine and three boxcars filled with men arrived just in time to save the depot, but little else. The fire spelled the end for Cushing.

LINCOLN, Pop. 70

This railway hamlet was named after President Lincoln when it was platted in 1893. It sits in a region of lakes that over the years has become a popular summer cabin area.

MOTLEY, Pop. 444

Motley was first laid out in 1870 by the Lake Superior and Puget Sound Company, a townsite organization formed in the East. In 1872, the Northern Pacific Railroad, a line that was being built from Lake Superior west to the Pacific Ocean, crossed the Crow Wing River and established a station. A railway employee named Calvin Priestly was Motley's first resident. The town was named by railroad officers and soon became one of the major lumber towns of the north.

In 1875, a steamboat to haul wheat was in operation between Motley and Long Prairie, on the Long Prairie River. But after three years, a dry season permanently ended its trips.

In 1878, H. B. Morrison came to Motley and lumbering began in the county. Morrison is considered the father of Motley, since his mills attracted lumbermen from all over the state. These mills could turn out 40,000 feet of lumber in a ten-hour day. Other companies also came here for lumber. The forests were filled with hundreds of men, cutting and floating logs down the Crow Wing River to Motley.

The town boomed, and in 1905 close to one thousand people lived here. In those days the railroads transported as many as 200,000 lumberjacks through the Twin Cities, as they sought work in the woods. The townspeople boldly predicted that Motley would be the center of trade for the region. In 1910 the streets were lighted by gasoline lanterns and in 1915, electricity came to town.

Situated behind the Motley High School is the Motley Castle House. This 18-room, four-story structure topped with a moorish onion-shaped dome, was built in 1905 by Alfred Wilson. It was originally intended for summer boarders who sought the curative powers of the north woods. Today it is a private residence.

CROW WING RIVER

This river begins in Hubbard County and flows about 100 miles to the Mississippi River, where the old Crow Wing Village used to exist. It was along this river that the slow-moving oxcarts followed a trail through the tall white pines on their 20-mile-a-day passage to the Red River Valley. These carts carried furs, buffalo robes, and other materials from their communities to trade for goods in St. Paul.

There were other trails besides this "Woods Trail." One of the earliest ones passed through the plains along the Minnesota River to Traverse des Sioux, just north of St. Peter. But traveling across the open prairie left these merchants vulnerable to hostile attacks by the Dakota Indians. Consequently, more secure and shorter routes were established in the 1840's and were heavily used after the Sioux Uprising of 1862.

The Crow Wing River was called "Kagiwegwon," or "Raven's Wing" by the Ojibwe Indians. The French named it "River of the Wing of the Raven." At some point it was erroneously translated into English as Crow Wing. This probably happened because the English-speaking traders and settlers of this region, were more familiar with the term crow.

STAPLES, Pop. 2,887

This town was first founded in 1885 and named after two Stillwater brothers who had lumbering interests in the area. Staples is one of the county's youngest towns. It formed shortly after the Northern Pacific decided to shorten its run 24 miles, building a cutoff from Little Falls to Staples, bypassing Brainerd. The town became a division point for the railroad and was mostly dependent on the company's employees. Staples later became an agricultural trading center and claims to be the geographical center of the state.

ALDRICH, Pop. 88

This small village grew up as a railway station along the tracks of the Northern Pacific. In 1874, Aldrich consisted of

Minnesota farm family.

MHS

several small stores and a nearby Ojibwe camp. One day, a settler claimed that two Indian boys had stolen a sack of flour. The accused boys claimed they had legally purchased the flour. Not believing their story, the settler beat them. The boys' brother, "Big Moose," went to town to reclaim their honor. Pushed away by a man named Costello, Big Moose fired his rifle in return. The bullet took off Costello's finger, pierced the thin walls of the house and instantly killed a young girl inside. Big Moose was shot in the chest, yet still escaped to the safety of his camp. The residents called for Sheriff McKay and his marshal "Slippery Bill," who had recently lynched an Indian in Brainerd.

A posse entered the Ojibwe camp late that night and tried to talk the Ojibwe chief into giving up Big Moose. The posse was outnumbered, two to one, and left without their man. Big Moose recovered and lived out his days at Leech Lake.

MHS

Oxcarts provided a link between St. Paul and communities along the Red River Valley, 1858.

VERNDALE, Pop. 504

Verndale was named for a granddaughter of Lucas Smith, one of the town's first settlers. The town was the termination point for a road called the "Wheat Trail." A prairie of flat, unforested land north of Verndale in the vicinity of Park Rapids, became known as the Shell Prairie. This name was from the ancient sea shells occasionally found there.

Early settlers began to grow wheat on these rich lands, hauling it down to the shipping center at Verndale. Caravans of up to 30 wagons would wind their way down to this town, unloading the wheat both night and day. For many years, this prairie was covered with the golden grain that grew right up to the edge of a forest called Pine Heights, known today as Smokey Hills State Forest.

The farmers knew little about preserving the nutrients of the soil and eventually the fields gave a lower yield. The dark prairie soil lightened, and the pines began to creep out across the prairie. The Wheat Trail became history.

During the late 1800's, Verndale carried on a bitter fight with Wadena for the county seat. Both villages hired temporary residents to bolster up their populations. Wadena won the election, but it wasn't until 1887 that the courts made their final decision.

WADENA, Pop. 4,699

Wadena began as a trading post, 15 miles east of the present village. It became the next important stop after Crow Wing Village on the Red River "Woods Trail." Old Wadena was situated between the mouths of the Leaf and Partridge rivers. A French post was first established here and the Ojibwe came to trade. During the winter of 1782-83 a band of Dakota attacked the post, marking one of the first armed battles between the white man and the Dakota. Later, a well-stocked store and an inn named the "Halfway House," were located here. Some one hundred people lived at the old Wadena post during its peak years of 1855 to 1860.

Travelers along the trail looked forward to stopping at old Wadena, since this portion of the trail was the most difficult. Stumps, sloughs and mosquitoes constantly tested their patience. But like the villages of Crow Wing and Otter Tail, old Wadena faded away as the Red River carts were replaced by the "iron horse."

When the Northern Pacific crossed the county in 1872, a town formed around a depot 15 miles west of the old post. It took the name Wadena. Wadena is an Ojibwe word meaning "little rounded hill," probably referring to the bluffs located near the old town. Follow the signs to the park at "Old Wadena," where camping and picnicking are available. A walk across the suspension bridge to a small hill, brings you to an area where the building depressions of the town can be seen.

Just west of today's Wadena is a beautiful park called Black's Grove, a tract of pine saved from the lumberjack.

OTTER TAIL COUNTY, Pop. 51,937

This county name has Ojibwe origins dating back to the days when the Indians camped by a lake they called Otter Tail. There they fished from a spit of sand created by sediments from the Otter Tail River. This sandbar resembled the tail of an otter, an animal once common to the streams of Minnesota. Lumbermen eventually came through forcing the Indians from their camp and destroying this sandbar, so as to better maneuver their logs.

FIRST WHITES

French and British traders and explorers trekked through this county in the late 1700's, with some trading at a small post on Otter Tail Lake. The Columbia and American Fur Companies were each represented. Joseph Nicollet's map, drawn as a result of his explorations in 1836, detailed this county for the first time. An expedition under Major Samuel Woods, came to Otter Tail Lake in 1849 and camped at the

Early fisherman enjoyed a bountiful catch.

MHS

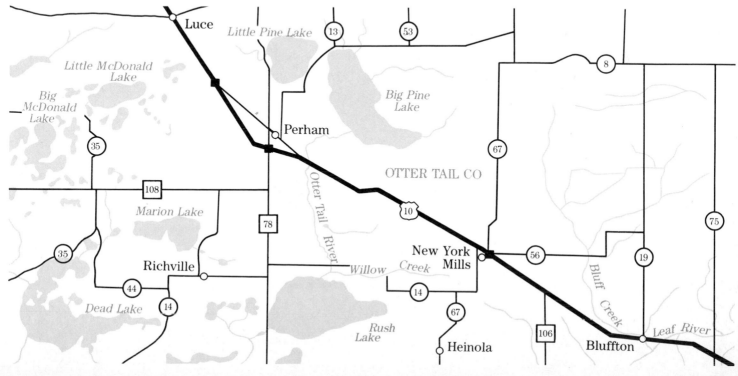

ruins of the old trading posts. They found the lake clear and full of fish. Woods claimed that "for fifty miles in all directions, this lake is among the most beautiful and fertile in the world," and "this region is the garden spot of the northwest."

EARLY SETTLEMENT

It wasn't until the middle 1850's that the white man staked out his claims across Otter Tail County. But even then, it started slowly. During the winter of 1859-60, a report came out of St. Paul stating that 48 persons in the county were attending school. From the same report, 36 people were listed as illiterate.

The Sioux Uprising of 1862 had scattered the settlers in a panic, with many seeking refuge at Ft. Abercrombie, a number of miles west on the Red River. It took the settlers a couple of years after the Uprising to gather enough nerve to return.

The first settlement of any consequence was accomplished by a group of Mormons, seeking a secure place to live after the upheaval in their Bringham Young Church in Illinois. They arrived on the north side of Clitherall Lake in 1865, and lived peaceably among the Ojibwe for many years.

The colony had to be self-sufficient since the nearest store was 65 miles away, requiring a 12 day trip behind their slow-moving oxen. The Mormons made all their own tools and furniture and managed fairly well.

With the Dakota banished from the state after the Uprising, the settlers began complaining that the Ojibwe Indians were wandering from their reservations, hunting and trapping around Otter Tail County. The whites complained that the Indians were getting to the furs before them and frightening the game, making it difficult for them to hunt.

BLUFFTON, Pop. 206

The village of Bluffton was settled shortly before Wadena, when James Valentine started a sawmill here in 1872. During the early 1870's, this town was larger than Wadena and showed more promise because of its wheat and lumber interests. The town received its name from the bluffs that run along the Leaf River, just east of town.

NEW YORK MILLS, Pop. 972

New York Mills was named by Van Aernams, a New Yorker, who had bought extensive timberlands in this region and established a sawmill here. In the late 1800's, New York Mills became a favorite settlement area of the Finnish immigrants. Accustomed to the lumber economy of the region, the Finns took jobs in the mills and woods during the boom years of lumbering. Today New York Mills is a trading center for a rich agricultural area.

PERHAM, Pop. 2,086

This town was first laid out by members of the Lake Superior and Puget Sound Land Company in 1873. It was named after the first president of the Northern Pacific Railroad, Josiah Perham. The important businesses in the town during those early days, were the Globe Milling Company and the Schmidt Wagon Works. Perham marks the beginning of the Lake Park region of Minnesota.

MHS

Wheat was an important crop to early Minnesota farmers.

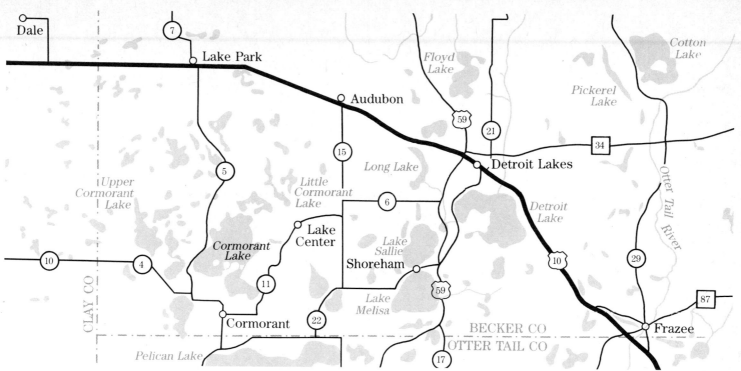

LUCE

At one time, Luce had a population of 180 residents which supported a co-op creamery and the Monarch Grain Elevator.

The Ojibwe of this area used more than 40 species of plants for food. Wild ginger was used as an appetizer. The Indians used berries and the leaves of the bearberry as a flour to thicken gravy. Dried corn silk gave the flavor of salt. Aster leaves could be boiled like spinach and eaten with fish. Wild potatoes, celery, pumpkin, squash, flower of milkweed, roots of bulrushes, the sap of basswood and aspen, and dried berries, provided sustenance for them.

AREA GEOLOGY

This famous region of hills and lakes was created by the movement of glaciers across Minnesota during the latest ice age, some 12,000 years ago. The rough topography marks the farthest advance of the ice sheet. The glacier was much like a shovel, pushing great amounts of dirt and gravel along its frontal edge. Lakes formed in many of the valleys and in some cases, large ice-blocks detached from the retreating glaciers to form basins which filled with water.

FRAZEE, Pop. 1,284

Before this town was settled, it was only a ford in the Otter Tail River, passed by the crude carts from the Red River

Valley. One of the first to stay here was Patrick Quinlan, in 1868. From the beginning Quinlan's luck failed him. During that winter the snow was so deep he couldn't take his oxen for supplies. Quinlan walked to Ottertail City, some 24 miles to the south. He returned with enough pork, flour and potatoes to survive another month.

That next summer Quinlan spent his time cutting some 30 tons of hay, hoping to sell it to the traders and their livestock as they traveled to the White Earth Indian Reservation. But a new trail went by Leech Lake, leaving Quinlan with mounds of unbought hay. The final blow came when the Northern Pacific claimed his land for the right-of-way. Quinlan packed his bags and headed for a cabin further north. He later wrote, "I took a claim at White Earth…my health has been very poor and I do not expect to get rich…but I am content."

DETROIT LAKES, Pop. 7,106

In 1868 five men left their farms in Otter Tail County in search of better grazing land for their cattle. When they reached Frazee, they were told that all the land was taken but the "promised land" was only another 14 miles to the north. They were also told that this area was full of strawberries, waiting only for the cows and their cream. When the men arrived in the area of Detroit Lakes, they liked what they saw. Without

MHS

(left) The small
railway village
of Detroit short-
ly after 1868.
(bottom) Station
at Audubon.

leaving their wagons, they headed back for their families.

A French priest was traveling through this area visiting new settlers when he camped for the evening, along a lake. As the sun set, he could see the highlights of a sandbar stretching across part of the lake. He turned to one of his companions and said, "see what a beautiful detroit," (detroit is French for "narrows or strait"). From then on, the lake and town were called Detroit, until 1927 when the town added "Lakes" to its name.

Detroit Lakes is known as the capital of the Lake Park region, and tourism is its major revenue producer.

WHITE EARTH RESERVATION

The White Earth Indian Reservation begins ten miles north of Detroit Lakes. It was named for the white clay that is found along the shores of White Earth Lake. This area was laid out in accordance with the terms of the White Earth Treaty, signed in 1867. The first group of Indians were moved here the following year and were paid an annuity of $10 per person.

The economic pressures of the whites for lumber, furs, and farmland, left little room for the Indians in this society, except to be moved to reservations. James Bassett, the Indian agent for the first group of Ojibwe that settled here wrote, "My experience with the Indian Department shows to my mind the most incomprehensible absurdity that a civilized people ever attempted to impose upon an uncivilized race. To attempt to civilize a people and at the same time prevent them from adopting any of the arts or advantages of civilization, is to my mind, absolutely absurd and ridiculous."

MHS

AUDUBON, Pop. 383

In 1871, a small group of people passed through this area and camped for the night where the railroad tracks would eventually be laid. It was the time of year when the prairie was covered with flowers and lilies. A woman in this group was quite impressed with the area's natural beauty. She commented to her friends that, "if a station should ever be located here, call it Audubon." It turned out that she was the niece of John J. Audubon, the famous American naturalist. The following year the townsite of Audubon was surveyed.

BUFFALO

The western part of Becker County was once part of the summer range of the buffalo. Though skeletons have been found as far east as Little Falls, the main herds ranged in the western parts of Minnesota. An area settler wrote, "we have had a terrible snow storm. I can count from the top of my oak tree, 20 or 30 herds of buffalo feeding out on the prairie. It is surprising how the cow buffalo resists the cold, piercing, north winds, which for a human is impossible to face for any short time. Still, these animals will stand grazing on these open fields."

It's hard to pinpoint just when the last buffalo disappeared from Minnesota, but it appears that the fall of 1868 was the date when the last bull crossed the Red River into Dakota Territory, with a bullet in its side.

"The last buffalo I saw was just north of Moorhead and within rifle shot. I got one shot off and followed the trail, but I could only find the drying blood on the grass. That was the last one (buffalo) I saw," wrote a settler in 1868.

LAKE PARK, Pop. 716

Lake Park was first settled in 1870 and had the honor of trying the first court case in the county. It seems that a man named Harvey Jones married in his late 50's and was not particularly accustomed to having his authority questioned. One day, during a heated argument with his wife, he decided to administer "some family discipline, with the aid of a sapling." Jones was arrested, tried and convicted of assault. Since there was no jail in Becker County, the sheriff decided to walk him to Ottertail City.

Somewhere along the way, Jones managed to steal the conviction papers from the sheriff and then refused to walk

A fallen buffalo.

MHS

any further without seeing the papers. Finding none, the sheriff had no recourse but to let Jones free. The historian doesn't tell us what happened to Jones' wife.

BIG CORMORANT LAKE

On the north shore of Big Cormorant Lake, ten miles south of Lake Park, the so-called "anchor stones" were found. These stones are actually three large granite boulders, each with a drilled hole nine inches deep by one inch wide. Interestingly enough, these stones are some 300 feet from the present lake, situated on an earlier shoreline. It is believed by many that these stones were used to anchor the boats of Norse explorers who came here in 1362. Possibly these were the same Norsemen that inscribed the Kensington Runestone, left in a field 70 miles to the south near Kensington in Douglas County. Many historians have discounted the likelihood of these early visits, but in this region, you'll still find many believers.

Portrait of a farm crew around 1900.

MHS

LAKE AGASSIZ GEOLOGY

Eleven thousand years ago, when the last glacier from this most recent ice age began melting and receding to the north, a large body of water began forming along its melting edge. Eventually the ice receded from central Iowa toward the north, across the continental divide near Browns Valley, in west-central Minnesota. Browns Valley is the divide where water flows either north to Hudson Bay, or south to the Mississippi River and the Gulf of Mexico.

Because the ice had retreated to the Hudson Bay side of the divide, the water was blocked on one side by the divide and on the other side by ice. Thus, Glacial Lake Agassiz was created. The lake's maximum depth was 700 feet and it was larger than the combined area of today's Great Lakes. Large prehistoric animals ranged along the shores of the cool water, feeding on the new vegetation. These mammals were hunted by prehistoric people who most likely crossed from Asia, along the Bering Straits land bridge.

The outlet of the lake was at Browns Valley and it flowed through the valley of the present Minnesota River. (Years ago this river was called Glacial River Warren.) The northern ice-dam in Canada eventually melted and the lake started draining into Hudson Bay. Left behind was a rich sedimentary deposit that now makes up the soils of the Red River Valley region.

The lake's level fluctuated as the ice blockage to the north melted, creating beaches which after years of wave action formed ridges of gravel and sand. Many settlers used these ridges to travel along. Over fifty have been identified, with most of them being in Canada. In Minnesota, there are two main beaches that can be discerned. One is called Herman Beach, the outermost beach of the lake which held this shore-line for 500 years. The next is Campbell Beach. This level existed for 2,000 years, thereby creating the most extensive and visible beach in Minnesota. The lake finally disappeared altogether, about 6,000 years before the birth of Christ.

HAWLEY, GLYNDON, AND DILWORTH

These three towns were settled when the Northern Pacific passed through the region in the early 1870's. At Hawley the road crosses Herman Beach, the first of two beaches of Lake Agassiz, then descends down some 200 feet into the lake bed of this ancient inland sea. This fertile valley was once roamed by the buffalo. Its grasses were alive with the colors of wild roses, poppies, goldenrod, bell-flowers, daisies, sunflowers, morning glories and clover. Today the rich black earth makes Clay county one of the top potato, sugar beet and sunflower producing areas.

Hawley is the town where Robert Asp spent 10 years building a full-scale replica of a Viking ship. The old potato ware-

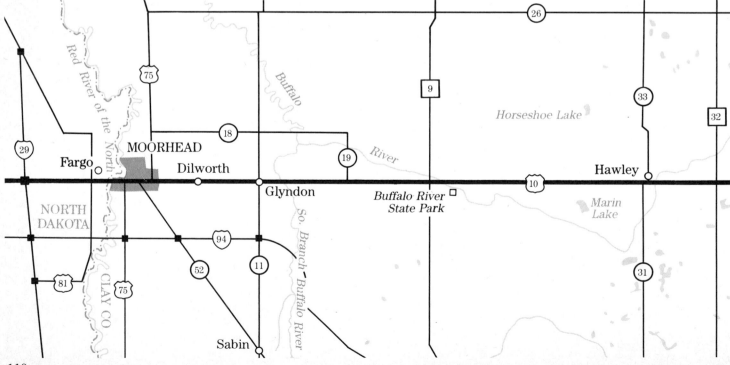

house once situated next to city hall, was torn down so the 76 foot ship could be transported to Lake Superior. Although Asp died in 1980, his children carried on his dream by sailing the "Hjemkomst" to Norway during the summer of 1982. Hjemkomst is Norwegian for "homecoming."

BUFFALO RIVER

This river runs some 88 miles from Becker County to the city of Georgetown on the Red River. It is thought by some that the Vikings might have traveled down the Buffalo in their explorations of this region. The Ojibwe called it "Pijik-iwi-zibi," or "Buffalo River," after the buffalo that wintered along its protective banks.

Buffalo Creek State Park, located off U.S. 10, is a 1,000 acre park situated on the shoreline of ancient Campbell Beach of Glacial Lake Agassiz. There are some 300 acres of virgin prairie here, with trails following along the rock-strewn shoreline of this ancient lake.

MOORHEAD, Pop. 29,998

Because it was a natural terminus for all forms of transportation, Moorhead developed into one of Minnesota's larger cities. The early routes of the Red River oxcarts passed through here along the east bank of the river. Moorhead became a

Railroad construction approaches Detroit Lakes.

steamboat landing for the Hudson Bay Company steamers, which plied the Red River of the north. The town was soon connected to Duluth and the Twin Cities by railroads and highways.

This muddy frontier settlement was named Moorhead in 1871, after Dr. William G. Moorhead, a director of the Northern Pacific Railroad. The Northern Pacific was chartered by the U.S. Congress to connect the port city of Duluth to some future spot on the Pacific coast. The project was financed by the Jay Cooke Company.

Northern Pacific brakemen gather for a photograph in 1908.

In the meantime, early visitors to this fertile Red River region didn't realize the possibilities of farming this flat land. Many believed that this treeless prairie had no agricultural value. In fact, General Sibley wrote of the territory, "It is fit only for the Indians and the devil." One historian told of a settler who came into the barroom of a local hotel, proudly showing off his vegetables. The man was laughed at, since nobody believed he could have grown crops here. Outraged, the farmer pulled a gun out from among his carrots and peas and shot one of the disbelievers.

A license to run a ferry across the river to the "lawless" hamlet of Fargo cost $15, with a toll of 25 cents per horse-drawn wagon; additional animals cost five cents a head. One of the first bills submitted to the county commissioners was a $12 fee by Sheriff J. B. Blanchard, for notifying the Indians to leave Clay County.

By 1882, Moorhead had become one of the important trading centers of the state, with 14 hotels and restaurants. Among those was the pride of Moorhead, "the Grand Pacific Hotel." It cost $165,000 and had 140 rooms.

RED RIVER STEAMBOATS

In 1859, the St. Paul Chamber of Commerce offered $2,000 to anyone who could establish steamboat service on the Red River, which would connect with the stage lines that were operating between Breckenridge and St. Paul. That winter, Anson Northrup dismantled his small steamer at Little Falls, and with 34 teams and some 60 men, hauled the boat in pieces across the frozen state. The lumber-bucket was hastily assembled and started to operate along the river. Northrup soon lost interest and sold the boat to the Minnesota Stage Company.

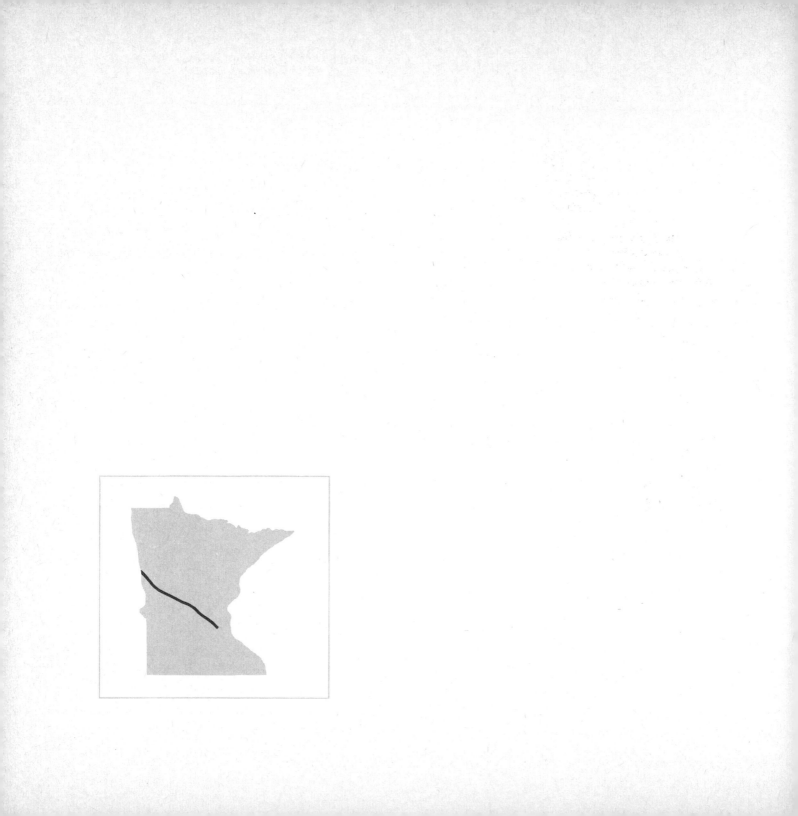

ROUTE I-94, TO MOORHEAD

Spending a warm afternoon with friends at a Minnesota lake.

WRIGHT COUNTY, Pop. 58,962

This county is named after Silas Wright, a New York states-man. It was chosen by a friend of his, W. G. McCrory, who settled along the Mississippi at Monticello in 1855.

Most of the county was originally covered with a variety of hardwoods. This forested area was part of the Big Woods, a 40-mile-wide band of deciduous trees. The woods started 100 miles northwest of the Twin Cities and continued south to Mankato. This great forest was interspersed with numerous lakes and marshes and some natural meadow-lands along the Mississippi. Cranberries grew in the marshes and were picked by the Indians to sell in St. Paul, long before the whites settled in this county.

Wright County was crossed by glaciers several times. In their slow movements, these glaciers dumped debris and scoured out depressions that formed the irregular hills and valleys. Many of the valleys filled with water and became the lakes of today.

If you look at a state map, you can see an arching belt of lakes, beginning at Lake Minnetonka and extending westward towards Willmar, then continuing up to Alexandria and Fergus Falls. This band of lakes was formed near a point where one of the last glaciers stopped. These lakes belong to a terminal moraine system, an area where glacial debris was left along the glacier's outer edge.

INDIAN OCCUPANCY

When Father Hennepin was in this region in 1680, most of Minnesota was occupied by the Mdewakanton band of Dakota Indians. Around 1740 the Ojibwe, armed with weapons from the French, pushed across Lake Superior, driving the Dakota from their strategic locations at Mille Lacs and Sandy Lake to the southern half of Minnesota. From then on, the Dakota became a people of the prairie until their expulsion from the state following the Sioux Uprising in 1862. Wright County was the dividing line between the warring tribes of the Dakota and Ojibwe. In 1772 and 1773, major battles between these two nations were fought at the mouth of the Elk River.

The first white man to establish himself in the county was Edmund Brissett, a French trader who had a post near Lake Harriet. In 1850, Brissett cut a trail from Lakes Harriet and Calhoun, through the Big Woods north of Buffalo to Lake Pulaski. There he maintained a post, trading with the Winnebago Indians until 1855. His trail greatly aided the settlers as they moved westward into Wright County during the 1850's.

EARLY ROADS

Unlike many of the southern Minnesota counties, where wagons could pass easily on the prairie, the new Wright County settlers had difficulty moving westward through the dense woods. Those that left the trading trail carved out by Brissett, had to cut their own way. In 1856 a road between Minneapolis and Rockford, known as the Rockford Road, was laid out by way of Hamel. For two years the men of

Wright County worked in neighboring Hennepin County, building bridges over the many streams and trying to keep the road clear. The project became a sore point, however, since many felt that the residents of Hennepin County gave little help to this endeavor.

CROW RIVER

Just past County 25, the South Fork of the Crow River passes on its journey 30 miles north to the Mississippi. This river begins just west of here in Meeker and Kandiyohi Counties, then empties into the Mississippi south of Elk River at Dayton. The Dakota called it "Wak-pah Kahn-ghe-toka," or "River of the Crows."

During the early years when roads through Wright County were still crude, steamers landed supplies at Dayton on the Mississippi. From there, good-sized row boats carried the freight up the Crow River to Rockford, Delano and Watertown. This form of river traffic continued for several years before the roads were improved.

OTSEGO

Otsego, an Indian word meaning "welcome water," was one of the first areas to be settled in the county. Samuel Carrick established a trading post here along the Mississippi, to trade with a group of Winnebago Indians that made camp

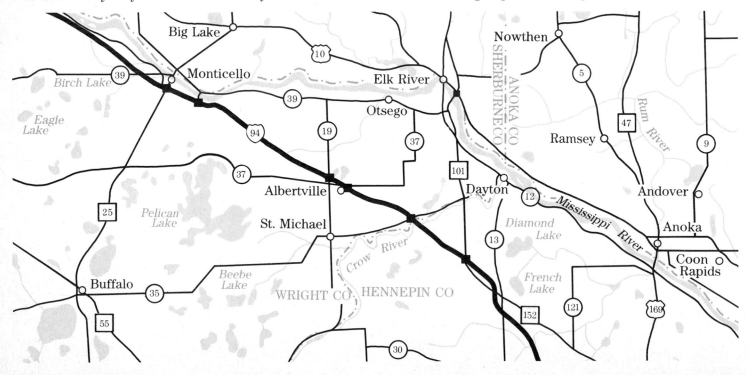

Main Street of Monticello in 1905.

in this region. Carrick also broke ground for the county's first farm. In 1852 only one Indian trail existed between Otsego and Monticello, but in the spring of 1854, a wagon road was cut along the Mississippi between these two towns.

The town of Northwood, a village promoted as the "Great Emporium of the Northwest," was located at the mouth of the Crow River. It had a large hotel, store and freight house. The town has long since rotted away.

ALBERTVILLE

For many years, Albertville was known as St. Michael's Station, a stop on the Great Northern Railroad that came through in 1882. Albertville is located near a natural prairie that was called Winneshiek Prairie, after the Winnebago chief who spent several years in this vicinity. In 1855 the Winnebago were sent to a reservation on the Blue Earth River, south of Mankato. Later they were moved again to a reservation along the Missouri River in South Dakota.

ST. MICHAEL

By 1856 most of the land around this region was occupied. Many German Catholics moved into the area and the church of St. Michael's was established that same year. The town took its name from the church. Besides the church, a hotel was raised, creamery started and a sawmill opened. At one point, daily stages moved between Albertville and St. Michael.

MONTICELLO, Pop. 3,111

The first settlers found a rolling, open prairie around this area, as compared to the almost impassible Big Woods of

the nearby region. The first settlers to stop at this prairie township were Herbert W. McCrory and Frederick Cadwell, who came here in the fall of 1852. The experiences of these pioneers were similar to those that were settling to the south of them, except that the settlers on the Monticello Prairie did not have to clear the land like those in the Big Woods. Unfortunately, when the great grasshopper plague came in August of 1856, the farmers here had larger fields and more money invested in crops, so their loss was greater. At one point in the early 1850's, this settlement was divided into two rival towns. The lower town was called Moritzious and competed aggressively for trade and river traffic from Monticello. Two small steamboats called the "Cutter" and the "Time and Tide," made stops at the towns on their runs to the mouth of the Crow Wing from St. Anthony.

Litigation between the two towns continued for some years. It wasn't until 60 legal cases later, in 1861, that the two towns united. Monticello had expectations of being a great town, but the removal of the county seat to Buffalo and years of courtroom battles with neighboring Moritzious, slowed its early growth.

During the Sioux Uprising in 1862, Monticello was overrun with frightened settlers, filled with the news that the woods were teaming with murdering Indians. People were sleeping in hallways, barns and sheds because of lack of space. The temperance element was strong during those first years. In 1858 Hull Hotchkiss started a local saloon, much to the displeasure of the people. Hotchkiss was a quiet man but his patrons raised quite a noise. One night the temperance people, dressed as Indians, broke into his saloon and destroyed most of his stock. Soon after, Hotchkiss left town.

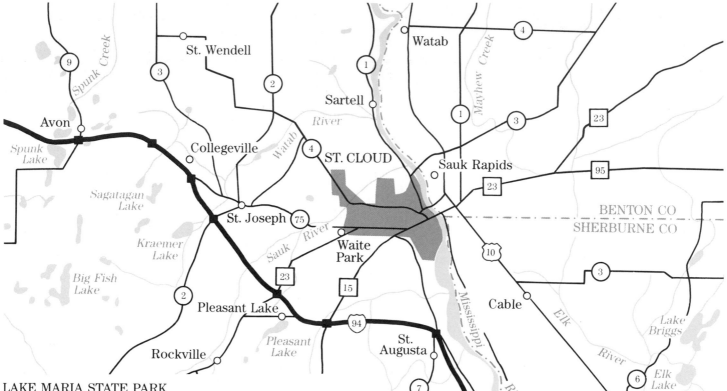

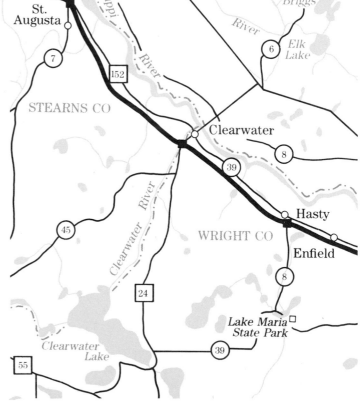

LAKE MARIA STATE PARK

This park, situated in a rolling landscape covered with deciduous trees, covers over 1,300 acres. The park maintains 25 campsites for backpackers and 13 miles of trails for hiking or cross country-skiing.

ENFIELD & HASTY

These two railway villages were platted during the late 1800's, when the railroad connected Monticello, Clearwater and St. Cloud. It was known as the Osseo branch of the St. Paul, Minneapolis and Manitoba Railway Company, which later became the Great Northern and finally the Burlington Northern Railroad.

GINSENG

After a hard winter in 1859, many of the early settlers were short of food and feared another year of locusts. A number had left the county in search of work.

That May, a Virginian named Robert Blain came to Wright County at Rockford, to buy the roots of an herb called ginseng. The Chinese used this herb for medicinal purposes. No one knew about the herb, so Blain showed them how to find the root with a hoe. In a short time almost everyone in the county was scouring the woods for this small root, which was worth up to six cents a pound. The settlers carried their bundles of ginseng to Monticello, Rockford, or Buffalo. From there the root was washed, and dried then shipped to the East Coast. A fair day's labor could bring up to five dollars, which in those days was a good sum. After a couple of years the ground became overworked, and ginseng dropped in popularity after 1861. But had it not been for the temporary relief of ginseng, many more farmers would have been forced to give up their land and their dreams.

CLEARWATER, Pop. 379

Clearwater was first settled in 1854 at the mouth of the Clearwater River, a stream that has its beginnings in Meeker County. The river provided the power for the first sawmill in 1856, the same year that ferry traffic crossed the Mississippi. Asa White, one of the first settlers, named the site El Dorado, but when he was out of town during the winter of 1855, others changed the name to Clearwater.

At one point Clearwater had the potential of becoming one of Minnesota's major cities because of its proximity to the river, the woods and the fertile country to the southwest. It all began when the Burbank Stage Company was operating between St. Paul and the Red River of the North, by way of St.Cloud. In 1856, the stage company made a proposal to the people around Clearwater; they could bring goods up the river to Clearwater, skirt St. Cloud by way of Cold Spring, and save some 15 miles. The Red River carts would then come to Clearwater and load onto barges, avoiding the low water problems at St. Cloud.

All that was needed in return was some land and stables to be donated to the stage company. But the townsite owners would not provide the free land, consequently, the stage maintained its St. Cloud connection. Clearwater today is still a small trading center.

STEAMBOAT TRAFFIC

It was during the 1850's that steamboat traffic flourished on the upper Mississippi. The first regular boat trips above the Falls of St. Anthony to Sauk Rapids began in 1850. Even after the railroads started chugging up the Mississippi, considerable effort was made to compete with the railroad lines. But rail rates were finally cut and the steamers went out of business. The last regular steamboat churned past St. Cloud in 1874.

STEARNS COUNTY, Pop. 108,161

A primitive people lived in this area shortly after the last glacier left the region, some 11,000 years ago. Numerous artificial mounds of varying shapes, give evidence that these people did occupy Stearns County and were most likely ancestors of the Dakota Indians.

Stearns County is one of the original twelve counties created by the territorial Legislature in 1855. The county should have been named "Stevens," but was misspelled by the enrolling clerk as "Stearns." Since there was a Charles Stearns with a good political reputation in the county, it was decided to let the name stand, rather than change it.

The Dakota already roamed this region when the first explorers came on the scene. Lake Mille Lacs was considered one of the capitals of this great Dakota nation; a nation that stretched westward as far as the Tetons. During the 1740's, the Ojibwe pushed into the Minnesota Territory from Lake Superior. With their more sophisticated weapons, they easily

Waiting for the train at Enfield, 1911.

MHS

pushed the Dakota from their long-held territories around Mille Lacs. It wasn't until 1825, that the two warring nations agreed upon a dividing line running through the middle of Stearns County.

Trading posts were established along the Mississippi River in the late 1700's, with Jean Baptiste Perrault setting up shop at a place he called "Grand Rapids". Today it is known as Sauk Rapids.

The explorers Cass, Schoolcraft, Beltrami and Nicollet, all passed through Stearns County in their search for the source of the Mississippi. Schoolcraft eventually recorded his discovery of the source at Lake Itasca, 140 miles to the north, during the summer of 1832.

Settlement began along the Mississippi and slowly spread westward across the county during the 1850's. Trade was well established as the Red River oxcarts creaked down from Winnipeg on the "East Plains Trail." This trail was relocated and improved upon in 1859, by the Minnesota Stage Company. Today, Interstate 94 follows much of this old stage route.

A short time later the government sponsored a survey team from St. Paul to help find a good railway route to Puget Sound. The surveyor used the route of the Red River stage trail, which later became the route of the Great Northern Railroad. Today it is one of the major routes for the Burlington Northern Company.

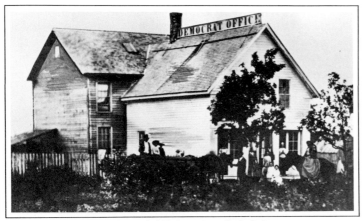

MHS

The St. Cloud office and home of editor Jane Swisshelm.

TOWN NAMES

There are many towns and villages in Stearns County named after saints. The reason for this is that many of the early settlers were German Catholics who named their communities after their churches. The German influx continued steadily from 1855 to the early 1900's. They settled in St. Cloud, St. Augusta, St. Joseph and other communities. Some Germans were craftsmen who continued in their trade, but the majority were farmers.

ST. AUGUSTA

This small village was settled by Germans in 1854, and first took the name Berlin and then Neenah. In 1856, it came to be known by its present name when Father Pierz established the St. Augusta Church here. Father Pierz was an Indian missionary at Crow Wing who believed that Stearns County was desirable for settlement. He wrote in German journals, promoting the region. Father Pierz made his rounds by foot, carrying a knapsack that contained everything necessary for a church service. Congregations at St. Cloud, St. Joseph, St. James, St. Augusta, Lake Henry, Richmond and others, claimed Father Pierz as their founder.

ST. CLOUD, Pop. 42,566

Early in 1853, a Norwegian named Ole Bergeson took claim to what is now the business district of St. Cloud. That summer, he sold his claim to John Wilson for $250. Wilson soon laid out plans for a new town. Wilson was a great admirer of Napoleon and insisted that the place be called St. Cloud

(bottom) St. Germain St., St. Cloud, 1920.

MHS

after the city Napoleon built for the Empress Josephine.

During this early period, Red River carts were crossing Stearns County to St. Cloud, where they forded the river and rested their oxen. It was this continual stream of furs from the northwest that helped St. Cloud grow. Steamboats soon met the carts here and shortened the long trip down the "East Plains Trail" by shuttling goods to St. Paul. The boats returned with supplies to be carried back to the Red River Valley on the carts.

Early St. Cloud was divided into three towns; Upper, Middle and Lower. Upper town was organized by General Sylvanus Lowry, a Southerner. Middle Town was settled by Easterners, such as John Wilson, and Lower Town was occupied by Germans. General Sylvanus, and a number of his neighbors in Upper Town owned slaves, as did their friends who brought them when they came to visit. Jane Grey Swisshelm, a feminist and editor of the local paper, wrote many scathing editorials about this situation, which was destined to plunge the nation into civil war. Soon after one of her editorials, a night raid, led by some people from Upper Town, destroyed Swisshelm's press and scattered the expensive type. With the approach of the Civil War, the Southerners left the area.

A stage route, which today is followed by I-94, carried the mail from 1851 to 1859. This mail was the only form of communication with the outside world. The stage drivers were usually big-hearted, fun-loving men, who were sought out when they rode into town. They became the eyes and ears of these new settlements.

St. Cloud, also called "the Granite City," is an important quarrying center. Its fine-grained granites have been used in notable buildings across the nation as well as the Minnesota State Capitol and the St. Paul Cathedral. The granite was first quarried in 1868. In a few short years, thousands of tons were being used annually. Some of Minnesota's granites are among the oldest rocks on the earth's surface. They were formed under mountain chains that eroded away millions of years ago, ultimately exposing this granite. Today, the State Reformatory occupies the site of St. Cloud's first quarry.

ST. JOSEPH, Pop. 2,994

Peter Loso was the first of a number of Germans that settled in this spot in 1854. Later this area took its name from a church started here by Father Pierz. The College of St. Benedict's, run by Benedictine nuns, is located at St. Joseph. This order began in Italy during the sixth century.

The nuns came here from St. Cloud in 1864, and always kept a small number of boarders, many of which were prospects for sisterhood. After 1875, many young women came here wishing to be educated. Because of their small facilities,

Columbian Book Store, St. Cloud, 1901.

MHS

St. Benedict's began constructing the main school building in 1879 and soon, this was a favorite school for women in Stearns County.

COLLEGEVILLE

South of the Interstate, in a thick stand of evergreens, lies St. John's University and Abbey, established in 1856. A small group of Benedictine Fathers came to St. Cloud when it was advertised as a city with 200 inhabitants. All they found were a few crude buildings and a general store. The Fathers accepted some land south of St. Cloud on the banks of the Mississippi and applied for a state seminary charter. In 1857 they held the first class, which consisted of only five students.

St. John's moved to their present location in 1865, with many of the present buildings erected during the early 1900's. Today St. John's University is one of the largest of the Benedictine order and the school is highly respected throughout the nation.

AVON, Pop. 804

Avon, a small railway village situated on Spunk Lake, was first settled by Nick Keppers, who moved his claim from St. Joseph in 1863 and built a one room shanty here. A small lake northeast of town is named after him. In 1880 his brother constructed the first grain elevator along the tracks of the St. Paul, Minneapolis and Manitoba Railroad.

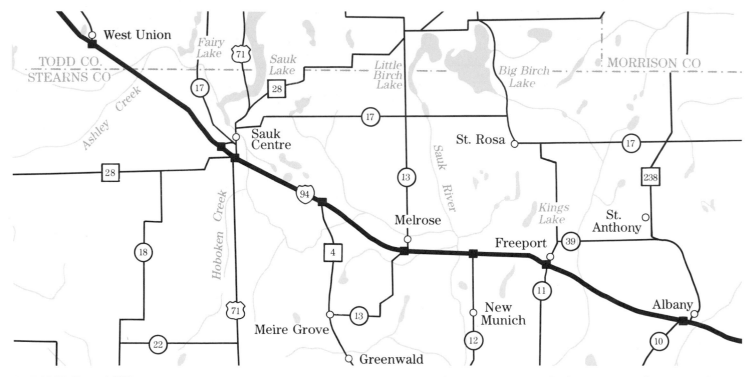

ALBANY, Pop. 1,569

Most of the region around Albany was covered with oak and maple when John Schwinghammer came here looking for a home in 1862. The St. Paul, Minneapolis and Manitoba line was constructed through here in 1871, after which a station was built and named Albany. A hotel was quickly built that same year. The Soo Line came through the town in 1907, connecting it to Duluth.

FREEPORT, Pop. 563

The village of Freeport came into existence shortly after the railroad came through in 1871. John Hoeschen, a German immigrant, opened the first store, while his brother opened a hotel. The town was first named Oak Station, but many were concerned that their mail would be confused with the town of Osakis, 30 miles northwest, so it was changed to Freeport, the home town of some settlers from Illinois.

MOSQUITOES

During the early days of this region, the population was small. On the average, there was about one family to each four square miles. The only company they had were birds, animals, and during the summer, mosquitoes. Because of the many marshes, millions of insects hatched daily. With no screens, the settlers found little rest from the pests, day or night. Many were driven permanently from the region because of these insects.

NEW MUNICH, Pop. 302

As early as 1855, two men named Burns and Sutton built a few small buildings, just south of the present village of New Munich. They also ran a small "wayside" inn for the stage that ran north-south through this part of the county. The town actually settled around the church, which was built

Farm boys and their favorite cattle. Photo/H.D. Ayer.

MHS

halfway between the homes of two early settlers he town received its name from a Bavarian hunter, who came from Munich and lived in this region for several years. In 1861 John Hroehler, from Ohio, built a small brewery whose beer became quite popular throughout the county.

At one time, New Munich had a school, bookbindery, brewery, creamery, harness maker, elevator, lumberyard, gristmill, drug store, two hardware shops, two hotels, three general stores and three shoemakers.

SAUK RIVER

This river was named after a small band of Sauk Indians that occupied the region at one time. The river has its beginnings in Lake Osakis, in the hill area of Douglas County. The Sauk flows some 100 miles, passing through many natural lakes of unusual clarity and finally empties into the Mississippi at Sauk Rapids. A dam is located at Melrose.

MELROSE, Pop. 2,409

This town was settled at a ford in the river on the stage trail between the Red River Valley and St. Cloud. It was named after Melissa Rose, the daughter of an early settler. For seven years, beginning in 1871, Melrose was the terminus of the railroad, making the town a marketing center and a jumping-off spot for the Red River Valley.

SAUK CENTRE, Pop. 3,709

Located on the southern tip of Big Sauk Lake, this town, like Melrose, grew up around a ford in the river. Because the town was considered the center point between Lake Osakis and Sauk Rapids, it was named Sauk Centre. A boulder on the corner of 7th and South Main St. marks the site of a stockade put up during the Sioux Uprising in 1862.

Sauk Centre was also the home town of Sinclair Lewis, one of the most influential authors of his time. His novel, MAIN STREET, upset many locals because it stripped away the facade of charm and innocence of small town life. Many Sauk Centre residents took the book personally. Sauk Centre disowned Sinclair for some time, but after becoming the first American to win the Nobel Prize in literature in 1930, the town's appreciation grew. Now there is a street and interpretive center named after him. The center is located at the junction of I-94 and Highway 71. Lewis wrote 16 novels, six of which were best-sellers.

Alexandria to Melrose stage, 1876.

MHS

Early Sauk Centre school buses.

MHS

STAGE LINES

The Minnesota Stage Company was formed in 1859 by J.C. Burbank, with several other men. The wooden coaches were usually pulled along by a four-horse team and scheduled to run from St. Paul to St. Cloud, then up the Sauk River Valley northwest to the state border. Stage stops were located about every 20 miles, where horses could be changed and patrons given a rest from their bumpy ride. The stops were little more than crude shacks, where salt pork and bread were often served. Many of the travelers carried guns with them and when a lake was passed that contained waterfowl, the stage stopped so a passenger could shoot a few ducks.

Red River carts started using this newly improved stage route instead of their "Middle Trail," some ten or so miles to the south. Their passage to the St. Cloud settlement did much for the development of that city. At West Union, the old stage trail swings a couple of miles north to Osakis and parallels the Interstate to Fergus Falls.

DOUGLAS COUNTY, Pop. 23,839

Douglas County was named for Stephen A. Douglas, a Senator from Illinois who was influential in admitting Minnesota to the Union in 1858.

When the first settlers came across this region, many were taken by the beauty of the land and its many lakes. But no land was homesteaded until the late 1850's. For many years this region was crossed by the Red River carts on their trips to St. Paul and later to St. Cloud. Word of the lake region began to attract many new arrivals to this country and by 1859, a number of new settlers had come. In spite of this settlement, much of the county remained a wilderness. The main source of food and money was hunting, furs and fishing. But the Sioux Uprising of 1862 scattered many of these pioneers, slowing early settlement.

OSAKIS, Pop. 1,355

This town, and the lake it was named for, were originally called "Sakis," an Ojibwe word meaning, "place of danger." The area was on the dividing line between the lands of the Dakota and Ojibwe nations. For years Sakis was a dangerous place for any Indian to visit. Settlers began to move here in 1859 and added the "O" to Sakis. Osakis became a stage stop on the route to Fort Abercrombie, located on the Red River in North Dakota. The town also produced flour for a number of years called O-Sa-Kis, and was sold throughout the state.

In 1866, there were hardly any women eligible for marriage in this town filled with men. That year, quite a scene developed when Mrs. Tannehill came into town on the stage with five "charming" daughters. It was reported that in a few short months she was living alone in Osakis.

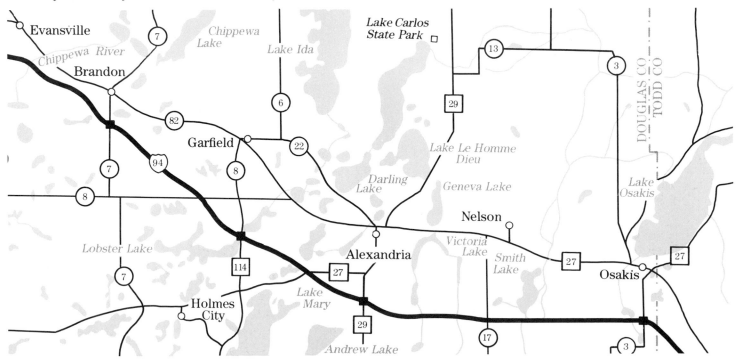

ALEXANDRIA, Pop. 7,608

During the summer of 1858, two brothers, Alexander and William Kincaid, moved up from a settlement they had started at Lake Minnewaska (Glenwood City), pitching their tent on the shores of Lake Agnes. Here they built a log cabin on a knoll just south of where the Burlington Northern station stands. Others followed them to this beautiful spot and a townsite committee soon formed. The area was named Alexandria, in honor of Alexander Kincaid. Most of the settlers came up along the edge of the woods from the south. The townsite company put up a log hotel named the "Gregory," and for many years this was a favorite resort for settlers.

In 1859, a trail was cut through the woods, connecting St. Cloud and Breckenridge by way of Alexandria. Interstate 94 follows much of this route. With its location along this trail, Alexandria soon became a convenient stopping place on the route, assuring this new community's success. In just a few short years, over 2,000 Red River carts passed down its streets. Today, Alexandria is a popular fishing and resort area.

KENSINGTON RUNESTONE

Alexandria is the home of the famous and controversial Kensington Runestone, a runic stone many claim is proof that America was visited by Norsemen before Columbus.

This interesting story begins in 1898 when a Swedish farmer, named Olaf Ohman, dug out a 250 pound tablet from under the roots of a poplar tree. The stone aroused excitement, since no one could read the inscription. But experts at the University of Minnesota claimed that it was not authentic, so Ohman used the stone as a doorstop for some time.

The inscription reads: "8 Goths (Swedes) and 22 Norwegians, upon a journey of discovery from Vinland westward. We had a camp by 2 skerries (islands) one day's journey north of this stone. We were out fishing one day. When we returned home we found 10 men red with blood and dead. Ave Virgo Maria, save us from evil." On the edge of the tablet was a further inscription: "We have 10 men by the sea to look after our vessel 14 days' journey from this island. Year 1362." To this day, reputable scholars disagree as to the stone's authenticity.

PRAIRIE FIRES

During the fall and early spring when the prairie grasses and fields were dry, the threat of fire made every farmer nervous. Many nights the sky would light up with the ominous orange of a nearby fire. Farmers would rush to help their neighbors and try to protect their farms and homes. Much has been written about these horrible fires which raged uncontrollably across miles of prairie and farmland.

A temporary duck pond on Alexandria's Main Street in 1876.

BRANDON, Pop. 473

Two miles north of the present village, Henry Gager maintained a farm and stage station along the route between Breckenridge and St. Cloud. After the Sioux Uprising, people began to settle here, and the small town was called Ojibwe. Later, a few stores went up, and a post office was established. The name was changed to Brandon, the Vermont birthplace of Stephen Douglas, after whom the county is named. In 1878, tracks of the St. Paul, Minneapolis and Manitoba Railroad were laid just two miles south of Brandon. This, of course, spelled the end of old Brandon, as people began moving down to the tracks where the town exists today.

CHIPPEWA RIVER

The Chippewa River, a tributary of the Minnesota, has its beginning in Fish Lake in Otter Tail County. Occasionally, warring Ojibwe would travel down this 130-mile-long river, making raids on the Dakota (Sioux) who lived along the Minnesota. The river, in effect, became a war road and was named by the Dakota after their hated enemies. Chippewa was the white man's mistranslation of the Indian name, Ojibwe.

EVANSVILLE, Pop. 571

Evansville is situated in a rich farming area of Douglas County. A stage driver, named Evans, maintained a log cabin shanty here in 1859, as a resting place between Fort Abercrombie and St. Cloud. Evans was killed four years later during the Sioux Uprising. Most people in this region fled for their safety, taking along everything they owned. Ten years after the Uprising, Jacob Shaner came here and was captivated by this prairie surrounded by groves and lakes. A town was laid out, and by 1879 the railroad reached the area.

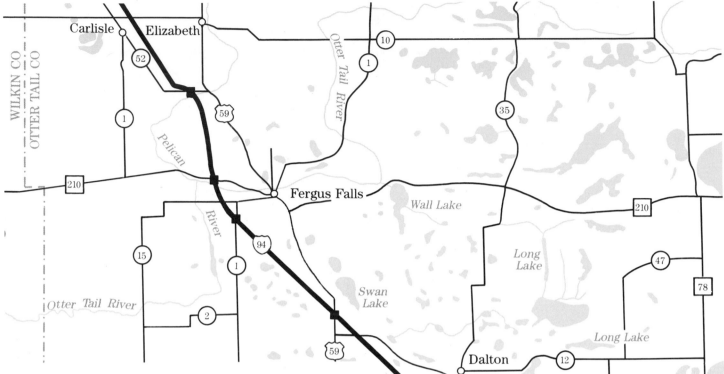

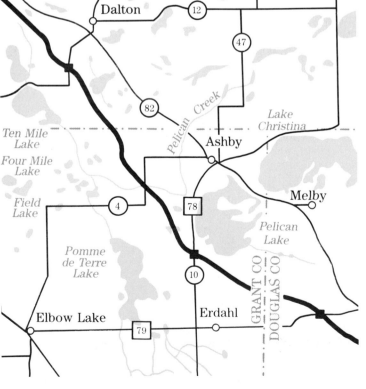

THE DAKOTA NATION

By the time the white man happened upon the scene, this Indian nation of 7 loosely-aligned tribes, calling themselves Dakota, roamed the region from Minnesota to the Tetons. They became known as the Sioux, from the term "Nadouessioux"–meaning enemy, a name given to them by the Ojibwe. These seven different bands represented several areas of the West. In Minnesota the primary tribes were: the Mdewakanton, Wahpekute, Wahpeton and Sisseton. By the 1700's the Ojibwe had pushed into Minnesota from the East. Equipped with newly-bought guns, they forced the Dakota further south, creating a division in the state that lasted until the banishment of the Dakota, after the Uprising of 1862. Bloody encounters continued for many years between these two powerful nations.

But it was the Dakota, more than any other Indian nation, that resented the intrusion of the white man: the whites hunted their sacred grounds, cut down the forests, wiped out the buffalo, and drove many other species of animals from the woods and prairie. The Dakota negotiated some poor and certainly questionable treaties, and soon found themselves on small reservations along the Minnesota River, having received little else in return. They quickly developed a dependency on the white man, with whiskey creating a

Dakota women and children, 1880.

MHS

particularly devastating effect upon their culture.

Still, the settlers feared the Dakota who roamed from time to time back to their old hunting grounds. Few understood their culture, let alone respected it. It was a case of two cultures with two different needs and philosophies competing for the same space. The simple, hardworking immigrants who were looking for a new life, could not allow the Indian to stand in their way. They had sacrificed everything to make a new start. It was a matter of survival. But to the Dakota it became a matter of survival as well.

In August of 1862, they took a final stand which became known as the Sioux Uprising. The Indians lashed out against the unsuspecting whites with such ferocity, that the southern and western part of the state went into a panic that took years to overcome. But as Little Crow, leader of the Dakota, had predicted, "Kill one, two, or ten, and ten times ten will come to kill you." Indeed, the Dakota paid dearly. Those that were not killed, lost their land, forfeited all payments due them, and were ultimately banished from the state. It was only 120 years ago that this state paid a bounty of $500 for each Dakota Indian scalp. Little Crow finally said, "We are only little herds of buffalo. The great herds that covered the prairies are no more."

POMME DE TERRE LAKE & RIVER

This lake and river were named from a French word meaning "apple of the earth." In reality it referred to a prairie turnip, with eyes like a potato. These were a highly-valued food by the Dakota, who harvested them on the upland prairie of the southwest. The Pomme De Terre River begins in the lake region northwest of Dalton, in Stalker Lake. Flowing some 100 miles to the south, it winds its way through many clear lakes and marshes abundant with waterfowl. Southwest of Appleton it enters Marsh Lake, a part of the Minnesota River. It is also a part of the Lac qui Parle Wildlife Area.

PELICAN LAKE

The early maps called this Lake Ellenora. But sometime later, locals began referring to it as Pelican Lake because of the large number of pelicans that stopped here during migration.

POMME DE TERRE VILLAGE

In 1870, a village named Pomme de Terre was laid out in Section 24, along the river by the same name. The village was located a short distance from a stockade which had been erected by soldiers in 1862. The village seemed to be getting a good start, boasting of two stores, two blacksmiths, a grist-mill, elevator, hotel and saloon. But the railroad passed to the north and this town, like so many others, faded away.

LEAF HILLS

On the north shore of Lake Christina are the Seven Sisters, a series of hills extending northeastward some 20 miles. This range, known as the Leaf Hills, are the only hills in this part of the state that can be seen for any distance. The Leaf Hills represent the farthest advance of a glacier. Hundreds of lakes were formed along this ridge. Some of the hills reach up to 350 feet in height.

CONTINENTAL DIVIDE

Five miles northwest of the Dalton exit, the Interstate crosses the continental divide, separating the Minnesota River drainage basin from the Red River basin. In other words, if you took a cup of water and poured it on this divide, one half would flow north up the Red River into Hudson Bay, then on to the North Atlantic. The other half would drain into the Minnesota River, then to the Mississippi and eventually into the Gulf of Mexico.

OTTER TAIL COUNTY, Pop. 51,937

The county name has an Ojibwe origin, dating back to a time when the Indians had a camp by a lake called Otter Tail. There they fished from a spit of sand, created by the stream that washed its sediment into the lake. This sandbar resembled the tail of an otter, an animal once common to the streams of Minnesota. The lake and river came to be known by the Indians as Otter Tail. When the lumbermen came through, forcing the Indians from their camp, they destroyed this sandbar so as to better maneuver their logs.

FIRST WHITES.

French and British traders and explorers trekked through this county in the late 1700's, with some trading at a small post on Otter Tail Lake. The Columbia and American Fur Companies were each represented. Joseph Nicollet's map, drawn as a result of his explorations in 1836, detailed this county for the first time. An expedition under Major Samuel Woods, came to Otter Tail Lake in 1849 and camped at the ruins of the old trading posts. They found the lake clear and full of fish. Here they also found the Ojibwe making large quantities of maple sugar. Woods claimed that "for fifty miles in all directions, this lake is among the most beautiful and fertile in the world…this region is the garden spot of the northwest."

EARLY SETTLEMENT.

It wasn't until the middle 1850's that the white man staked out his claims across Otter Tail County. But even then, settlement started slowly. During the winter of 1859-60, a report came out of St.Paul stating that 48 persons in the county were attending school. From the same report, 36 people were listed as illiterate.

The Sioux Uprising of 1862 had scattered the settlers in a panic, with many seeking refuge at Fort Abercrombie on the Red River. It took the settlers a couple of years after the Uprising to gather enough nerve to resettle.

A central Minnesota fishing party gathered along the shore in 1917.

MHS

The first settlement of any consequence was accomplished by a group of Mormons, seeking a secure place to live after the upheaval in their Bringham Young Church, in Illinois. They arrived on the north side of Clitherall Lake in 1865, and lived peaceably among the Ojibwe for many years. The colony had to be self-sufficient since the nearest store was 65 miles away, requiring a 12-day trip behind their slow moving oxen. The Mormons made all their own tools and furniture and managed fairly well.

With the Dakota banned from the state after the Uprising, settlers began complaining that Ojibwe braves were wandering from the reservations, hunting and trapping around Otter Tail County. The whites felt the Indians were getting to the furs before they were and frightening the game, making it more difficult for them to hunt.

FERGUS FALLS, Pop. 12,519

This town was named after a Scotchman called James Fergus, who actually never set foot in the area. However, Fergus did supply a dog team and a half-breed guide to a man named Joseph Whitford, who set out from Little Falls in 1857 to settle a new town. Whitford worked his way west to the Red River, where he staked out a town he called Graham's Point. But a short time later, an Indian family told him of a better site, some 20 miles east, near a falls on the Otter Tail River. Whitford investigated the spot and liked what he saw. He staked out this claim and named it after his friendly supplier, Mr. Fergus.

An 1860 census said this about Whitford. "Age, 35; farmer; real property worth, $500; born in Vermont; insane." Five years later, James Whitford was killed by Indians during the Sioux Uprising, as he poled his boat along the Red River near Fort Abercrombie.

The Fergus Co-op Creamery 4th of July float, circa 1900.

Lincoln Avenue in Fergus Falls, 1900.

In 1866, Ernest Buse and his family passed the Clitherall settlement and stopped by the roaring falls where Whitford had his cabin. "Live or die, this is our home," said Buse. Settlers soon followed and a log cabin served as the first post office. The German postmaster couldn't read English, however. So when someone came for their mail, he emptied the sack on the floor and let the person sift through it.

Fergus Falls, needing an economic boost, waited desperately for the railroad to reach them from the Twin Cities. Rumors had the line coming in 1872. By the following year though, not even a work crew could be seen on the horizon. Some of the citizens decided to take matters into their own hands and formed the Red River Slack Water Navigation Company. Its purpose was to ship goods up the Otter Tail River some 35 miles northeast, to the Perham railroad station. The trip was made on a small barge, but funding was impossible to get and during dry months the trip was hopeless. The idea was eventually scrapped. In 1879, the railroad of James J. Hill finally reached Fergus Falls.

In 1919, a devastating June tornado destroyed much of Fergus Falls, killing 60 people.

CARLISLE, ROTHSAY AND LAWNDALE

These towns are railway villages that grew up along the St. Paul, Minneapolis, and Manitoba line, built in 1879. This line later became the Great Northern and finally the Burlington Northern Railroad.

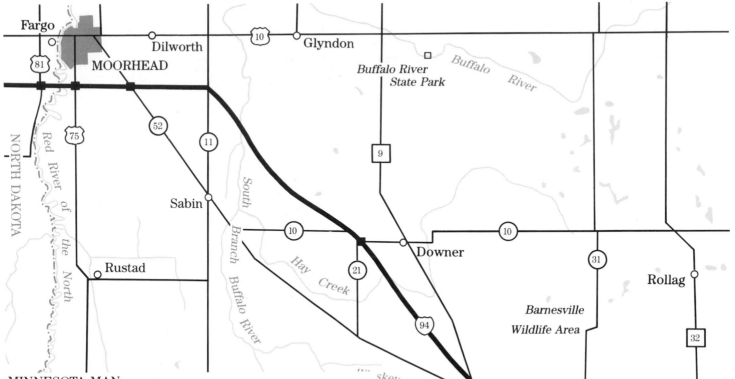

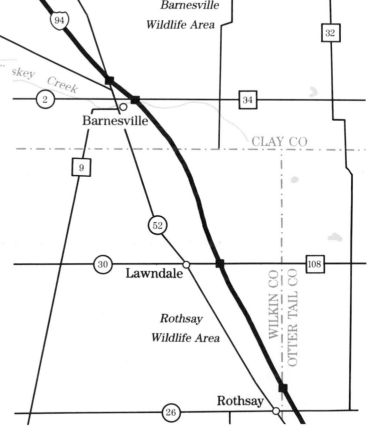

MINNESOTA MAN

Just north of Pelican Rapids a road crew unearthed a skeleton in 1931. The importance of this discovery was that the skeleton was buried under nine feet of silt, laid down by an ancient glacial lake some 11,000 years ago. Called the Minnesota Man, the skeleton was actually a young woman, who apparently drowned in this lake. She became the first proof that a prehistoric people occupied this region of North America, and that these people might have used the Bering Strait land bridge in Alaska, to enter North America from Asia. Found with the skeleton was an elk antler knife and an interesting conch shell. The shell indicated to historians that there had been contact with southern regions, since the Gulf of Mexico is the closest source of conch shells.

BARNESVILLE, Pop. 2,207

Started as a railway village in 1879, Barnesville was named after George S. Barnes, a wheat farmer. Today, Barnesville is a shipping center for wheat, potatoes and livestock. Its grain elevators dominate the horizon.

Barnesville is located on the Campbell beach level of prehistoric Lake Agassiz. Northwest of Barnesville, the Interstate traverses the now-dried lake bed of Agassiz.

LAKE AGASSIZ GEOLOGY

Toward the close of the last stage of glaciation about 11,000 years ago, the ice receded from central Iowa toward the north, across the continental divide, near Browns Valley in west-central Minnesota. The divide sends the flow of water north to Hudson Bay or south to the Mississippi River.

Because the ice had retreated to the Hudson Bay side of the divide, the melting ice was blocked on one side by the divide and on the other side by ice. Thus, Glacial Lake Agassiz was created. Its maximum depth was 700 feet and it covered an area larger than today's combined Great Lakes.

The outlet of this glacial lake flowed through the valley of the present Minnesota River. It was called Glacial River Warren and was responsible for the deep, broad river valley we see today. When the northern ice eventually melted, the lake drained into Hudson Bay, leaving behind a rich sedimentary deposit which now makes up the soils of the Red River Valley.

The lake's level slowly dropped as the ice blockage to the north melted. Many of the early settlers traveled over the ridges formed by years of wave action. More than fifty ridges have now been identified, with most of them in Canada. In Minnesota, two main beaches can still be discerned. One is Herman Beach, the outermost beach of the lake which held this shoreline for 500 years. The other is Campbell Beach. This beach existed for 2,000 years, thereby creating the most extensive and visible beach in Minnesota. The lake finally disappeared altogether, about 6,000 years before the birth of Christ.

MOORHEAD, Pop. 29,998

Moorhead developed into one of Minnesota's larger cities because of its natural terminus for most forms of transportation. The early routes of the Red River oxcarts passed along the east bank of the river. This gradually became a steamboat landing for the Hudson Bay Company steamers, which plied the Red River and the town was connected to Duluth and the Twin Cities by railroads and highways.

This muddy frontier settlement was named Moorhead in 1871, after Dr. William G. Moorhead, a director of the Northern Pacific line. The Northern Pacific was chartered by the U.S. Congress to connect the port city of Duluth to some future spot on the Pacific coast. It was formed in Duluth by the Jay Cooke Company. Because of financial problems, however, the line did not pass Moorhead until 1878.

In the meantime, early visitors to this fertile Red River region didn't realize the farming possibilities of this flat land. Many believed that the treeless prairie had no agricultural value. In fact, General Sibley wrote of the territory, "It is fit

Steamboats still plyied the Red River in 1880.

MHS

only for the Indians and the devil."

One historian told about a settler who came into the barroom of a local hotel proudly showing off his vegetables. The settler was laughed at, since nobody believed the vegetables were grown there. Outraged, the farmer pulled a gun from his bundle of carrots and peas and shot one of the disbelievers.

A license to run a ferry, across the river to the "lawless" hamlet of Fargo, cost $15. A toll of 25 cents was required per horse-drawn wagon, with 5 cents a head for additional animals.

By 1882, Moorhead had become one of the important centers of the state with 14 hotels and restaurants. Among those was the pride of Moorhead, the Grand Pacific. It cost $165,000 and had 140 rooms. The hotel eventually began to lose money and was later closed by James J. Hill.

RED RIVER STEAMBOATS

In 1859, the St. Paul Chamber of Commerce offered $2,000 to anyone who could establish steamboat service on the Red River, connecting it with the stage lines that operated between Breckenridge and St. Paul. That winter, Anson Northrup dismantled his small steamer at Little Falls, and with 34 teams and some 60 men, hauled the boat in pieces across the frozen state. It was hastily reassembled and put into operation. But Northrup lost interest in the venture and sold the boat to the Minnesota Stage Company.

ROUTE 55, TO GLENWOOD, ALEXANDRIA

MHS

Fishing from the dock at an early Minnesota resort.

WRIGHT COUNTY, Pop. 58,962

This county is named after Silas Wright, a New York statesman. The name was chosen in 1855 by a friend of his, W. G. McCrory, who settled along the Mississippi at Monticello.

Most of the county was originally covered with a variety of hardwoods. These forests were part of the Big Woods, a 40-mile-wide-band of deciduous trees that started 100 miles northwest of the Twin Cities and continued south to Mankato. In this area, the forest was interspersed with numerous lakes, marshes and some natural meadow lands along the Mississippi. Cranberries grew in the marshes and were picked by the Indians to sell in St. Paul, long before the whites settled in this county.

Wright County was crossed by glaciers several times. In their slow movements these glaciers dumped debris and scoured out depressions that formed the irregular hills and valleys. Many of the valleys filled with water and became the lakes of today.

Looking at the state map, you can see an arching belt of lakes, beginning at Lake Minnetonka and extending westward towards Willmar, then continuing up to Alexandria and Fergus Falls. This chain of lakes was formed near a point where one of the last glaciers stopped. The lakes belong to a terminal moraine system, an area where glacial debris was left along its outer edge.

EARLY EXPLORERS AND TRAPPERS

The first whites found this county richly forested with red and white oak, sugar maple, elm and basswood. They called this region the Big Woods, since it spread over a 40-mile-

131

wide band that started 100 miles northwest of the Twin Cities then down to Mankato. The woods separated the prairie of the southwest from the spruce and pine forests of the northeast.

When Father Hennepin was in this region in 1680, most of Minnesota was occupied by the Dakota Indians. Around 1740, the Ojibwe, armed with weapons from the French, pushed across Lake Superior and drove the Dakota from their strategic locations at Mille Lacs and Sandy Lake to points south and west. From then on, the Dakota became a people of the Minnesota prairie until their expulsion from the state in 1862. Wright County was the dividing line between the warring tribes of the Dakota and Ojibwe.

The first white man to establish himself in the county was Edmund Brissett, a French trader with a post near Lake Harriet. In 1850, he cut a trail from Lakes Harriet and Calhoun through the Big Woods, north of Buffalo to Lake Pulaski. There he maintained a post, trading with the Winnebago Indians until 1855. His trail greatly aided the settlers as they moved westward into Wright County during the 1850's.

EARLY ROADS

Unlike counties to the south, where wagons could pass anywhere on the prairie, the new settlers of Wright County had difficulty moving west through the dense woods. Those that left the trail carved out by Brissett had to cut their own way. In 1856, a road between Minneapolis and Rockford, known as the Rockford Road, was laid out by way of Hamel. For two years the men of Wright County worked in the neighboring Hennepin County, building bridges over the many streams and trying to keep the road clear. The project became a sore point with the Wright County workers, who felt that the Hennepin County residents gave little help to this endeavor. The following year, the road was continued to Buffalo, and basically follows today's Highway 55.

ROCKFORD, Pop. 2,028

This area was settle in 1855 near a rocky ford in the Crow River (from which the town received its name). The first settlers came by way of Hamel, cutting a road which enabled them to transport parts for a steam sawmill. That was in 1856. This road later became known as the Rockford Road. The sawmill was an important source of construction lumber used in the building of new homes. Two years later, a dam was built on the Crow River, providing power for the new grain and feed mill. There was little doubt by the founding fathers that Rockford would be an important city.

In those early days, a band of Winnebago Indians set up a winter camp near Rockford to hunt deer. Many of the settlers thought the Indians were taking too many, leaving

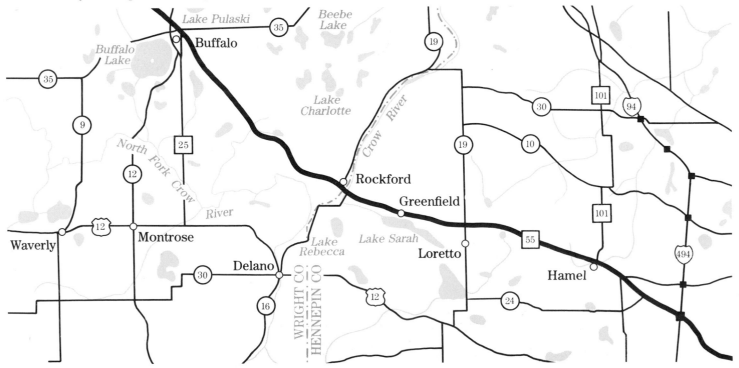

(left) Rockford July 4th reunion of Civil War veterans, 1896. (bottom) Early Minnesota farmers.

few for them. But the situation eased when the Winnebago were forced onto a reservation along the Blue Earth River, south of Mankato. The Winnebago were once a strong Indian nation who lived in Wisconsin. But white settlement pushed them south onto reservations in Iowa. From Iowa, they were forced to resettle in Minnesota, until their lands were appropriated and they were finally moved to the Dakotas.

CROW RIVER

The South Fork of the Crow River passes through Rockford on its journey some 30 miles north to the Mississippi. This river has its beginnings west of here in Meeker and Kandiyohi Counties, emptying into the Mississippi, south of Elk River. The Dakota called it "Wak-pah-Kahn-ghe-toka," or "River of the Crows."

In the days when roads were still crude, steamers landed supplies at Dayton, on the Mississippi. From there, good-sized rowboats carried freight up the Crow River to Rockford, Delano and Watertown. This form of river traffic continued for several years before the roads were improved.

GINSENG

After a hard winter in 1859, many of the early settlers were short of food and feared another year of locusts. Many had left the county in search of work. That May, a Virginian named Robert Blain came to Wright County at Rockford, to buy the roots of an herb called ginseng. The Chinese used this herb for medicinal purposes. No one knew about the herb, so Blain showed them how to find the root with a hoe.

In a short time, almost everyone in the county was scouring the woods for this small root, which was worth up to six cents a pound. The settlers carried their bundles of ginseng to Monticello, Rockford, or Buffalo. From there, the root was washed and dried, then shipped to the East Coast. A fair day's labor could bring up to five dollars, which in those days was a good sum. After a couple of years, the ground eventually became overworked, and after 1861, ginseng dropped in popularity. Had it not been for the temporary income from ginseng however, many more farmers would have been forced to give up their land and their dreams.

SOO LINE RAILROAD

The Minneapolis, St. Paul & Sault Ste. Marie Railway Company, eventually became known as the "Soo Line." It was chartered in 1884 and made its first run between Sault Ste.

Marie, Michigan, and Minneapolis, a distance of 500 miles. The Soo stretched into Wright County in 1886, on its way to North Dakota. The railroad was undoubtedly the most important factor in the development of Wright County. Now lumber could be hauled cheaply, along with all the other supplies necessary for the growing settlements. Farmers could also begin raising food for distant markets, which were now as close as the nearest railway station.

BUFFALO, Pop. 4,560

This town was named from nearby Buffalo Lake, a lake noted by early fur traders for its large number of buffalo fish. The location was once the favorite camping spot of the Dakota before it became settled by whites. During the summer they picked cranberries and fished, while in winter they

Annandale Main Street, 1903.

returned to hunt deer. By 1855, the Winnebago Indians had a large village here, where the women tended the corn while the braves hunted. The town's first settler was Augustus Prime, who stopped here among the Indians and built a cabin.

MOSQUITOES

During the early days of this region, the population was small. On the average, there was about one family to each four square miles. The only company these settlers had were birds, animals and during the summer, mosquitoes. Because of the many marshes shaded by the Big Woods, millions of these insects hatched daily. With no screens, the settlers found little rest from the pests, day or night. Many were driven permanently from the region because of these insects. But as the woods were cleared, some of the pools began to dry, reducing the number of mosquitoes.

Sunday afternoon ride, 1900.

A quiet afternoon on a Stearns County lake.

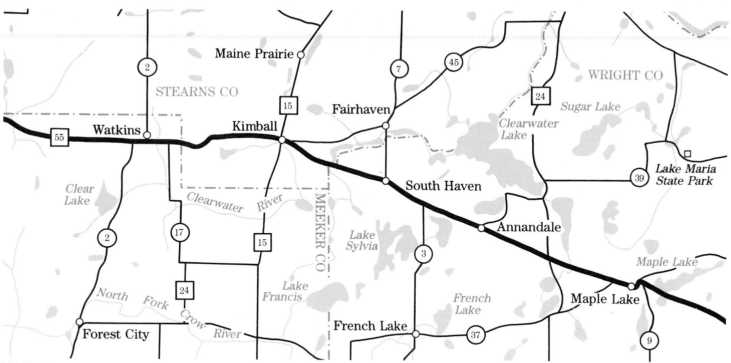

MAPLE LAKE, Pop. 1,132

The area around Maple Lake was originally timberland, interspersed with lakes and meadows. One of the larger lakes was named for the maples that lined its shore and it was from this lake, that the town later took its name.

A road from Monticello to Forest City was cut through this region during the winter of 1855-56, providing an important link to the Mississippi River.

The following year, Dr. Rufus Sargent laid out a village on the northwest shore of Maple Lake and called it Geneva. Two hundred acres were platted and shares were sold to people out East. A man named McCord, from Reading, Pennsylvania, bought what he thought would be a store, hotel and home in this new town of Geneva. But when he arrived, all he found was an unfinished shanty with a few scattered goods. Geneva never really developed, but before it folded, its name was changed to Maple Lake. The present village is located two miles south, where the Soo Line built a station in 1866.

Before the railroad came, many settlers were ready to leave the Maple Lake region. Then word came from Rockford that people were making good money picking the ginseng root. The settlers started their search for this mysterious root that lies one to four inches below the ground. A good number of destitute settlers made enough money to keep food on the table until better times arrived.

ANNANDALE, Pop. 1,568.

There are several versions of the way Annandale received its name, but the one proposed in the history of Wright County, explains that in 1886, the town was originally called Abbyville. This name caused problems with the post office, since another city in the state had the same name. So Senator Washburn, one of the townsite founders, was asked to pick a different name. Soon afterwards, he gazed upon a poster promoting a stage show featuring Izzie Annandale—hence the name Annandale was given to the town. Another version states that the town was named after the Annan River in southern Scotland.

The first winter was one of the most severe in this young town's history. For most of the winter, the snow depth stayed at three feet and the temperatures below zero. It was a desolate and lonely sight, with the railroad tracks passing the two small buildings that marked the town. A narrow sleigh trail passed by the buildings and out again into the empty countryside.

During the Sioux Uprising, wide-scale panic swept the western part of the county and many of the settlers sought refuge at the small village of Clearwater. However, most of the real property damage was done by whites who vandalized the homes left vacant by the frightened settlers. There was a second scare in 1863, a year after most of the Dakota had

135

been chased from the state. Two or three Indians had been spotted near the future site of Annandale. It was reported by a farmer named Charles Dakin, that the Indians fired bullets and arrows at his cows. Upon closer inspection, Dakin found a calf with an arrow in its back, and a cow with a bullet in its throat. Nothing further is said about what happened as a result of this incident.

SOUTH HAVEN, Pop. 205

This village began shortly after the Soo Line Railroad was built in 1887. They called it South Haven, since it sat a couple of miles below the town of Fair Haven in Stearns County.

CLEARWATER RIVER

This stream has its beginnings in Meeker County. It passes under Highway 55 and continues another 16 miles northeast to the Mississippi, at Clearwater. Some small tributaries of the Clearwater are trout streams.

MHS

Farm family portrait.

STEARNS COUNTY, Pop. 108,161

Stearns is the largest county in the southern half of the state, with an area of 1,393 square miles. Forests cover a good portion of it, with the remainder made up of rolling prairie, lakes and streams. Today, Stearns is one of the top dairying counties in the state.

After the last glacier retreated from this area about 11,000 years ago, a primitive people lived here. Numerous artificial mounds of different shapes have been found here and in the area near Paynesville. Most likely, these people were ancestors of the Dakota. By the time the first explorers came on the scene, this was the land of the Dakota nation. Lake Mille Lacs was considered one of the capitals of this great nation that extended westward to the Tetons. During the 1740's, the Ojibwe pushed into the upper Mississippi region from Lake

Superior, and with their more sophisticated weapons, they easily pushed the Dakota from their long-held territory. It wasn't until 1825 that the two warring nations agreed upon a dividing line that ran through the middle of Stearns County.

Trading posts were established along the Mississippi River in the late 1700's, with Jean Baptiste Perrault setting up a post at a location he called "Grand Rapids", later named Sauk Rapids.

The explorers Cass, Schoolcraft, Beltrami and Nicollet, all passed along Stearns County in their search for the source of the Mississippi. In the summer of 1832 Schoolcraft recorded his discovery at Lake Itasca, 140 miles to the north. Development began along the Mississippi and slowly spread westward across the county during the 1850's. By that time, trade had been well established by the Red River oxcarts creaking down from Winnipeg on the "East Plains Trail." This path was relocated and improved upon in 1859 by the Minnesota Stage Company. Today Interstate 94 follows much of this old stage route.

A short time later, the government sponsored a survey team from St. Paul to find a good railroad route to Puget Sound. The surveyor's choice of a route along the Red River stage trail, had an important impact on the Northwest. It would later become the route of the Great Northern Railroad.

KIMBALL, Pop. 651

Known as Kimball Prairie, this small railway village was founded in 1866. It was located on the Soo Line tracks and named after Frye Kimball, one of the early farmers that settled here. Kimball lies in Maine Prairie Township.

MAINE PRAIRIE.

Just north of Kimball is the small hamlet known as Maine Prairie Corners. In 1854, a group of Massachusetts people were determined to locate a colony in the West, where they could devote their energies to the "human spirit and its achievements." Agents were sent to find such an area. One of them came to this spot, and staring out across this beautiful prairie, decided to call it "Paradise." The colony never got fully organized, however, but many pioneers from Maine and Massachusetts came to this region to settle. The town took its name from the predominant group. In their first year of 1856, not enough crops were harvested to carry the settlers through the winter. The next year's crops were destroyed by locusts. Much of their food was corn, ground in coffee grinders and cooked as mush. Their stories reflected the many hardships of pioneer settlement.

During the Sioux Uprising of 1862, local farmers defended themselves by building a stockade at the site of Maine Prairie Corners.

WATKINS & EDEN VALLEY

These two towns were platted in 1886 when the St. Paul, Minneapolis & Sault Ste. Marie Railway Company laid their tracks through this area.

PAYNESVILLE, Pop. 2,140

Early records show that there were at least two attempts to locate townsites here. The first was in 1856, when a party of settlers came from St. Cloud and founded Onawa. But for some reason, they left without even filing a claim. The last attempt at settlement was made in the spring of 1857 by the Paynesville Townsite Company, which named the area after Edwin Payne, one of its officers and first residents.

In 1861, the village became part of the mail route between St. Peter and St. Cloud. Paynesville continued to grow and attracted settlers and business development from St. Paul. But life at Paynesville changed quickly on August 21, 1862, when news reached town that a massacre had taken place 17 miles west of here, at Norway Lake. It was reported that a group of settlers returning home from a wedding, were attacked, and thirteen had been killed by Dakota Indians.

At Paynesville, construction began immediately on a fortification. The sod fort, five feet high with some frame buildings inside, attracted so many settlers from the surrounding prairie, that crowded conditions rendered it unsafe. The fort was quickly abandoned, and the entire population moved up to Richmond and St. Cloud. Paynesville was later burned by the Indians.

Following the Uprising, German settlers arrived to rebuild the town. A fort was once again maintained in Paynesville by U.S. soldiers until 1864. Twenty-three years later, the Great Northern Railroad Company built a station at Paynesville. This was followed by the Soo Line Railroad which put up a station one mile east of town, calling it New Paynesville. Competition between the two towns continued for the next several years, with New Paynesville eventually winning out. In March of 1905, a popular vote by the citizens dropped the word New and the town was once again called Paynesville.

THE DAKOTA NATION

By the time the white man happened upon the scene, this Indian nation of loosely-aligned tribes, calling themselves Dakota, roamed the region from Minnesota to the Tetons. They became known as the Sioux, from the term "Nadouessioux"—meaning enemy, a name given to them by the Ojibwe. These seven different bands represented several areas of the West. In Minnesota the primary tribes were: the Mdewakanton, Wahpekute, Wahpeton and Sisseton. By the 1700's the Ojibwe had pushed into Minnesota from the East. Equipped with newly bought guns, they forced the Dakota further south,

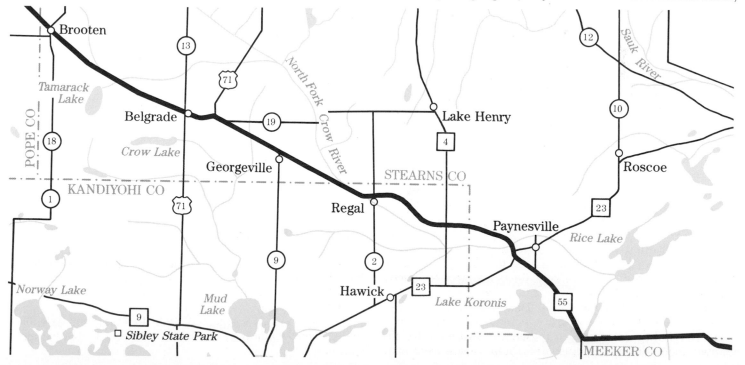

creating a division in the state that lasted until the banishment of the Dakota, after the Uprising of 1862. Bloody encounters continued for many years between these two powerful nations.

But it was the Dakota, more than any other Indian nation, that resented the intrusion of the white man: the whites hunted their sacred grounds, cut down the forests, wiped out the buffalo, and drove many other species of animals from the woods and prairie. The Dakota negotiated some poor and certainly questionable treaties, and soon found themselves on small reservations along the Minnesota River, having received little else in return. They quickly developed a dependency on the white man, with whiskey creating a particularly devastating effect upon their culture.

Still, the settlers feared the Dakota, who occasionally returned back to their old hunting grounds. It was a case of two cultures with two different needs and philosophies, competing for the same space. The simple, hardworking immigrants who were looking for a new life, would not allow the Indian to stand in their way. They had sacrificed everything to make a new start. It was a matter of survival. But to the Dakota it became a matter of survival as well.

MHS

The railroads reached west-central Minnesota in 1886, giving farmers incentive to increase their production for shipment to new markets.

In August of 1862, the Dakota took a final stand which became known as the Sioux Uprising. The Indians lashed out against the unsuspecting whites with such ferocity, that the southern and western part of the state went into a panic that took years to overcome. But as Little Crow, leader of the Dakota, had predicted, "Kill one, two, or ten, and ten times ten will come to kill you." Indeed, the Dakota paid dearly for the Uprising. Those that were not killed, lost their land, forfeited all payments due them, and were ultimately banished from the state. It was only 120 years ago that this state was paying a bounty of $500 for each Dakota Indian scalp. Little Crow finally said, "We are only little herds of buffalo. The great herds that covered the prairies are no more."

KANDIYOHI COUNTY, Pop. 36,703

Historians believe that in early years, the Indians used this word to name several lakes that were the sources of the Crow River. Kandiyohi means, "where the buffalo fish come." It wasn't until 1856 that white settlers discovered first hand the beauty of the many lakes in this region.

Kandiyohi County was promoted by several land companies. At one time, an Englishman named Whitefield proposed that the county become the capital of Minnesota. The measure actually passed both Legislative houses but was vetoed by the governor. The county was divided into two sections in 1858, with the top half called Monongalia. In 1870 the two sections were united.

REGAL & GEORGEVILLE

These small railway stations were developed after the Soo Line came through in 1886.

The North Fork of the Crow River runs along State 55 from Regal to Paynesville. Eventually, it connects to the main body of the Crow River at Rockford.

BELGRADE, Pop. 805

A railroad village on the Soo Line, Belgrade was named after the capital of Yugoslavia and a county in the state of Maine. It is located just north of Crow Lake, the source of the Middle Fork of the Crow River, which flows south into Kandiyohi County, and westward to the Mississippi.

BROOTEN, Pop. 647

Brooten is named after one of the early Scandinavian farmers that settled in the area. The town grew up around the Soo Line that came through in 1886. In 1907, the Soo linked Brooten to Duluth, connecting this rich agricultural area to the ports of Lake Superior.

POPE COUNTY, Pop. 11,657

This county was created in 1862 and named after General John Pope. In that same year, Pope was ordered to Minnesota to take up the fight against the Dakota Indians who had declared war on the United States Government.

Pope County is situated in the area called the "Park Region," an area of beautiful lakes, groves and streams. As early as 1855, settlers became aware of the beauty of this area around Lake Minnewaska. A town was eventually laid out one mile west of the present city of Glenwood and was called Winthrop. But the little hamlet failed and soon faded away. A few settlers lived in the county prior to the Sioux Uprising of 1862, but they left as soon as word spread of the conflict.

GLENWOOD, Pop. 2,523

The county slowly began to resettle after the Uprising. Many feared the Indians might attack again from their position in the Dakotas. Glenwood wasn't platted until 1866 and named for the wooded valley Lake Minnewaska occupies. Minnewaska is the state's thirteenth largest lake and is bordered by many Indian mounds and burial sites. It is recorded that Chief White Bear and Princess Minnewaska are buried at one of these sites. Lake Minnewaska, which was named after an Indian Princess, can be seen from Mount Lookout, just off Highway 55.

The view from Mount Lookout reveals the effects of glaciation that occurred some 11,000 years ago. When the last glacier receded slowly to the north and west, it paused here long enough to deposit rocks and sand that formed the hills around Lake Minnewaska. This ridge of hills and lakes continues in an arch from Willmar to Fergus Falls. The basin of the lake itself was formed when a portion of the glacier became detached from the main ice sheet.

ALEXANDRIA, Pop. 7,608

During the summer of 1858, two brothers, Alexander and William Kincaid, moved up from a settlement they had started at Lake Minnewaska (Glenwood City), pitching their tent on the shores of Lake Agnes. Here they built a log cabin on a knoll just south of where the Burlington Northern station stands. Others followed them to this beautiful spot and a townsite committee soon formed. The area was named Alexandria, in honor of Alexander Kincaid. The townsite company put up a log hotel named the Gregory, and for many years this was a favorite resort for settlers. Most of the settlers that first year came up along the edge of the woods from the south. In 1859, a trail was cut through the woods, connecting St. Cloud and Breckenridge by way of Alexandria. Interstate 94 follows much of this route. Today, Alexandria is a popular fishing and resort area.

(TO CONTINUE THE ROUTE ON I-94   SEE PAGE 123)

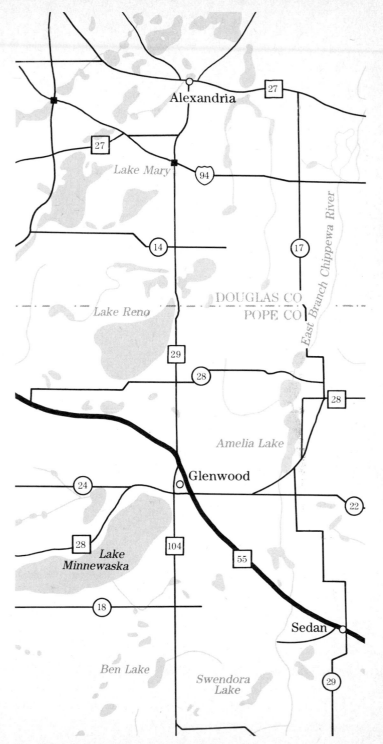

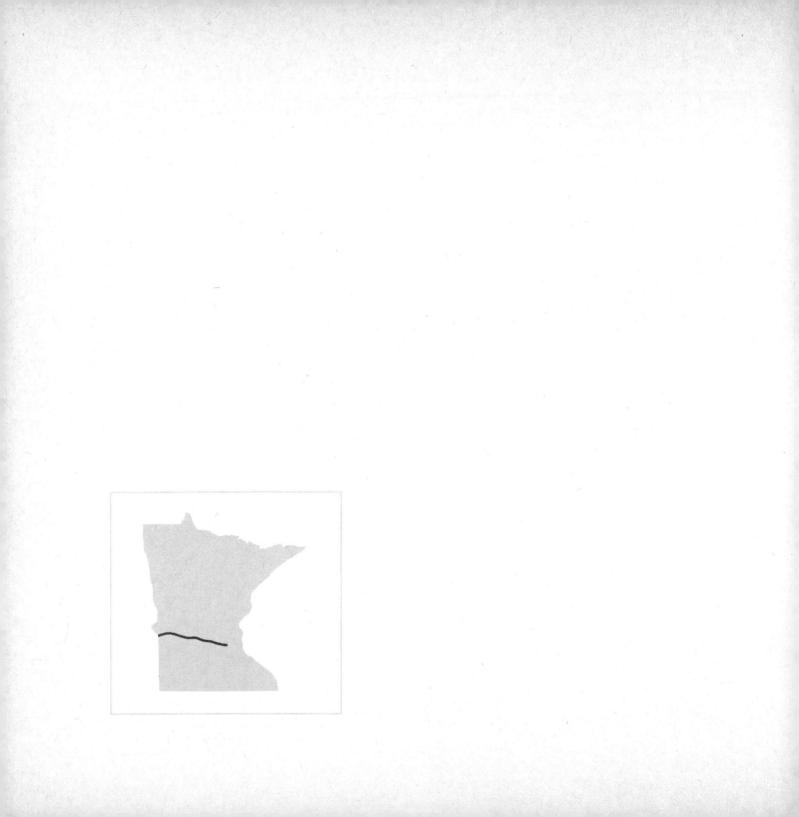

ROUTE 12, TO ORTONVILLE

Watching Sunday afternoon sailboat races on Lake Minnetonka, circa 1900.

This route runs through the picturesque lake region of south-central Minnesota and into the broad farming country of western Minnesota. The rolling, irregular landscape, so typical of this lake region, was caused by the retreating glaciers as they left behind their debris. Many lake basins were scooped out by the ice and later filled with water. In some cases, large chunks of glacial ice broke off, creating "kettle lakes" or depressions that later filled with water.

WAYZATA, Pop. 3,621

This name comes from a Dakota word meaning "god of the north," or "a fabled giant that lives to the north and blows cold from his mouth." Wayzata, the largest town on Lake Minnetonka, was platted in 1854. The lake's romantic beginnings, start with the Dakota and Ojibwe who came here to worship the great spirit, Manitou, ruler of the waters of "Me-ne-a-ton-ka." During all the years of exploration by Hennepin, Le Sueur, Catlin, Pike and Nicollet, Lake Minnetonka remained undiscovered. It wasn't until a 17-year-old drummer boy named Joseph R. Brown, hiked up Minnehaha Creek and discovered, or at least made the first record of this lake, in 1822. Thirty years later the lake was explored by Governor Ramsey and given its present name which means "Big Water."

Wayzata, located on the north side of the lake, became a stopping place for the street cars arriving from Minneapolis. Eventually, multi-decked steamers plied the lake, bringing people out to Big Island or the amusement park at Excelsior. Large resorts attracted vacationers from all over the country. The scene has changed of course, but the value of the land around Minnetonka still commands a premium price because of the lake's beauty and its proximity to the Twin Cities.

LONG LAKE & INDEPENDENCE.

These two towns, lying alongside the Burlington Northern tracks, were settled in the mid-1850's and named after adjacent lakes. Lake Independence was named during a Fourth of July party on the lake.

141

WRIGHT COUNTY, Pop. 58,962

Wright county was named after a New York statesman whose friend lived in Monticello, Minnesota. The county was crossed by glaciers over 11,000 years ago, creating many of the irregular hills and depressions that make up this region. There is hardly one township here without a lake.

Early explorers and trappers found the county extensively forested with red and white oak, sugar maple, elm and basswood. This area later came to be called the Big Woods. These woods separated the prairie of the southwest from the spruce and pine forests of the northeast. Unfortunately, the early settlers cut the Big Woods rapidly and in a few short years, they were destroyed. Most of the trees were burned to clear the land for farming.

When Father Hennepin was in this region during 1680, most of Minnesota was occupied by the Dakota Indians. Around 1740, the Ojibwe, armed with rifles from the French, easily drove the Dakota from their strategic locations on Mille Lacs and Sandy Lakes. From that point on the Dakota became a people of the prairie, until their expulsion from the state in 1862.

The first white man to establish himself in this county was Edmund Brissett, a French trader with a post near Lake Harriet. In 1850, he cut a trail from Lakes Harriet and Calhoun through the Big Woods, to a spot north of Buffalo on Lake Pulaski. There he maintained a post, trading with the Winnebago Indians until 1855. His trail greatly aided the settlers as they moved westward into Wright County.

RAILROAD

The railroad known as the Breckenridge division of the St. Paul and Pacific, cut through the Big Woods of Wright County in 1866. During the next three years, tracks were laid to Wayzata, Delano and Cokato. The line eventually reached Breckenridge on the Minnesota-North Dakota border in 1870, giving the Twin Cities a railway connection with the Red River Valley. The line brought in little revenue though, and went bankrupt in 1879.

James J. Hill, working as a station agent for the St. Paul and Pacific, had a dream to reorganize the railroad and extend across North Dakota, Montana, Idaho and on to the Pacific coast. Hill was named president of the company in 1883, and ten years later his newly consolidated "Great Northern Railroad," reached the Pacific. Instead of having a line that ran too far to the north, as some had feared, Hill's railroad crossed the rapidly developing wheat fields of North Dakota. His line also carried back lumber from the rich forests of Idaho and Washington, to the wood-hungry eastern markets.

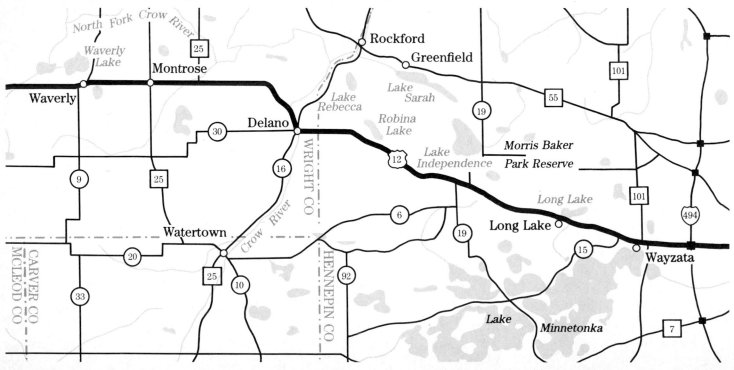

A farmer plows his field, 1910. Photo/H.D. Ayer.

MHS

DELANO, Pop. 2,480

Delano was platted the same year that the railroad reached the crossing of the Crow River in 1868. First called Crow River, the town was later named in honor of Francis Delano, a pioneer lumberman and administrator of the St. Paul & Pacific Railroad. The line is now run by the Burlington Northern Company. Many German and French Catholics settled in the Delano area around 1855.

CROW RIVER

At Delano, the South Fork of the Crow River flows 20 miles north to the Mississippi. This river has its beginnings west of here, in Meeker and Kandiyohi Counties. It empties into the Mississippi south of Elk River, at Dayton. The North Fork of the river runs parallel to Highway 12, a few miles to the north. The Dakota called it "Wak-pah Kahn-ghe-toka," or "River of the Crows."

WAVERLY & MONTROSE

These two railroad towns grew up when the St. Paul & Pacific Railroad passed through the county in 1868. The village of Waverly was once called Waverly Station. This dis-

tinguished it from Old Waverly, a pioneer village that existed about a mile or so from the present site. Old Waverly attracted considerable attention and many lots were sold for development. There was even a chance for the placement of the county seat here. But the financial crash of 1857 forced the investors from the town, leaving it to die. Waverly was once the residence of Hubert H. Humphrey. While he was vice president, this quiet little town was overrun by the "press" during his stays. While Waverly has lost population during the last ten years, neighboring Montrose has doubled in size.

WRIGHT COUNTY SETTLEMENT

The settlements continued in Wright County and land in the east, south, and central portions was all taken by the end of 1857. In the fall of that year, however, the financial collapse of the nation forced many to leave their claims for the next couple of years. During that time the medicinal herb ginseng (used in great amounts by the Chinese), was discovered in Wright County. Great amounts of it were picked here and around the state. Selling ginseng to buyers from the East Coast kept many families from starving during those difficult times.

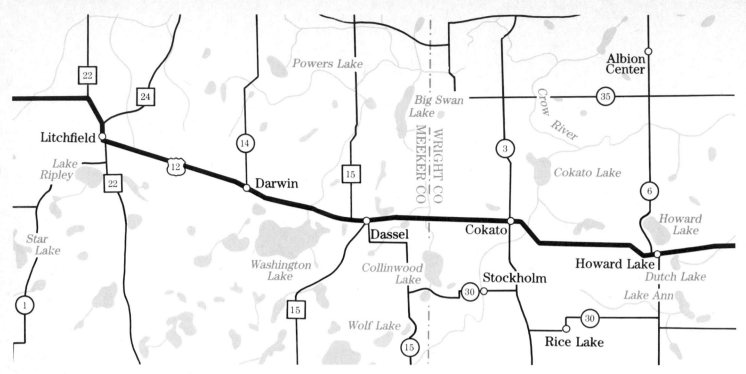

HOWARD LAKE, Pop. 1,240

The town takes its name from the lake, which was named after John Howard, an English philanthropist and prison reformer. Starting in 1873, the Rocky Mountain locusts blew into Minnesota from the West. Farmers in the area of Howard Lake, like so many others in the state, were devastated. In 1878 the pests ate everything that had leaves. Some claimed that the grasshoppers were even eating their clothing. The farmers participated in a state-wide day of prayer, hoping to rid themselves of this plague. Soon afterwards, without any explanation, the locusts departed.

In August, 1862, word of the Sioux Uprising spread like a prairie fire. Wright County settlers were terrified, since most lived in isolated clearings in the deep woods. People gathered at central locations and built crude stockades, preparing for the worse. Many miserable nights were spent cramped in these cold, dingy fortifications. Some watched their children die of diphtheria. It took several years for the fear to subside completely, and a year after the Uprising, in June of 1863, a Howard Lake family was killed by Dakota warriors who were passing through the area.

COKATO, Pop. 2,056

This Dakota name meaning "at the middle," or "stopping place" has the same name as its township. The area used to be called Mooers Prairie, after Josiah Mooers, the first settler who came here in 1856. Ten years later, there was a large influx of new settlers. Reports were coming in that the railroad would be put through and employment could be had by anyone willing to wield a pick. The city attained the title of "Gem City of the West." But plans for the railroad were delayed. Worse yet, the following year there was a wet spring, making planting impossible. Reports started coming in that people were starving, with some subsisting on elm bark alone. Many of the destitute lived in the Mooers Prairie region.

The railroad finally reached here in 1869, followed by an influx of Swedish and Finnish immigrants.

MEEKER COUNTY, Pop. 20,594

Trappers and hunters moved through this area for years, prior to white settlement. During the summer of 1855, three men poled their way up the Crow River, through the Big Woods and into what is now Meeker County. They were John Huy, Benjamin Brown and a man named Mackenzie who were scouting for pine for a lumber company. Pushing through the thick woods, they emerged upon the prairie just east of today's Forest City. Huy was impressed with the open, rolling land where shadows from the clouds skimmed across the waving grass.

Huy returned that same fall and spent the winter in this pathless wilderness. He lived in a small cabin with two other men. That spring, Huy moved down the river a short distance to what eventually became known as Forest City. This small hamlet was the county seat for 12 years, until it was moved to Litchfield. A number of settlers came through the Big Woods during the summer of 1856, on their way to California's golden shores. Pleased by the numerous lakes and richness of the soil, many stopped and settled at Kingston, Forest City and further west at Harvey. The tide of immigration continued on through the late 1850's. The smoke curling from the cabins and the neatly plowed lands, signaled that the white man was here to stay.

BIG WOODS BOUNDARY

Meeker County marks the region where the Big Woods ended and the natural prairie began. The rolling terrain, shaped by glaciers and the debris they left behind, is covered with a rich loam, making this a profitable farming area. Southwest of here, the prairie flattens and then rises to the Coteau des Prairies, or "highland of the prairie".

The early settlers were awed by the open vistas as they wandered from the Big Woods. The shoulder-high grasses of bluestem and indiangrass appeared like the rolling surface of the ocean. The many lakes and marshes ringed by stands of trees, harbored many animals and waterfowl.

Buffalo wandered across the prairie in large herds. Some were so large, in fact, that during the winter, huge frost clouds drifted above them. The Indians had difficulty killing the beasts even with their spears and arrows. It wasn't until the introduction of firearms that buffalo could be killed easily for food. Still, it wasn't the Indian that the buffalo had to fear. During the 1850's, the white man relentlessly slaughtered the buffalo, leaving the prairie strewn with their carcasses.

DASSEL & DARWIN

These two towns were named after railroad officers. Darwin, settled in 1856, was named in honor of E. Darwin Litchfield, principle stockholder in the St. Paul & Pacific Railroad. The towns still remain as shipping centers for local farmers.

LITCHFIELD, Pop. 5,904

Prior to the "iron horse" steaming across Meeker county, Litchfield was nothing more than a wheat field. The area was first called Ness, after one of the early Norwegian farmers that settled here during the summer of 1856.

But it wasn't until the tracks reached as far as Ness in July 1869, that a new village called Litchfield was platted. It was named after E. D. Litchfield, an English capitalist and financier of the St. Paul & Pacific Railroad. The town was settled quickly and became an industrial and farming center, with the railroad enabling local farmers and merchants to exchange their goods in Minneapolis and St. Paul. The new town wasted little time in calling for a vote to move the county seat from Forest City, which lies six miles to the north on the western boundary of the Big Woods.

LAKE RIPLEY

That first winter when John Huy was huddled in his cabin on land that would later become Forest City, two other men, by the names of Dr. Frederick Ripley and John McClelland, built a cabin on the shores of Cedar Lake in southern Meeker County. By March, Ripley and McClelland's supplies were running short, so they headed north to seek help from Huy. Before long, a terrible blizzard developed, forcing them to spend the night in a snowbank. By morning they were lost and backtracked through the deep snow to find their own cabin. With their matches wet, they had no choice but to continue on for shelter. Dr. Ripley became too weak and insisted his friend continue on alone. Ripley soon froze to death but wasn't found until spring. McClelland survived, but had to have both legs amputated to save his life. Lake Ripley, in Litchfield, was named after Dr. Ripley.

Rain-In-The-Face, Dakota Indian. Photo/F.B. Fisk.

MHS

PANIC OF 1857

With the rapid increase of settlement came a great land speculation which reached a climax in 1857. Great tracts of prairie land were obtained for as little as $1.25 an acre. This land was "improved" by building small cabins on it or turning over a few acres of land to be resold for $5 an acre. Townsites were platted by the hundreds. St. Paul bankers found ready borrowers at three percent. But with the nation-wide collapse of the economy in August 1857, hopes for these new towns of the future were dashed. Lack of money forced many to return to homes in the East, temporarily stalling the growth of Minnesota.

GROVE CITY, Pop. 596

Numerous tracts of groves in this area were the inspiration for the town's name. Like most of the towns along Highway 12, Grove City received its life from the St. Paul & Pacific Railroad that came through this section in 1869.

SIOUX UPRISING OF 1862

After the Panic of 1857, the economy of the county began to improve. In August of 1862, larger fields were being cultivated, cattle were fattened on the broad pasture land and the corn was ripening. It was reported that the songs of children filled the air. But as an early historian put it "sud-denly there fell upon the peaceful settlers a disaster more harrowing than can be described by words."

A couple of miles south of Grove City, four Dakota Indians killed five settlers on a dare. Their deaths marked the beginning of one of the more important events in Minnesota history, the Sioux Uprising. After the murders, the frightened braves rode 40 miles south to their village on the Redwood River, by the Lower Sioux Agency. They told their leaders (one of whom was Little Crow), what they had done. The Indians knew that these murders would not go unanswered. The real reasons for the Uprising were many, but most of them stemmed from a growing disatisfaction with the 1851 treaties at Traverse des Sioux and Mendota.

This once proud people, who hunted the prairie for their food, were now cramped along the Minnesota River, waiting for handouts that, most often, never came. A fear of reprisal for the Grove City murders, plus the collection of injustices heaped upon this nation of 7,000 people, were major factors in the Uprising. In a few short months over 400 whites had been killed, towns and fields burned, and cattle scattered by bands of Dakota warriors that roamed the counties of this region. But as Little Crow had predicted, "We will die like rabbits when the hungry wolves hunt them in the hard moon." The war ended a few months later. The Dakota were driven from the state; their reservations were sold, and their money

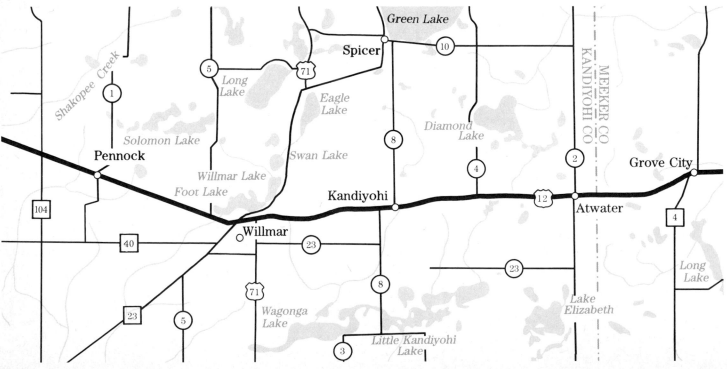

The steam-thresher increased the production of Minnesota wheat fields during the late 1860's.

MHS

never paid. There was even a bounty paid for Indian scalps for the next few years.

Little Crow, leader of the Uprising, met his end while picking berries with his son, just west of Hutchinson. His body was dragged into town and maliciously desecrated. Little Crow's son escaped, but was later captured in the Dakotas.

FOREST CITY

During the first days of the Uprising, most residents of Meeker County headed further east. Those that remained behind fled to Forest City, where a stockade was constructed. Not anticipating an immediate attack, most slept in a nearby hotel. A sentry, hearing horses approach at three a.m., sounded the alarm. It was a scene of mass disorder and confusion as everyone rushed for the stockade, leaving most of the ammunition behind. But the settlers held off the attack, as the Indians burned the town and left for easier prey.

KANDIYOHI COUNTY, Pop. 36,703

Kandiyohi takes its name from a chain of lakes that extends through the county from northwest to southeast. The Dakota referred to these lakes as "Kahn-Dee-O-He," meaning "abounding in buffalo fish." This meaning referred to the time each spring when many of these fish moved up the rivers and streams to spawn in the lakes. Joseph Nicollet was the first white man to refer to this region by that name. Kandiyohi Lake appears on his map of 1842.

Not until 1856 did the people of Minnesota gain any knowledge of this region and its many lakes. At that time, Edwin Whitefield, an artist and promoter for the newly founded Kandiyohi Townsite Company, traveled into the county, painting scenes and picking future townsites. Whitefield was fond of this part of the state and felt it was a haven for the people "from the consumptive East and the fever-stricken South".

Settlers began to arrive on trails running up from Carver and Henderson on the Minnesota River, and one other coming in from St.Cloud. Mail routes developed between Glencoe and St.Cloud in 1857, then curved west to service the settlements of Kandiyohi and Spicer on Green Lake. The county was actually divided into two parts in the early days. The top half was called Monongalia County until 1870, when it was united with Kandiyohi. County promoters went to extremes in platting almost the entire county for settlement. One group advertised a mythical paper town, with it's new railway station situated next to a non-existent railroad line.

At one point in 1869, a proposal passed both houses of the state Legislature to move the capital of Minnesota to a site near Little Kandiyohi, a town that has since faded away. Unfortunately for the little town, the governor vetoed the bill.

FIRST SETTLER

With a horse, a light wagon and some camping gear, Elijah Woodcock, 23, set out for a new beginning somewhere west of Faribault. It was 1856, and when he rode past Young America and Hutchinson there were only a dozen cabins in each. Following the wagon trail of some previous traveler, Woodcock worked his way northwest, past the numerous lakes and groves of Kandiyohi County. He eventually stopped by a lake with the most beautiful shade of bottle green, and built his cabin. The town became known as Spicer and the lake was called Green Lake. Woodcock went East to marry and brought his wife back to the site, making her the first woman in this county.

EARLY FARMING

The first farmers had to turn over the tough, unbroken sod and then plant enough to live on. Since the closest markets were in St. Paul and roads were non-existent, surplus farming was unheard of. Eventually, roads were developed, and trips to St.Cloud and Sauk Rapids were made for supplies. Trapping was also important, since furs were a more dependable form of income in those days. Four to five hundred dollars a season was considered a fair return for one man's efforts. Occasionally, caravans of farmers would take their grain and furs of muskrat, mink, and otter to St. Paul.

WILLMAR, Pop. 15,895

Once the site of a disputed hunting grounds between the Dakota and Ojibwe, Willmar was settled before the Sioux Uprising of 1862. During that event, 13 settlers were killed along present-day Highway 12, just west of Willmar. Foot Lake was named after one of the first residents. But it wasn't until after the Indian scare subsided and the railroad was completed, that Willmar started coming to life. The St. Paul & Pacific line reached the town in 1869 and the village was named after Leon Willmar, a London bondsman who handled investments in the railroad for Englishmen. Willmar's son was given land on the northeast side of Willmar Lake, where

Plowing a straight furrow. Photo/H.D. Ayer.

Largest clothing store in Willmar, 1900.

he constructed elaborate buildings and spent 10 years trying to make a go of it before he returned to Europe.

RAILROADS

The railroads were not only instrumental in populating the state, but their routes determined the placement of towns. Following the Civil War in 1865, railroad executives established an immigration bureau and sent agents to Europe to entice families to come to Minnesota. Many of these immigrants worked on the railroads. By 1880, 71 percent of the state's population was first or second generation European, with the highest majority of Scandinavian and German descent.

WILLMAR REGION GEOLOGY

The soil of the Willmar region has a history dating back 60 million years, when an inland sea covered the Great Plains from the Gulf of Mexico to the Arctic Ocean. As the adjacent land was eroded, sandstone, shale and limestone accumulated as sediment on the sea floor. Much later, great earth movements caused the sea to withdraw by raising the sea floor of this newly formed sedimentary rock above the water level.

Thousands of years later, the glaciers swept southward pushing great quantities of this sediment from Canada and northwestern Minnesota toward the Willmar area. These deposits, rich in lime, magnesia and potash, became the basis for the fertile soil of this region.

PENNOCK, Pop. 255

This small railway village used to be named St. Johns, but was changed to Pennock, after the Willmar superintendent of the Great Northern Railroad.

SWIFT COUNTY, Pop 12,920

This county was named after Henry Swift, governor of Minnesota in 1863.

U.S. 12 crosses a flat plain where early settlers lived an almost primitive life during the years of 1866-68. A small group of Norwegians were the first to settle in this county and they chose the northeast area by Camp Lake. Because trees were scarce, the dwellings were often just holes, carved out of small hills. If no hills were to be found, the homes were made from sod chunks.

By the time autumn came around, the sod roofs sprouted a rich growth of grass and prairie flowers. The floors of these dwellings were also made of dirt. After heavy rains, the dirt walls proved ineffectual. But some inventive pioneers soon discovered that a mixture of cow manure and wood ashes, in the right proportions, withstood the downpours much better.

There wasn't much room inside these huts and most of the furniture was homemade. Five to ten-acre sites were broken up and planted with wheat and potatoes. But for many of these early farms, the markets of New Ulm, St. Cloud and Sauk Center were too far away to trade, using slow moving oxen. Subsistence farming was all that could be done. The winters were dreaded the most because of the fierce snow and isolation that they brought.

RAILROADS

U.S. 12 runs parallel to the Burlington Northern tracks. In 1864 this line was designated as the first division of the St. Paul & Pacific Railroad. The line reached Willmar in 1869, and Benson the following year. The construction of the railroad across the flat, treeless plains of Swift County was relatively easy. Many of the workmen came from Scandinavia, trying to eke out a living in this promised land. The crews worked long hours under the hot sun, using ox teams to move the dirt for building up the beds and hauling in the rails from the last station. It wasn't until 1885 that James J. Hill developed the extensive railway system that would eventually reach the Pacific Ocean and be called the Great Northern.

TOWN LOCATIONS

By picking townsites at intervals of approximately eight miles, the railroad was the determining factor in the development of Swift County's trading centers in the 1870's. The first town was Kerkhoven, named after one of the company's stockholders; next came De Graff, which honored the railroad builder; then came Benson, named after a prominent politician and citizen of Anoka.

As the railroad was being laid, many immigrants purchased tickets as far as the line would carry them and then pro-

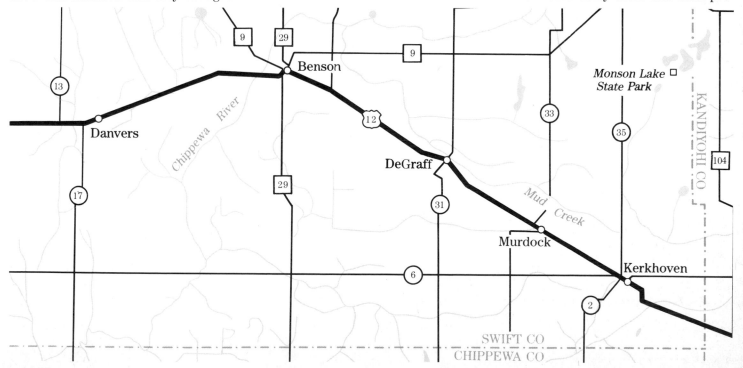

Main Street of Benson, 1882.

MHS

ceeded by oxcart to their final destinations. Many Irish settled in the proposed towns along this stretch of railway. But settlement could be a slow and miserable process. One woman wrote about leaving the train in Willmar and trekking west across a flat prairie "dotted with sloughs and inhabited by millions of mosquitoes." She said she saw but one person, and he crawled out of his sod hut in true gopher-like fashion, giving them only a cold stare.

RED RIVER OXCARTS

As the railroad pushed into Swift County, many of the oxcarts carrying merchandise between Manitoba and St. Paul, came to meet the train. These crudely built carts, consisting of wheels with a large basket-like box built over the axles, could carry from 600-700 pounds. Most of the goods were choice wines, brandies, whiskeys, tea, tobacco and hardware. On some days, 40 to 50 carts, their un-greased wheels squealing, would creak into town and deposit their goods on the train. This system of transportation faded rapidly after the railroad was connected to Breckenridge.

KERKHOVEN, Pop. 761

Kerkhoven, named after a Scottish stockholder in the railroad, began when the railroad was built here in 1870. The railroad gave the small settlement incentive to build a hardware store, hotel and grain dealership. But five years later, there were still only 50 people living here.

BENSON, Pop. 3,656

This town was named in honor of Norwegian, Ben Benson, who settled here with a group in the 1860's. Ten years later, the St. Paul & Pacific Railroad was laid through here, and for the next two years Benson remained the terminus of the line. In 1885 it became part of James J. Hill's Great Northern Railroad.

During those few years, an economic boom had begun, with Benson building its first store—a sod shanty. The town served as a grain market for all the territory 100 miles to the west, north and south. Wheat was hauled in from the nine surrounding counties. Many immigrants began seeking the long-promised visions of productive fields. The area was so crowded with claim seekers, that sleeping space, even on the dirt floors, was at a premium. Many staked their claims during the winter, only to find that come spring—they owned a marsh.

Benson flourished. Each train that brought new people, returned to the Twin Cities with loads of wheat. In 1875 Benson exported 260,000 bushels. Then, one hot August day in 1880, a fire started next to Fountain's Saloon. By the time it had burned out, most of the 20 buildings which comprised downtown Benson, were left in ashes.

CHIPPEWA RIVER

The Chippewa River, a tributary of the Minnesota, runs 130 miles north from Fish Lake in Otter Tail County. This was Ojibwe territory, and occasionally warring Ojibwe would use this river to make raids on the Dakota who were living along the Minnesota. The river, in effect, became a war road, thereby getting its name from the Dakota. It was near this river that a hunting party of Dakota from the Lac qui Parle region were attacked and scalped by Ojibwe. The Dakota never forgot it, later avenging those murders at the Rum River near Anoka. Many miles of the Chippewa have been channelized, but there are still marshes and wildlife areas in this county protected by the state.

CLONTARF, Pop. 196

In 1876, Bishop John Ireland, a Catholic priest, promoted the town of Clontarf by distributing brochures in the poverty-stricken areas of the East coast. An Irish-Catholic prohibition colony emigrated from Pennsylvania and took the train as far as Benson. Here they took oxcarts to the 117,000 acres under the Bishop's jurisdiction. They named it Clontarf after a watering place in Dublin, Ireland.

There was a terrible grasshopper infestation that first year, destroying most of the crops. But colony churchmen were opposed to killing the pests, believing that grasshoppers were "heaven's punishment for their sins."

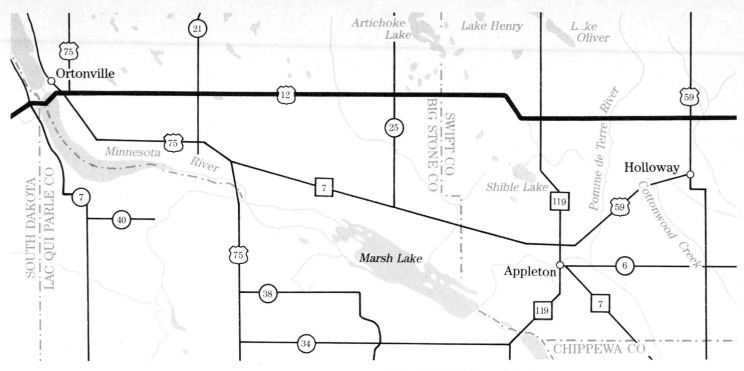

POMME DE TERRE RIVER

The Pomme de Terre River, the French word for potato, was named for a prairie turnip with eyes like a potato. These turnips were harvested by the Dakota. The Pomme de Terre has its beginnings in the lake region, 100 miles to the north. The river winds its way through many clear lakes and marshes, abundant with waterfowl. Southwest of Appleton, it enters Marsh Lake, which is part of the Lac qui Parle Wildlife Area.

BIG STONE COUNTY, Pop. 7,716

Organized in 1862, this county took its name from the lake which the Dakota called "Inyan tankinyanyan", meaning "very great stone." This name comes from the granite outcroppings along the Minnesota River near Ortonville.

Big Stone Lake was created by sediment deposited across its outlet by the Whetstone River of South Dakota. Marsh and Lac qui Parle lakes were also created by this process. Now all three lakes have dams to regulate their levels.

Big Stone Lake is 25 miles long and is the source of the Minnesota River which flows 270 miles to St. Paul. At the head of Big Stone Lake is the town of Browns Valley, located on the continental divide. Here a small rise in the land separates the Red River, which drains north into Hudson Bay, from the Minnesota River basin, which eventually flows to the Gulf of Mexico.

ORTONVILLE, Pop. 2,548

Ortonville is located on the southern shore of Big Stone Lake. The surrounding area was a favorite hunting and fishing spot for the early Dakota Indians. Many Indian mounds have been discovered in this region.

Though the town was not settled until 10 years after the Sioux Uprising, this spot was heavily traveled. In the early 1800's, noisy Red River carts were heading for Traverse des Sioux from their settlements near Winnipeg and Pembina. Trading posts were also established along Lake Traverse down to Lac qui Parle. French and English traders bought many furs from the Indians here.

In 1872, Cornelius Orton traveled from Wisconsin to this spot on the Big Stone and laid out a townsite. The town began to flourish and became known as Ortonville. It grew into a major trading center, even though the nearest railroad station was 40 miles away at Benson. At one time, grain was shipped down the 25-mile long Big Stone Lake on steam-driven barges.

A ruby-red granite has been quarried here for many years, supplying stone for buildings such as the Minneapolis City Hall. A canning company in Ortonville was also the originator and patent-holder of equipment used in canning whole kernels of corn. Ten miles north of town is the Larson Round Barn, probably the largest round barn in Minnesota.

151

ROUTE 7, TO ORTONVILLE

The steamboat "Excelsior" departs the town dock on Lake Minnetonka.

LAKE MINNETONKA

Lake Minnetonka lies just out of sight on the north side of Highway 7. This lake was formed along the receding edge of glaciers over 11,000 years ago. Glacial debris, ice blocks and irregular melting helped to create the numerous bays and channels of this lake that contains over 114 miles of shoreline. For many years the lake was undiscovered, except for the Indians that camped along its shores and on Big Island. It wasn't until 1822 that a 17-year-old drummer boy from Ft. Snelling and his companion, followed the Minnehaha Creek and discovered what many considered to be, the most beautiful lake in Minnesota. Thirty years later it was explored by Governor Ramsey and given its present name which means "Big Water".

Lake Minnetonka became one of the major tourist spots in the nation. During the late 1800's and early 1900's, large hotels and resorts lined its shores. Multi-decked steamers provided transportation around the lake, and one, named the "Belle of Minnetonka," was equipped to carry 3,500 people. Today the area's valuable lakeshore has been heavily developed.

EXCELSIOR, Pop. 2,523

In 1853, a horticultural group called the Excelsior Pioneer Organization was formed in New York City. Many of their members arrived at this site in 1853. The group was primarily interested in seeing if their crops of apples, peaches, plums, cherries and pears, could be grown here successfully. Gideon Bay, located just off of Excelsior, is named for Peter Gideon who developed the "Wealthy" apple while operating the state fruit farm here, in 1879.

153

GRIMM'S ALFALFA

In 1857, a German farmer immigrated to this area with 20 pounds of alfalfa seed. Through repeated plantings, he was able to acclimate the plant and increase its yields enough to begin selling it to other farmers. The new alfalfa was hardier than other strains and able to survive the rigorous Minnesota winters. During the 1890's Carver County supplied 50 percent of all alfalfa grown in Minnesota and dominated the market for many years. The German farmer's house, built in 1876, still stands in the Carver Park Reserve.

ST. BONIFACIUS, Pop. 857

In its early days, this small community was a thriving center for bee-keeping. The activity was led by Father Jaeger, a priest of St. Bonifacius Church. The town takes its name from the church which was named after a German saint. For a short time in the early 1970's, St. Bonifacius was also the site of a Nike missile base; part of the Twin Cities defense strategy.

CARVER COUNTY, Pop. 37,065

The county was named after Jonathan Carver, who explored this area along the Minnesota River in 1766.

Thousands of years before Carver's travels, glaciers covered the county, advancing into southern Minnesota and beyond. When these ice sheets began to melt, they left behind a rolling, irregular surface of sand, gravel and clay. Large blocks of ice that had broken from the main glacier left depressions in the earth that eventually formed lakes.

Early explorers and trappers found the county to be extensively forested with red and white oak, sugar maple, elm and basswood. This came to be called the Big Woods. The thick forest separated the prairie of the southwest from the spruce and pine forests of the northeast. But in a few short years most of the Big Woods were destroyed, either for lumber or for farming.

Land was opened to white settlement after the important treaties of Traverse des Sioux and Mendota in 1851. A short time later some 25 settlements spread throughout the county. Today, only 12 remain. The towns that developed owed their success to the railroad lines that entered the county in 1880. Those that faded away found themselves miles from any railroad grading. The first immigrants were mostly German and Scandinavian, with strong religious backgrounds. East Union, on County Road 40, was one of the first Swedish communities in the state. A church built there in 1859 still stands among the cornfields of this small rural community.

WACONIA, Pop. 2,638

The major factor in Waconia's growth was its lake. Waconia became a resort community largely because of a French wine

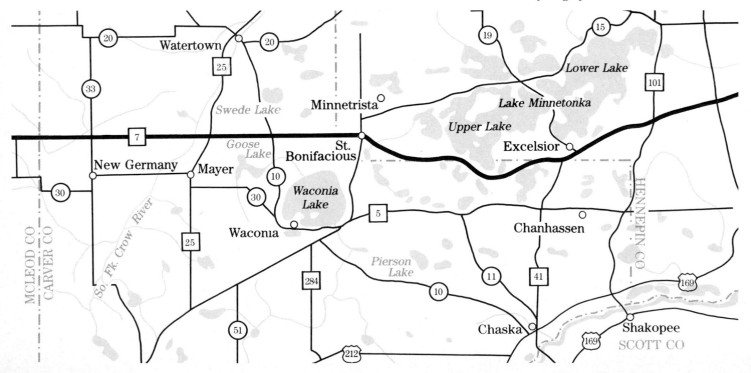

importer named Amblard. Amblard purchased an island in the lake in 1877, then built villas and a resort which attracted many visitors. This island is called Coney Island. E.H. Mack started a large, cigar-manufacturing business in Waconia, selling to local resorters.

MAYER AND NEW GERMANY

These two towns sprang up along the railroad running to Hutchinson and points beyond. But after the depression, priority was given to building a state highway system. Soon trucks started shipping more of what used to go exclusively by rail. A decrease in rail freight marked the economic decline of these towns. Without banks or stores, Mayer and New Germany are now basically bedroom communities of Minneapolis. One interesting note. During World War I, New Germany changed its name, temporarily, to Motordale because of the general disdain for Germans.

CROW RIVER

Just past County 25, the South Fork of the Crow River passes on its journey 30 miles north to the Mississippi. This river has its beginnings in Meeker and Kandiyohi Counties and empties into the Mississippi, south of Elk River. The Dakota called it "Wak-pah Kahn-ghe-toka," or "River of the Crows."

The wedding portrait, 1908. Photo/John Runk.

A Carver County field of Grimm Alfalfa.

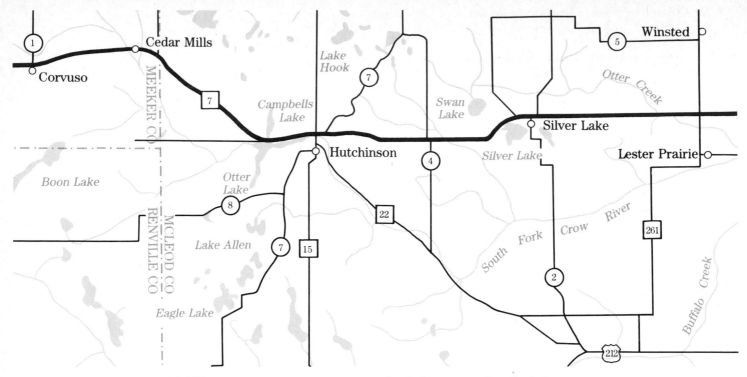

MCLEOD COUNTY, Pop. 29,657

McLeod County is drained by the South Fork of the Crow River which joins the North Fork at Delano, and travels up to the Mississippi at Dayton. The other major stream is Buffalo Creek which drains into the Crow, south of Lester Prairie. The surface contour of McLeod undulates with swells rising to 25 feet, formed by glaciers 11,000 years ago.

Originally, forests covered about half of the county and were called the "Chahn-tonka," or "Big Woods." The woods ended just east of Glencoe. The rest of the county was natural prairie that extended all the way to the Rocky Mountains.

In 1769 at a major battle on Lake Mille Lacs, the Dakota were routed by the Ojibwe. The Dakota moved southward to the plains, but often traveled back to these rich woodlands of oak, maple, basswood, and elm to hunt and trap. Loaded with furs, they traveled to the Minnesota River for trading at Mendota or Traverse des Sioux.

Germans became the first white settlers here during the early 1850's. The settlers immediately began clearing the Big Woods which was no easy task. Eventually, as the woods were destroyed, the bear, wolves, panthers, and lynx disappeared. It took two men, one whole winter to clear two acres. Most of the wood was then burned in large piles. The early pioneers later regretted the waste of wood when they real-

ized the money they had thrown away.

Buffalo were plentiful, but the early Indians had difficulty killing the beasts with spears and arrows. The introduction of firearms enabled them to easily take buffalo for food. The white man, however, killed largely for sport and this wanton slaughter continued into the 1850's, until only a few small herds remained.

HUTCHINSON, Pop. 1,090

In the fall of 1855, the Hutchinson brothers (a family of singers), along with some other men, left Minneapolis to explore the country west of the Big Woods. If a suitable location could be found, they would establish a settlement. After winding their way for three days up Minnehaha Creek, over to Carver and then on to Glencoe, they stood on a hill overlooking a spot by the Crow River and exclaimed, "We have found it." That night they camped by the river, where the town of Hutchinson would one day be located.

The next spring, a road was cleared through the Big Woods from Rapid Water (known now as Watertown), making the trip from Minneapolis much shorter.

The following winter, only six houses occupied the site. The weather was particularly severe with snow, three feet deep, making travel almost impossible. Hutchinson was very

MHS

Little Crow, A leader of the Sioux Uprising of 1862.

MHS

Little Crow's son, Wo-Wi-Na-Pe, after his capture in 1864.

quiet that winter, with most of the town's efforts spent in trying to keep from freezing.

Hutchinson continued to grow, however, with farming the major activity. The Hutchinson brothers dictated the early political sentiment which advocated complete abolition of slavery, equal rights for women, no gambling, and the founding of a church called the "Humanities Church." During those days, this type of thinking was considered anarchy.

The Sioux Uprising of 1862 caught the settlers by surprise and many families in this area were killed. Hutchinson was one of the few towns that did not panic. Residents built a stockade, saved their crops and held their ground during the attacks. But the scene was not a pretty one. Because of the cold fall and winter, many of the children died in the stockade. Huddled together without bodily comforts, medicine or medical help, some families lost two and three children to diphtheria.

After the Uprising, Hutchinson was a military post for a couple of years. In 1863 Nathan Lamson and his son, traveling five miles west of town in search of deer, happened upon an Indian and his young son picking berries. Lamson crept up and fired, wounding what turned out to be Little Crow, leader of the Uprising. Little Crow was then killed by Lamson's son but Little Crow's boy escaped.

The body of Little Crow was dragged into town and since it was the Fourth of July, some young boys put firecrackers in the ears and nostrils. Later Little Crow's head was cut off by a soldier. The skull was later retained by the Historical Society. Lamson's son received $75, the going bounty for an Indian scalp. Little Crow's son was captured later near Devil's Lake, North Dakota in a starving condition. He was 16.

MEEKER COUNTY, Pop. 20,594

For years prior to white settlement, trappers and hunters moved frequently through this area. During the summer of 1855 three men poled their way up the Crow River, through the Big Woods and into what is now Meeker County. These men were John Huy, Benjamin Brown and a man named Mackenzie. All were scouting pine for a lumber company. Pushing through the thick woods the men came upon the prairie, just east of where Forest City stands today. Huy was impressed with the rolling prairie and the shadows from the clouds skimming across the waving grass.

Huy came back with two others that same fall and spent the winter inside a small cabin, in the pathless wilderness. The next spring he moved down the river a short distance to what became known as Forest City. A number of settlers came through the Big Woods during the summer of 1856 on

Dakota . Photo/Edward Curtis.

MHS

their way to California's golden shores. Pleased with what they saw in Minnesota, they settled at Kingston, Forest City and further west at Harvey. The tide of immigration continued, with many delighted by the numerous lakes and richness of the soil. The curling smoke from the cabins and the neatly plowed grounds, signaled that the white man was here to stay.

SIOUX UPRISING OF 1862

On August 17, 1862, in Acton township west of Litchfield, four Dakota Indians killed five settlers on a dare. The Indians had been in the Big Woods on a hunting expedition. After the murders, they sped south to their village at the mouth of the Redwood River, by the Lower Sioux Agency. Fear of reprisal for their murders, plus a collection of numerous injustices by the white man, persuaded this nation of 7,000 people to wage war against the whites. The Dakota swept through Renville County first, killing many of the German settlers. Those that escaped through the grass and thickets, brought word of the disaster to Fort Ridgely, along the Minnesota River. Most of the fighting was over by summer's end, but not before 400 settlers had been killed, with some reports as high as 800. (This author found no figures listed for the Indians.)

LAKE RIPLEY & CEDAR LAKE

That first winter when John Huy was huddled in his cabin near what would become Forest City, two other men by the names of Dr. Frederick Ripley and John McClelland, built a cabin on the shores of Cedar Lake. By March, Ripley and McClelland's supplies were running short, so they headed north on a beautiful sunny day, seeking help from Huy. Before long a terrible blizzard had engulfed them, forcing them to spend the night in a snowbank. By morning they were lost, and backtracked through the snow to find their own cabins. Eventually, Dr. Ripley became too weak to continue and insisted his friend go on alone. Ripley soon froze to death but his body was not found until spring. His companion survived, but both legs had to be amputated. Lake Ripley, in Litchfield, was named after the doctor.

CEDAR MILLS, Pop. 73.

This town was named after a lake located two miles to the northeast. Cedar Mills Lake was first referred to on old maps by explorers, Fremont and Nicollet. The lake had the Indian title of "Ranti-tia-wita," or "Lake of the Red Cedar Island." Daniel Cross settled here with his family in 1856, but was later killed during the Sioux Uprising. Both Cedar Mills and Cosmos are located on the South Fork of the Crow River, which empties into the Mississippi by Dayton. It drains one of the largest watersheds (over 2700 square miles) in central Minnesota.

Dakota family.

MHS

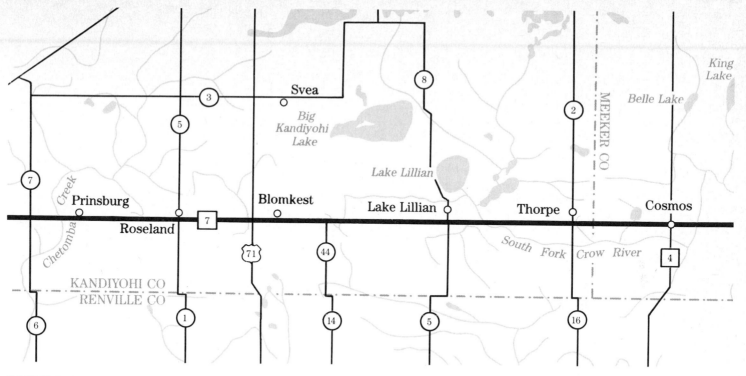

COSMOS, Pop. 571

This town takes its name from a Greek word that defines harmony in the universe. Daniel Jackman was the first settler here in 1867. Jackman settled by the Crow River where the prairie was level and the soil rich. Several others followed him that first year. Isaac Layton and H.W. Young became the first farmers and planted wheat.

KANDIYOHI COUNTY, Pop. 36,703

Kandiyohi takes its name from a chain of lakes that extends through the county, from northwest to southeast. The Dakota referred to these lakes as "Kahn-Dee-O-He," meaning "abounding in buffalo fish." This meaning referred to the time each spring when many of these fish moved up the rivers and streams to spawn in the lakes. The Dakota took advantage of this and speared them for food. Joseph Nicollet was the first white man to refer to this region by that name. Kandiyohi Lake appears on his map of 1842.

Not until 1856 did the people of Minnesota gain any knowledge of this region and its many lakes. At that time, Edwin Whitefield, an artist and promoter for the newly founded Kandiyohi Townsite Company, traveled into the county, painting scenes and picking future townsites. Whitefield was fond of this part of the state and felt it was a haven for the people "from the consumptive East and the fever-stricken South."

The county was actually divided into two parts in the early days. The top half was called Monongalia County until 1870, when it was united with Kandiyohi. County promoters went to extremes in platting almost the entire county for settlement. One group advertised a mythical paper town, with it's new railway station situated next to a non-existent railroad line.

At one point in 1869, a proposal passed both houses of the state Legislature to move the capital of Minnesota to a site near Little Kandiyohi, a town that has since faded away. Unfortunately for the little town, the governor vetoed the bill.

LAKE LILLIAN, Pop. 329

Lillian was named after the wife of Edwin Whitefield, one of the state's first artists. Whitefield painted scenes around Kandiyohi County and also became a promoter for moving the state capital to this county.

PRINSBURG, Pop. 557.

This town was named after Martin Prins, a member of a land company that bought 35,000 acres of railroad land here in 1884.

CHIPPEWA COUNTY, Pop. 14,941

Chippewa County lies in the Minnesota River basin with the large, Lac qui Parle Lake and the Minnesota River forming its western border.

Explorers, traders and trappers passed along the natural pathway of the Minnesota River, traversing Chippewa county many years before permanent settlement took place. Joseph Renville was one of the early, important settlers in the region. Renville built a stockade named Fort Adams, near the end of Lac qui Parle Lake, where he lived like a Baron until his death in 1846. He was surrounded by a coterie of old voyageurs, Indian relatives and half-breeds. His fort was a welcome spot for those that traveled over the monotonous prairie. In 1835 Renville invited missionaries, Williamson and Huggins to come into the county and establish a mission. Renville assisted them in translating the Bible, textbooks and hymns into the Dakota language.

EARLY TRAVEL

The earliest settlers moved across the broad prairie in covered wagons (also called prairie schooners) which were pulled by dependable ox-teams. Oxen, besides being more durable than horses, were steadier and less subject to fright. The families plodded along during the day through all kinds of weather, stopping at night to sleep under tents or the bowed cover of the wagon. During the day, the intrepid settlers had to skirt swamps and lakes and ford streams, all the time making sure that their wagons didn't tip over.

When they found a site to claim, they either dug out a hole in the prairie and covered the walls with logs, making a roof of canvas or brush; or they lived in their wagons, until they could cut timber from stream beds and bring in lumber from Glencoe, Willmar or Benson. The faithful oxen were also used to turn over the thick prairie sod which had built up a tough, almost impenetrable root system.

CLARA CITY & MAYNARD

When the survey for the Great Northern Railroad came through Chippewa County in 1887, the towns of Clara City and Maynard were formed. Clara City was platted on a rise and named after the wife of Theodore Koch, a well-known Dutch businessman. Koch exported Holstein cattle from Holland in 1884, and for several years he purchased hundreds of thousands of acres of Minnesota prairie in this area. Koch actively encouraged Hollanders to settle here, with Clara City being one of his favorite sites.

UPPER SIOUX AGENCY

South of Maynard about 15 miles, is the Upper Sioux Agency. After the treaty of Traverse des Sioux in 1851, when the

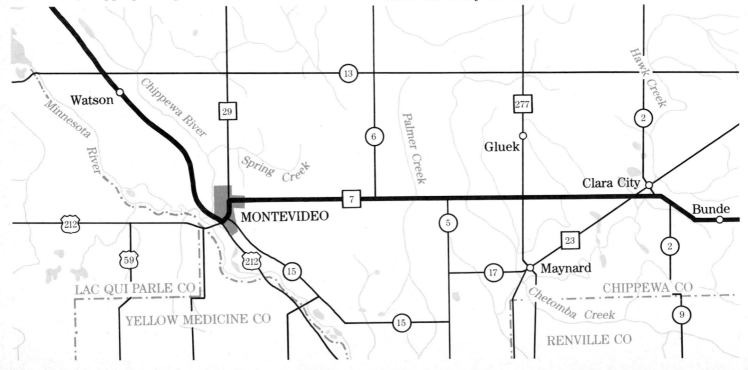

1880 view of Montevideo's Main Street.

Sisseton and Wahpeton Dakota gave up 24 million acres of land, the Indians moved to a narrow reservation along the Minnesota River. Upper Sioux Agency was their capital, while the Lower Sioux Agency, 30 miles to the south, was the capital for the Wahpekute and Mdewakanton Dakota who signed their treaty at Mendota.

The agency was to disperse the goods and payments due the Indians, but due to the cumbersome bureaucracy, these payments were most often delayed. Just before the Sioux Uprising, some 5,000 Indians had gathered at the agency, many near starvation, waiting for food.

For this unjust treatment, the lack of promised payments and a painful realization of what they had given up, the Dakota started the Sioux Uprising in August of 1862. For the next few months the Dakota waged war against the white settlers, killing over 400. Battles were fought up and down the Minnesota, as far as New Ulm and across the prairie into Meeker county.

One of the last battles of the brief war was at Wood Lake, just south of the agency. After this battle, many of the Dakota warriors, including Little Crow, slipped into the plains of Dakota Territory, defeated. After the war, the reservations were opened to the whites since the Dakota were exiled from the state and all treaties were considered null and void. But the Dakota continued their resistance against the white

man for another 30 years. The final blow came in 1890 at Wounded Knee, South Dakota, when government troops tried to disarm a band of Dakota heading for the Pine Ridge Reservation. When the shooting had stopped, some 200 Indian men, women and children lay dead.

MONTEVIDEO, Pop. 5,845

Montevideo, situated at the confluence of the Chippewa and Minnesota rivers, was named for a city in Uruguay. The meaning of the town is Latin for "to view from a mountain," and was probably inspired by a view from its bluffs of the Minnesota and Chippewa valleys. In 1862 a couple of men built a cabin where Montevideo would grow, but one was later killed and the other seriously wounded during the Sioux Uprising. The little cabin was still there in 1865 when permanent settlement began.

Claims were staked on the west bank of the Chippewa where it emptied into the Minnesota. The town was called Chippewa City until almost everyone moved across the river in 1870 to a site that became known as Montevideo.

CHIPPEWA RIVER

The Chippewa River, a tributary to the Minnesota River, has it headwaters 130 miles north in Fish Lake of Otter Tail County. This was once Ojibwe territory. Occasionally, war-

MHS

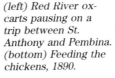

(left) Red River ox-
carts pausing on a
trip between St.
Anthony and Pembina.
(bottom) Feeding the
chickens, 1890.

ring Ojibwe would use the river to make raids on the Dakota, living along the Minnesota. The river, in effect, became a war road and was named by the Dakota for their enemy.

WEST PLAINS TRAIL

One of the early land routes between the Red River Valley settlements and Mendota, on the Minnesota River, passed through Chippewa County. This was the West Plains Red River Trail, traveled by carts loaded with furs and other products of the wilderness and bound for Mendota. The travelers put up a constant battle with the mosquito, which was more than a slight inconvenience. At night they could barely sleep as they fought to keep the bugs out of their tents. Even worse, the oxen were often so bothered that they had trouble eating and were dangerously weakened.

MHS

WATSON, Pop. 238

Watson, a railway village on the Chicago, Milwaukee, St. Paul & Pacific Line, was platted in 1879. Watson calls itself the "Canada Geese Capital," since every fall thousands upon thousands of these honkers fly down the Red River from Canada descending on the Lac qui Parle game refuge. During the day they fly out to feed in the surrounding cornfields, filling the skies in their traditional formations. Watson boasts

of a grain elevator dating back to 1886.

Running parallel to the highway, just north of Watson, is an old glacial river channel known as the Watson Sag. During dry periods, the southeast part is used as pasture land. Much of this channel, however, is a rich marsh spotted with dead trees and known locally as the "Big Slough." Engineering was completed to divert floodwaters from the Chippewa, if if needed, through the slough.

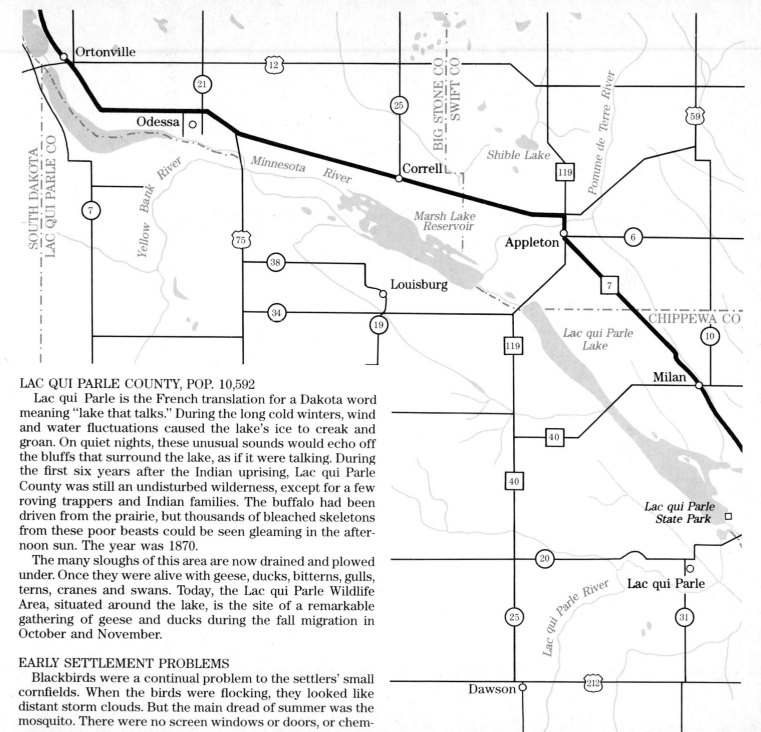

LAC QUI PARLE COUNTY, POP. 10,592

Lac qui Parle is the French translation for a Dakota word meaning "lake that talks." During the long cold winters, wind and water fluctuations caused the lake's ice to creak and groan. On quiet nights, these unusual sounds would echo off the bluffs that surround the lake, as if it were talking. During the first six years after the Indian uprising, Lac qui Parle County was still an undisturbed wilderness, except for a few roving trappers and Indian families. The buffalo had been driven from the prairie, but thousands of bleached skeletons from these poor beasts could be seen gleaming in the afternoon sun. The year was 1870.

The many sloughs of this area are now drained and plowed under. Once they were alive with geese, ducks, bitterns, gulls, terns, cranes and swans. Today, the Lac qui Parle Wildlife Area, situated around the lake, is the site of a remarkable gathering of geese and ducks during the fall migration in October and November.

EARLY SETTLEMENT PROBLEMS

Blackbirds were a continual problem to the settlers' small cornfields. When the birds were flocking, they looked like distant storm clouds. But the main dread of summer was the mosquito. There were no screen windows or doors, or chem-

Railroad hunting excursion, 1880.

MHS

ical sprays for the cattle. Only the use of smoke could give a little relief. Each fall, the grasses of the prairie became dry, and during the first half of October a fire always seemed to start. Everything in its path was burned to the ground, even the sedges and reeds of the marshes. The view on a dark, windy night of a fire sweeping through the blackness, was a sight few forgot.

During the winter when heavy snowfalls occurred, travel became nearly impossible. The landscape became one great, white ocean where the wind pushed the snow into drifts that could bury cabins. It was not unheard of for settlers to climb out of a chimney to free themselves.

SNOWSAILING

West of here, the land had few fences and was flat enough for an interesting sport called snowsailing. Sleighs resembling ice boats, with some room for supplies, shot across the snow at great speed, a few covering distances as great as a 100 miles in a day.

LAC QUI PARLE VILLAGE

First settled in 1868, this village once boasted of a population of 600. Today it has dwindled to a few houses. The town was situated near the Lac qui Parle River, on a trail that led from Big Stone Lake to Redwood Falls. Settlers had been attracted here by glowing pictures of a western metropolis that one day would become an economic center of the region. When the Wisconsin, Minnesota & Pacific Railroad entered the county in 1884, it missed the town by many miles. Citizens recognized that this was the beginning of the end, and moved their stores and houses across the prairie to the towns of Dawson and Madison, both situated on the new railroad line.

The final blow came in 1886, when the county seat was moved from here to Madison. There was much tension when a posse from Madison came into town to literally move the small courthouse away. The residents watched as the building, resting on a large wagon, rumbled across the prairie. It was only a few miles out of town when this bizarre procession was stopped by a snowstorm and a broken axle.

MILAN, Pop. 417

Milan is another railway village, platted in 1880 and named after an Italian city. No one knows for sure how that happened, since 90 percent of the town is Norwegian. The residents are very proud of their Norwegian potato flatcakes called "lefse."

LAC QUI PARLE PARK

This 529-acre park is situated along the Minnesota River, where a 300-foot dam regulates its flow. The dam has created one of the major waterfowl areas in the upper Midwest. Each fall, the lake is covered with geese that fly out to feed in nearby fields. It is quite a sight.

The park is also the site of the earliest Protestant Indian mission, dating back to 1835. Joseph Renville established a post here in 1826. His mother was a Dakota and taught Renville the Indian ways. With his bilingual abilities, Renville helped the missionaries translate the Bible and other necessary materials. Renville also assisted Reverend Riggs in compiling the first grammar and dictionary books in the Dakota language. These books were later published by the Smithsonian Institute in 1852.

SWIFT COUNTY, Pop. 12,920

This county was named after Henry Swift, governor of Minnesota in 1863. The county is mostly a flat plain. Settlers lived an almost primitive life here during the early years of 1866-68. A small group of Norwegians was the first to settle in the northeast part of the county, by Camp Lake. Because trees were scarce, the dwellings were often holes carved out of small hills. If no hills were to be found, they built their homes out of sod chunks. By the time autumn came around, the sod roofs had sprouted a rich growth of grass and prairie flowers. After heavy rains, the dirt walls proved ineffectual. But inventive pioneers soon discovered that a mixture of cow manure and wood ashes, in the right proportions, withstood the downpours much better.

There wasn't much room inside these crude dwellings, and most of the furniture was homemade. Five to ten acres of land were planted with wheat and potatoes. For most of these early settlements, the markets of New Ulm, St. Cloud and Sauk Center were too far away to trade. Consequently, most of the food was raised for subsistence living only. The winters were dreaded for the fierce snow and isolation that they brought. Gauging how much food to store for the winter was extremely difficult.

Settlement here didn't begin in any great numbers until after the Sioux Uprising and the Civil War. By picking townsites at intervals of approximately eight miles, the railroad became the determining factor in settlement. Swift County's trading centers developed in 1870–only after the rails were laid. The first was to be Kerkhoven, named after one of the company's stockholders; next came De Graff, which honored the railroad builder; and then Benson, named after a prominent politician and citizen of Anoka.

As the railroad was laid, many immigrants purchased tickets as far as the line would carry them, then proceeded by ox-team to their final destinations. Many Irish settled in the proposed towns along this stretch of railway. But settlement was often a slow process. One woman wrote about leaving the train in Willmar and trekking west across a flat prairie "dotted with sloughs and inhabited by millions of mosquitoes." She wrote that she saw only one person, and he crawled out of his sod hut in true gopher-like fashion, giving them only a cold stare.

APPLETON, Pop. 1,842

Appleton is the former site of a Dakota camp on the Pomme de Terre River. But it wasn't until five years after the Sioux Uprising that settlers began to move in slowly. Addison Phelps was one of the first to call this place home in 1868. The township became known as Phelps until, by his own request, it was renamed Appleton after the Wisconsin town of the same name. The town itself didn't get started until 1871, when a dam and mill were constructed. Three years later this village contained one store, a blacksmith shop, a mill and half a dozen buildings.

Today, Appleton is a shipping center crossed by lines of the Burlington Northern and the Chicago, Milwaukee, St. Paul & Pacific Railroads.

MHS

The Minnesota River was one of the first major routes of the Red River oxcarts.

POMME DE TERRE RIVER

The Pomme De Terre River, from the French word for potato, was named for a prairie turnip with eyes like a potato. These turnips were harvested by the Dakota. The Pomme De Terre River has its beginnings in the lake region, some 100 miles to the north. The river winds its way through many clear lakes and marshes, abundant with waterfowl. Southwest of Appleton, it enters Marsh Lake, which is part of the Lac qui Parle Wildlife Area.

BIG STONE COUNTY, Pop. 7,716

Unorganized until 1862, this county took its name from the lake which the Dakota called, "Inyan tankinyanyan," meaning "very great stone." This comes from the granite outcroppings once quarried along the Minnesota River near Ortonville.

Big Stone Lake was created by sediment deposited across its outlet by the Whetstone River of South Dakota. Marsh and Lac qui Parle Lakes were created by this process. Now all three lakes have dams to regulate their levels. Big Stone Lake is 25 miles long and is the source of the Minnesota River which flows 270 miles to St. Paul.

At the head of Big Stone Lake is the town of Browns Valley, located on the continental divide. Here, a small rise in the land separates the Red River, which drains north into Hudson Bay, from the Minnesota River basin, which eventually flows to the Gulf of Mexico.

MHS

Early quarrying in Minnesota.

ORTONVILLE, Pop. 2,548

Ortonville is located on the southern shore of Big Stone Lake. The surrounding area was a favorite hunting and fishing spot for the early Dakota Indians. Many Indian mounds have been discovered in this region.

Though the town was not settled until ten years after the Sioux Uprising, this spot was heavily traveled. In the early 1800's, noisy Red River carts were heading for Traverse des Sioux from their settlements near Winnipeg and Pembina. Trading posts were also established along Lake Traverse down to Lac qui Parle. French and English traders bought many furs from the Indians here.

In 1872 Cornelius Orton traveled from Wisconsin to this spot on the Big Stone and laid out a townsite. The site began to flourish and soon became known as Ortonville. It grew into a major trading center, even though the nearest railroad station was 40 miles away at Benson. At one time, grain was shipped down the 25-mile-long Big Stone Lake, on steam-driven barges.

A ruby-red granite, quarried here for many years, supplied the stone for buildings such as the Minneapolis City Hall. A canning company in Ortonville was also the originator and patent holder of equipment used in canning whole kernels of corn.

MHS

Drought in Swift County during the depression.

166

A farm family takes their lunch in the field.

ROUTE 169, 60 SOUTH TO WORTHINGTON

Travel was slow and arduous on a Red River oxcart.

MHS

This highway follows the Minnesota River some sixty miles down to Mankato. It lies inside a valley carved out over 12,000 years ago by a glacial river larger than the present Minnesota River. The Minnesota, like the Mississippi, provided a passageway for Indians, traders with their Red River oxcarts and finally, the settlers themselves. A rich history runs along this river; stories of settlers who climbed off keel boats and steamers to begin a new life, and the sad demise of the proud Dakota Nation which lost its land in the Traverse des Sioux Treaty, signed along these quiet river banks near St. Peter.

The second half of route 169 leaves the Minnesota River where food and water were always plentiful, and stretches out across an area of tallgrass prairie. To the west, the land climbs slowly to Coteau des Prairies, or "highland of the prairies," an area some 800 feet higher than the central plains. Through the shoulder-high grass, the farmers came across southern Minnesota in their covered wagons called prairie schooners. Eventually they stopped by streams and built cabins, breaking the thick sod to raise food. Their's was a story of blizzards, locusts, and generally hard times. A fear of nature equaled their fear of the Indians that roamed the prairie. Much of southwestern Minnesota wasn't settled until some twenty years after land was first opened to the whites in 1851.

EDEN PRAIRIE, Pop. 16,263

Settled in 1852, Eden Prairie was named because of its prairie-like qualities in contrast to the rolling hills of the Minnesota River Valley.

MINNESOTA RIVER VALLEY

Highway 169 traverses a broad valley covered with backwater marshes dotted with muskrat houses. During the mid-1800's this route was one of the main trade routes for communities of the Red River Valley and Winnipeg.

It hardly seems possible that the Minnesota, a quiet river hidden from view by the stately cottonwoods, could erode a valley as wide and deep as the one we see here today. Twelve thousand years ago, glacial meltwater in northwest Minnesota created Glacial Lake Agassiz, a body of water larger than the combined Great Lakes and covering most of northwest Minnesota, eastern North Dakota and the Canadian province of Manitoba. Because ice to the north blocked the normal drainage into Hudson Bay, the water flowed south to the Mississippi as a massive river named Glacial River Warren.

Glacial River Warren was the major river in the state until the ice dam on the north side of Lake Agassiz melted, and the lake started draining north. Today the humble Minnesota

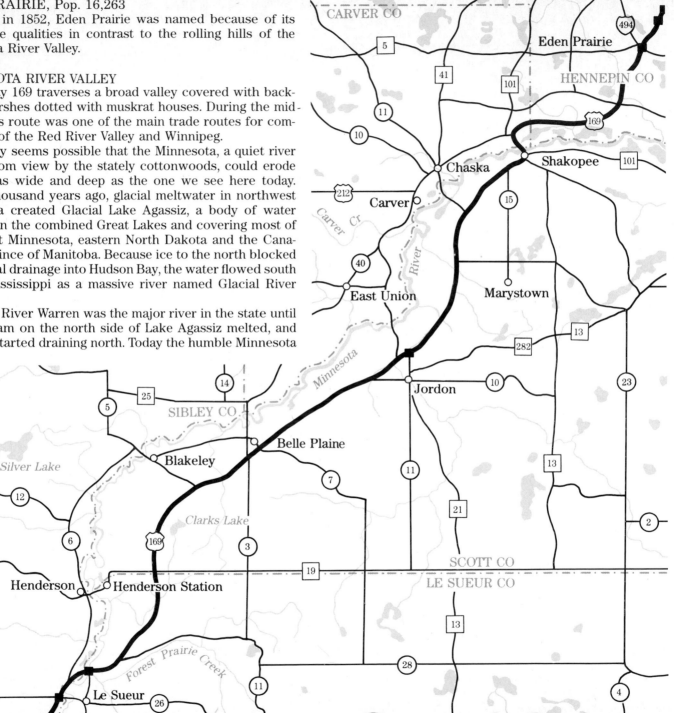

River runs through the broad valley of this ancient glacial river. In some places the valley is five miles wide and over 250 feet below the surrounding hills. Prior to 1849, the Minnesota River had been called the St. Peter River by French and British explorers. The name St. Peter is thought to refer to Pierre Charles Le Sueur, an early explorer of the river.

The Minnesota River flows from Big Stone Lake between Browns Valley and Ortonville and continues for 328 miles before it joins the Mississippi at Fort Snelling. The Minnesota's watershed draws 14,751 square miles, close to one-fifth of the state's area. The river takes its name from the Dakota word meaning "cloudy waters." After the 1851 treaty of Traverse des Sioux, it became the highway to the southern and western part of the state for thousands of settlers that streamed in. At one time, steamboats plied the Minnesota, leaving St. Paul and traveling as far upstream as New Ulm.

SCOTT COUNTY, Pop. 43,748

This county, established in 1853, was named for General Winfield Scott, commander-in-chief of the U.S. Army during the Mexican War. Scott visited Fort St. Anthony in 1824, shortly after it was built, and proposed changing its name to Fort Snelling, in honor of the fort's builder, Colonel Josiah Snelling. The name was changed the following year. Ironically, that was the closest Winfield Scott ever came to Scott County.

Pierre Le Sueur, a French fur trader and explorer, was probably the first white man to pass through this region in 1700. Le Sueur was on his way up the Minnesota River in search of copper ore and furs. Jonathan Carver, a Connecticut Yankee, passed along the Minnesota some 60 years later to make peace with the Indians and search for a passage to the Pacific Coast. In the next few decades traders began to locate along the river, and by 1820 the Minnesota Valley had become an established route between St. Paul, Mendota and the communities along the Red River of northwestern Minnesota and Canada.

SHAKOPEE, Pop. 9,941

For many years, the present town of Shakopee was the site of a Dakota village led by a line of chiefs with the name of Shakopee. The last Chief Shakopee was one of 38 Dakota Indians hung in Mankato for their part in the Sioux Uprising of 1862.

Eventually traders and missionaries settled near Chief Shakopee's village. One of the first was Oliver Faribault who started trading there in 1844. His father, Jean Baptiste Faribault, had a post near Carver as early as 1803.

In 1851, Thomas Holmes, a townsite promoter set up a trading store in Shakopee and is credited with being the founder of the town. Stagecoaches were running between St.Paul and Shakopee by 1853, but for 15 years, the river and stage trails were the only routes of transportation. It wasn't until the winter of 1865 that the Minnesota Valley Railroad reached Shakopee, connecting it with St. Paul.

Meanwhile, steamboats traveling up the Mississippi began exploring the Minnesota, even though it was shallow, unpredictable and crooked. The first steamboat left Fort Snelling for Shakopee's village in 1842. Sixteen years later over 400 departures from St. Paul were recorded, with many boats traveling as far as New Ulm. Settlers flooded this area after the 1851 Mendota and Traverse des Sioux treaties were signed. The Dakota ceded most of their Minnesota lands and were then relocated on reservations along the Minnesota above New Ulm. But during the summer months, Indian braves still roamed their old hunting grounds. In 1858, the year Minnesota was given its statehood, about 150 warriors of Shakopee's band were camped near the town when an Ojibwe raiding party attacked. A bloody battle followed until the Ojibwe finally retreated north. This battle at Shakopee marked the end of almost 150 years of conflict between these two tribes.

CARVER COUNTY, Pop. 37,065

This county was named after Jonathan Carver, who explored the region and wrote his impressions while traveling along the Minnesota River in 1766. Thousands of years before Carver's travels, glaciers covered the county, advancing into southern Minnesota and beyond. When these ice sheets began to melt, they left behind a rolling, irregular surface of sand, gravel and clay. In addition, large blocks of ice that had broken from the main glacier left depressions in the earth that eventually formed lakes.

Early explorers and trappers found the county to be extensively forested with red and white oak, sugar maple, elm and basswood. This area was later called the Big Woods. The thick forest separated the prairie of the southwest, from the spruce and pine forests of the northeast. But the early settlers took advantage of the forest's abundance, and in a few short years most of the Big Woods were destroyed, either for money, or just by clearing them for farming.

Land was opened for white settlement after the important treaties of 1851 were signed. A short time later, some 25 settlements spread over the county. Today, only 12 remain. The towns that grew, owed their fate to the railroad lines that entered the county in 1880. Those that faded away, in most cases, had found themselves miles from any railroad grading.

Most of the first immigrants were Germans and Scandinavians, whose strong religious backgrounds provided fertile ground for the missionaries that developed the early religious communities. East Union was one of the first Swedish communities in the state. A church was built there in 1859.

CHASKA, Pop. 8,346

This name is taken from a Dakota word generally given to their first born son. It is possible that the first Indians camped here as long ago as 3,000 B.C. Today, the only record of their visits are some mounds located in the public square. The first white man was Thomas Holmes, who came in 1851. But the Chaska Land Company, an eastern enterprise, bought most of the land and planned the town.

The proximity to the river provided the needed boost to this town, which was one of the first settled in the county. Chaska, along with Carver, was the major trading center for the next 20 years, at least until 1872, when the railroads diminished the importance of the river. Although Carver eventually became a sleepy little community, Chaska remained economically strong, with its pickle and sugar-beet processing plants, breweries and brickyards. In 1866, the town produced 800,000 bricks that were used in the construction of many state buildings, including Fort Snelling.

A few days before the James-Younger gang made their raid on Northfield in September of 1876, they entered Chaska. Not easily recognized, they were invited to play poker with the sheriff, newspaper editor, and other prominent citizens.

CARVER, Pop. 642

Carver, named after the explorer Jonathan Carver, was settled around the same time as Chaska by a crusty Norwegian named Axel Jorgeson. With its spot on the river, Carver soon became an active town. There was daily stage service and between its grain shipping, brickyards and farm businesses, Carver had a bright future. But railroads in the region during the 1870's slowed the prosperous steamboat traffic and like so many other stream-side villages during the turn-of-the-century, Carver struggled to stay alive. Today, a number of nineteenth century homes have been restored, and a drive down into this old rivertown is well worth the time.

EAST UNION

In 1852 this became the site of one of Minnesota's earliest Swedish settlements, called King Oscar's Settlement. A church was built seven years later, which still stands today amid the cornfields of this fertile region.

JORDAN, Pop. 2,663

Jordan, when it was settled around 1854, took its name from the biblical Jordan River of the Mideast. It was an early attraction to German immigrants, partly due to a German writer named Carl Schurz. Schurz wrote that this part of the Minnesota River, with its gently sloping banks, was as beautiful as the Rhine.

Two miles east of Jordan, Samuel Strait built a hotel in 1857 at what was to be the town of St. Lawrence. But the town never really materialized and the elaborate three-story building with a dance hall on the top floor was used as a barn.

BELLE PLAINE, Pop. 2,754

Most of Scott County was covered by the Big Woods, except for the Minnesota River bottom lands between Jordan and Belle Plaine. This stretch of level grassland became known as Shakopee Prairie and was the site of Broken Arm's village during the 1830's. But in 1852, the site became home for a trading post run by Louis Robert and was given a French name meaning "beautiful prairie." Today Belle Plaine, a classic turn of the century town, is an agricultural trading center.

In 1976, the Minnesota National Wildlife Refuge was established, running for the most part from Belle Plaine to Fort Snelling. This refuge of marshes, oxbow lakes and river bottom, appears much like it did when the Dakota hunted for their food. It is rich in song birds, deer, and many species of waterfowl .

BLAKELEY

Situated along the Minnesota River is the small hamlet of Blakeley, founded in 1867 as a railroad village. The old stone bank, a couple of wooden stores and a handful of homes are all that remain of the town today.

LE SUEUR COUNTY, Pop. 23,434

This county, established in 1853, was named after Pierre Charles Le Sueur, a French-Canadian. Le Sueur became one of this area's first explorers as he searched for minerals and furs. Hearing about some copper ore embedded in the banks of the Blue Earth River, Le Sueur traveled up the Minnesota River to present-day Mankato in search of it. It is unclear if Le Sueur meant to use the ore as a means to obtain financing for his fur-trading business. Nevertheless, he managed to mine 4,000 pounds of some blue-green clay. Unfortunately, he hauled the ore all the way to France only to discover it was worthless.

Most of the county is drained by the Minnesota, except for a southeastern portion drained by the Cannon River east to the Mississippi. The Minnesota River, flowing some 200 feet below the bluffs, is two to four miles wide in some places. Before the settlers cleared the land for agriculture, the county was covered by an extensive forest (40 to 50 miles wide) that ran north to south through central Minnesota. The forest was mainly basswood and sugar maple, but also included red and white oak, elm, ash and many others.

The first permanent settlers in this region lived in the villages of Le Sueur, Ottawa and Kasota.

LE SUEUR, Pop. 3,763

The highway drops down into the broad valley of the ancient Glacial River Warren and past the town of Le Sueur, an active village with a number of stately homes. Le Sueur was the first county seat and the second stop up from St. Peter, along the Chicago and Northwestern Railroad. In the early days there was much squabbling as to where the actual town was to be located. At one time there were three villages; Le Sueur, Le Sueur City and Middle Le Sueur. But the town finally formed where George Thompson built his log cabin in the spring of 1852. Thompson never really saw Le Sueur grow because he was accidentally shot on the prairie the following year.

During the formation of local governments, intense competition for the county seat developed between neighboring villages. Le Sueur was no exception. In the fall of 1859, a group of armed men from Cleveland, a town ten miles to the south, marched to Le Sueur to take the county records, thus making Cleveland the county seat. But Le Sueur city officials were forewarned and hid with the records and cocked rifles in a store. The frustrated Cleveland group made off with only a few maps, a desk and some legal papers.

Le Sueur was also the home of Dr. William W. Mayo while he practiced as a country doctor, from 1858 to 1863. Mayo was founder of the world famous Mayo Clinic in Rochester. The home Mayo built is preserved on the city's main street. A plaque on the building gives a brief history.

The early activities of Le Sueur were centered around milling and farming, but since 1903 the region has produced large amounts of corn and peas. The main economic activity has centered around the multi-million dollar Green Giant Company, which runs a processing and canning plant in town. At one time Le Sueur had a community of pastel-colored adobe houses lived in by Mexican-Americans who came north to work the fields during the summer.

ARROW PRAIRIE

This flat grassland which extends along the east side of the river from Ottawa to Le Sueur, was once a campsite used by Dakota braves hunting buffalo or waiting to trade with travelers moving along the Minnesota River.

Crossing the Minnesota River by ferry near Ft. Snelling. Photo/Ingersoll.

MHS

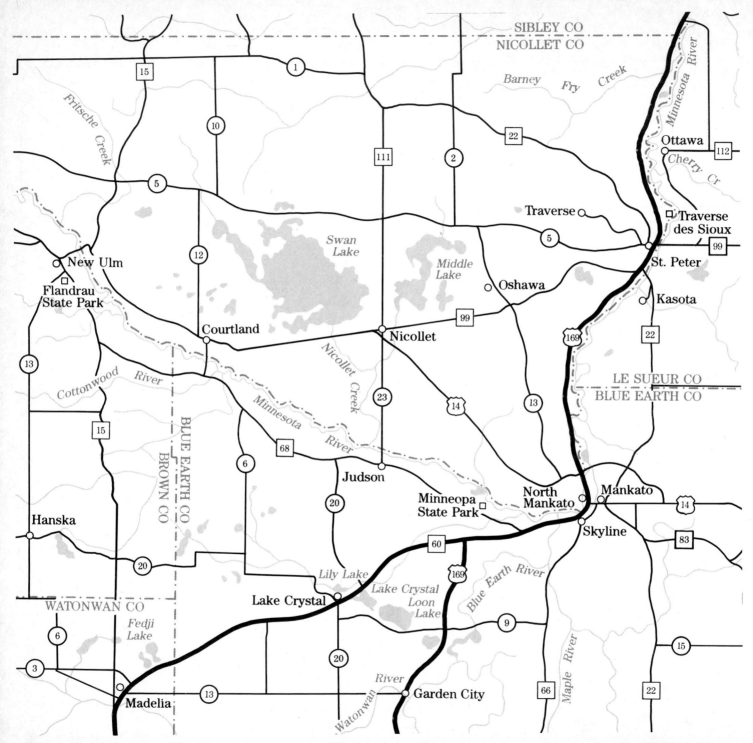

ALTERNATIVE ROUTE TO ST. PETER

From Le Sueur, a winding country road runs down the east side of the Minnesota River bottoms to the village of Ottawa and on to St. Peter. The road is in good shape, not busy, and offers a view of the Minnesota Valley not seen from U.S. 169. Take County Rd. 36 from Le Sueur to Ottawa, then 23 south from Ottawa to State 99 into St. Peter.

OTTAWA, Pop. 100

Ottawa was founded in 1853 by a Frenchman named Antoine Young, who built the first saw and gristmill in the county. After a few years of back-breaking work, Young moved to western Minnesota where he was killed during the Sioux Uprising.

The hamlet was named after the Ottawa Indian tribe, which was related to the Ojibwe. Today, only a small collection of homes makes up this town. The old brick school #12, built in 1915, sits empty; its windows broken. The schoolyard, scattered with rusted farm implements, is now used for storage by a local farmer. Still preserved, however, is the stone Methodist church built in 1859. It is one of the oldest Methodist churches in Minnesota. The church was used until 1958 and is still open Sunday afternoons during the summer.

NICOLLET COUNTY, Pop. 26,929

Established in 1853, Nicollet County is bounded on three sides by the Minnesota River. It was named after J. Nicholas Nicollet, a French astronomer who traveled the region and drafted the first authentic map of the territory. The county is nearly flat and covered with glacial drift some 100 to 200 feet thick. The major feature of this county is the deep valley in which the Minnesota River lies. Most of the timber in the county lies along the Minnesota River and consists of white and red elms, basswood, sugar and silver maples, butternut, hickory, black ash, aspen, cottonwood, willows and paper birch.

TRAVERSE DES SIOUX

An 1100 acre park now marks the location of one of the most important historic moments in Minnesota history.

Traverse des Sioux was, at first, the location of a small Sisseton Indian village located near a shallow, sandy spot on the Minnesota River. This natural land feature made it an easy crossing for the Dakota and his pony. Louis Provencalle, a Canadian fur-trader, was the first white settler here as an agent for the American Fur Company. Provencalle knew this was an ideal place for an Indian trading post, since it was here that their trail led from the western plains to their hunting grounds in the Big Woods.

As the oxcarts began traveling down the Minnesota from the Red River Valley, Traverse des Sioux became an important transfer spot, where goods were loaded onto keel boats to finish the trip to Mendota. The Big Woods were too thick in those early days to make an overland trip to Mendota feasible.

Because of settlement pressures extending from the East in the early 1850's, the U.S. Government desired acquisition of the vast lands owned by the Dakota Nation. It was at this crossing in the river during the summer of 1851, that the Dakota chiefs signed away 24 million acres of land in Minnesota and Dakota Territory. They further agreed to move to a reservation running along a narrow stretch of the Minnesota River from Granite Falls to Lake Traverse. The total price paid to the Dakota averaged 12.5 cents an acre, payable over a 50-year-period. But it didn't really matter, since after the Sioux Uprising in 1862, the government voided the treaty and the Dakota were banished from the state. All annuities were denied them and a bounty was offered for all Dakota scalps. The Dakota continued their futile battles with the white man until 1890 when the Massacre of Wounded Knee took place near Rosebud, South Dakota.

Today a park run by the city of St. Peter is located one-half mile north of town on the east side of U.S. 169, opposite the treaty site which is located just across the highway. Here a trail runs from the parking lot along a grassy plain where depressions from the old trading posts, missions and hotels can still be seen.

ST. PETER, Pop. 9,056

St. Peter was founded in 1853 by Captain William B. Dodd who built the first section of a military road near Traverse des Sioux to Mendota. With two ox-teams and ten men, Dodd cleared a narrow path through the Big Woods in just over

Jacoby's Photo Gallery in St. Peter, 1867.

MHS

175

three months. He was killed during the defense of New Ulm in the Sioux Uprising. The city got its name from the Minnesota River, which during the 1700's was called Riviere St. Pierre by the French and the St. Peter River by the British. In 1852, Congress changed it to the present Minnesota.

Early settlers in 1857 tried to move the territorial capital from St. Paul to St. Peter. The settlers had anticipated that this new state of Minnesota might be a horizontal state, with its northern boundary running along the 46th parallel, just above the Twin Cites and west to the Missouri River. If this were the case, St. Peter would become a centrally located capital in this long horizontal farming state.

Land was quickly donated and residents hastily built a frame structure at the corner of Third and Walnut streets. The bill to move the capital passed both House and Senate, but was spirited away by Joseph Rolette before the governor could sign it. Rolette hid in a hotel room until the constitutional time limit was passed and St. Peter lost out in its bid.

St. Peter, though not directly attacked during the Sioux Uprising, was on the edge of a battle where up to 500 whites were killed. The newspaper here was the first to hint at possible troubles with the Dakota just before the uprising. Gustavus Adolphus College and the St. Peter Security Hospital are located here. St. Peter is also the home of five state governors.

KASOTA, Pop. 739

Kasota is named after a Dakota word which describes a nearby prairie ridge. The town was settled in 1851 by Reuben Butters and J. W. Babcock. Babcock and his son, Charles, built a mill and started a quarry, while Butters started raising potatoes. A short time later, Butters harvested 900 bushels of fine Irish potatoes that sold for one dollar a bushel. The next year it seemed that the whole area planted spuds and the price fell to 10 cents a bushel.

This river village became well-known for its pink colored limestone, soon called Kasota Stone. These quarries supplied the stone for the Minnesota and Wisconsin State Capitals, Kansas City Railroad Terminal, Hotel St.Paul, and many other major buildings from coast to coast.

Aided by the busy quarries, Kasota grew rapidly. At one time the town had a very popular dance hall, a hotel, general store, blacksmith and wagon shop, plus a sawmill and one hundred homes. Today all that remains are a few homes and a couple of interesting old stone buildings. But on a county road south of town, there is still some quarrying going on. Here you can see the booms that lift out huge limestone blocks as they are drilled and cut from the bedrock.

Portrait of a threshing crew, 1890.

MHS

BLUE EARTH COUNTY, Pop. 52,314

Blue Earth County is laced with a number of rivers, each cutting a deep valley out of the level prairie. These rivers are: the Minnesota, Blue Earth, Watonwan, Le Sueur, Maple, Big Colb, and Minneopa. Timber grew along their banks, offering shelter and fuel for the early pioneers that followed them from Iowa and Wisconsin. These same rivers powered early saw and gristmills and harbored the first settlements.

Glaciers pushed across the county over 11,000 years ago, leaving up to 150 feet of rich soil. A tallgrass prairie sprung up from this soil, providing grazing for the vast buffalo herds and other animals that roamed the land. When Indians began to appear, they used the rivers and made trails to hunt this fertile area. They called the Minnesota River "Watapa Minnesota" or "river of cloudy waters." But today many translate it as the "land of sky-tinted waters."

Le Sueur was probably the first white man to pass this area in search of minerals and furs. Paddling up the Minnesota in 1700, into the mouth of the Blue Earth River, he sighted blue-green clay along the banks. The Indians used this clay to paint themselves, in the belief that it protected them from arrows. But Le Sueur thought the clay was copper ore. He built a fort a couple of miles up from the mouth of the Blue Earth and named it Fort L'Huillier. Le Sueur wintered there with nineteen men and subsisted by trading with the Indians and living off the kill of 400 buffalo. The following spring, Le Sueur left twelve men at the fort while he made the long trip back to France with 4000 pounds of what turned out to be worthless clay. The twelve men later abandoned the fort in 1702 after an attack by the Fox Indians.

For the next 64 years there was little written history about this region, until Jonathan Carver passed by in 1766 and spent the winter with Indians in New Ulm. To be sure, there were other trappers and explorers that wandered this rich area during this time, but it was Carver who published the first English narrative about the land and the Indians. It wasn't until 1838, that Joseph Nicollet, a cartographer, initiated the first mapping and factual recording of this region. Impressed by the number of streams in this area, Nicollet named it the "Undine Region," after a folklore water spirit.

MANKATO, Pop. 28,642

Mankato is southwestern Minnesota's leading metropolis. Industry merges here with agriculture, as its location has made it a natural trade center for all of southwestern Minnesota, parts of Iowa and South Dakota. The diversity ranges from soy-bean processing to a state university.

Mankato, a Sioux name meaning "Blue Earth," was named for a colored clay found along the banks of the Blue Earth River near its confluence with the Minnesota. The town was first settled in January, 1852, by three St. Paul men named Parson Johnson, Henry Jackson and Daniel Williams. These three men made the six day journey on sleighs and were stopped along the way by Chief Sleepy Eye, who was upset

because the government had not paid him for the land he gave up in the 1851 treaty. The men offered him a barrel of pork, along with other items, and they were soon allowed to pass. Finally, they stopped at a spot covered with tall waving grass, unsusceptible to spring flooding. There they built a 12-foot square shanty without floor or windows.

It wasn't long before this spot developed into a booming frontier town and steamboats were transporting people and goods to supply them. Each time the shrill whistle of the boat was heard, everyone in ear-shot, including the Indians, would rush to the Mankato landing. As in all new towns, there were many hardships to overcome, such as the mosquitoes. One summer, a farmer claimed that after his mule died it was carried away by these pesky bugs.

The town grew, roads were built, and river traffic during the late 1800's continued to increase. Hundreds stopped at Shakopee, Chaska, St. Peter and Mankato, carrying a large amount of goods. Fort Ridgely was established up the river in 1853 to help keep peace between the Dakota and Ojibwe. The fort also provided protection for settlers residing on the lands that the Dakota gave up at Traverse des Sioux in 1851.

MINNEOPA STATE PARK

This 917-acre State Park was named after the Dakota word for "two falls." It is situated along Minneopa Creek where two scenic waterfalls drop 50 feet into a gorge surrounded by steep bluffs. Included in the park is an old stone windmill built by Louis Seppman in 1864. The mill is 32 feet high and has a millstone that Seppman brought from St. Louis at a cost of $6,000. Seppman's mill ground flour until 1880 and

Harvesting wheat, 1882.

MHS

was used as a feed mill for local residents until 1890.

The park was donated by the Blue Earth Historical Society to the state park system in 1931. It is only a short drive down into the Minneopa Valley. There you can park and walk the one hundred or so feet to the falls.

MANKATO EXECUTIONS

In August 1862, after years of insensitive treatment by the government, and seeing their once-vast domain condensed to a narrow stretch of land along the Minnesota River, the Dakota began their war against the white man. The Uprising was squelched, but not before 500 whites had been killed. The panic of the settlers was fueled by rumors of spearings,

MHS

Big Eagle, one of the leaders during the Sioux Uprising.

scalpings and mutilations. Revenge was quickly taken when some 307 warriors out of the 2,000 captured were sentenced to death.

It was a bitterly cold day after the Christmas of 1862, when President Lincoln approved the hanging of 38 Dakota Indians, out of the original 307. Every vantage point was taken at the

Mankato site of Front and Main Streets. W. H. Dooley, whose entire family was killed at Lake Shetek, cut the two-inch rope that plunged the entire group to their death. This multiple hanging marked the largest wholesale execution that ever took place in the United States.

NEW ULM, Pop. 13,755

The German village of New Ulm is located on high land that was once an island in the Glacial River Warren. Today the Cottonwood River, one of the major streams flowing from the highland prairie of southwest Minnesota, enters the Minnesota River at New Ulm. The city was built on three different terraces formed by these rivers.

New Ulm was founded in 1854, when members of the German Land Society from Chicago came here to lay out a town. Officially they named it New Ulm after the town of Ulm in Wurttemberg, Germany. The town struggled along for a year before the German Land Society merged with a Cincinnati group. They then became known as the German Land Association of Minnesota. New Ulm developed around highly efficient craftsmen, bankers, brewers and farmers. By 1860 there were over 653 Germans living here who maintained their native language and customs.

New Ulm was the site of an important battle during the Sioux Uprising of 1862. As word spread that Chief Little Crow was leading a large number of Dakota warriors in strikes against the whites, families rushed in from the prairie to New Ulm for protection. Frustrated by their repulsed attacks on Fort Ridgely, just up the river, the Dakota braves mounted a major attack against New Ulm on August 23, 1862. Under the guidance of Charles Flandrau, a St. Peter Judge, the residents of New Ulm fought off a prolonged attack by some 800 warriors. But before the Indians retreated up the Minnesota River, much of New Ulm had been burned, twenty-six residents killed, and scores wounded. Dr. William W. Mayo of Le Sueur was one who gave aid to the wounded. A short time later, Judge Flandrau decided to evacuate the entire town of 1200 or so people thirty miles to Mankato.

FLANDRAU STATE PARK

Located just south of New Ulm, is an 800-acre state park situated in the heavily-wooded Cottonwood River Valley. In this park there are 90 campsites, seven miles of trails, boat rentals, and a park naturalist to answer questions.

BIG WOODS

As the highway climbs from the Minnesota River Valley to the uplands, the traveler leaves what was once the western

MHS

Settlers fled for safety as word of the Sioux Uprising spread rapidly.

edge of the Big Woods and enters the tallgrass prairie. Today this is all farmland and most of the trees mark homesteads or windbreaks planted by farmers.

LAKE CRYSTAL, Pop. 2,078

Lake Crystal grew around the St. Paul and Sioux City Railroad that came through in 1869 on its push into Iowa. A line also ran from Lake Crystal south to Blue Earth. The town was so named because of the clarity of the surrounding lakes. Along the city's main street you will see a number of brick stores built in the late 1800's.

WATONWAN COUNTY, Pop. 12,361

The gently waving surface of the county shows that the glaciers moved through here in a slow continuous current, leaving slightly rolling slopes that collect water and drain into the tributaries of the Watonwan River. The Watonwan River lies in a valley some 40 feet below the general surroundings. The county, like most of the region, is covered by a rich soil laid down by the glaciers. This area was also part of the tallgrass prairie that extended through much of southwest Minnesota. Most of the original trees in this region were located along river and stream bottoms.

Watonwan settled slowly until the railroads entered the county in 1870. The northern part was first settled by Germans, Swedes and Norwegians, with the south settled by emigrants from Indiana and Wisconsin.

MADELIA, Pop. 2,130

Settled in 1857, Madelia was the first county seat of Watonwan before it was transferred to St. James in 1878. It is hard to imagine what it was like to live on the broad open prairie in an area such as Madelia. The early settlers were without phone or mail, roads or railroads. The long cold winters and the forced isolation pushed many into a deep depression. After a winter or two here, a good number packed their bags and headed back East.

It was the railroad that brought the outside world to these people. At the same time, it also freed the farmer from his long and sometimes dangerous trips to Mankato, St. Peter and St. Paul where he sold his products and then resupplied. An excitement filled these prairie towns when the tracks reached them. Their products could now feed Boston and New York. Travel to other cities was easier now, and mail delivery could be carried on year round.

In September 1876, Missouri outlaws Jesse and Frank James, led a gang of eight men into Northfield to rob the First National Bank. Failing to open the safe, they sprayed the town with bullets, killing two people. Gang members Clel Miller and Bob Stiles were also killed, but the rest of the men headed west, chased by a thousand-man posse. The gang was finally cornered in a marsh north of Madelia, where Charlie Pitts was killed and the Younger brothers wounded. Frank and Jesse James somehow managed to escape through the tallgrass into South Dakota.

ST. JAMES, Pop. 4,346

A historian of Watonwan County wrote that "in the midst of wild prairie grass and weeds there was no sign of human habitation of white men until the St.Paul and Sioux City Railroad, pushing southwest from Lake Crystal, decided to make this a station." The train entered this newly platted town in November, 1870.

General Henry Sibley was asked by the president of the line to name this town. Sibley selected a rather long and confusing Dakota Indian name which he himself couldn't pronounce. The president of the line angrily responded, "if you can't pronounce the town you were allowed to name, I have one that can be both pronounced and remembered...St. James."

This town is also the location of the stately Watonwan Court House built in 1895. The town has preserved the old Chicago & Northwestern Depot in a park located on the southwest side of town on St. James Lake.

COTTONWOOD COUNTY, Pop. 14,854

The county was established by the territorial Legislature as early as 1857, but the region had only an occasional tepee and one white trapper named "Dutch Charlie." At the time of the Sioux Uprising in 1862, only a dozen families had settled in this county, but they rapidly left, leaving no record as to who they were or where they went.

No settlement occurred here until after the Civil War. Many settlers were soldiers who, unable to be paid their bonuses in cash by the government, received 160 acres of land under the Veterans Homestead Law. According to this law, settlers had to break at least 10 acres of prairie sod for farming and remain on this land for 5 years before they could have title to it.

During those first years, the settler had very little to sell except for the furs he trapped along the streams. Because of the prairie fires, there were few trees with which to build log homes. Many homes were built of sod instead and during the winter, heat was obtained by twisting hay and slough grass into stove lengths for burning. There was a shortage of everything during those long cold months. Roasted wheat was a substitute for coffee and candles or wicks sitting in lard were the only lights. To buy supplies, a five to seven day trip to Mankato by oxen was needed. Most feared the journey lest they be caught in a blizzard.

MOUNTAIN LAKE, Pop. 2,277

The first white settler came here in 1865. He was a trapper named Mason, who lived on an island in what is now called

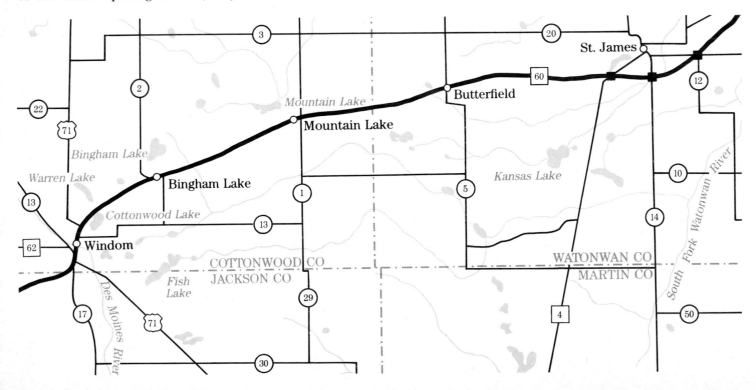

The railroad reached the Windom area in 1871.

MHS

Mountain Lake. The island, forty feet high and covered with trees, was visible for many miles and was used as a landmark for travelers. The landmarks for today's traveler are the "prairie castles" or grain elevators that can be seen for many miles.

The area of Mountain Lake turned out to be the mid-point between St. Paul and Sioux City and the railroad wanted to have a station here named Midway. Mason protested and the station retained the name of Mountain Lake. After the railroad was built in June, 1870, there was a sizeable influx of Mennonites from Russia into Mountain Lake.

WINDOM, Pop. 4,666

Windom formed along the St. Paul and Sioux City railroad in 1871 when the line was completed into the region. By fall, eight trains passed daily through the town.

Windom was named after William Windom who served in the U.S. Congress and was secretary of the treasury. Windom moved to Winona in 1855 where he practiced law and was elected to public office. He is said to have visited Windom only once.

The first years for this farming community were difficult ones. On June 14, 1873, the westerly winds carried the Rocky Mountain locusts into the region. They came by the millions; darkening the sky, devouring the cultivated crops, and bringing disaster to nearly every resident. The following year grasshopper eggs hatched again, resulting in ten times as many pests. A second successive crop failure was a terrible blow to Windom and the entire region. Wild ducks and prairie

chickens were the only meat. The county became bankrupt, immigration ceased, and emigration from the area began. Most traded their homes and land for a good team of horses to take them back East. It wasn't until 1878 that the area returned to normal and new people began to move into southwestern Minnesota.

Windom's downtown is built around a town square, in a fashion unlike other Minnesota towns. Located just off the square is the Cottonwood Historical Society and museum. The museum is free and contains an outstanding collection of historical items from the region.

DES MOINES RIVER

The Des Moines, a French term meaning "River of Monks," starts its flow some 60 miles to the north in Lake Shetek, one of the largest lakes in southwestern Minnesota. Located at Lake Shetek is a state park and the site of an Indian massacre during the Sioux Uprising. The river flows slowly through cultivated farmland. Ten miles below Windom it flows through a stretch of the Kilen Woods State Park, where it passes through a forest of oak and basswood. Twenty campsites located on a bluff here, overlook the river and several trails wind down along the river bottoms. The river gorge with its banks over 150 feet in some places, follows the river to Jackson. The Des Moines River Valley marked the edge of the Minnesota frontier during the 1850's.

MHS

Snow blocked a train after a southwestern Minnesota storm in 1909.

JACKSON COUNTY, Pop. 13,690

The county was founded in 1857, and there is still some confusion as to whom it was named after. The most popular belief is that it was named for Henry Jackson, who established the first general store in St. Paul. Jackson became the first justice of the peace and also the state's first postmaster. Early whites visiting the county were mostly trappers in search of pelts, and traders seeking business with the Dakota. Just north of the county there was a trading post on Lake Talcott in 1835, but that was abandoned in 1837. Members of the Sisseton band of Dakota Indians, and a small number of trappers had the county to themselves for several years.

One of the most obvious physical features of this prairie county is a prominent north-south ridge, crossing just west of the Des Moines River. This ridge was formed by glacial drift deposited during the ice ages 11,000 years ago. Its crest rises in some places to 1,500 feet above sea level.

HERON LAKE, Pop. 783

Heron Lake takes its name from the Dakota word "Oka-bena," meaning "nesting place of the heron." This lake was once connected to its lower lake, making it the largest lake in southwestern Minnesota. At one time it was eleven miles

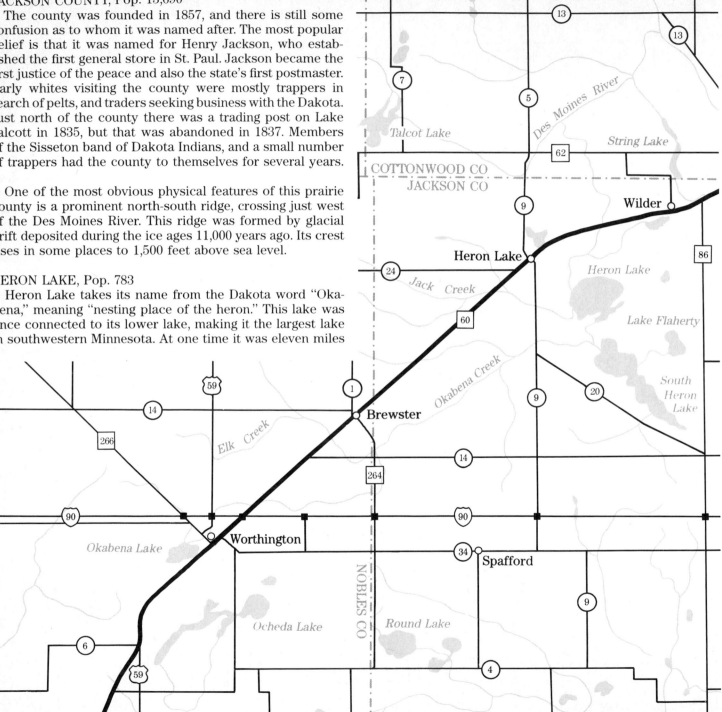

long and two miles wide. Now extensive marshes around it provide cover for geese, ducks and other waterfowl. The town was mostly settled by German and Irish farmers around 1870.

When a rumor circulated that a railroad was to lay tracks through here, homes grew up around what is now the town. But the fast growing town and the local economy suffered from the locusts of 1873. The pests were so thick that they covered the sun, and the sound at night was like the roaring wind. Property became useless and many settlers lacked the funds to leave on the train. Happily, the county made a comeback and today is one of the top agricultural producers in the state.

NOBLES COUNTY, Pop. 21,840

Nobles was organized in 1857 with its county seat planned and named "Gretchtown." The town existed on paper only. By 1860, only 65 people, mostly trappers and fur agents, were living there. The Sioux Uprising, which followed in 1862, had much to do with the slow settlement of this area.

At the beginning of the 17th century, there were, perhaps, as many as 130 million buffalo roaming the grasslands of the west. On cold winter mornings, Dakota warriors told of frost clouds that hung over giant herds that spanned 15 or 20 miles. When the white man came, wholesale slaughtering began. In many cases only the tongues were taken because of their delicacy. River boats were filled with buffalo hides and sent up the Red River, eventually carted down from Pembina to St. Paul. By the late 1800's, man had succeeded in all but wiping out this proud beast of the prairie.

WORTHINGTON, Pop. 10,234

Worthington was settled in 1871 by the National Colony Company, a temperance group that first named the town Okabena, an Indian word meaning "nesting place of herons." Although the sale of liquor was prohibited, one could still find it tucked behind the counters of some stores.

The nearby lake retains the name Okabena, but the town changed its name to Worthington in honor of one of the founders of the National Colony Company. In 1873, grasshoppers were carried in by westerly winds, making the first of several destructive visits. Farmers around Worthington that year were lucky to average nine bushels per acre in wheat, oats and corn. Money was in such short supply that the local newspaper offered to take anything in trade for subscriptions, except grasshoppers. Appeals went out to the nation to help the thousands of destitute families. Many farmers turned to trapping as a means of subsistence. In the winter of 1874-75, some 28,000 muskrat skins were shipped from Worthington.

Worthington used to have a local polo team that attained excellent national ratings. The town also boasted of the Okabena apple, which was developed in orchards on the southern shore of Lake Okabena. In the vicinity of Worthington, a series of north-south valleys and ridges mark the western expansion of the Keewatin Glacier during the last ice age. It was the Coteau des Prairies, a rise of land in southwestern Minnesota, that offered resistance to any further westward glacial movement. The French traders gave it a name which means "highland of the prairies." The plains here are some 800 feet higher then the central prairie of Minnesota.

MHS

The tallgrass prairie had given way to the plow by the 1870's.

ROUTE I-90, LA CRESCENT TO LUVERNE

The harsh and lonely winters on the prairie drove many early settlers back East.

Interstate 90 follows the bluffs of the Mississippi River Valley for a few miles before it climbs to the fertile and gently rolling farmland of southcentral Minnesota. The road eventually passes through a level area of prairie, crossing occasional brooks, streams, and scattered lakes by Fairmont and Albert Lea. It then passes through the Coteau des Prairies area, the highland prairie of southwestern Minnesota. This area is up to 800 feet higher then the central plains and divides the great Missouri and Mississippi drainage basins. The plateau rests on an eroded mountain range that crossed the state millions of years ago. Today of course, the prairie has been plowed and towns have formed along the old stage routes or railroad lines.

As the eastern part of Minnesota became populated, new settlers began to hopscotch further west from the Mississippi River settlements towards the prairie. The first pioneers moving inland during the 1850's were awe-struck by this vast treeless prairie. They compared it to being on the deck of a ship, with its undulating grasses stretching as far as the eye could see. The wind blew unhindered from the Rockies, and for many, its unrelenting force was too much. Still for most, this was an exciting start of a new life on a land they could call their own. The determined settlers faced many hardships though, like the long winters, where prolonged isolation and the struggle to obtain supplies, tested their perseverance. This great tallgrass prairie arched from southeast Minnesota, diagonally up its western edge, north to Canada. The prairie was composed of many grass species like switchgrass, big and little bluestem and indiangrass, to name a few. The prairie also supported an incredible variety of birds, animals and insects. Vast herds of bison, elk, and deer roamed the open land and reared their young in sheltered places along the streams. The prairie was, for the most part, formed by the glaciers that melted and reformed, each time leaving a rich deposit of soil, sand, and gravel over the hard base-rock. The last glacier retreated over 11,000 years ago.

185

WINONA COUNTY, Pop. 46,256

When Winona County was established in February 1854, it was given a name that the Dakota often gave to their first born daughters. Legend has it that an Indian woman named Winona, a cousin to chief Wabasha, threw herself from "Maiden Rock," on Lake Pepin's east shore, to keep from marrying a brave she didn't love.

Early settlement in the county started along the Mississippi during the 1850's, trade from the steamers and lumber from the St. Croix, boosted the frail economy. Flour mills went up quickly as settlers started shipping wheat in from the prairies. The Mississippi was heavily used for shipment to markets south—until the railroads came and opened up the eastern seaboard to Midwestern products.

LA CRESCENT, Pop. 3,383

When a rivalry developed with the town of La Crosse on the Wisconsin side of the Mississippi, the settlers of the small hamlet of Manton, on the Minnesota side, petitioned to change the village name to La Crescent. This stemmed from their belief that La Crosse was named for the crusader's emblem, the cross. So Manton picked the crescent, a Mohammedan emblem for power, to symbolize their competition.

Because of the fertile soil and the late frost that comes to the valley, settlers began to plant apple trees around La Crescent. The town is called the apple capital of Minnesota. During the fall it promotes the local orchards with an apple festival. The back roads of this area are stunning, and make for a beautiful autumn drive.

DAKOTA, DRESBACH

At age 17, Jeremiah Tibbitts started trading here with a band of Dakota Indians, as early as 1853. The town of Dresbach formed a few years later when George Dresbach quarried a limestone called Winona Travertine from the nearby bluffs. The bluff overlooking Dresbach is called Mineral Bluff, a sandstone hill rising 405 feet. Traces of coal, lead and silver have been found here, as was a skull with a copper hatchet protruding from it.

This part of the state is known as the "driftless area," a region untouched by glacial action. The terrain is representative of how Minnesota looked prior to glaciation. The meltwater of the glaciers did flow down the various streams however, cutting deep channels through the hillsides.

O. L. KIPP STATE PARK

One of the best kept secrets of the state park system is the 1600 acre O. L. Kipp Park, located on the bluffs of the

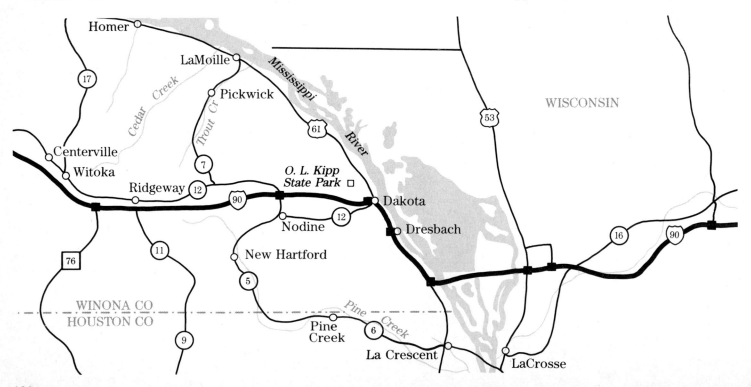

Mississippi. The park has 31 camping sites which connect nine miles of hiking and cross-county ski trails. These trails cross through deep hardwood forests and out to cliffside vistas overlooking the Mississippi and the sun-warmed hills of La Crescent. Owls, hawks, deer and an array of wild-flowers are abundant. During the fall migration, the night sky is filled with ducks and geese. Bring binoculars to watch the birds silhouetted against the harvest moon. The park is accessed from I-90 and Winona County 12.

RICHARD J. DORER STATE FOREST

In 1961 this state forest was created in southeastern Minnesota. It covers an area of two million acres; 460,000 of which are hardwoods, making it the state's largest forest. In 1974 it was named after Richard Dorer, the man who during the mid-1900's witnessed the wholesale destruction of the

HOMER, Pop. 230

A man named Francois du Chouquette tried to establish trade here with Chief Wabasha's tribe in 1830, but raids by the Sac and Fox Indians forced him to move to a safer location at the settlement of Prairie du Chien, Wisconsin.

Located on the south side of the highway is the historic Bunnell House, maintained by the Winona Historical Society. Willard Bunnell was a townsite planner and speculator who became the first permanent settler in the county. He moved off the river flats and built his house on this hillside in 1849. Bunnell named the townsite after his birthplace in New York.

DRIFTLESS AREA

Some of the most rugged terrain in Minnesota occurs south of Winona, in Houston County. It is here that a small portion

MHS

Reaching across the Mississippi, the railroads took trade from the steamboats and promoted settlement further west.

beautiful river valleys of the Whitewater, Zumbro and Root rivers. The hills were stripped clean for their lumber, and coupled with unwise farming practices, there was rapid erosion of the region's fragile topsoil. Major flooding had become an annual event, threatening what little wildlife was left. Dorer worked through his Minnesota Department of Conservation job to restore the valleys that were being washed away. Through his efforts, this region of rivers and hills has recovered and is now one of the most beautiful parts of the state.

PICKWICK

Located two miles from Lamoille on County 7, rests the picturesque village of Pickwick with its old gristmill located along Trout Creek. This beautiful drive climbs up through wooded valleys and hillside farms to O.L. Kipp State Park.

of southeast Minnesota, eastern Wisconsin, and northwest Iowa remained untouched by glaciers. Hence, it is called the driftless area since it is void of glacial debris.

As the glaciers melted to the west and east, their waters gushed down the rivers to the Mississippi, eroding the land into deep valleys and coulees. (A coulee is a gorge or valley whose stream is usually dry during the summer). When the melting was finished, the winds blew a fine silt called loess, over the the barren limestone hills. It was from this loess that the forests grew. The forests though, were abused by the early settlers, and serious erosion and flooding began to take place. Subsequent replanting during the early 1900's has restored this area's natural beauty. Because of the hills, streams and small farms with grazing herds, this region has picked up the nickname of "Little Switzerland."

SOUTHEASTERN MINNESOTA

This was one of the first areas to be settled in the new territory. By 1850 there was pressure on the U. S. Government to open more land for white settlement. The Dakota had control of most of southern Minnesota, while the Ojibwe held the north. The government drew up treaties at Mendota and Traverse des Sioux in 1851. These treaties were read to the Indians in English. When they signed, they had given up 24 million acres of land in Minnesota, Iowa and South Dakota. Eleven years later, the Dakota would be banned from the state because of the war they waged in the Sioux Uprising of 1862. Now that southern Minnesota was legally open for settlement, people were attracted by the fertile soil, plentiful lumber, and numerous streams providing water power. The level plains above the Mississippi were soon heavily planted with wheat.

By the late 1850's however, the forests were nearly depleted, causing large-scale erosion, floods, and almost total destruction of the land. Drought and diseased wheat showed the farmers that one-crop agriculture was unwise. Today this area commands over $1500 an acre for top farmland.

WYATTVILLE, WILSON, CENTERVILLE, WITOKA, RIDGEWAY, NODINE

Situated along the freeway are a series of small hamlets that mainly consist of a few homes, an occasional store, gas station, creamery, church and abandoned schoolhouse.

Southeast Minnesota homestead, 1855.

MHS

The Winona levee at night.

MHS

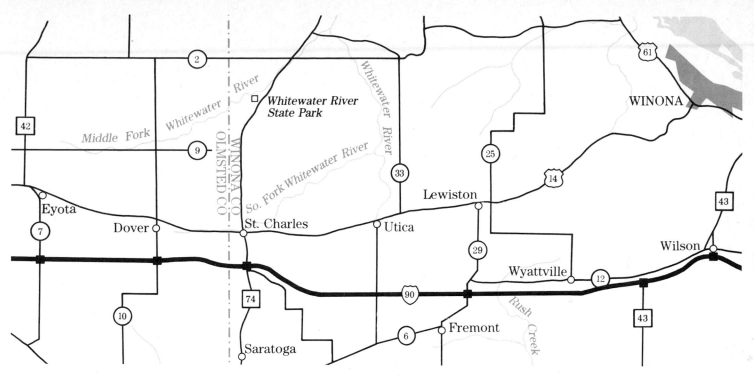

WINONA, Pop. 25,075

A prairie, devoid of any trees, once occupied this area along the Mississippi. At that time, it was the original site of Chief Red Wing's band and French traders referred to it as Wing's Prairie. Later, when Chief Wabasha resided here, it became known as Wabasha's Prairie. Around 1850, Wabasha traded these rich bottomlands for six barrels of flour. Eventually, a small collection of shanties formed on the prairie and was called Montezuma after the Mexican Aztec chief. In 1853, this growing town was renamed Winona. Legend has it that a Dakota woman, related to Chief Wabasha and named Winona (a name often given to a first born Indian girl), threw herself from a cliff on Lake Pepin's east shore, to keep from marrying a brave she didn't love. The rock became known as "Maiden's Rock."

At first Winona attracted little interest, except from a handful of traders and settlers. In 1851 the steamboat Nominee stopped here to take on wood from the hillsides for its boilers. Soon after, Winona became an important stopping place for steamboats taking on freight and wood. By 1856 settlers from Germany and New England were coming to the area. Together, these two groups planted trees along this prairie stretch, developing Winona into one of the primary sawmill towns on the Mississippi. By the late 1850's, Winona was

firmly rooted in sawmills, steamboats and wheat. At one time Winona had 10 sawmills with some 2,000 loggers and 1,500 mill hands in the workforce. During one year in the late 1800's, 8,585 steamboats rounded the bend at Winona. By 1868 Winona had become the fourth largest wheat market in the country.

In 1862, The Winona and St. Peter Railroad replaced the grain wagons and started tapping the grain fields of South Dakota. By the early 1900's, the sawmills closed down as lumbering stopped on the upper St. Croix. But economic help came from nearby quarries that developed along the sandstone bluffs. Brick-making also became an important industry. One plant produced three million bricks during the 1920's. Today Winona is a diversified agricultural and industrial center.

LEWISTON, Pop. 1,226

Lewiston was the first stop for the stage on its way from Winona to Rochester. It continued to grow as a railway village along the line between Mankato and Minnesota City.

UTICA, Pop. 240

Like St. Charles, Utica developed as a railway village on the Chicago & Northwestern Railroad line.

MHS

A farm couple gathers corn and pumpkins, 1915.

WHITEWATER STATE PARK

Nine miles north of St.Charles, is one of Minnesota's most popular parks. Whitewater is located along the steep and picturesque bluffs of the Whitewater River Valley. This valley, now covered by a hardwood forest, was eroded by glacial meltwater as it descended from the highlands into the flood plains of the Mississippi River.

During various periods the Whitewater slowed, allowing the valley to silt up. As the water velocity increased again, it carved deeper into the hillsides, forming terraces of sand and gravel. Some 96 campsites and 15 miles of trails are located here in one of the most varied forests in the state. The forests contain red and white oak and black walnuts, as well as basswood, butternut, ash, black cherry, hickory, maple, hackberry, birch, and juniper.

ST. CHARLES, Pop. 2,184

Built into hills along the Root River is St. Charles, a quaint town of old brick buildings that date from the 1890's. Before the town formed, several ministers left the river bottoms of Winona in 1853, to explore the prairie beyond the bluffs. They traveled westward, a distance of 75 miles, across the plateau separating the Root and Whitewater rivers. Along the way, they took notes of all the places they considered to be choice farming spots, such as the land around Blooming Prairie, High Forest and St. Charles. When passing through this region, a Sunday church service was held on a hill overlooking the river. This was the first service held off the river bottoms in southeastern Minnesota. When the town was settled in 1854, it was named after an Italian cardinal, and the founders offered free land to every Christian Democrat who settled here.

GEOLOGY OF OLMSTED COUNTY

Rock outcroppings are numerous in Olmsted County because it lies on the edge of a system of deeply eroded valleys which extend westward from the Mississippi. These valleys were formed by the Zumbro, Whitewater, and Root rivers. This part of southeastern Minnesota was hardly touched by the ice ages; the beautiful valleys and ravines were carved out by years of rain and the erosion of the rivers and their tributaries. In western Olmsted, rich glacial deposits have created a fertile farming area. A historian writing about Olmsted before the land was cultivated said, "of the rolling prairies and romantic hills covered with flowers and trees, it is doubtful if the eye of man ever rested on a spot of earth which for the fertility of the soil, beauty of landscape and healthfulness of climate, could ever be duplicated."

This region of southeastern Minnesota is also underlaid by limestone, a rock which is easily penetrated by rain and surface waters. Many underground streams exist in this limestone formation and surface pollutants often find their way into the groundwater of southeastern Minnesota. There are no natural lakes in this county, and there are several streams which disappear into the ground, never to be seen again.

DOVER, Pop. 312

Philo S. Curtis, became Dover's first resident in 1853. He opened the first hotel, became the town's postmaster and eventually the sheriff. The town was named for Dover, New Hampshire, where some of the early settlers had come from. Both Dover and Eyota lie along the South Fork of the Whitewater River.

EYOTA, Pop. 1,244

Eyota was first settled in the early 1850's, and took its name from a Dakota word meaning "the greatest." Eyota was one of several towns that grew up along the old Winona to Rochester stagecoach line. This route was later followed by the railroad that came up from the Mississippi near Winona, and continued on to Rochester and Mankato.

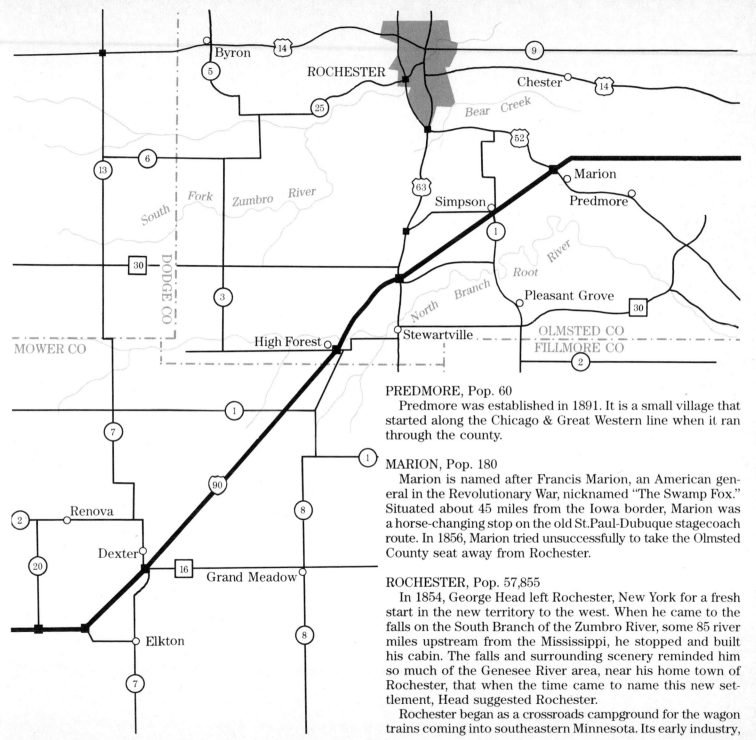

PREDMORE, Pop. 60

Predmore was established in 1891. It is a small village that started along the Chicago & Great Western line when it ran through the county.

MARION, Pop. 180

Marion is named after Francis Marion, an American general in the Revolutionary War, nicknamed "The Swamp Fox." Situated about 45 miles from the Iowa border, Marion was a horse-changing stop on the old St.Paul-Dubuque stagecoach route. In 1856, Marion tried unsuccessfully to take the Olmsted County seat away from Rochester.

ROCHESTER, Pop. 57,855

In 1854, George Head left Rochester, New York for a fresh start in the new territory to the west. When he came to the falls on the South Branch of the Zumbro River, some 85 river miles upstream from the Mississippi, he stopped and built his cabin. The falls and surrounding scenery reminded him so much of the Genesee River area, near his home town of Rochester, that when the time came to name this new settlement, Head suggested Rochester.

Rochester began as a crossroads campground for the wagon trains coming into southeastern Minnesota. Its early industry, like most of the towns in this region, was flour milling. Three mills were established between 1856-1871. The Winona and St. Peter Railroad reached Rochester in 1864 to help ship out the crops and fancy foodstuffs being grown in this fertile region. In 1865, one of the state's first dairy farms was started here, and the area soon became the focus of the dairy industry.

Rochester would have remained like any other busy midwestern town, if it weren't for a man named Dr. William W. Mayo, who moved his practice from Le Sueur to Rochester in 1863. Twenty years later on a hot August night, a tornado swept across the plains into Rochester, killing 26 and seriously injuring several hundred others. This tragedy was compounded because the closest hospital was 100 miles away. The injured were taken to hotels, private residences and the Convent of St. Francis. As a result of this storm, the nuns of the convent were motivated to build and operate a hospital, if Mayo and his two sons, also doctors, would direct it.

A 40-bed unit was built and became known as St. Mary's Hospital. But that was only the beginning for a nucleus of hospitals that, together with the famed Mayo Clinic, would eventually employ over 11,000 people and treat 200,000 patients annually.

STEWARTVILLE, Pop. 3,925

This still-growing town situated along the North Branch of the Root River, was named for Charles N. Stewart, who established a mill along the river in 1858. Here the river flows through a valley, 100 feet below the plain. At one time there were 32 flour mills located along the Root River alone.

During World War I, people had to cut back on their use of flour. Barley, oat and rice flour were used as substitutes. Because of the scarcity of milled flour, people started buying their bread instead of making it. After the war was over, the habit couldn't be broken and bakeries across the state began to flourish, causing small mills along the streams to fade away.

The mill-dam at Stewartville created Lake Florence, named after Stewart's wife. The lake attracted many people from around the area and a steam-powered launch called the "Idle Hour" once operated on the lake. Stewartville is also the birthplace and boyhood home of Richard W. Sears, the founder of Sears and Roebuck Company. Sears worked for the railroad in Minnesota for 15 years as a telegrapher. He started selling watches through the mail to other employees, and from that, his business grew into one of the world's largest retailing firms.

HIGH FOREST, Pop. 90

Situated along the North Branch of the Root River, is the once busy town of High Forest. In this hamlet in 1857, a posse from Frankford caught up with two commissioners from Austin as they tried to escape with Frankford's county records. The commissioners were arrested and brought back to Frankford, but not before they hid the box of records in a snowbank. This incident stemmed from a desire to move the county seat from eastern Mower county to Austin. The general belief was that wherever the county records were located, so was the county seat. High Forest, located on the southern stage route, was also the site of a Methodist Seminary for a short time. Today, only a small collection of homes make up this village.

GRAND MEADOW, Pop. 965

Founded by Erlund Olson in the fall of 1854, Grand Meadow didn't really exist until the rails approached the town in 1870. Thirty years later, a fire destroyed the town, even though some buildings were dynamited trying to contain the blaze. The town proper was rebuilt, this time with bricks. Fire was a serious threat to many of these small towns, since their stores and granaries were constructed of wood and closely spaced. Buckets of water had little effect on a fire with a good start.

FIRST RESIDENT OF MOWER COUNTY

In July 1852, Jacob McQuillian, his wife and nine children, entered Mower county from the northeast. Before unhitching his team of oxen, McQuillian nailed a coffee-mill to a tree as his claim to this site. The family lived in the wagon while they planted crops and built a rough cabin of poplar logs. Unfortunately, McQuillian lost a good portion of his land to another settler, causing him financial ruin and forcing him to move to another part of the county.

DEXTER, Pop. 279

Dexter was settled in 1857 by Mahlon Parritt and his son Dexter. They lived alone in this area for several years before they were joined by others. The year 1876 was the beginning of a number of boom years for Dexter, as the railroad pushed through on its way west from La Crescent. In 1897, a fire pushed along by high winds, destroyed all the buildings on the west side of main street. Today the railroad is gone; the town has only a few stores, a feed elevator and a school which was converted into apartments.

AUSTIN, Pop. 23,020

During the early 1850's a half-broken trail led from Iowa to Mendota, passing through what is now Mower County. At one point, the road turned to take a ford in the Cedar River. It was a beautiful spot and the prairie schooners with their passengers would stop here to rest their oxen. The Dakota also camped along the river banks and began watching with wary eyes the never-ending stream of travelers.

Austin Nichols, a fur trapper working the river, first settled here in 1853. The next year, Chauncey Leverich came, pitched his tent, and proclaimed that "here I will start a city." That year a number of people settled near the ford along with Leverich, and struggled through the first winter, subsisting on wild game. One person wrote "I have never seen a place where the game was so plentiful. We can go out at any hour and kill a deer, and we did kill all we wanted." The town developed quickly with the help of Leverich's sawmill. But when he built the town's first frame house, he was immediately criticized for "putting on airs."

An interesting story surrounds the naming of Austin as the county seat in 1857. In northeastern Mower, a town by the name of Frankford was the original county seat. But Frankford neglected to build a courthouse. Newly elected commissioners from Austin were unhappy about the distance they had to travel for meetings. They reasoned that since a courthouse had never been built, wherever the "tin box" containing the county records was kept, would be the site of the county seat. One day they stole the box while attending a meeting at Frankford and rode for Austin with the sheriff and townsfolk of Frankford following in hot pursuit.

The posse caught up with the men at the stage way-station in High Forest and arrested them. The hotel was searched, but not before the tin box had been ditched in a snowbank. The people of Austin, some carrying guns, gathered in Frankford to insure a fair trial for the jailed commissioners. The men were eventually released and a county-wide election in 1857 turned the county seat over to Austin. Today, besides being an agricultural trading center, Austin is the site of a large meat-packing plant.

MOWER COUNTY, Pop.40,390

The county of Mower is situated in a rolling sweep of farmland that used to be covered by a tallgrass prairie, interspersed with groves of trees. During the 1800's, this area was a popular spot for hunting parties venturing south from Fort Snelling. Some men who joined these hunts were Henry Sibley, Alexander Faribault, John Fremont, Major Taliaferro, and Dred Scott, a slave later made famous in the "Dred Scott Case." During the 1841 winter hunt, 2,000 deer, 50 elk, 50 bear, five panthers and a few buffalo were killed.

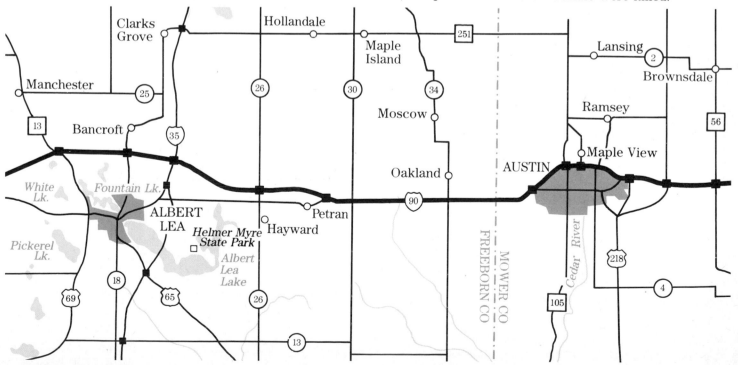

The first settlers in the county were farmers, and with few exceptions they were very poor. They had no alternative but to make a success of their farming. The first crops were wheat and subsistence gardens. One settler wrote, "new arrivals are coming every day and houses went up as if touched by a magic hand. In the morning there would be a clearing made, by nightfall the gleam of a lighted candle could be seen from the windows of a crude, yet cozy cabin."

From 1857 to 1877, the farmers planted wheat. It seemed they could do no wrong and after years of successful wheat farming, this became the land of "Eldorado" for the settlers arriving from the East. But for the next five years, starting in 1878, rain and chinch bugs (small black and white bugs that ate the wheat juices), destroyed the crops. Farmers paid the price for all the years of intensive one-crop farming. Broken and penniless, many left the county and headed for a new start in the Dakotas.

POST OFFICE

In the days of the earliest settlers, there were no post offices in the county, except for the letters brought in by travelers. The roads then were scarcely more than a trail, and often passengers had to leave their wagons to pry the wheels from the mud with poles cut from roadside saplings. Jacob McQuillian became the first postmaster for Mower County in 1855, when he took mail in at Elkhorn, a small hamlet situated along the stage route. Other post offices were soon opened in Frankford and Austin.

MOSCOW

This small hamlet received its name when a thick stand of oak burned during a dry year. The stand burned with such intensity, that to locals it suggested scenes from the terrible fires in Moscow, Russia, during the Napoleon invasion.

HAYWARD, Pop. 294

This farming area covered with deep rich loam, was settled in 1856 by David Hayward, an emigrant from Iowa. There once was a two-story mill here that was driven by the wind and capable of grinding 200 bushels of wheat per day. Just east of Hayward, was the site of an old Indian camp, where many Indian artifacts have been found over the past few years, especially when the freeway was constructed during the late 1960's.

ALBERT LEA, Pop. 19,190

The city of Albert Lea was platted in 1856 around a number of lakes, the largest of which is Albert Lea Lake. The lake was first called Fox Lake, when a young lieutenant named Albert Lea, approached this body of water for the first time and saw a white fox run across his path. Lea was part of an 1835 expedition into Minnesota, from which he published a journal and maps of the area. Lea was also the first to use the word "Iowa" in his narrative to describe the region below Minnesota. Joseph Nicollet, the French explorer, later renamed Fox Lake in honor of Lea. Nicollet's map, published in 1843, was the most complete map of Minnesota during this period. The area around Albert Lea was also a favorite hunting ground of the Dakota, and they defended it aggressively.

One of the first settlers, William Rice, started delivering mail for the new homesteaders in the region. That first winter of 1856, Rice was caught in a blizzard and died from exposure. The winter seemed to have no end, sending many of the new settlers into a deep depression. That next spring, many packed their bags and headed back east to their former homes. But in the summer, those that left were replaced by a new flood of settlers who pushed the population of the once empty county to a total of 2,500. Few agricultural regions have ever witnessed such rapid growth or general material wealth as this area.

Main Street, Albert Lea, 1900.

MHS

The treeless farmsteads could be seen for miles across the level prairie.

At first, the straggly little town of Albert Lea was nothing more than a collection of log houses and frame shacks. Its main street, Broadway, was flanked by stores whose homemade shingles announced their wares. Albert Lea, one of the early railroad towns on the Southern Minnesota Railroad, was connected to the Mississippi River in the 1860's. The once laborious trip to the river was past. Now shipments of wheat could be made to the elevators that were being built along the tracks. Today, Albert Lea is serviced by four railroad companies and has a major packing and food-processing plant in town.

ALBERT LEA LAKE

This lake lies in a pre-glacial valley of the Shell Rock River which was later filled in by the glaciers. Today the lake is the headwaters for the Shell Rock River. Located on the northeast side of Albert Lea Lake is the Helmer Myre State Park, where 1,500 acres of prairie land exist, along with a wooded lake island. Over 450 different varieties of wildflowers have been found in the park. There are 120 sites available for camping and 12 miles of hiking trails. Also located at the park is the Owen Johnson Interpretive Center. The center contains one of the largest collections of Indian artifacts in the United States.

The park was named after a Minnesota senator from the district when is was created in 1947. A number of lakes are situated around Albert Lea because it rests on the eastern margin of the most recent glacier that formed here 12,000 years ago. The glacial deposits blocked the old drainage channels so most of the land east of Albert Lea to the Mississippi is devoid of lakes.

DES MOINES AND CEDAR RIVER BASIN.

In Freeborn County, the river drainage changes from its eastward flow into the Mississippi, southward to streams such as the Upper Iowa, Cedar, Shell Rock and Des Moines rivers. There are over 30 lakes in this county of rolling farmlands. It was the large number of marshes, especially around Albert Lea, that served as a barrier to the prairie fires that swept in from the west. This in turn enabled the trees to take root and grow, eventually forming the forests that begin east of Albert Lea. These marshes were filled with water most of the year and underlaid by heavy peat deposits, unlike the western marshes that dried out during the summer, offering little protection from the prairie fires.

Freeborn County was believed to be underlaid by significant amounts of coal, and exploration began in 1879. Though some thin layers were found, nothing in commercial amounts was discovered.

STAGE DRIVER

The rugged stage driver was an important person during those early days. He was the one who, being well traveled, saw the changes that were rapidly occurring, and had been to places most had only heard of. When he stopped in towns, people gathered around to hear his stories and ask his opinion on important matters.

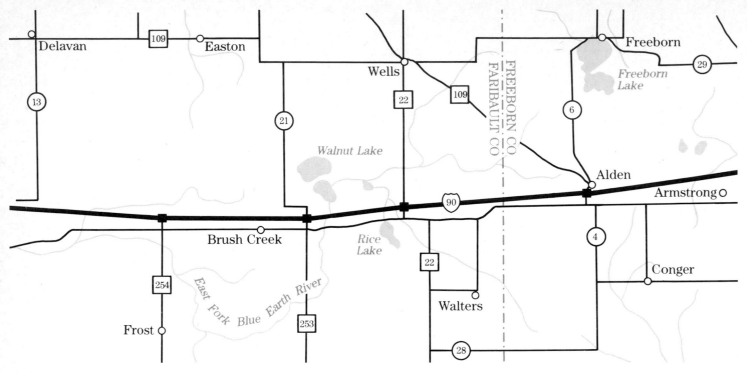

ALDEN, Pop. 687

This once treeless prairie town did not develop like most other towns. There was no squabbling for the county seat or lobbying for a rail connection. The town was formed only after the Southern Minnesota Railroad passed here in 1869. Trees were planted, stores built, and the town organized the first Grange chapter in this part of the state. The Grange, a national organization, began in Little Falls, Minnesota to help promote the advancement of farming.

The county's first doctor lived here, but he was not very popular. One of the more interesting stories tells how the doctor once billed his brother, who had gone insane, for the service of delivering him to an asylum.

FREEBORN COUNTY, Pop. 36,329

Ole Gulbandson became the first settler of this county in 1853, when he built a small cabin along the Cedar River in the southern part of the county near Gordonsville. The county was named after William Freeborn, a member of the territorial Legislature during the late 1840's. Today Freeborn County ranks as one of the state's top corn and hog producers.

WALNUT LAKE.

The name Walnut Lake is taken from the Dakota name "Tazuka," referring to the Butternut trees that lined the lake.

WELLS, Pop. 2,777

The town of Wells developed as a railway village in the 1870's around the tracks of the Southern Minnesota Railroad. Wells was a robust trading center which was once connected to Mankato by rail.

In 1933, Wells showed the first talking pictures in the county. Wells is also the home of Larry Buendorf, a secret service agent who blocked an attempt on President Gerald Ford's life in 1975.

FARIBAULT COUNTY, Pop. 19,714

Established in 1855, Faribault County was named for Jean Baptiste Faribault, a French-Canadian, who for a good portion of his life traded with the Indians through the Northwest Fur Company. The first white settler in the county was Moses Sailor, who built a cabin where the city of Blue Earth now stands.

An 1859 Faribault County resident wrote, "we have as a community, arrived at a period more depressing financially and full of gloomy foreboding, than any other time in the history of the county. There is no money, provisions are scarce and many families are almost out of food. But it is said, the darkest hour is just before the break of day..it is never best to give up in despair."

The following year, historian Jacob Kiester wrote, "the times are still hard and money very tight. Yet a marked change has come over the community, a more hopeful and healthful spirit; a new life, and new energy seems to animate the people. Immigration is very considerable and some building is being done in the villages; large amounts of land are being broke and farmed, schools started, roads laid, regular church services have begun and to crown all, the crops are abundant and harvested in good season."

For the next couple of years considerable progress was made in the county, until the start of the Sioux Uprising. In August 1862, settlers west of Blue Earth City began pouring into town, seeking security from the Dakota braves that were attacking the town of New Ulm, some fifty miles to the north. This panic prevailed across southern Minnesota, all the way to the Mississippi River Valley. The population of the county before the Uprising was 2,500, but in a few short days less then one hundred settlers remained in the Blue Earth City fortification. One story is told about two persons rushing wildly into Blue Earth, screaming that a whole line of Indians were approaching the town. Terror struck the city and "people became panic stricken, running wild, screaming and crying. Teams were hitched up and wagons filled with men, women and children, filling the road to Albert Lea."

Soon after, the so-called Indians turned out to be a line of cattle, driven by the settlers who were trying to save their herds by going east. This report gives us good insight on how afraid the people were of the Dakota. As it turned out, no attack was ever made in the county; no murders were committed, and no property was directly destroyed by the Indians. Yet fear and uncontrolled panic prevailed and it took many months for the area to recover.

As the economy recovered in the 1870's, most of the towns in this county developed every five to seven miles along the railroads that were laying their tracks westward. The first railroad went to Wells in northeastern Faribault County in 1870. These railroad villages provided markets where farmers could barter eggs and butter at the general store, sell their grain to elevators and offered a place from which to ship their cattle to eastern markets.

FARIBAULT COUNTY GEOLOGY

Thousands of years ago most of Faribault County was under a lake called Glacial Lake Minnesota. This lake was formed by meltwater from the last glacier which retreated northward across the county. Since normal drainage was also to the north, the ice created a dam and formed the lake. After the ice retreated, water began to drain through the Blue Earth River into Glacial River Warren, or what is now the Minnesota River.

There are many hills in the county, formed by silt and debris left behind as the glaciers melted. These rich soils have helped the county become a top corn and soybean producer.

Many settlers had to build their homes of sod, since trees could only be found along the rivers.

MHS

BLUE EARTH, Pop. 4,123

Pushing through the shoulder-high prairie grass from Iowa, Moses Sailor finally stopped his oxen at a spot on the West Fork of the Blue Earth River and staked a claim. This spot, once known as Blue Earth City, later became shortened to Blue Earth. It was spring when Sailor arrived and his first duty was to break up five acres of tough prairie. Sailor wanted to plant corn and potatoes in order that his family might survive the winter. The Sailors lived in a covered wagon until the crops were planted, then efforts were concentrated on building a cabin, which later served as the county headquarters, a hotel, resort and scene of many social gatherings. During those long winter months, dancing was one of the chief social pastimes of these small prairie towns. Blue Earth City was no exception, for a dance was held at least once a week.

The early years of Blue Earth City were like most others, with settlers being in dire need of money. The new homesteaders were soon broke. Most of their cash was invested in getting started, buying seed, livestock, and food. Little capital was left to help develop these new communities. Gold and silver were exchanged since paper money had little value. Unfortunately, times got worse. In the late 1800's money was being loaned to settlers and arriving immigrants at interest rates of 30 to 60 percent. The region was being drained by these payments. What hurt most was that almost all of the payments went to out-of-state creditors. Many farmers and businessmen defaulted and lost their land.

Blue Earth's stately courthouse, built in 1891, is now the government center in a town of interesting turn-of-the-century buildings. The city is also the location of a large food-processing plant.

BLUE EARTH RIVER

The Blue Earth River, whose headwaters begin just inside Iowa, drains through the town of Blue Earth, north to Mankato. The interesting feature about this river is that its drainage basin is wider than the river is long. Tributaries such as the Watonwan are as long as Blue Earth itself.

As early as 1700, French explorer, Charles le Sueur was digging along the river near Mankato, extracting a blue-green clay thought to be copper ore. Some historians believed that he used the ore as a ploy to interest others in financing his travels, while he pursued a fur trade with the Dakota. In any case, when Nicollet traveled up the Blue Earth one hundred years later, he could find no trace of the excavations, except where the Indians extracted clay to paint their faces. All that remains now is the beautiful Dakota word, "Mankato," meaning "blue-green earth."

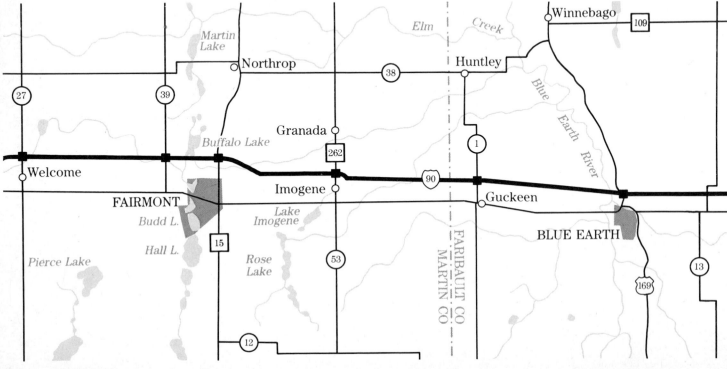

The river, with its hardwood-lined banks, provided the early settlers with wood for shelter and fuel. It was an oasis on a prairie of shoulder-high grasses.

GUCKEEN

In 1900, the Iowa, Minnesota and Northwestern Railroad extended their tracks west from Blue Earth to Derby, a trading center that eventually changed its name to honor the farmer on whose land the town was built. During the early 1900's, Guckeen grew with small businesses, a bank, and a busy blacksmith. Today little remains of this once active village except the grain elevator. Down a dusty side street stands the vandalized old school house and several decaying stores.

FAIRMONT, Pop. 11,506

This town was first called Fair Mount because of its view of Lake Sisseton. Fairmont is located on a north-south chain of 18 lakes which used to be deeply-eroded valleys before they were filled by glacial deposits.

In 1856, shortly after Calvin Tuttle settled near here, William Budd began farming at what is now Fairmont. He sowed turnips for his first crop, built a small house, put up hay, and erected a stable for his cattle. Budd had a difficult time breaking the tough prairie sod though, and was forced to make the long trip to Mankato to repair his broken plow. That first winter was bitterly cold for the handful of settlers who lived at Fairmont. Little food had been raised for them and their cattle and frequent trips into Iowa were necessary.

Three to four feet of snow covered the trackless prairie, making passage extremely difficult. Settlers spent their winters searching for wood to keep warm, finding food for themselves, hay for their cattle and keeping a road open to their barns. By the end of the winter, two-thirds of the pioneers had their fill and packed up, never to return. For those that remained, that next summer was spent tending crops of corn, potatoes, beans, rutabagas, melons, carrots and squash. According to William Budd, "we learned the lesson that we must work or the ship will sink."

Fairmont and the county grew rapidly during the next few years. But suddenly things came to a grinding halt. The severe winter of 1862 was followed by spring floods and the Sioux Uprising. These events had a profound effect on Fairmont. On an August day in 1862, news arrived like a prairie fire that Dakota warriors were advancing on Fairmont. This started a widespread panic. So complete was the eastward stampede of homesteaders, that soldiers who later passed through the region scouting for Indians, found houses with tables still

set and items left as if the settlers had merely stepped out for a while. For those that remained behind, a stockade was constructed on a hill overlooking Lake Sisseton. The present-day Martin County courthouse is constructed on that site.

Eventually the town returned to normal, when an English farming colony settled here in 1873. Many of this group were Cambridge and Oxford graduates and some even carried titles. But their timing couldn't have been worse. That June, the prairie winds carried the dreaded Rocky Mountain locusts into the county. An eyewitness wrote that, "like an army in a strange land, they lost no time in commencing business. Gardens were soon destroyed and of the English colony's beans…they were gone in 24 hours without a beanstalk remaining."

The attempts to make Fairmont a "bean" capital in the west, barely survived. Though many left the colony, some elected to stay. This colony eventually recovered and later became known throughout the state as the Fairmont Sportsmen. They developed an active fox hunting club, boat club, football team (English style), and organized racing.

WELCOME, Pop. 855

This town is named after Alfred Welcome, an early farmer in the area. Today the Chicago & Northwestern Railroad from South Dakota meets the Chicago, Milwaukee, St. Paul and Pacific line from Jackson.

A Sunday outing along a shaded southern Minnesota stream.

MHS

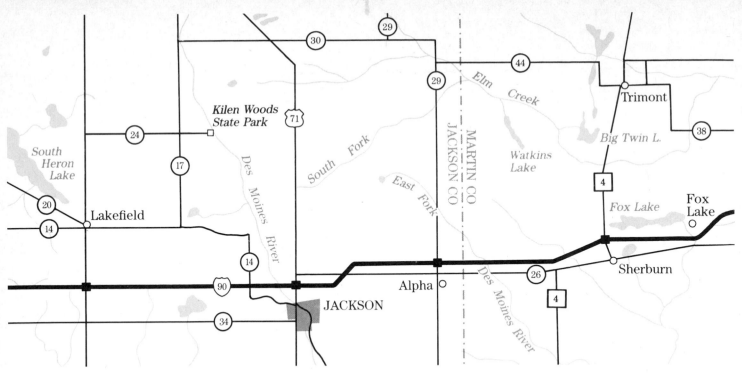

FOX LAKE AND LAST BUFFALO

Fox Lake, a railroad village established in 1872, was named after a lake and system of marshes that now comprise the Fox Lake Game Refuge. The first murder in Martin County was committed just north of this lake when a man named Charles White passed here on his way from Yankton (Dakota Territory) to Mankato to buy supplies for his store. White left his small traveling caravan and headed north from Fox Lake to find a shorter route up to Mankato. He never returned. A year later, after a prairie fire burned off the grass from a nearby slough, his body was found with a hole in his skull. The marsh became known as "Dead Man's Slough," but has since been drained and plowed.

In 1863, on a crisp autumn day a few miles north of Fox Lake, a soldier slowly rose from the tall grass, carefully took aim and shot the last remaining buffalo in this region.

SHERBURN, Pop. 1,275

Sherburn is a village named after the wife of an officer of the Chicago, Milwaukee and St. Paul Railroad. In 1878 Sherburn began to grow with the addition of a store, warehouse, mercantile building and creamery that reoccupied the local brewery building.

MARTIN COUNTY GEOLOGY

The county has three chains of lakes that lie in a north-south direction, giving geologists much to speculate about. It is thought that these lakes were once a long valley, eroded away by glacial streams and eventually filled by debris pushed along by new glaciers. Some depressions became marshes while others became lakes.

JACKSON, Pop. 3,797

Here along the fertile, tree-lined valley of the Des Moines River is the site of the first white settlement in this area. In 1856, a dozen or so people settled around a shanty store near a ford in the river and named it Springfield. William Wood opened a log store on the west bank of the river, while most of the other cabins were scattered on the east side. Their first winter here was severe since the hurriedly-built cabins were drafty and hard to heat.

Food was scarce and fresh game was hard to find. The closest village was fifty miles away and being caught in a prairie blizzard meant almost certain death, particularly if one couldn't make the protection of a wooded river bottom. But after surviving that first winter, a different kind of problem arose for the hamlet, which had changed its name to

Jackson. Settlements had been budding across the prairie, farther and farther into what had been, for thousands of years, the Indians' hunting grounds. The Dakota had ceded southern Minnesota in the treaties of 1851 made at Mendota and Traverse des Sioux. But during the spring of 1857, a small band of Dakota became uneasy about the influx of whites to this region. Led by an Indian named Inkpaduta (Scarlet Point), the band attacked a small settlement eight miles south of Jackson at Spirit Lake, Iowa. Inkpaduta's appearance was frightening to the settlers. He was 60 years old, six feet tall, and his face was badly scarred from small pox.

It was a bloody encounter at Spirit Lake. Thirty-two pioneers and their children were killed by Inkpaduta's warriors. From there, the chief and his band escaped north towards Springfield (Jackson), where they attacked the scattered cabins along the river. At one site, the two Wood brothers and all their livestock were killed as their small store was looted. Several others were also killed at Springfield. Inkpaduta fled to South Dakota with 12 braves, their women and children, and three captives. Their escape was successful, but it was still cold that March and several of their horses starved before they reached South Dakota. Inkpaduta's notorious reputation grew and since he was never captured,

Jackson County was devoid, of settlers until the fall of 1863, when small groups started to trickle back.

Besides the whites' fear of Indians and their struggles with fierce weather and claim jumpers, they also had to contend with prairie fires and insects. In 1872, Jackson residents fought a raging prairie fire to the outskirts of town, barely saving it. A year later grasshoppers destroyed the crops and continued to plague the settlers for the next several years. There was little joy to prairie life during those early years.

DES MOINES RIVER

The Des Moines, a French term meaning "River of Monks", has its beginnings at Lake Shetek, one of the largest lakes in southwestern Minnesota. Located at Lake Shetek is a state park and site of an Indian massacre during the Sioux Uprising. The river flows southward through cultivated land as a slow stream with low banks. Ten miles below Windom though, the river flows through a stretch of the Kilen Woods State Park where it passes through an oak and basswood forest. There are 20 campsites in the park located on a bluff overlooking the river. Five miles of trails wind along the river bottom which is abundant with wildlife.

Buffalo bones were collected across the prairie and shipped to St. Paul to be ground into fertilizer.

fear spread among the settlers of southwestern Minnesota. (Inkpaduta was later reported to have aided in the battle against General Custer at the Little Big Horn. Today, a replica of Inkpaduta's camp can be found in Jackson.)

Five years later in 1862, the Sioux Uprising reached this region. A cavalry unit was dispatched to the county. Soldiers found nine pioneer bodies, buried them, and reported that the rest of the county was entirely deserted. For one year,

The Des Moines River, with its high wooded banks, once provided shelter to early settlers crossing the prairie. These oak savannah forests survived the prairie fires and winter winds by growing on the protected hillsides and moist valleys of the river. The burr oaks became the source of lumber for the rustic cabins that began to appear. The Des Moines River Valley became part of the Minnesota frontier during the 1850's when such towns as Windom and Jackson were established.

White-Man-Bear, a Dakota brave.

JACKSON COUNTY, Pop. 13,690

The county was founded in 1857, but today there is still some confusion as to who it was named after. The most popular version is that it was named after Henry Jackson who established the first general store in St. Paul, became the first justice of the peace and later, the state's first postmaster.

Trappers in search of pelts were the first whites in the county. In 1835 a trading post was established on Lake Talcott, just north of the county. The Indians (members of the Sioux or Dakota nation), along with a few trappers and traders, had the county to themselves for a number of years. As late as 1857 a political party named the Moccasin Democrats tried to gain additional votes by showing that they had 50 inhabitants in four non-existent Jackson County villages.

GEOLOGY

West of Jackson, the freeway runs along the division of the Des Moines River basin draining south into Iowa, and the Missouri River basin draining west into the Missouri River. One of the most obvious physical features of this prairie county is a prominent ridge crossing the region north to south, just west of the Des Moines River. Glaciers deposited this ridge during the most recent ice age. In some places its crest rises to 1,500 feet above sea level. Jackson, along with

Nobles, is one of the top farm income counties in Minnesota; strong in corn, soybeans, hogs and cattle.

WORTHINGTON, Pop. 10,234

Worthington, county seat of Nobles, was settled in 1871 by the National Colony Company, a temperance group that first called their settlement "Okabena," an Indian word meaning "nesting place of herons." Liquor sales were prohibited in Okabena, but if one tried hard enough, the illegal "firewater" could still be found behind some store counters. The nearby lake is still called Okabena, but the town was renamed Worthington in honor of a founder of the National Colony Company.

In 1873, the grasshoppers made the first of several destructive raids to southwestern Minnesota. Farmers showed an average yield that year of just nine bushels per acre in wheat, oats and corn. Money was in such short supply that the local newspaper offered to take anything in trade for subscriptions, except grasshoppers. Appeals went out to the entire nation seeking relief-aid for the thousands of destitute families. When farming failed, many of the pioneers turned to trapping as a means of existence. In the winter of 1874-75, 28,000 muskrat skins were shipped from Worthington.

During the early 1900's, Worthington had a local polo team that maintained a national rating. The Okabena apple was

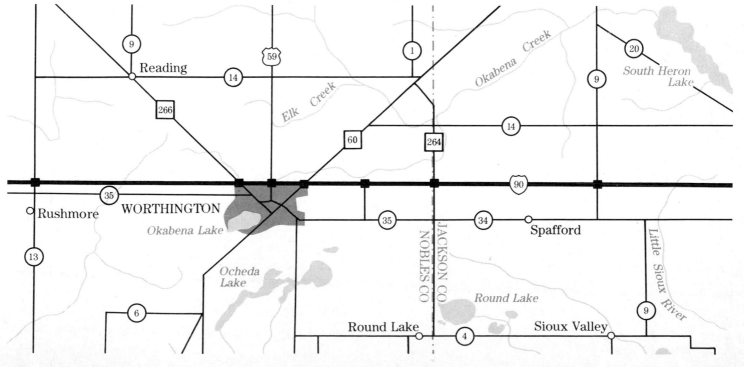

also developed in orchards on the southern shore of Lake Okabena. Today Worthington is the major trading center in southwestern Minnesota., with turkey production a major income producer.

In the vicinity of Worthington, a series of terminal moraines, or north-south valleys and ridges mark the western extension of the Keewatin glacier. (Terminal moraines are the rolling hills and debris formed along the edges of a glacier.) This natural phenomenon occurred during the last ice age that ended some 11,000 years ago. It was the Coteau des Prairies, or "Highland of the Prairies," that resisted any further westward glacial extension.

NOBLES COUNTY, Pop. 21,840

This county was organized in 1857 around a place called "Gretchtown", which existed on paper only. By 1860 only 65 people were living in the county and these were mostly agents or trappers for fur companies. The Sioux Uprising in 1862 contributed greatly to the slow settlement of this area. The county takes its name from William H. Nobles, a member of the 1856 territorial Legislature. Nobles advocated the construction of a road running from southern Minnesota through a pass he discovered in the Sierra Nevada mountains a few years earlier. This road would be built for the purpose of helping California immigration. Eventually trains connected St. Paul to California through that same pass.

WATERSHED BOUNDARY

West of Worthington the freeway crosses the divide that separates the Mississippi River basin to the east, from the Missouri River basin to the west. This area where the land drains to a central river, is called a watershed.

RUSHMORE, Pop. 387

Rushmore formed by the tracks of the St. Paul & Sioux Falls Railroad in 1878 and was named after S. M. Rushmore, one of the town's first merchants.

MHS

Raising turkeys has become big business around Worthington.

MHS

An early view of Kenneth, just north of Magnolia.

ADRIAN, Pop. 1,336

Platted in 1876, this town was named after Adrian Iselin, a relative of one of the St. Paul and Sioux City Railroad Company directors. Adrian was established by Archbishop John Ireland who acquired 70,000 acres from the railroad to start a farming colony of German and Irish Catholics. During the 1880's, Adrian was an ambitious contender for the county seat which belonged to Worthington.

ROCK COUNTY, Pop. 10,703

Rock is one of the few counties in the state devoid of lakes. It is generally flat and covered by a rich deposit of glacial till. The terrain changes only in the valleys made by Beaver Creek, the Rock River and other smaller streams.

During the late 1600's when Father Hennepin was crossing this unexplored land along the Mississippi, the region around Rock County was held by the Yankton band of Dakota Indians. Several decades later when trappers and explorers journeyed across the state in search of furs and trade, the Sisseton band of Dakota took possession of this western county. But before all of these newcomers, a primitive people had occupied this region as far back as 10,000 years ago. A number of human-made mounds have been found in the county. These early people felt all living things contained a special power and spirit. They painted their stories on the rocks often depicting animals.

Rock County was extensively explored by Joseph Nicollet in 1839. It was Nicollet's descriptions of the northwest that awakened interest in the region. His maps were the standard guide for many years. But the fear of the prairie Indians (called Sioux by the early whites), kept settlers from this territory for the next 30 years.

MAGNOLIA, Pop. 234

This small village developed along the Chicago & Northwestern Railroad as a small agricultural center. It was named for a village of the same name in Wisconsin.

One of the few recommendations in this book is for the Magnolia Steak House located on the main street of town. It offers great steaks selected from a herd maintained by the owner. The restaurant has moved from a little run-down cafe to a newer, somewhat non-descript building, but the food has remained the same and draws people from around the region.

ROCK RIVER

This river starts 30 miles to the north in Pipestone County and meanders southward, draining some 500 square miles in

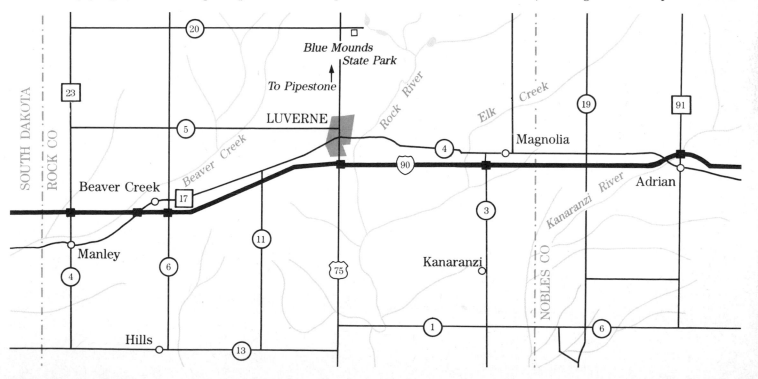

MHS

(left) Grazing cattle
in southwestern Minn-
esota, 1890.
(bottom) Raising a
barn was most often
a community effort.

Minnesota. Rock River has the distinction of being the only major Minnesota stream to drain into the Missouri River. The rest of the state's streams empty into the Hudson Bay, Lake Superior, or the Mississippi.

LUVERNE, Pop. 4,568

The business of mail delivery brought the county's, and this town's, first settler. A mail carrier named Philo Hawes, whose duty was to deliver mail between Blue Earth City and Yankton, South Dakota, settled here and built a post office in 1868, at a spot where the Yankton road crossed the Rock River. Hawes planted oats, and that winter his threshing yielded 20 bushels, which he promptly sold to travelers for one dollar a bushel.

In 1871, with help from an agricultural community in Worthington called the National Colony Company, settlers in large covered wagons, called prairie schooners, began moving into the county. In the fall of 1876, the St. Paul & Dakota Railroad reached into Rock county, bringing a large number of settlers every day. By 1890 the region had some 7,000 people, 27 percent of whom were Norwegian-born.

PIPESTONE QUARRY

Sixteen miles north of Luverne is the Pipestone quarry, sacred Indian grounds that were first described in 1836 by an artist-explorer named George Catlin. Catlin came here from New York, painting Indian scenes and studying their culture. Joseph Nicollet, a French scientist and explorer, visited the quarry in 1838, where he described the "three maid-

MHS

ens" rocks and a number of Indian petroglyphs. Nicollet (along with several others), also left his mark by carving his name on a boulder called Inscription Rock. The initials can still be seen.

This quarry was the source of the unusual reddish-colored stone used by the Indians for centuries to make pipes. For generations, bitter warfare was waged to maintain possession of this quarry. The legend is that Wahegela, an Omaha wife of a Yankton Dakota, discovered the stone while trailing a white bison whose hoofs uncovered the red stone. Ultimately, an agreement was reached by the warring tribes, making the quarry neutral ground, to be shared by all Indians.

The stone is a soft clay of aluminum silicate, with some iron impurities. The chemist who first analyzed the stone, named it Catlinite, in honor of Catlin and his explorations of 1836. The 280-acre site, one mile northwest of Pipestone, became the Pipestone National Monument in 1937, making it Minnesota's first national monument.

BLUE MOUNDS STATE PARK

Seven miles north of Luverne on the Rock River, is the Blue Mounds State Park and Interpretive center. It is situated in a beautiful prairie setting where 76 campsites are provided. The interpretive center is located on the south edge of the park, looking out across the Rock River Valley. A small buffalo herd is maintained in the park, along with four miles of trails. The park took its name from the massive bluff of red quartzite that is flecked with blue from weathering. Early explorers like Nicollet, could see this bluff for miles on the level horizon and used it to guide their travels. The bluff was affectionately known as the "rock", and the county took its name from it. Indians drove herds of buffalo over the bluff to obtain food and hides. It was also in these hills that Jessie and Frank James hid after their raid on Northfield in 1876. The rest of their gang had already been captured in a marsh northwest of Madelia.

BEAVER CREEK, Pop. 260

This village was organized in 1872 when a small group of settlers gathered in the sod shanty of Eli Grout to decide on a name for their newly-founded settlement. They decided to name the town after the large number of beaver that lived along the creek which flowed west to the Big Sioux River in South Dakota. The settlers lived in their covered wagons or in crude sod houses as they directed their energies to breaking up the tough prairie sod.

It is remarkable that Beaver Creek ever survived at all, since it was founded during the great grasshopper plague that began in 1873. What few crops were grown were eaten by the pests.

A branch of the Omaha Railroad eventually reached the town and used Beaver Creek as its terminus for several years. During this period, Beaver Creek became the distribution point for the frontier towns of eastern South Dakota. The town grew rapidly and was quite lively as stores popped up along its main street. But eventually, the rails continued on past the town and trade dropped off. Several fires almost destroyed the town and competition from other nearby villages kept it from becoming more than just a small trading center.

MANLEY

Once a small hamlet platted in 1899, today Manley is only a railway crossing for the Burlington Northern, and Chicago & Northwestern Railroads. The town was named for W. P. Manley, a leading stockholder of the early Sioux City & Northern Railroad Company.

MHS

An 1880 government survey train stretches across the open prairie.

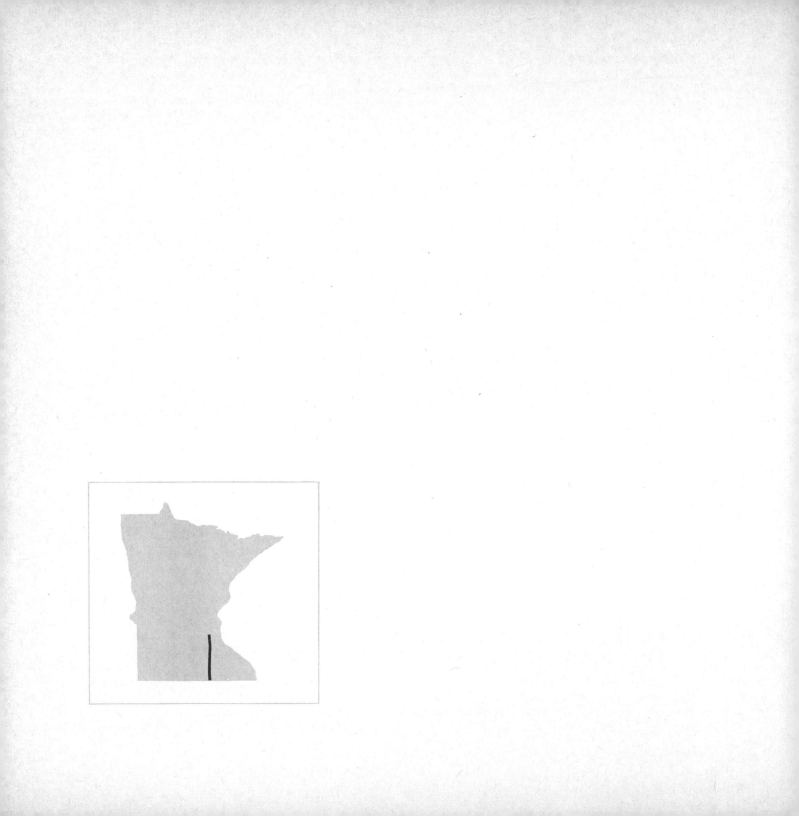

ROUTE I-35, SOUTH TO ALBERT LEA

Pausing along the Minnesota River. Photo/E.A. Bromley

MHS

BLOOMINGTON, POP. 81,831

Bloomington was first settled around 1843, but was originally the home of Dakota Indian bands that lived on the bluff overlooking the Minnesota River flats. The village was named in 1852 by settlers from Illinois. The largest growth for Bloomington came between 1950 and 1970, when some 19,000 homes were constructed.

MINNESOTA RIVER.

Approaching the Minnesota River on the Interstate, the road descends into a broad valley covered with backwater marshes, rushes and cottonwoods. It seems strange that this quiet river could erode a valley so deep and wide. Well, it didn't. About 12,000 years ago, glacial meltwater created Glacial Lake Agassiz, a body of water larger than today's combined Great Lakes. Agassiz covered most of northwest Minnesota, eastern North Dakota and the Canadian province of Manitoba. Because ice blocked the normal drainage north into Hudson Bay, Agassiz's water flowed south to the Mississippi as a massive river named Glacial River Warren.

Glacial River Warren, while draining Lake Agassiz, was the major river in the state. But the ice dam in Canada finally melted and the Agassiz began draining to the north. Today the humble Minnesota River runs through the River Warren's broad valley, which in many places is five miles wide and over 250 feet below the surrounding hills. Prior to 1849, the Minnesota River had been called the St. Peter River by French and English explorers. The name St. Peter is thought to have referred to Pierre Charles Le Sueur, an early explorer of the river.

Today, the Minnesota flows out of Big Stone Lake between Browns Valley and Ortonville and continues on some 328 miles before it joins the Mississippi below Fort Snelling. The Minnesota's watershed draws from 14,751 square miles in Minnesota, close to one-fifth of the state's area.

The Minnesota River is a Dakota name meaning "cloudy waters." Some have interpreted the name to mean "land of sky-tinted waters." In any case, the river was an important

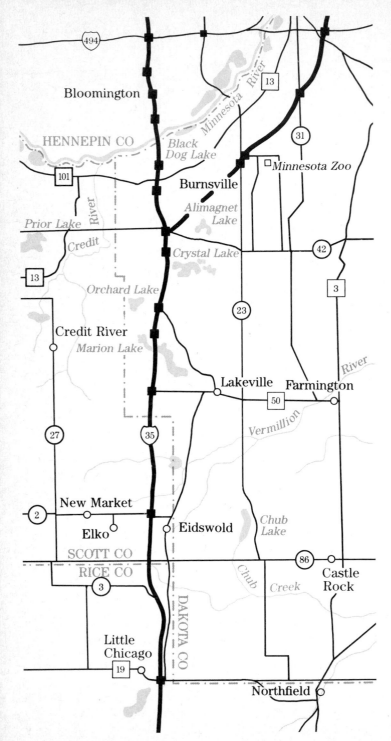

route for the Dakota in the southern and western parts of the state. the famous Red River oxcart trail followed the Minnesota and allowed supplies to flow from the Red River colonies of Winnipeg and Pembina to Mendota. Eventually, thousands of settlers steamed up the river after the Dakota had given away most of southern Minnesota in the 1851 treaties of Traverse des Sioux and Mendota. The steamboats traveled upstream as far as New Ulm, making stops at all the sprouting river towns.

DAKOTA COUNTY, Pop. 194,111

This county, established in 1849, was named for the Dakota Indians. The Dakota, comprised of seven allied Indian tribes, originally occupied most of Minnesota and the adjoining western states. The Ojibwe, no friend of the Dakota, began calling them, Nadouessioux, or "enemy." It was in this way that the Dakota became more commonly known as Sioux.

The Dakota maintained three villages in what is now Dakota County. One was Kaposia on the present site of South St. Paul. Another was Medicine Bottle's village at Pine Bend on the Mississippi. The third was Black Dog's village near the northeast end of Black Dog Lake on the Minnesota River bottoms, now part of Burnsville. The Dakota of this area were constantly fighting with the Ojibwe, who had pushed them from their traditional hunting and fishing grounds in the north. In 1842 the Mille Lacs Ojibwe came south and attacked the Kaposia village. The main battle took place at Battle Creek Park and the Ojibwe were repulsed with heavy losses. Father Louis Hennepin was probably the first white man to pass along the Mississippi here in 1680, after he had been captured by the Dakota on Lake Pepin.

DAKOTA COUNTY GEOLOGY

The hilly regions of Dakota County were formed by a great ice sheet, that shaped this region 12,000 years ago. The Wisconsin stage of glaciation (last of the great ice age glaciers), moved southward from Canada through the valleys of the Red and Minnesota rivers. The ice, which in Canada was several thousand feet thick, pushed into central Iowa like a stubby finger.

As rising temperatures brought a gradual end to glaciation, the ice border melted back and floodwaters spread widely. The Glacial River Warren (today called the Minnesota River), was still blocked by ice in the area of what is now Fort Snelling. The water overflowed its valley, sweeping eastward across Dakota County into the Vermillion and Cannon rivers. Today these rivers are but remnants of the once powerful streams that eroded their present channels with the melting of the last glacier.

BLACK DOG LAKE

Approximately four miles long, Black Dog Lake is part of the Minnesota River backwaters. The lake was named after a Dakota Indian who camped on its east end. The flood plain of this area retains much of the same wildlife and vegetation as first encountered by the early settlers. Muskrat, mink, wood duck, blue heron, deer, red-winged blackbirds, and a variety of game and rough fish are plentiful in this area.

BURNSVILLE, Pop. 35,647

This fast-growing area dates back to 1858 when it was named for William Burn who emigrated from Canada and settled here with his family at the mouth of the Credit River— an area now known as Savage.

BUCK HILL

This hill, some 1170 feet above sea level, was used by the Dakota to watch deer drink from Crystal Lake, across from today's Interstate. Subsequently, it was known as Buck Hill.

SCOTT COUNTY. Pop. 43,748

The county, established in 1853, was named after General Winfield Scott, commander-in-chief of the U.S. Army during the Mexican War. Scott's prominence in Minnesota peaked when he visited Fort St. Anthony in 1824. At that time, Scott

MHS

Picking raspberries.

proposed changing the fort's name to Fort Snelling, in honor of Colonel Josiah Snelling who built the outpost in 1819. Scott's advice was taken and the following year Fort St. Anthony became Fort Snelling. It was the closest Winfield Scott ever came to the county that bears his name.

For many years, the present town of Shakopee was the site of a Dakota village ruled by a line of chiefs with that name. The explorer, Le Sueur, passed through Scott County as early as 1700 on his way up the Minnesota to the Blue Earth River in his search for copper ore and furs.

The next white man, Jonathan Carver, passed along the Minnesota River some 60 years later. Carver was hoping to make peace with the Dakota and also to find a route to the Pacific. He ended up spending the winter with the Indians near New Ulm. Carver was important to Minnesota because he was the first person to publish a book in English that described the Indians and the new interior regions of the country.

CASTLE ROCK

The village of Castle Rock was named for an eroded bluff of sandstone just east of town. This bluff was noted on Nicollet's map of 1844 and served as a landmark for Indians and settlers as they traveled along the level plains.

ELKO, Pop. 274

Elko began as a railway town located on the now-vacated branch of the Chicago, Milwaukee, St. Paul & Pacific Railroad. This line once reached Mankato and Farmington.

RICE COUNTY, Pop. 46,087

This county was first established in 1853 and named after one of Minnesota's first senators, Henry Mower Rice. After moving west from Detroit, Rice became a fur agent at Fort Snelling. Here he negotiated several treaties with the Dakota that opened settlement to the whites in Minnesota.

Rice County is primarily an agricultural area. The story of its farming development is similar to that of neighboring counties. The first settlers broke enough land for crops to sustain their families and to trade for necessities which they couldn't produce. As more land was broken, wheat became the principal crop. Following the wheat failure in 1877, and the decline of wheat prices through the next few years, the farmers turned their attention to diversifying their crops and many began dairying.

CANNON RIVER VALLEY

The Cannon River played an important role in the milling history of this state, and is the most important topographical feature of the county. One of the more unusual features of this area is the grouping of approximately 2,000 man-made mounds within a 10 mile radius of Northfield. They are low (one to three feet), and round, with a diameter of 20 to 50 feet. What is unusual about these mounds is that although they appear to be of human origin, excavation has revealed very few artifacts.

MILITARY ROADS

For a number of miles, the Interstate follows the same route as the old Mendota-Big Sioux military highway, constructed in 1855 to connect the Mississippi and Missouri rivers. The road ran from Mendota to Mankato, but funds were exhausted before the highway ever reached the Missouri River. Another road was established by the territorial Legislature in 1852 to run west from Reads Landing on the Mississippi, to Kenyon, Faribault and then on to Traverse des Sioux at St. Peter.

NORTHFIELD, Pop. 12,594.

This picturesque village situated on the Cannon River, was founded in 1855 and incorporated as a city in 1875. It was named after two principal founders, John W. North, a lawyer, and I.S. Field, a blacksmith and farmer. The city grew rapidly around its three water-powered mills that produced up to 3,000 barrels of flour a day. Because of its quality, the flour received a $2 per barrel premium in eastern markets. The town still retains a nineteenth century look and is the home of Carleton and St. Olaf colleges established in 1866 and 1874 respectively. For many years the town's motto was "Cows, Colleges and Contentment."

Northfield takes great pride in the fact that the James Brothers held up the First National Bank here on September 7, 1876. Bullet holes can still be seen on the old building's stone walls. Two townsfolk were killed as were gang members Clel Miller and Bill Stiles. Up to 1000 men pursued the gang as they retreated west. The Younger Brothers were captured north of Madelia in a marsh, while Jesse and Frank James escaped across the prairie into South Dakota.

Northfield developed around the Cannon River and there are several lovely views of the river in the city. Between Northfield and Faribault, the Cannon River flows through a maple and basswood forest which has been designated as the Cannon River Wilderness Area. There is a profusion of wildlife in the area.

The James brothers paused for portraits during a lull in their escapades.

DUNDAS, Pop. 422.

Just east of the freeway lies Dundas, a railway town platted in 1857 and named by two millers, John and Edward Archibald, emigrants from Dundas, Ontario. The brothers built a mill along the Cannon River which helped develop Dundas as the wheat milling center of Minnesota during the 1850's. The Archibalds also pioneered a new method of making flour. It was the Archibald Mill that produced a whiter, finer flour by using sifters, blowers and silk sieves. This process soon became the standard for the Minneapolis mills located at the Falls of St. Anthony. Farmers, ladened with wheat, traveled long distances to the Archibald Mill because of its quality milling. The mill has long vanished, but its foundation can still be seen south of the bridge on the east side of Main Street. Dundas was once a bustling town, but today, only consists of several buildings and a few homes.

WAHPEKUTE INDIANS

The Cannon River Valley was once the hunting grounds of the Wahpekute Dakota who were situated at the mouth of the Cannon River near Red Wing. In 1835 Alexander Faribault persuaded a number of the Wahpekute to settle and trade with him at the present site of Faribault. The Indians continued to roam the area between Faribault and Redwood Falls, but were required to live on a reservation after the 1851 Mendota and Traverse des Sioux treaties were signed. Following the Sioux Uprising of 1862, the Wahpekute were expelled from the state and sent to the Santee Reservation in Nebraska.

NERSTRAND WOODS

The eastern part of Rice County is gently rolling land that was once covered by a large forest of hardwoods called the "Big Woods" by early explorers and settlers. These woods, some 45 miles wide and running from central Minnesota to the southeast, consisted mainly of maple, basswood, white and red elm and red oak. The early settlers wasted no time in clearing these woods for farming, leaving little to be remembered except for an occasional grove. A remnant of these woods, standing east of Faribault, is known as Nerstrand Woods State Park, a thousand-acre memorial to the Big Woods.

CANNON RIVER

The Cannon River from Faribault to Red Wing is part of the state's Wild and Scenic River System, enacted in 1973. From this point, the Cannon flows 60 miles to the Mississippi just above Red Wing. The early French called this the "river of canoes." The river still draws many canoeists today and the stretch from Cannon Falls to Red Wing is the most pop-

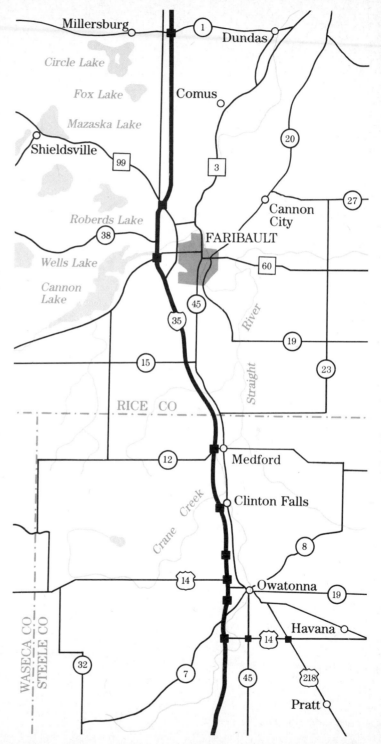

ular. The Cannon is slightly more than 100 miles from its beginning at Shields Lake in Rice County, to its confluence with the Mississippi just above Red Wing. It is one of four major streams of southeastern Minnesota that drains into the Mississippi. The others are the Zumbro, Whitewater, and Root.

The Cannon drains a total watershed of 1,462 square miles. The upper portion flows through many lakes and dams, descending some 400 feet by the time it reaches the Mississippi. Towns grew rapidly along the Cannon because of the milling power that the river provided. As farming developed during the 1850's, centers for trade and mills for grinding wheat into flour were needed. During the land boom of 1856, the small towns along the Cannon filled with transients, claim hunters and land speculators.

But with the collapse of the wheat market in the late 1870's, the 15 or so mills along the Cannon disappeared. Now only a few crumbling foundations can be found among the shrubs and cottonwood that line the banks of the river. Today, all the paper towns whose promoters once sold lots that commanded $100 a running foot, have been plowed under in the fields of this rich farming area.

FARIBAULT, Pop. 16,241.

Faribault rests on a low flood terrace in the valleys of the Cannon and Straight rivers. This area was a favorite trapping ground for Indians and fur traders, with Alexander Faribault being one of the first whites to set up trade here. Faribault worked the Cannon River area during the 1820's and by 1835 had set up a post. French-Canadian trappers and traders joined Faribault at this trading post and for the next twenty years, Faribault's creaking fur-carts were the only commerce in this region. An invoice for goods at Faribault's post in 1828, gives some insight as to what was important then. The list includes blankets, scalpers, guns, black silk handkerchiefs, tomahawks, combs, needles, flour, pork, corn and whiskey.

By the 1850's area settlement was rapidly increasing with milling and wheat farming the predominant trades. Together, the Cannon and Straight rivers provided power for the town's grist and sawmills.

GINSENG

In addition to building homesteads, cutting timber, and breaking soil, many settlers also engaged in gathering ginseng, a spicy root highly sought after by the Chinese. In 1859 it was reported that six tons of ginseng were brought to Faribault for export in one week.

BISHOP WHIPPLE

In 1860 a clergyman named Henry Benjamin Whipple was named Minnesota's first Episcopal bishop. Whipple held the first services in Faribault in the spring of 1860 at a site later occupied by Seabury Divinity School, Shattuck School and St. Mary's Hall, a school for girls, all of which Whipple founded.

But much of the bishop's time was devoted to the problems of the Indians, whose degradation and squalor he blamed on

MHS

Ruins of the Castle Mill on the Cannon River at Dundas. Photo/E. Larsen.

MHS

Bishop Whipple and his wife.

the whites. Whipple was one of the few men of the times that understood the injustices being done to the Indians. He was harshly denounced because he offered a defense for the Sioux Uprising of 1862. Yet in his 40 years as Episcopal bishop of Minnesota, Whipple's counsel was favored by England's Queen Victoria as well as many presidents of this country.

STEELE COUNTY, Pop. 30,328

Steele County was formed in 1855 and named after Franklin Steele, who came from Pennsylvania to Fort Snelling in the early 1800's when he was only 25. Steele developed land around the Falls of St. Anthony and was instrumental in the growth of the Minneapolis lumber and sawmill industries. He was also one of the first regents of the University of Minnesota.

MEDFORD, Pop. 775

In 1853 five men erected houses on the east bank of the Straight River, making that the first settlement in Steele County. William K. Colling, an Englishman, named the town after the ship Medford which had carried him to the United States.

CLINTON FALLS, Pop. 80

Named after a stretch of rapids on the Straight River, the falls developed in the late 1850's as an important milling stream. The Clinton Mill ground flour and animal feed for much of the surrounding area until it burned down in 1896.

One of the buildings still stands today by the river.

OWATONNA, Pop. 18,632

Owatonna is the present seat of Steele County and was founded in 1854. Chief Wadena is said to have moved his entire village to this site in order that his frail daughter might drink from one of its mineral springs. The water, rich in iron and sulphur, was described as similar to the Vichy Springs in France.

The city developed around the Straight River where Maple Creek joins it from the east. Despite its crookedness, the Dakota named the river Owatonna, meaning "straight." In 1866 the Minnesota Central Railway entered Owatonna from the north and the St. Peter and Winona line came from the east, assuring this village as an important shipping center. The town sits in a rich agricultural area where wheat fields long ago gave way to corn and dairy farms.

Owatonna has many old and interesting buildings, one of which is the National Farmers Bank erected in 1908, (now the Northwestern National Bank). The building was designed by Louis Sullivan, a nationally-known architect. Sullivan was given free hand to design the bank in any style but the traditional Greek and Roman. One writer called it a "jewel box set in a prairie town." The bank is still considered one of Minnesota's more interesting buildings and is a must for anyone making a serious national tour of important architecture.

Covered wagons entering Owatonna in 1864.

MHS

215

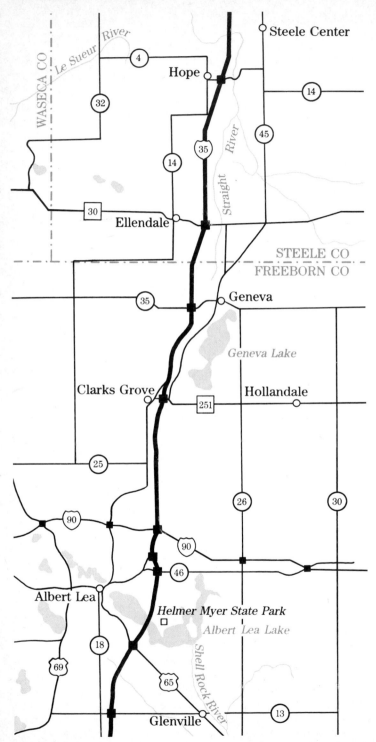

HOPE, Pop. 140
A small railway village located on the Chicago Rock Island and Pacific Railroad.

ELLENDALE, Pop. 555
This town, which was incorporated in 1901, is situated along the Chicago, Rock Island and Pacific Railroad. The town was named after Ellen Dale, the maiden name of the railroad president's wife. Mrs. Dale was well known for her interest and concern over the employees of the line and it was said she knew many by name. When the station was built, it seemed fitting to honor her.

GENEVA, Pop. 417
Geneva was settled in 1855 and named by its postmaster for Geneva, New York.

FREEBORN COUNTY & CEDAR RIVER BASIN
As the freeway passes Ellendale and continues into Freeborn County, the lakes and streams begin to drain southward into Iowa through the Des Moines and Cedar rivers. Freeborn County is a region of rolling farmland interspersed with some 30 lakes. Before the land was plowed and the marshes drained, these wetlands served as a barrier to the prairie fires that swept in from the west. This in turn enabled a steady growth of forests that began to the east of Albert Lea and Austin.

The Freeborn County marshes were different from those to the west, which invariably dried up during the hot summer months. Here, the marshes were mostly filled with water and underlaid by a heavy deposit of peat.

In 1879 the county was explored for coal, which was believed to exist in significant quantities. Although some thin layers were found, commercial amounts have yet to be discovered.

CLARKS GROVE, Pop. 620
This town was founded in 1880, some ten years before the Chicago, Rock Island and Pacific Railroad came through. The town was named after a grove of trees, just east of the town where a man named Clark settled. A number of Danish settlers began farming in the area. In 1889 they became the first group in the state to develop the cooperative concept. This important marketing idea revolved around farmers bringing their products to a central location and selling them under a cooperative label. The profits were distributed according to the individual production. The idea spread.

Twenty years later there were 1400 co-ops in the United States, with nearly 50 percent of them in Minnesota alone. All of this began here in Clarks Grove.

ALBERT LEA, Pop. 19,190

The city of Albert Lea was platted in 1856 around a number of lakes, the largest of which was Albert Lea Lake. The lake and city were named after Albert Lea, an explorer who traveled through southern Minnesota in 1835, mapping the area's lakes and streams. Albert Lea Lake was first called Fox Lake by Lea, when he saw a white fox run across his path as he approached the lake for the first time. These lakes were a favorite hunting ground of the Dakota.

That first winter of 1856 was severe and many of the settlers suffered from depression. A man named William Rice tried delivering mail to the lonely pioneers, but he was soon

ALBERT LEA LAKE

This lake lies in a pre-glacial valley of the Shell Rock River. It was later filled in by glaciers and is now the headwaters of the Shell Rock River. Located on the northeast side of Albert Lea Lake is the Helmer Myre State Park, where 1,500 acres of unplowed prairie exist, along with a wooded, lake island. Over 450 different varieties of wildflowers have been found in the park. There are 120 sites available for camping and 12 miles of hiking trails. Also located at the park is the Owen Johnson Interpretive Center. This center contains one of the largest collections of Indian artifacts in the United States.

Minnesota wheat, stacked and waiting to be threshed.

MHS

caught in a blizzard and died from exposure. As soon as the snow began to melt, many packed their belongings and returned to their former homes back East. However, that summer they were replaced by a new flood of settlers that pushed the population of Albert Lea to 2,500. The straggly little town became a collection of log houses and frame shacks. Broadway, the town's main street, was flanked by stores whose home-made shingles announced their wares.

Albert Lea was one of the early railroad towns on the Southern Minnesota Railroad line which in the early 1860's connected it to the Mississippi River. Because of the rich farmland and the number of railroads that served Albert Lea, few agricultural regions have ever witnessed such rapid growth in settlement or material wealth.

When Helmer State Park was created in 1947, it was named after a Minnesota senator from this district. A number of lakes are situated around Albert Lea because it rests on the eastern margin of the most recent glacier that formed here 12,000 years ago. Glacial deposits still block the old drainage channels, so most of the land east of Albert Lea to the Mississippi is devoid of lakes.

HAYWARD, Pop. 294

This area, covered with a deep rich loam, was settled in 1856 by an Iowan named David Hayward. There was once a two story windmill here jutting up from the prairie, capable of grinding 200 bushels of wheat daily. Just east of Hayward is the site of an old Indian camp. Many Indian artifacts have been found there over the years.

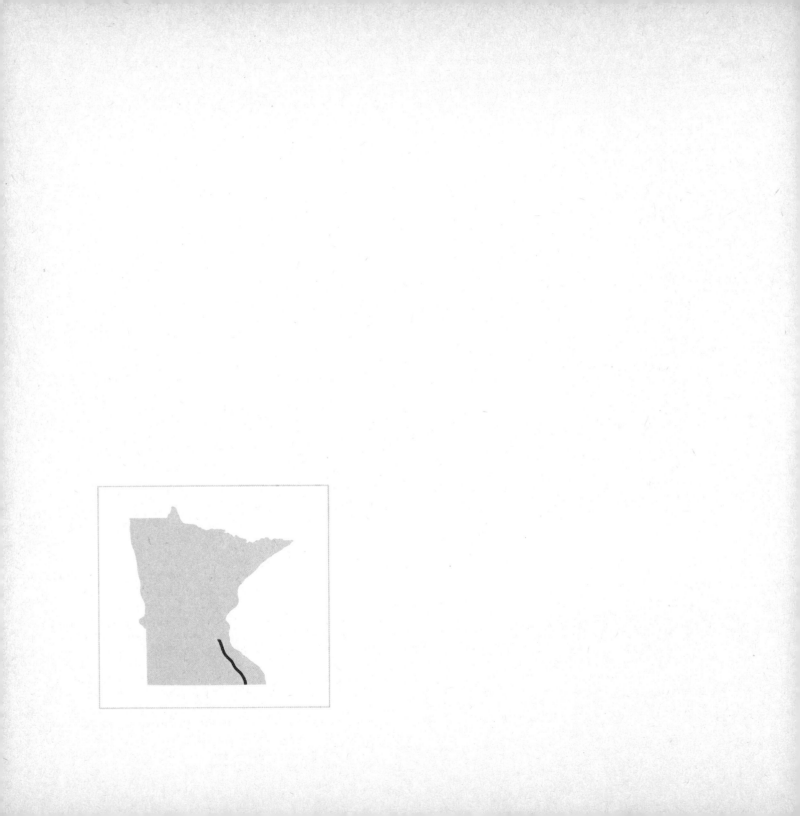

ROUTE 52, TO HARMONY

After the Sioux Uprising, many Dakota Indians were imprisoned at a stockade below Ft. Snelling. Photo/B.F. Upton.

MHS

FORT SNELLING

It wasn't long after the Louisiana Purchase of 1803, that the U.S. Government felt the need to obtain land for a military post in this new region. Its purpose was to block British expansion and influence in the Northwest. The strategic location was to be at the crossroads of two important waterways, the Minnesota and Mississippi rivers. In 1805, land across from Mendota was purchased from Chief Little Crow, a Dakota Indian whose grandchild later led the 1862 Sioux Uprising. This tract of land was bought for 60 gallons of whiskey and the promise of $2,000 in cash or merchandise.

But the wheels of government turned slowly. It was some fourteen years later before payment was finally made on the plateau where Fort Snelling would be built. Gathered there were a half-dozen chiefs including Little Crow and Wabasha. That fall some 200 soldiers came up the river and camped at Mendota. It was a cold, miserable winter and by spring some forty soldiers had died of scurvy. During the spring of 1820, they moved across the river and began working on Fort St. Anthony (later renamed Fort Snelling). Once built, Fort Snelling remained the farthest northwest Army post for the next thirty years. After other forts were built, Fort Snelling lost its importance and was only a supply post.

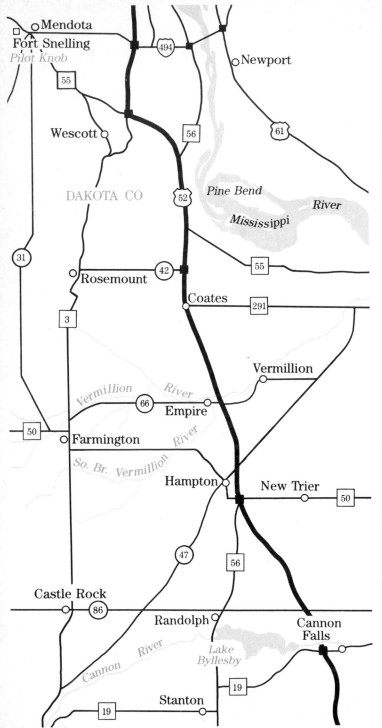

DAKOTA COUNTY, Pop. 194,111

This county was established in 1849 and named for the Dakota Indians. The Dakota were comprised of a number of allied tribes (seven in all), who originally occupied most of Minnesota and the adjoining western states. The Ojibwe, no friend of the Dakota, began calling them, "Nadouessioux," meaning "enemy." The name was eventually shortened to Sioux by whites.

The Dakota maintained three villages in what is now Dakota County. One was Kaposia, on the present site of South St. Paul. Another was Medicine Bottle's village at Pine Bend on the Mississippi and the third was Black Dog's village near the northeast end of Black Dog Lake on the Minnesota River bottoms. The Dakota of this area were constantly fighting with the Ojibwe who had pushed them from their traditional hunting and fishing grounds in the north. In 1842 the Mille Lacs Ojibwe came south and attacked the Kaposia village. The main battle took place across the Mississippi at Battle Creek Park, with the Ojibwe suffering heavy losses.

Father Louis Hennepin was probably the first white man to pass along the Mississippi in 1680 after he had been captured by the Dakota on Lake Pepin.

DAKOTA COUNTY GEOLOGY

The hilly regions of Dakota County were formed by a great mass of glacial drift that covered this area 12,000 years ago. The last of the great ice age glaciers moved southward from Canada through the valleys of the Red and Minnesota rivers. The ice, which in Canada was several thousand feet thick, pushed into central Iowa like a stubby finger.

When rising temperatures ended glaciation about 11,000 years ago, glacial floodwater spread widely. The Glacial River Warren (today's Minnesota River), was blocked by ice in the area of Fort Snelling. This caused its water-filled valley to overflow and sweep eastward across Dakota County to the Vermillion and Cannon rivers. Today these rivers are but remnants of the streams that once carved out their steep-walled valleys.

MENDOTA BRIDGE

Built in 1926, the Mendota Bridge, with its commanding view of the valley, sits 120 feet above the Minnesota River.

MENDOTA, Pop. 219

The word Mendota is Dakota for "where the waters mingle." It's an appropriate name, for here the Minnesota River ends its 330 mile journey from Browns Valley in western Minnesota. The Mississippi itself has traveled 500 river miles to this point, where it is joined by the Minnesota.

MHS

(left) Medicine Bottle, who was executed for his part in the Sioux Uprising. Photo/Whitney.
(bottom) An 1895 view of the Sibley house in Mendota.

MHS

Mendota (known as St. Peter's until 1837), was the site of the first permanent white settlement in Minnesota. It became a gathering spot for traders and trappers and in 1834, became the headquarters for Henry H. Sibley of the American Fur Company. Here in 1836, Sibley built the first stone house west of the Mississippi. Sibley, known as the "Squire of Mendota," became the territory's first representative in 1849 and the first governor of the state. Mendota became the focus for the area's exchange of furs and other supplies. A number of famous Minnesota people lived here, including Jean Baptiste Faribault, Alexis Bailly, and Lawrence Taliaferro, the regional Indian agent.

The Sibley house, which has been called the "Mount Vernon of Minnesota," can still be seen in Mendota. It is presently maintained by the Daughters of the American Revolution. Here in 1849, Alexander Ramsey lived with Sibley and issued the proclamation which officially recognized Minnesota as a territory. Next to the Sibley House is the Faribault House, home of the early fur trader, Jean Baptiste Faribault. This similar structure was built about 1840. Also located in Mendota (visible from the Mendota bridge) is St. Peter's Catholic Church, built in 1853. It is the oldest church in continuous use in Minnesota. Mendota's importance declined as the fur trade diminished. It is now listed in the National Register of Historic Places.

PILOT KNOB

Located across from Mendota on a hilly plain overlooking the Minnesota River, was a Dakota burial ground call Pilot Knob. Pilot Knob later became the site of an important treaty signed by the Dakota Nation in 1851. It was here under an arbor bush on a warm summer day, that Chiefs Little Crow, Wacouta, Cloud Man, Gray Iron, Wabasha (the head chief), Good Road and Shakopee met with Territorial Governor Alexander Ramsey, among others, and relinquished 24 million acres in what came to be called the Treaty of Mendota.

With this treaty and one signed a number of days earlier at Traverse des Sioux (just north of St. Peter), the Dakota ceded southern Minnesota and parts of Iowa and South Dakota. The price to be paid was three million dollars. Little of it ever reached the Dakota however, and after the Sioux Uprising of 1862, the treaty was nullified and the Dakota were banned from Minnesota.

In the fall of 1863, Little Six and Medicine Bottle were

captured near Grand Forks and returned to Minnesota because of their participation in the Sioux Uprising. They were hung at Pilot Knob, which today is a cemetery.

EAGAN TOWNSHIP

Named in 1861 after Patrick Eagan, one of the first settlers in this area.

PINE BEND

Where the Mississippi takes a sharp bend in its course, a stand of pines once covered its banks. Hence the area name. Here on the plain above the river, Chief Medicine Bottle and his band of Dakota maintained a camp. In 1851, shortly after the Treaty of Mendota was signed at Pilot Knob, the government relocated them on a reservation near Redwood. Old Chief Medicine Bottle died just before the Sioux Uprising of 1862, and his son was hung at Pilot Knob a short time later for his part in the conflict. Presently a refinery and other chemical companies make up Pine Bend. An aging limestone marker on the east side of the road is the only reminder of the past.

EMPIRE, Pop. 100

First known as Empire City in 1854, this small community was named after Empire, New York, the home town of one of its early settlers. Here the South Branch of the Vermillion River joins the main stream and flows fourteen miles further into the Mississippi near Hastings. The total length of the stream is about 35 miles and starts west of here in Scott County. The Vermillion River was once an important power source for the Hastings grist mills.

HAMPTON, Pop. 299

Established in April 1858 and named after Hampton, Connecticut, this town, along with Inver Grove Heights and Rosemount, started as a local banking and trading center.

Cannon Valley Mill, Cannon Falls, 1915.

MHS

CANNON FALLS, Pop. 2,653

Cannon Falls township was first settled around 1854 and derived its name from the falls of the Cannon River which is now covered by the reservoir of Lake Byllesby. Like many other southeastern Minnesota towns along the Cannon, Vermillion and Zumbro rivers, Cannon Falls was founded and prospered as a milling town.

In 1857 the first flour mill was completed in the new village. It wasn't long before several mills were grinding over 3,100 bushels of wheat per day. Today the buildings along Main Street retain much of their original flavor from the late 1850's and 1860's. The towering building visible from the highway is the Minnesota Grain Pearling and Malting Company.

CANNON RIVER

The Cannon River some 100 miles long, flows past the towns of Faribault and Northfield before it empties into the Mississippi just north of Red Wing. The river is now part of the state's Wild and Scenic River System enacted in 1973. East of Cannon Falls the river meanders slowly through a wooded valley of maple and basswood. As the river passes Cannon Falls, its low banks give way to a beautiful deep gorge where limestone and sandstone cliffs rise up 250 feet. Glacial waters had much to do with the formation of this valley, creating one of the more beautiful canoeing streams in the state, particularly the stretch from Cannon Falls to the Mississippi.

It is no surprise that the early French called this the "Riviere aux Canots," meaning "River of Canoes." But it was the English that thought the Dakota were trying to say Cannon rather than Canots, and the name Cannon River stuck. The Cannon is slightly more than 100 miles from its beginnings at Shields Lake in Rice County to its confluence with the Mississippi. It is also one of four major streams in southeastern Minnesota that drain into the Mississippi. The others are the Zumbro, Whitewater and Root.

As agriculture developed in this area during the 1860's, a need arose for farm trade centers and flour mills. The Cannon provided water power for these mills and towns began to form along its shores. Most of the early farmers planted wheat and during the 1860's they had a string of successful crops. But disease, drought and lower prices forced many to diversify into other crops. With the advent of the railroads, wheat was shipped to Minneapolis, which soon became one of the largest milling centers in the world. Thus the 15 or so small mills along the Cannon disappeared, leaving only a few crumbling foundations that can still be found hidden under the shrubs.

Farm chores. Photo/Carl Graff.

MHS

Milkmaid poses with her stool and pail.

MHS

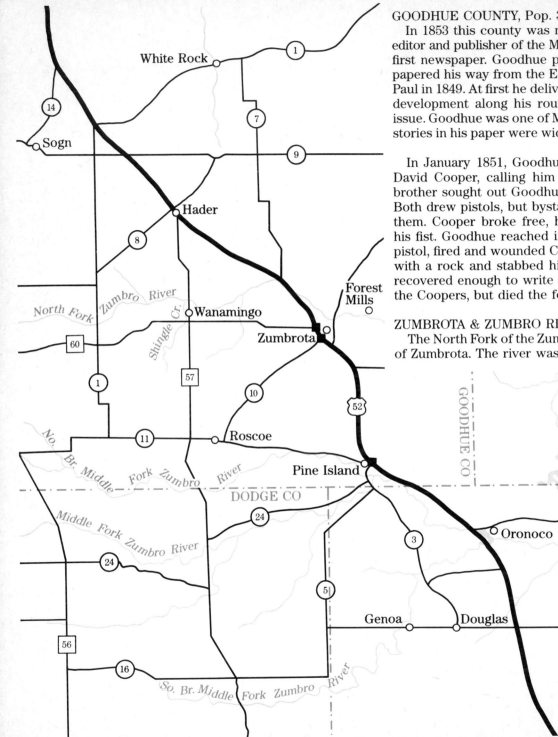

GOODHUE COUNTY, Pop. 38,749

In 1853 this county was named after James M. Goodhue, editor and publisher of the MINNESOTA PIONEER, the state's first newspaper. Goodhue practiced law, farmed and news-papered his way from the East before he opened shop in St. Paul in 1849. At first he delivered papers by hand, noting new development along his route and recording it in the next issue. Goodhue was one of Minnesota's early supporters, and stories in his paper were widely reprinted around the nation.

In January 1851, Goodhue wrote an article about Judge David Cooper, calling him an "arrogant ass." The judge's brother sought out Goodhue to defend his brother's honor. Both drew pistols, but bystanders intervened and disarmed them. Cooper broke free, however, striking Goodhue with his fist. Goodhue reached into his coat, pulled out another pistol, fired and wounded Cooper. Cooper then hit Goodhue with a rock and stabbed him twice with a knife. Goodhue recovered enough to write another scathing editorial about the Coopers, but died the following year.

ZUMBROTA & ZUMBRO RIVER

The North Fork of the Zumbro River runs through the town of Zumbrota. The river was first named by the Dakota who

Royal Hose Company, firefighters of Zumbrota, 1884. Photo/A.F. Raymond.

MHS

called it "Wazi Oju," meaning "pines planted." At one time a stand of pines did grow a few miles to the south of what is now the village of Pine Island. Later the French called it "Riviere des Embarras," referring to driftwood obstructions that created problems as they paddled along its winding course. The river's name was eventually translated by the English into Zumbro. When the town was settled in 1854 they added the Dakota suffix "ta," meaning at, or on, giving them Zumbrota, or "on the Zumbro."

Zumbrota was settled and platted between 1854 and 1856 by the Strafford Western Emigration Society. The group's aim was to strictly reinforce prohibition in order to maintain a Puritan community. Zumbrota grew as a milling town, utilizing the power of the Zumbro's North Fork. The town also claims Minnesota's only covered bridge. Unfortunately, it is now land-locked at their county fair grounds.

The Zumbro River flows some 74 river miles from here to the Mississippi, where they converge near the town of Kellogg. The North Fork joins the Zumbro just west of Zumbro Falls. The Zumbro with it's North, Middle and South Forks, drains a total of 1,400 square miles in Goodhue, Olmsted, Dodge and Wabasha counties. As the highway periodically drops from the level farmlands into broad wooded valleys,

you can be sure a stream or creek feeding into the Zumbro will be found at the bottom. These valleys were largely eroded away by glacial meltwater that followed these present streambeds some 12,000 years ago.

PINE ISLAND, Pop. 1,977

This town was established at about the same time as Zumbrota and Cannon Falls. The town's name was derived from the Dakota word "Wa-zee-wee-ta," or "pine island." The Middle Fork of the Zumbro circles the present town where at one time a large stand of pines could be seen for many miles across the prairie. It was a favorite winter camping spot for the Dakota that lived along the Mississippi near Red Wing.

Pine Island was settled by Swiss immigrants during the 1800's, who immediately began making their traditional cheeses. With 30 cheese factories in the area during the early 1900's, it was considered the "cheese center of Minnesota." In 1914 a 6,000 pound cheese was loaded on a flatcar and shipped to the State Fair in St. Paul. Today cheese is still an important product of this active farming community. Lying slightly west of Highway 52, Pine Island is still a quaint village with store fronts dating back to 1895.

225

OLMSTED COUNTY, Pop 91,971

Founded in 1855, Olmsted County was named after David Olmsted, the first mayor of St. Paul. Southeast Minnesota was one of the first areas to be settled in the state. The 1851 Treaty of Mendota removed control of the land from the Dakota, legally enabling whites to settle in this region. People were attracted by the fertile soil, lumber and water power available from the numerous streams. As the settlers started to move across the state, the level plains above the Mississippi became heavily planted with wheat. The streams and creeks provided the power for mills that seemed to be built at every turn of the river.

It wasn't long past the 1850's that soil erosion, floods and depletion of the forests nearly destroyed the land. Moreover, drought and diseased wheat showed the farmers that one-crop agriculture was unwise. Farmers diversified their income with corn, small grains and dairy cattle. Today this area commands over $1500 an acre for good farmland and Olmsted is one of the state's leading agricultural regions.

GEOLOGY OF OLMSTED COUNTY

This county lies just at the edge of a system of deeply eroded valleys extending westward from the Mississippi. These valleys were formed by the Zumbro, Whitewater, Root rivers and their tributaries. This area was hardly touched by the ice age, but glacial water and years of rain and erosion were responsible for the beautiful valleys and ravines of today.

An early traveler once wrote about Olmsted County that "of the rolling prairies and romantic hills covered with flowers and trees, it is doubtful the eye of man ever rested on a more beautiful spot." This area is underlaid by limestone which is easily penetrated by rain and surface waters. In these limestone formations many underground streams exist, and surface pollutants can easily filter into the groundwater of southeast Minnesota. There are no natural lakes in this county and several streams flow into the ground never to be seen again.

ORONOCO, Pop. 574

Settled in 1854 by millers wanting to harness the power of the Zumbro River, Oronoco was organized as a town in 1858 and named after the 1,600 mile South American river, Orinoco. Highway 52 crosses two forks of the Zumbro here. Shady Lake, one of the few bodies of water in Olmsted County, is an old millpond created by a dam.

In 1857 prospectors found gold flecks in the river here, and hundreds rushed to Oronoco to make it rich. This short-lived boom gave birth to a mining company and a number of sluices to wash the gold found in the sand. Operations closed down that winter and when the spring floods came, most of the sluices were washed away. Frustrated by the bad weather and small amounts of gold found, Oronoco's gold fever quickly cooled.

MHS

A farmer moves cut hay back to the barn.

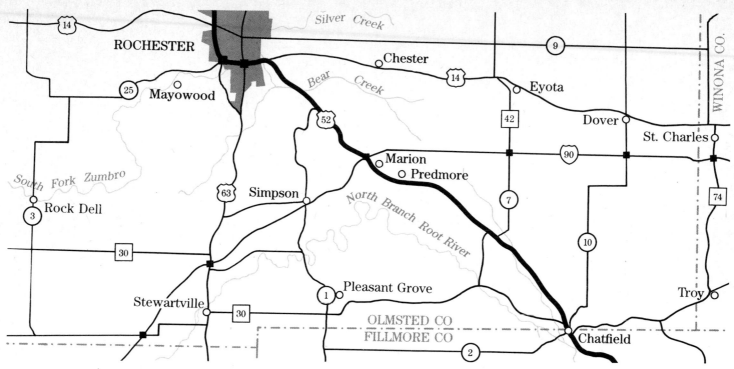

ROCHESTER, Pop. 57,855

In 1854, George Head traveled west from Rochester, New York in search of a new home. Near the falls of the South Branch of the Zumbro River, Head built his cabin. The falls and surrounding scenery reminded him of the Genesee River area near his home town. When the time came to give this new settlement a name, Head suggested Rochester.

Rochester began as a crossroads campground for the wagon trains coming into southeast Minnesota. Its early industry, like most of the towns in this region, was flour milling. Three mills were established here between 1856-1871. The Winona and St. Peter Railroad reached Rochester in 1864 to help ship out the crops and fancy foodstuffs being grown in this fertile region. In 1865, one of the state's first dairy farms was started here and the area soon became the focus of the dairy industry.

This town would have remained like other busy Midwestern towns if it weren't for a country physican named William W. Mayo, who moved his practice from Le Sueur to Rochester in 1863. Twenty years after his arrival in town, on an August night in 1883, a tornado swept across the plains into Rochester, killing 26 people and injuring hundreds more. The tragedy was compounded since the closest hospital was 100 miles away. The injured were taken to hotels, private resi-

dences and the convent of St.Francis. It was this storm that motivated the nuns of the convent to build and operate a hospital, if Mayo and his two sons, also doctors, would direct it. Subsequently, a 40-bed unit was built and became known as St. Mary's Hospital. But that was only the beginning for a nucleus of hospitals that, together with the famed Mayo Clinic, now employ over 11,000 people and treat 200,000 patients annually from around the world.

SILVER LAKE

A millpond dam was constructed in the mid-1800's forming Silver Lake near the center of Rochester. Today, the city's power plant keeps the water ice free and thousands of Canada geese make their winter home here. In 1960 a subspecies of giant Canada geese, thought to be extinct, was discovered wintering here. It is quite a sight to see these flocks of geese returning to the lake, after a day of feeding on the nearby fields.

MARION, Pop. 180

This town took its name from Francis Marion, the famed "Swamp Fox" of the Revolutionary War. Marion began about 45 miles from the Iowa border as a stage-stop on the old St.Paul-Dubuque stagecoach route. In Marion, horses were

MHS

Dr. C.H. Mayo, in the operating room at Mayo Clinic, 1913.

exchanged and passengers fed before they continued their bumpy ride to Rochester and St. Paul. In 1856, Marion tried unsuccessfully to wrestle the county seat from Rochester.

FILLMORE COUNTY GEOLOGY

Established in 1853, Fillmore County was named after Millard Fillmore, thirteenth President of the United States. The county's surface is much like the other hilly and wooded counties of Winona and Houston. A good portion of it lies within the Richard J. Dorer Memorial Hardwood Forest. Dorer worked for many years in the Minnesota Department of Conservation and was concerned with the way the land of southeastern Minnesota had been devastated by indiscriminate logging and farming. Through his efforts beginning in the 1930's, the region has once again become a valuable economic and recreational land. Several state parks are in this region, of which Forestville State Park is one. Forestville is located west of Preston on State 16 and situated by the South Branch of the Root River. Here you can still see the abandoned, though mostly intact, general store run by Thomas Meighen during the Civil War. The park also has excellent trout fishing.

IRON ORE

When one mentions iron ore, the Mesabi and Vermilion Ranges of the Arrowhead come immediately to mind. But few know about the ore deposits that were found near Spring Valley, southwest of Chatfield. The ore came as a surprise find in 1930, but mining didn't start until 1942 when the demand was high because of the war. Some five million tons have since been removed.

CHATFIELD, Pop. 2,055

On a hillside overlooking the North Branch of the Root River, is a town named for Andrew G. Chatfield, a judge who held the first court in the county in 1853. Chatfield was an important town to southern Minnesota during its early history. The all important government land office was located here in 1856 to handle all the immigrants who wanted to homestead in this region. The Minnesota census of 1860 recorded only 11 cities with populations over one thousand. Chatfield was one of them. Duluth counted only 80 people for that same year.

Chatfield was also the connecting point between two important stage routes, the St. Paul - Dubuque line and another territorial route that came from Winona. The stage road to St. Paul roughly follows present-day Highway 52. Hundreds of pioneer wagons followed these early roads, driving herds of cattle with them as they searched for suitable farmland. Today, Chatfield boasts of its nationally recognized, brass band.

ROOT RIVER

Named from the Dakota word "Hokah," in reference to the exposed tree roots along its banks, the river and its tributaries run through valleys lined by rugged hills. During the autumn, the colors of the forests make for spectacular canoe trips on the 35 mile stretch from Chatfield to Lanesboro. The Root River starts in Mower County, but its deep, erosive valleys begin in Fillmore County. In all, the watershed for the Root comprises 1,670 square miles and drops over 500 feet by the time it reaches the Mississippi.

Along its banks you can see birch, maple, willow, white oak and cottonwood. The river's valley widens shortly after it passes Chatfield. The Root is a mature river, where sediment has washed down from the level prairie and hillsides and been deposited along the valley floor. The early farmers found this to be a good place to grow corn, wheat, and even tobacco. In some valleys of the Root, the growing season is over five months long and the first frost arrives here later than most other parts of the state.

FOUNTAIN, Pop. 347

Fountain township was settled in 1853 and named for a large spring located one mile northwest of Fountain village. The village was platted when the Southern Minnesota Railroad came through in 1870.

WHITE SETTLEMENT

In 1850, many Norwegian immigrants were looking for public lands west of the Mississippi. After the Dakota Indians ceded southern Minnesota in the 1851 Treaty of Mendota, thousands of immigrants began to settle in southeastern Minnesota. They moved up from the Mississippi along the rivers and valleys that offered rich farmland, plentiful woods, needed waterpower and protection from harsh plains weather. These Norwegian settlements left a rich heritage to this region, as the Swedes did to the St. Croix Valley area. Fillmore County continued to grow while many parts of Minnesota were still uninhabited. As late as 1865, Fillmore had the largest population in the state with 17,500 people.

PRESTON, Pop. 1,413

This town, located in the center of Fillmore County, has been the county seat since 1856. The town was named after Luther Preston who ran the flour mill located along the South Branch of the Root River. Milling was common in this area because of the wheat grown on the prairie to the west. It's proximity to the many streams in southeastern Minnesota made it convenient for farmers to haul in their harvests.

From Preston eastward along State 16, the terrain is unlike any other part of the state, because it is the only area undisturbed by the glaciers. Here one can see southeast Minnesota as it appeared millions of years ago with its river-eroded terrain.

HARMONY & CANTON

In 1926 on a farm a few miles out of town, a number of pigs kept disappearing. One day while the farmer walked his fields trying to uncover the mystery, he heard some faint squeals. Following the sounds, he discovered a small opening which led to a vast underground network of caverns and his pigs. The caverns became known as Niagara Cave and opened to the public in 1933. Many caves exist in this area because the underlying limestone has been dissolved by underground rivers over many years.

Canton was incorporated in 1887 and named after Canton, China. The towns of Canton, Prosper and Harmony grew and prospered along the now-abandoned tracks which once connected them to the Mississippi.

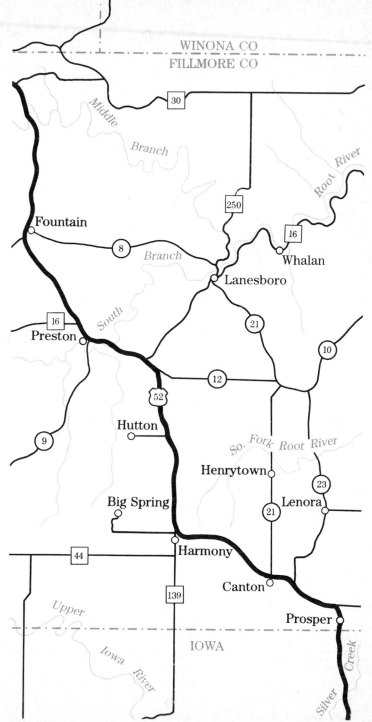

ROUTE 61, SOUTH TO LA CRESCENT

The steamer "Ben Hur" waited for passengers near the Mississippi River town of Winona. Photo/John Runk, 1911.

U.S. 61 traverses the broad Mississippi River Valley for some 134 miles to La Crescent, Minnesota. This beautiful region of rounded hills and steep bluffs was carved out over 10,000 years ago by two large glacial rivers. Together these powerful rivers drained the two largest bodies of fresh water that this continent has ever known, Glacial Lake Agassiz and Glacial Lake Duluth.

Lake Agassiz was located in northwestern Minnesota over 12,000 years ago and was originally formed by glacial meltwater. The lake occupied an area larger than the combined Great Lakes of today. The second body of water, Glacial Lake Duluth, is now occupied by the smaller Lake Superior. The two rivers that flowed from these lakes followed the present channels of the Minnesota and St. Croix rivers, cutting, scouring and widening the valleys we see today. As the water surged along these glacial rivers, the Mississippi River bedrock below Hastings was cut some 800 feet deeper than today. Eventually the waters eased, allowing the Mississippi to silt back to its present day level. Today a rich basin of backwater sloughs, alive with fish and waterfowl, extends all the way into Iowa.

It was on these same waters that Le Sueur, Du Luth, Hennepin, Nicollet and Carver explored Minnesota, the land of rivers and lakes. Subsequently, it was along the Mississippi that the first Minnesota towns were settled and land was farmed. Along with other rivers and lakes, the Mississippi became the conduit for furs coming from the Northwest and lumber from the rich pineries along the St. Croix. Quite naturally, the Mississippi became the vital artery from which this state's rich history developed.

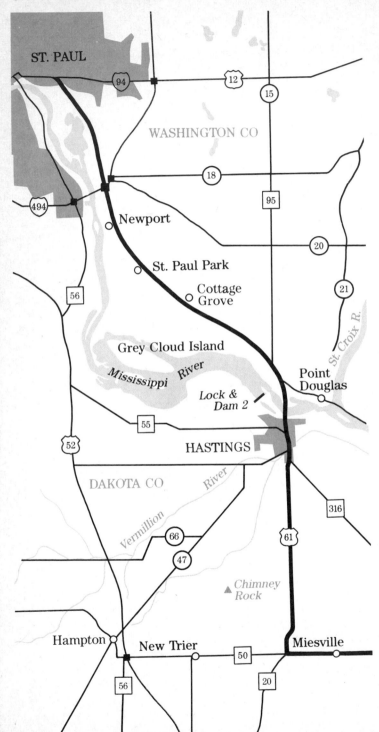

WASHINGTON COUNTY, Pop. 113,571

This fertile area, lying between the St. Croix and Mississippi Rivers northward to the Mille Lacs Lake region, has been known as the "St. Croix Delta" or the "Golden Triangle." The abundant furs and white pine of this delta were the leading attractions for the white man's expansion into the Northwest. In the early 1800's, pressure was exerted on the government to open more lands for settlers and the St. Croix delta became the prime target. Subsequently, in a treaty signed in 1837, the Dakota and Ojibwe Indians ceded 920,000 acres for which they were paid $500,000. Of this, $200,000 was given to traders to cover unpaid Indian bills. This event marked the first legal settlement by white men west of the Mississippi. In 1851, the Treaty of Mendota released the rest of southern and western Minnesota from Indian control. By the time Minnesota reached statehood in 1858, the Dakota and Ojibwe had ceded most of their land to the white man.

With the territory now open for settlement, the lush forests of eastern Minnesota started falling to the axe. The rest of the nation was also in need of wood, so white pine flowed down the St. Croix and Mississippi rivers to southern cities past an influx of settlers heading upstream to this new land. Because the tip of the delta (lower Washington County), had open prairie and a proximity to lumbering camps on the St. Croix, it was natural that the first farming in the state be done here. These small farms supplied the lumber camps with potatoes, corn and wheat. In 1834, the state's first grist mill began operations near Afton on Valley Creek. Settlement increased during the early 1850's as steamers pushed up the Mississippi, loaded with Easterners looking for a new beginning. Towns formed along the valleys of the Cannon, Zumbro, Whitewater and Root rivers. The rich soil, abundant timber and ample water power offered the necessary ingredients.

During the late 1850's, lumbering was the main economy of the St. Croix delta. Huge rafts of logs cascaded down the St. Croix to the Mississippi for milling in Winona and other nearby areas. Eventually, this lumber helped build the central cities of the U.S. such as Des Moines, Omaha, Kansas City and St. Louis. Later the Twin Cities became the major lumber and milling centers of Minnesota.

GREY CLOUD ISLAND

This island and slough area was named after a noted Indian woman named Grey Cloud, a member of a small band of Dakota Indians that camped in the vicinity. In 1695, Pierre Le Sueur, a French fur trader and explorer, maintained a small post on this island. Eventually, Le Sueur left Grey Cloud Island to explore the Minnesota River near Mankato in his search for furs and copper. U.S. soldiers also camped here in 1819 on their way up the Mississippi to build Fort Snelling. In 1838, a trading post was established by Joseph Brown who broke some sod and planted potatoes, probably making him the first white farmer in the region. Today there is little remaining on the island to suggest the activity of so many years ago.

NEWPORT, Pop. 3,323

Located at the United Methodist church in Newport is a large granite boulder called "Eyah-shaw," meaning "red rock." Over many years the Dakota revered this rock and painted various symbols across its surface. For a time the rock was located along the town railroad tracks prompting the name, Red Rock Station.

Rev. Benjamin Kavanaugh, one of the early Methodist missionaries, came here in 1839 to minister to Chief Little Crow's band. This large Dakota village, named Kaposia, was located a short distance up the river at the present town of South St. Paul. The rock, and the log mission were later moved to the Methodist church that sits on a hillside overlooking the valley.

Joseph Irish, one of the first permanent settlers, came to Newport with his family and 27 cows and soon became the first cheese-maker in Minnesota.

As wheat began to pour in from the prairie during the 1870's, Newport maintained a large flour and saw mill and soon became an important storage and shipping center on the Mississippi.

ST. PAUL PARK, Pop. 4,864

St. Paul Park was a railroad town that grew up along with Newport and Cottage Grove. When settlement began in this region, a few wealthy men wanted to develop a town here and name it St. Paul. But a disagreement between landowners and promoters resulted in the town of St. Paul being built 12 miles up river. Nevertheless, a town was formed here eventually and arrived at its name by combining the desired name of St. Paul with that of Charles Parker, a local settler. At one time St. Paul Park boasted of a knitting mill, wagon factory, paper mill and some six hotels.

COTTAGE GROVE, Pop. 18,994

This township was settled in 1844 and by 1851 it had become a busy agricultural center for the area. Because of its proximity to lumber camps and Indian agencies, Cottage Grove also became one of the first farming areas in Minnesota.

MHS

Employees of the Dudley Mill posed outside their boarding house in 1889 at Point Douglas.

POINT DOUGLAS

On U.S. 10, three miles east of Route 61, lies the site of Point Douglas, an abandoned pioneer town. It was once considered as a potential location for a new western fort, but in 1819, Fort Snelling gained that distinction. The first military road in this new territory was built from Pt. Douglas to the town of Superior, Wisconsin along the west bank of the St. Croix. Another was built from Point Douglas to St. Paul, then up to Fort Ripley. This road between Superior and Point Douglas, provided a vital commercial link between the boat traffic coming across Lake Superior and the supplies moving along the Mississippi.

Point Douglas also established the first post office in Minnesota in 1840. By the time mail and stage traffic was moving along the Point Douglas Road in 1861, a total of $120,600 had been spent developing the 185 mile road. A number of small stations developed along the route, such as Copas, Vasa, Sunrise and Chengwatana. Later when the railroad from Duluth to St. Paul was completed, traffic on the road stopped almost overnight and today only small sections of the old trail can be seen at various locations. At one time, Point Douglas also marked the northwest limit of the cardinal, but bird feeding today has drawn the species throughout the Northwest.

Most people thought that because Point Douglas was located at the confluence of the St. Croix and Mississippi rivers, it would become the most important town in the Northwest. Today only a few houses hug the shore, but it is said that several old building foundations can still be found along the hillside.

CARPENTER ST. CROIX VALLEY NATURE CENTER

North of Point Douglas a couple of miles on Washington County 21, is the newly developed St. Croix Valley Nature Center. It was once an estate and apple orchard situated on a beautiful tract of land overlooking the St. Croix Valley. The estate, previously owned by Thomas Carpenter, was donated and converted into a nature center in 1981. The center has some 15 miles of prairie and wooded trails, of which four miles are paved and handicap-accessible. The park also contains over 7,000 apple trees of some 45 varieties, making this a delightful fall visit.

Unique programs offered at this beautiful new center include raptor rehabilitation, beekeeping, bird-banding, orienteering, geology, orchard maintenance and many more. One weekend a month the park is open to the general public, while the rest of the time groups of 10 or more are welcome by reservation.

MISSISSIPPI & ST. CROIX RIVERS

At Hastings, the Mississippi has wound its way 520 miles from its source at Lake Itasca. Two miles east of the Hastings bridge, the St. Croix ends its 150 mile journey that began in northern Wisconsin. Where the Mississippi crosses the mouth of the St. Croix, a natural dam of sand and silt has been deposited by the Mississippi, creating a 20 mile pool of water called Lake St. Croix.

When one views the broad St. Croix Valley with its steep banks, it is apparent that a much larger volume of water flowed through here when it was an outlet of Glacial Lake Duluth. The sandstone, laid bare along the walls of the St. Croix Valley, were formed by an ancient sea that covered Minnesota 500 million years ago. Because of the thickness of this sandstone, and its exposure along the St. Croix and other areas throughout North America, it is referred to by geologists as the St. Croixian series.

DAKOTA COUNTY, Pop. 194,111

This county, established in 1849, was named after the Dakota Indians. The Dakota were comprised of seven allied Indian tribes who originally occupied most of Minnesota and the adjoining western states. The Ojibwe, never a friend of the Dakota, began calling them "Nadouessioux," or "enemy". The name was later shortened to Sioux. In 1680, Father Louis Hennepin, captured by the Dakota at Lake Pepin, became the first white man to pass along the Mississippi as he was taken north to Mille Lacs Lake by his captors.

The Dakota maintained three villages in the county. One was Kaposia, at South St. Paul, another was Medicine Bottle's village at Pine Bend on the Mississippi and lastly, Black Dog's village near the northeast end of Black Dog Lake on the Minnesota River bottom. The Dakota of this area constantly fought with the Ojibwe, who had pushed the Dakota from their traditional hunting and fishing grounds in the north during the mid-1700's. In 1842, the Mille Lacs Ojibwe ventured south, attacking the Kaposia village, with the main battle taking place across the river at Battle Creek Park. The Ojibwe retreated with heavy losses.

DAKOTA COUNTY GEOLOGY

The hilly regions of Dakota County were formed by a great mass of glacial drift shoveled in by ice sheets that covered this area 12,000 years ago. The last of the great ice age glaciers moved southward from Canada through the valleys of the Red and Minnesota rivers. The ice, which in Canada was several thousand feet thick, pushed across Minnesota into central Iowa like a stubby finger. With rising temperatures, glaciation ended about 11,000 years ago with meltwater flooding widely. The Glacial River Warren (today's Minnesota River), was blocked by ice in the area of Fort Snelling. This caused its water-filled valley to overflow and sweep eastward across Dakota County to the Vermillion and Cannon rivers. Today these small tributaries are only remnants of the streams that once carved out their steep-walled valleys.

MHS

Chimney Rock appears today as it did at the turn of the century.

HASTINGS, Pop. 12,827

During the early 1800's, this spot along the Mississippi was first known as Oliver's Grove. It was named after Lt. William Oliver whose boat full of supplies bound for soldiers building Fort Snelling, became stuck in an ice jam here in 1819. Joseph R. Brown, a 14-year-old drummer boy, was with Oliver during that fateful winter. Brown returned 12 years later and started a trading post with a small plot of spring wheat. By 1853 a village had grown and Oliver's Grove was renamed Hastings, from the middle name of Henry H. Sibley, Minnesota's first governor.

The convergence of the Mississippi, St. Croix and Vermillion rivers established Hastings as an important agricultural center. As the rivers provided power for its mills and an access to river markets, Hastings became one of the great wheat-marts of the Northwest. A large grain elevator on the Vermillion River is still functioning. The river flavor of this town can still be tasted on a short drive down Second St.

At the corner of Vermillion and 17th, stands the Le Duc House, one of the more noted nineteenth-century homes of Minnesota. The house was built by General William Le Duc, a Civil War veteran and owner of a Hastings mill.

VERMILLION RIVER

The Vermillion River, some 35 miles long, starts in Scott County, runs through all of Dakota County, and then into Hastings. In the 1850's, the Vermillion was an important milling stream for Hastings and the surrounding area. The river empties into the Mississippi at the Gores Wildlife Management Area, a collection of ponds, sloughs and backwaters abundant with wildlife and open to the public for recreational use.

CHIMNEY ROCK GEOLOGY

To see one of the best examples in Minnesota of this type of formation, travel six miles south of Hastings. Turn West at 220th St. and continue two miles to a T intersection. Just 1/2 mile further north you will see the rock. The 34-foot formation, surrounded by oak and birch, rests in an area of rolling farmland shaped by glaciers 12,000 years ago.

This sandstone rock is capped by a thin layer of limestone which helps protect it from rain. Chimney Rock was formed by a combination of wind and rain which eventually eroded away much of the sandstone around it.

MIESVILLE, Pop. 179

Miesville, settled in 1854, was first known as Douglas. Later it was renamed after John Mies who settled here in 1874 and built a hotel and saloon.

GOODHUE COUNTY, Pop. 38,749

Formed in 1853, this county was named after James Goodhue, editor of the MINNESOTA PIONEER, the territory's first newspaper. Goodhue farmed and newspapered his way from the East before he set up his small press in St. Paul. Goodhue often used his newspaper to verbally attack town officials. Eventually he was stabbed by a relative of a judge who had been ridiculed in one of Goodhue's editorials.

CANNON RIVER

The Cannon River, some 100 miles long, leaves the rolling farmlands and drops into the valley of the Cannon River. The river is now part of the state's Wild and Scenic River System enacted in 1973. The river meanders through the deep wooded valley lined with maple, basswood, oak and birch, its limestone hills rising 250 feet in some places. Glacial waters had much to do with the forming of this valley which also created one of the more beautiful canoeing streams in the state, particularly the stretch from Cannon Falls to the Mississippi.

It is no surprise that the early French called this the "La Riviere aux Canots," meaning "River of Canoes." But it was the English that thought the Dakota were trying to say Cannon rather than Canots, and the name Cannon River stuck. The river is also one of four major streams in southeastern

Minnesota that drain into the Mississippi. The others are the Zumbro, Whitewater, and Root.

WELCH

A narrow winding road descends into the small village of Welch which was settled along the Cannon River in 1857. Steep bluffs rise over the old buildings and antique shops of this once active milling town. There is a place here along the river to rent canoes or have a picnic .

RED WING, Pop. 13,736

Red Wing's name was derived from a series of Dakota chiefs named "Whoo-pa-doo-to," meaning "Wings of Scarlet." Indian camps were set on this level piece of land close to the Mississippi River. In 1837 Red Wing became the site of a Dakota mission run by two Swiss missionaries. But the Dakota preferred their traditional ways to the preaching of the Swiss. Discouraged by their inability to convert the Indians, the missionaries abandoned the site.

Soon after the Mendota and Traverse des Sioux treaties of 1851, Red Wing grew rapidly and in 1853 it became the county seat of Goodhue. Steamboats also began stopping regularly at the docks, helping this river town become a major trading center for the farms above the bluffs. Today

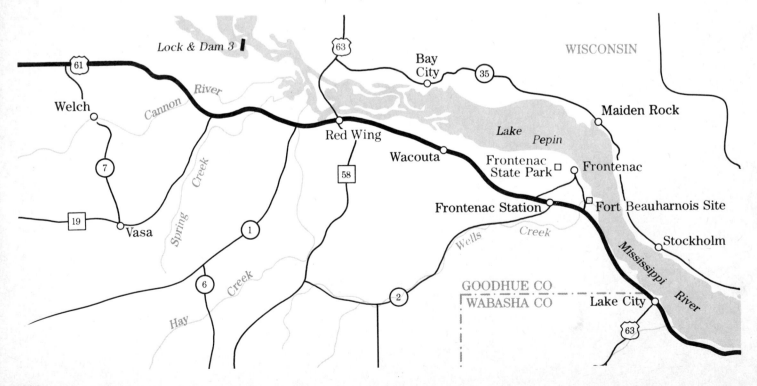

the town has actively restored many of its grand old homes and businesses. One recent example is the charming St. James Hotel. A large hill called Barn Bluff looms over the east end of Red Wing. This bluff was once an island in the post-glacial river channel. The resistant rock held its ground as the surrounding area was washed away. Eventually the river channel changed and today the bluff is connected to the city. A trail takes you to the top of the bluff for a view of the Mississippi River Valley. There is an unusual double Indian trail here that runs along the top of the bluff. This trail was noted by Henry Thoreau when he climbed here for a look in 1861, as he journeyed up the Mississippi.

WACOUTA, Pop. 80

This spot was first settled in 1853 by an Indian trader named Bullard. Plotting a village around his post, Bullard picked the name Wacouta from the last chief of the Red Wing band of Dakota Indians. Chief Wacouta was a kindly man who thought peace a virtue and advised his people accordingly. This small village once competed with Red Wing for the county seat when it was a town alive with lumberjacks and rivermen. Millions of logs were rafted together here to be sent down river to the growing towns of St. Louis and Kansas City. Today only summer homes mark this area.

LAKE PEPIN

Between Red Wing and Wacouta, the Mississippi widens to form Lake Pepin. The Indians called it "Pem-vee-cha-mday" or "Lake in the Mountains" because of the high bluffs that extend along this broad body of water. Pepin was formed by the Chippewa River which enters the Mississippi some 34 miles down stream. Sediment carried along by the fast moving Chippewa is deposited across the Mississippi, creating a sandbar that backs up the water and forms the lake. Only two other bodies of water are formed this way in Minnesota. They are Lac qui Parle Lake and Lake St. Croix.

Father Louis Hennepin became the first white man to explore Lake Pepin when he traveled north along the Mississippi during the summer of 1680. Captured by a Dakota hunting party, Hennepin was brought up the Mississippi along the Rum River to Lake Mille Lacs, the spiritual capital of the Dakota nation. This Franciscan priest, named Lake Pepin, "Lac des Pleurs" or "Lake of Tears." Inspiration for the name came from Indian braves who, unable to gain permission from their leaders to kill Hennepin, spent the night crying by the lake. Hennepin was eventually rescued by Sieur Du Luth, another French explorer. Lake Pepin took its present name from an unknown French trader some time during the 1700's.

FRONTENAC, Pop. 620

Frontenac Station and Frontenac are a railway village and river settlement of summer homes. Frontenac first started when Bully Wells pulled his canoe up on the shore in 1830 and opened a trading post. In 1854, Evert Westervelt and Lewis Garrard, a wealthy Southerner, bought Wells' land and developed a town which Garrard named after Westervelt.

In 1859 the name was changed to Frontenac after a French colonial governor of Canada. A number of large mansions were built here as well as a lodge called the Lakeside Hotel. The Lakeside, in operation by 1867, was one of Minnesota's first resorts. An Episcopal church was built at Frontenac in 1868 with the help of Bishop Whipple, Minnesota's first Episcopal bishop and staunch supporter of the Indian cause. This church is still used, as are the Garrard and Westervelt homes. Frontenac State Park is also located here on 1300 acres of rolling woodlands that border the river. The park has 59 campsites and six miles of trails.

FORT BEAUHARNOIS

During the 1600's, Minnesota was on the outer fringe of French exploration. By 1727 the French sought a more permanent base from which to explore, so they built a fort on the Mississippi on a spit of land called Sand Point. The post was named Fort Beauharnois and from here further explorations were planned for that elusive route to the western sea. This small compound also contained a Jesuit mission, making it Minnesota's first church. But flooding and continued fighting between the Dakota and Fox Indians led the French to abandon the fort in 1729. In 1750 the post was reestablished and trade with the Indians was carried on for the next several years before the French garrison was recalled to fight against the British in the French and Indian War.

LAKE CITY, Pop. 4,505

This small community was first settled in 1854. Besides growing as a resort area, the town thrived on its wood and flour trade. Nearby Lake Pepin, with its abundant supply of river clams, soon developed an important clamming industry. In the early 1900's over 500 clammers worked the riverbeds from their boats and supplied the button factories at Lake City. The production of synthetic buttons on the East Coast eventually killed this industry. It was at Lake City in 1922, that 18-year-old Ralph Samuelson tied eight-foot pine boards to his feet, proving that if one can ski on snow, one can ski on water. Pulled behind a boat on Lake Pepin, Samuelson became the world's first water skier. He also tried his luck skiing behind seaplanes, in order to reach faster water speeds.

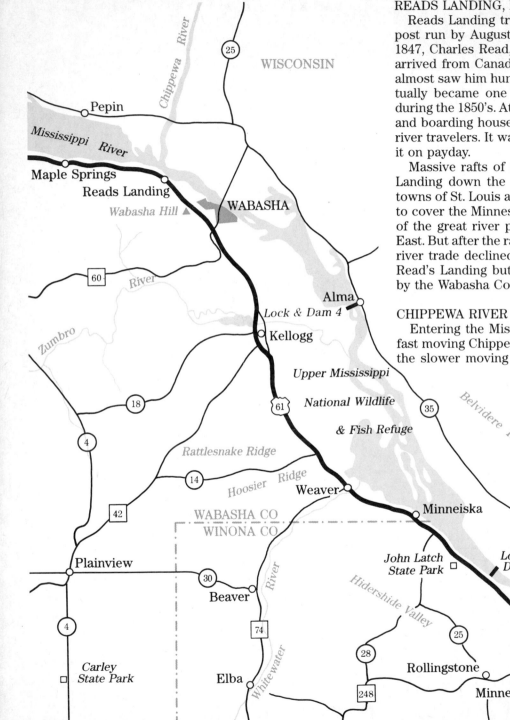

READS LANDING, Pop. 220

Reads Landing traces its beginnings to an Indian trading post run by Augustine Rocque from 1810 to 1830. Then in 1847, Charles Read, (from whom the town takes its name) arrived from Canada, taking refuge from a rebellion which almost saw him hung. The little post at Reads Landing eventually became one of the busiest sites on the Mississippi during the 1850's. At that time, some 20 saloons and 17 hotels and boarding houses catered to lumberjacks, raftsmen, and river travelers. It was a rough town and most locals avoided it on payday.

Massive rafts of St. Croix pine were floated from Reads Landing down the Mississippi River to build the booming towns of St. Louis and Kansas City. Then, when wheat began to cover the Minnesota prairies, Reads Landing became one of the great river ports for shipping flour and grain to the East. But after the railroad began hauling wheat in the 1860's, river trade declined rapidly. Today little remains of the old Read's Landing but a few buildings and an old school run by the Wabasha County Historical Society as a museum.

CHIPPEWA RIVER

Entering the Mississippi across from Reads Landing, the fast moving Chippewa River drops most of its sediment into the slower moving Mississippi. As a result, the Mississippi

(left) The Main Street of Reads Landing was lined with busy stores in 1872. (below) Rafted logs were steamed from Winona to towns along the Mississippi. When this photo was taken in 1910, the lumber industry along the St. Croix was near its end.

backs up, creating the Lake Pepin basin. Much of the Wisconsin pine harvested during the 1800's was sent down this river. The Chippewa was also an important waterway for trade coming up the Mississippi to towns such as Chippewa Falls and Eau Claire. In 1867 fights broke out between lumbermen who wanted to put booms across the mouth of the Chippewa to catch logs and those that wanted it to remain open for steamboats. Their solution was to construct a portable boom, allowing boats to enter.

WABASHA, Pop. 2,372

In 1838 this settlement along the Mississippi was named Cratte's Landing after an English blacksmith who worked out of a small shed along the river. Ten years later in 1843, Cratte's Landing was renamed Wabasha after a Dakota chief whose village was located up river near today's Minnesota City. Wabasha, located on the flood plain, was a favorite stopping spot for fur traders during the late 1700's. When steamboat traffic increased, other trading posts were established and farmers brought wheat to town from the prairie. Wabasha soon became one of the major wheat markets on the Mississippi. Located in Wabasha is the Anderson House, Minnesota's oldest operating hotel which opened for business in 1856. The hotel is now completely refurbished in

period furniture and decor.

Wabasha also marks the beginning of an extensive network of backwater sloughs and bayous reaching 300 miles southward to Illinois. This was once called the Winneshiek Bottoms and is now part of the Upper Mississippi Wildlife Refuge. In many places the river basin widens and is covered with a rich growth of willows, cattails, rushes, and water lilies. During the fall migratory season, the ponds and marshes are covered with waterfowl, including white pelicans and whistling swans. Because the Mississippi is too slow to move sediment deposited by its many tributaries, the river bottoms are constantly changing. The shifting sandbars and islands, create an endless battle to maintain a nine-foot channel for today's river barges.

ZUMBRO RIVER

The Zumbro River is an extensive system of tributaries draining the gentle farmlands from Rochester to Faribault. In its final run into the Mississippi Valley, its waters have cut a deep gorge through the bluffs. The French called the Zumbro, "Riviere des Embarras," meaning a "river clogged by driftwood and logs." Somehow through spelling and mispronunciation by the English-speaking settlers, it came to be called the Zumbro.

KELLOGG, Pop. 440

This village, founded in 1870, was named after a Milwaukee man who furnished wooden depot signs to the Chicago, Milwaukee and St. Paul Railroad Company. Today a number of old buildings remain vacant and in disrepair. Between Kellogg and Winona the broad river bottom is interspersed with farms and marshes. Look for egrets and herons that stalk these marshes.

WHITEWATER RIVER

This river is the shortest of four major southeastern Minnesota streams that feed into the Mississippi. The Whitewater runs through the limestone hills and valleys where over 25,000 acres of wildlife management land and two state parks have been put aside. Wild turkeys were successfully introduced to the rough, wooded terrain in 1964.

The steep bluffs along the Whitewater Valley consist of limestone deposits from a giant sea that existed over this region for millions of years. Erosion of these sedimentary rocks occurred during the ice ages when meltwater from the glaciers gushed from the level prairie into the Mississippi Valley.

MINNEISKA, Pop. 80

Minneiska, a Dakota word for the White Water River, was settled in 1851. It became one of many river towns that prospered during the 1870's when up to 330,000 bushels of wheat were being shipped from here annually. With the advent of the railroad, the town decreased in size, giving rise to the riverman's custom of spitting a curse every time he crossed the tracks. During the fall, a large variety of waterfowl gather along the river bottoms.

Main Street, Wabasha 1863.

MHS

JOHN LATCH STATE PARK

Jonathan Carver stopped at this spot in 1766 as he explored the Mississippi. Here he discovered a series of turf-covered Indian mounds resting along the marshy terrace below the present road. Carver's mission in Minnesota was to make friends with the Dakota Indians and invite them to a large peace council to be held at Mackinac, Michigan. He also was searching for a passage to the Pacific Ocean. The important result of Carver's travels was that he published the first English narrative that described the Indians and interior lands of this new region. Today this spot is occupied by a state wayside park.

MINNESOTA CITY, Pop. 265

This settlement was first called Rollingstone City and was platted in 1852. The city was formed by a number of New York mechanics who desired a new start in the west. The group, known as the "Western Farm and Village Association," began looking for a suitable place to build a town. Finding a spot along the Mississippi, they returned to New York, drew up maps and started promoting this new farming community. Before long settlers started heading for the town they thought already existed. River captains at Galena, Illinois were puzzled when people began asking to be taken to this nonexistent place called Rollingstone City. Nevertheless, the spot was identified on their maps and the settlers were deposited here, with nothing but the trees and river to greet them.

Within a couple of months this town grew to 400 people, most with little knowledge about farming or pioneer life. Many died during the winter and the colony eventually broke up. Some moved to Winona, while many returned to New York, leaving behind nameless graves and a few old buildings. The present village of Rollingstone has no connection to the early village.

WINONA, Pop. 25,075

This area along the Mississippi was once a prairie, devoid of trees. It was the original site of Chief Red Wing's band, but later became known as Wabasha's Prairie when Chief Wabasha ruled. Around 1850 Chief Wabasha traded these rich bottom lands to settlers for six barrels of flour. A small collection of prairie shanties began to form here and was called Montezuma, after the Aztec chief. But the town continued to grow and in 1853 it was renamed Winona. Legend has it that a Dakota woman, related to Chief Wabasha and named Winona (a name often given to a first-born Indian girl), threw herself from a cliff on Lake Pepin's east shore to keep from marrying a brave she didn't love. The bluff became known as "Maiden's Rock."

At first Winona attracted little interest, except to a handful of traders and settlers. In 1851 the steamboat Nominee stopped here to take on wood from the forested hillside for its boilers. Winona soon became an important stopping place for other steamboats taking on freight and wood. By 1856 a number of Germans and New Englanders began settling here. Together these two groups planted trees and developed Winona into one of the primary sawmill towns on the Mississippi. In the late 1850's Winona had 10 sawmills with some 2,000 loggers and 1,500 mill hands in the work force.

During one year's time in the late 1800's, 8,585 steamboats rounded the bend at Winona. By 1868 Winona had become the fourth largest wheat market in the United States. And in 1862, The Winona and St. Peter Railroad replaced the grain wagons and started tapping the grain fields of South Dakota.

By the early 1900's the sawmills shut down as lumbering stopped on the upper St. Croix. But economic help came from nearby quarries that developed along the sandstone bluffs. Brick-making also became an important industry to Winona. One plant produced three million bricks during the 1920's. Today Winona is a diversified agricultural and industrial center.

DRIFTLESS AREA

Some of the most rugged terrain in Minnesota occurs south of Winona, in Houston County. Only a small portion of southeastern Minnesota, eastern Wisconsin, and northwestern Iowa was untouched by the glaciers. It is called the driftless area, since it is void of glacial debris.

As the glaciers melted to the west and east, their waters gushed down the rivers to the Mississippi, eroding the land into deep valleys and coulees. (A coulee is a gorge or valley whose stream is usually dry during the summer). When the melting was finished, the winds blew a fine silt, called loess,

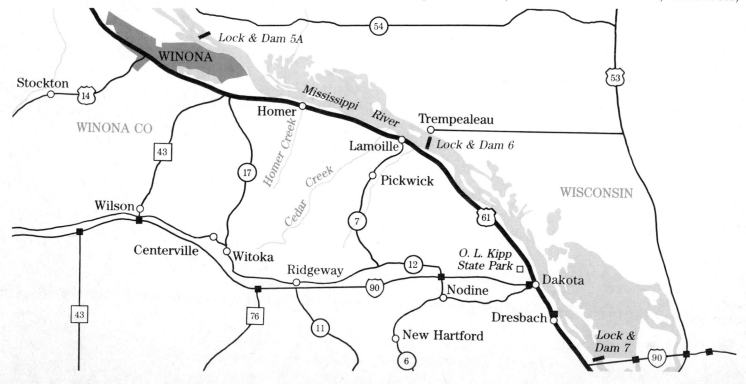

over the the barren limestone hills. It was from this loess that the forests grew. These same forests, though, were abused by the early settlers and serious erosion and flooding began to take place. Subsequent replanting during the early 1900's has restored this area's natural beauty. Today, these woods are among the most varied in the state. Here one can find red and white oak, black walnut, basswood, butternut, ash, black cherry, hickory, maple, hackberry, birch, and juniper. Because of the hills, streams and small farms with grazing herds, this region has picked up the nickname of "Little Switzerland."

SUGAR LOAF BLUFF

This bluff capped with a column of limestone, stands 500 feet above the city at the intersection of Highways 61 and 43. The Dakota, who ranged the Upper Mississippi area before the white man came, gathered at this bluff for celebrations. The bluff top was called Wabasha's Cap and lookouts alerted the nearby camp of any Ojibwe raiding parties. The stone knob on the top is a more recent remnant from a quarry that was once worked there.

MHS

Sugar Loaf Bluff, 1890. The frequent thawing and freezing of its sun-lit slopes makes it difficult for plants and trees to grow.

HOMER, Pop. 230

It was here that Francois du Chouquette tried to establish trade with Chief Wabasha's tribe in 1830, but raids by the Sac and Fox Indians forced him to move to a safer location at the settlement of Prairie du Chien, Wisconsin. Located on the west side of the highway is the historic Bunnell House, maintained by the Winona Historical Society. Willard Bunnell was a townsite planner and speculator who became the first permanent settler in the county. He moved off the river flats and built his house on this hillside in 1849. Bunnell named the townsite after his birthplace in New York.

PICKWICK

Located two miles from Lamoille on County 7, rests the picturesque village of Pickwick. The road through town, passes a decaying old mill situated along Trout Creek. From here, the road winds up from the wooded valley to nearby O.L. Kipp State Park.

O. L.-KIPP STATE PARK

One of the best kept secrets of the state park system is the 1600-acre O. L. Kipp State Park, located on the bluffs of the Mississippi. There are 31 camp sites here that connect to nine miles of hiking and cross-county ski trails. These trails lead through hardwood forests and out to cliffside vistas overlooking the broad Mississippi River Valley. Owls, hawks, deer and other wildlife are abundant. The autumn bloom of wild-flowers in the park is spectacular. During the fall bird migration, the night sky is filled with ducks and geese. The park is accessed off of I-90, at Winona County 12.

MHS

The steamer "Thistle", on a trip up the river from La Crosse.

DAKOTA, DRESBACH

At age 17, Jeremiah Tibbitts started trading here with a band of Dakota Indians in 1853. The town of Dresbach formed a few years later when George Dresbach quarried a limestone called Winona Travertine from the nearby bluffs. The bluff overlooking Dresbach is Mineral Bluff, a sandstone hill which rises 405 feet. Here traces of coal, lead and silver have been found, as was a skull with a copper hatchet protruding from it.

This area of southeastern Minnesota is called the "driftless area," a region untouched by glacial action. The terrain is representative of parts of Minnesota prior to glaciation. The glacial meltwater did flow down from the uplands however, cutting deep channels through the Mississippi bluffs.

with an apple festival. The back roads offer stunning scenery, making this a good autumn trip.

Frost comes late to the valleys near La Crescent, making it an ideal place to grow apples. Photo/H.D. Ayer, 1910.

The once treeless town of Winona as seen from the intersection of Center and Third Streets. Photo taken 1861.

LA CRESCENT, Pop. 3,383

When a rivalry developed with La Crosse on the Wisconsin side of the Mississippi, the settlers of the small hamlet of Manton petitioned to change the village name to La Crescent. They thought that La Crosse had been named for the crusader's emblem, the cross. So Manton picked the crescent, a Mohammedan emblem of power, to symbolize their competition.

Because of the fertile soil and late frost that comes to the valley, settlers began to plant apple trees around here. La Crescent has since been called the apple capital of Minnesota and during the fall, the town promotes the local orchards

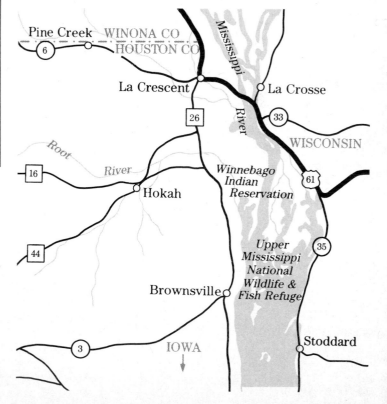

ST. PAUL & MINNEAPOLIS

View of original Capitol, taken from St. Paul Courthouse in 1857.

MHS

The rivers of the state were the vital pathways of trade and settlement in early Minnesota. Every river had its own distinct set of features which defined the type of development that occurred along its shoreline. So it is not surprising that a steamboat landing and a waterfalls, situated on the "Great River" the Mississippi, were the determining factors in the development of Minnesota's two major cities.

ST. PAUL, Pop. 270,230

Rising from a steamboat landing and spreading along the 80-foot-high sandstone bluffs, St. Paul began as a fur-trading and resupply center for the Red River settlements of northwestern Minnesota. Red River oxcarts delivered products of the frontier to St. Paul for shipment east. Side wheeler boats began to bring more immigrants to the region and left with furs, moccasins and dried buffalo tongue.

A French fur trader and bootlegger named Pierre (Pig's Eye) Parrant, built the first shack within the boundaries of St. Paul in 1838, after being expelled from the Fort Snelling military reservation. The nature of Parrant's business gave rise to the saying that "while Minneapolis was conceived in water power, St. Paul was born in whiskey."

The following year, Father Lucian Galtier built a small chapel where Kellogg Boulevard and Minnesota Streets now meet, and consecrated it to Saint Paul. At that time the closest settlement of Mendota was named St. Peter, as was the Minnesota River. For Father Galtier it seemed fitting to have the two famous saints represented side by side.

245

1869 view of Hennepin Avenue near Washington Avenue.

MHS

MINNEAPOLIS, Pop. 370,951

Today there is little trace of the wild, original beauty of the Mississippi's St. Anthony Falls. Named by Father Louis Hennepin for his patron saint in 1680, the falls provided the power for lumber and flour mills which firmly established this town as a rich commercial and agribusiness center.

By the 1840's the falls had attracted the attention of French trader Pierre Bottineau, as well as Henry Steele, the brother-in-law of Territorial Governor Alexander Ramsey. Steele and Bottineau were the first people to own land along the east bank of the Mississippi. In 1847 Steele began building a saw-mill and a dam. French Canadians began to settle near this new community which was called St. Anthony.

Steele encouraged his clerk, John Stevens, to stake out a claim on the west bank of the river above the falls. This was technically part of the Fort Snelling military reservation, but Stevens received a special permit and built the first frame house west of the Mississippi. Hennepin County politics and culture had their beginnings in the Stevens home. The name "Minneapolis" was suggested for the new community. The name is a combination of the Dakota word "Minnehaha" meaning "laughing water" and the Greek word "polis" for city. With 16 lakes within the city limits, the name was aptly chosen.

It was thought that St. Anthony would become the major community, but the beautiful lakes and spaciousness of the west bank, gave Minneapolis a decided advantage. While New England influence was strong in developing Minneapolis, as well as St. Paul, Scandinavians began to dominate the population by the late 1800's.

With increased mechanization, cheap land, railroads and expanded markets, the early subsistence farming gave way to more productive agriculture, with wheat becoming the predominant crop in the state. In the 1860's, over 500 flour mills were located in Minnesota. Minneapolis had an advantage over the towns because of its growing home market. But one thing set it apart form the others. New Englander, Cadwallader Washburn, helped Minneapolis achieve prominence when he developed a new technology which revolutionized flour milling. The "middlings purifier", produced a finer white flour with longer shelf life using the more abundant spring wheat. By the 1890's Minneapolis had earned the nickname "Mill City" and claimed to be the world's leading wheat market.

Rarely have two cities so close together, grown to such a degree of prominence as these.

St. Paul became the capital of the Territory in 1849 and of the state in 1858. After the Civil War, many educated and experienced "yankee's" came west to St. Paul, bringing a level of culture reflected in the schools, arts and social concerns that gave this town the nickname "Boston of the West." St. Paul was becoming a terminus for railroads fanning out across the state, increasing trade and settlement. Eventually, the railroad with its cheaper fares and varied routes, diminished the importance of the steamers.

By the 1870's James J. Hill was developing his railroad empire, with St. Paul as the capital. This extensive network of rail lines would eventually reach the Pacific Ocean, connecting the rich forests of the Northwest and the wheat fields of the Dakotas to the Midwestern markets.

Through the efforts of Bishop John Ireland, thousands of Irish immigrants settled in Minnesota, developing St. Paul into one of the largest Catholic dioceses in the country. Irish and German immigrants dominated the early population of St. Paul.

246

Nicollet Island view in 1870. Just to the left of the city's first suspension bridge, is the Stevens' house, the first frame house in Minneapolis.

Album of History and Biography of Meeker County, Minnesota. Chicago: Alden Ogle & Co., 1888.

Anderson, Antone A. and Clara A. McDermott. The Hinckley Fire. New York: Comet Press Books, 1954.

Anoka County History. A.M. Goodrich, 1905.

Anonsen, Stanley H. A History of Swift County. Benson: Swift County Historical Soc., (1929?).

Blegen, Theodore, C. Minnesota, A History Of The State. Minneapolis: Univ. of Minn., 1975.

Brown, John A., ed. History of Cottonwood and Watonwan Counties, Minnesota. Indianapolis: B.F. Bowen & Co., 1916.

Centennial History of Kandiyohi County, Minnesota, The, 1870-1970. (Willmar: Kandiyohi County Historical Soc.?), 1970.

Compendium of History and Biography of Polk County, Minnesota. Ed. by R.I. Holcombe and William H. Bingham. Minneapolis: W.H. Bingham & Co., 1916.

Costello, David F. The Prairie World, Thomas Y. Crowell Company. 1969.

Courtnay, Booth. Wildflowers and Weeds, Van Nostrand Reinhold. 1972.

Curtiss-Wedge, Franklyn, ed. History of Dakota and Goodhue Counties, Minnesota. Illustrated. Chicago: H.C. Cooper, Jr. & Co., 1910.

Curtiss-Wedge, Franklyn, ed. History of Fillmore County, Minnesota. Chicago: H.C. Cooper & Co., 1912.

Curtiss-Wedge, Franklyn, ed. History of Freeborn County, Minnesota. Chicago: H.c. Cooper, Jr. & Co., 1911.

Curtiss-Wedge, Franklyn, ed. History of Goodhue County, Minnesota. Chicago: H.C. Cooper, Jr. & Co., 1909.

Curtiss-Wedge, Franklyn, ed. History of Houston County, Minnesota. Winona: H.C. Cooper, Jr. & Co, 1919.

Curtiss-Wedge, Franklyn, ed. History of McLeod County, Minnesota. Chicago & Winona: H.C. Cooper, Jr. & Co., 1917.

Curtiss-Wedge, Franklyn, ed. History of Rice and Steele Counties, Minnesota. Illustrated. Chicago: H.C. Cooper, Jr.,& Co., 1910.

Curtiss-Wedge, Franklyn, ed. History of Wabasha County, Minnesota. Illustrated. Winona: H.C. Cooper & Co., 1920

Curtiss-Wedge, Frankln. History of Wright County, Minnesota. Illustrated. Chicago: H.C. Cooper, Jr., & Co., 1915.

Dunn, James T., The St. Croix. Holt, Rinehart and Winston. 1965.

Easton, Augustus B., ed. History of the St. Croix Valley. Chicago: H.C. Cooper, Jr., & Co., 1909

Fisher, Harold. The Land Called Morrison.

Folsom, William H.C. Fifty Years in the Northwest. Ed. by E.E. Edwards. (St. Paul): Pioneer Press Co., 1888.

Fritzen, John. Historic Sites and Place Names of Minnesota's North Shore, St. Louis Co. Historical Society. 1974.

Fuller, Clara K. History of Morrison and Todd Counties, Minnesota. Indianapolis: B.F. Bowen, 1915

Gebhard, Martinson. A Guide to the Architecture of Minnesota, Univ. of Minnesota Press. 1977.

Goodrich, Albert M. History of Anoka County and the Towns of Champlin and Dayton, Minnesota. Minneapolis: Hennepin Pub. Co, 1905.

Gresham, William G., ed. History of Nicollet and LeSueur Counties, Minnesota. Indianapolis: B.F. Bowen, 1916.

History of the Minnesota Valley. Comp. by George E. Warner and Charles M. Foote. Minneapolis: North Star Pub. Co., 1882.

History of the Red River Valley, Past and Present; by Various Writers. Grand Forks, N.D.: Herald Printing Co.; Chicago: C.F. Cooper & Co., 1909.

History of the Upper Mississippi and Saint Louis Valleys. Minneapolis: Minnesota Historical Co., 1881.

History of Winona and Olmsted Counties. Gathered from Matter furnished by Interviews with Old Settlers. Chicago: H.H. Hill & Co., 1883.

Holmquist and Brookins, Minnesota's Major Historic Sites. Minnesota Historical Society, 1963.

Hough, Jack Luin. Geology of the Great Lakes, University of Illinois. 1958

Hughes, Thomas. History of Blue Earth County. Chicago: Middle West Pub. Co., (1909?).

Knauth, Percy. The North Woods, Time-Life Books. 1972.

Larson, Constant, ed. History of Douglas and Grant Counties, Minnesota. Indianapolis: B.F. Bowen & Co., 1916.

Lass, William. Minnesota,A History, W.W. Norton & Company Inc. 1977.

Lund, Duane. Tales of Four Lakes. Nordell Graphic Communications, 1977.

Mason, John W., ed. History of Otter Tail County Minnesota. Indianapolis: B.F. Bowen, 1916.

Minnesota, A State Guide. Compiled and Written by the Federal Writer's Project of the W.P.A. New York: Hastings House, 1938.

Minnesota Arrowhead Country. Compiled by Workers of the Writer's Program of the W.P.A. Chicago: Albert Whitman & Co., 1941

Minnesota Historical Records Survey, 67 Volumes, 1941.

Morely, Sims. Geology of Minnesota, Minnesota Geological Society, Univ. of Minnesota.

Moyer, Lycurgus R. And Ole G. Dale, eds. History of Chippewa and Lac qui Parle Counties, Minnesota. Indianapolis: B.F. Bowen & Co., 1916.

Rose, Arthur P. An Illustrated History of The Counties of Rock and Pipestone, Minnesota. Luverne: Northern History Pub. Co., 1911.

Rosendahl, Carl O. Trees and Shrubs of the Upper Midwest, University Of Minnesota Press. 1928.

Sanford, Sidney. The Wheat Trail, 1958.

Schwartz, George, and Thiel, George. Minnesota Rocks and Waters. University of Minnesota, Minneapolis: 1963.

Turner, John and C. Knut Semling, eds. History of Clay and Norman Counties, Minnesota. Indianapolis: B.F. Bowen & Co., 1918.

Upham. Minnesota Geographic Names, Minnesota Historical Society. 1920.

Van Brunt, Walter, ed. Duluth and St. Louis County, Minnesota. Chicago & New York: Am. Historical Soc., 1921.

Wadena Pioneer Journal, 50th Anniversary, 1927.

Water, Thomas F. The Streams and Rivers of Minnesota, University Of Minnesota. 1977.

Wilcox, Alvin H. A Pioneer History of Becker County, Minnesota. (St. Paul): Pioneer Press Co., 1907.

INDEX

Book Designed by Richard Olsenius
Type set by Type House/Duragraph, Minneapolis, in 10 pt.
century book.
Paper is coated 65# matte
Book Printed at North Central Publishing, St. Paul